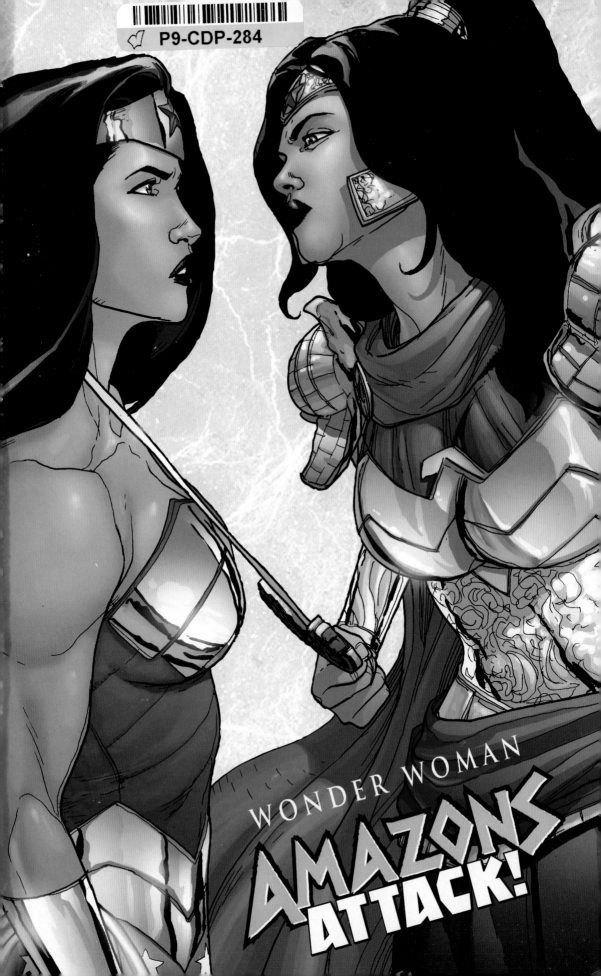

WONDER WOMAN

AMAZONS ATTACK!

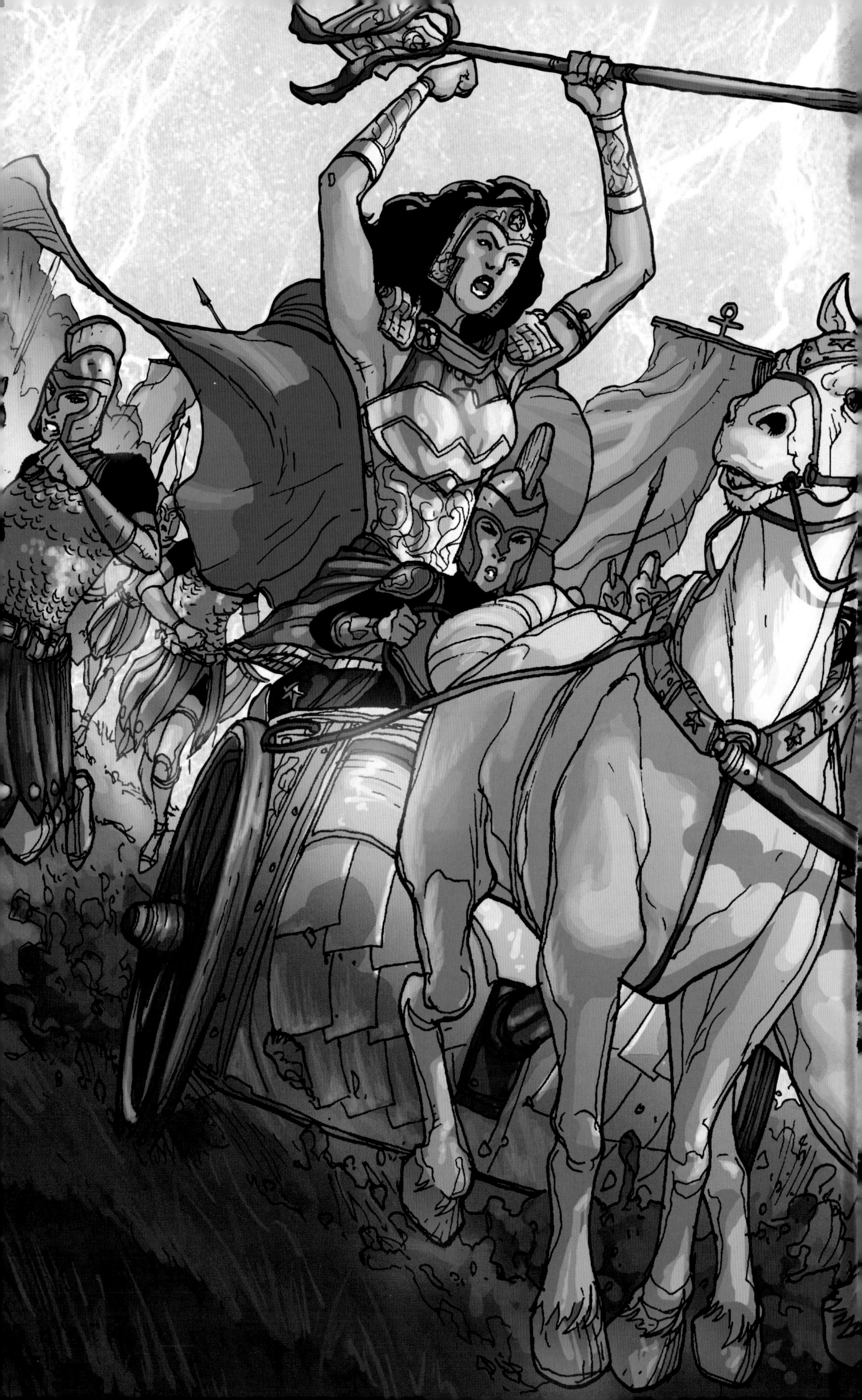

WONDER WOMAN
AMAZONS ATTACK!

Will Pfeifer
Writer

Pete Woods
Artist

Brad Anderson
Colorist

Travis Lanham   Rob Leigh
Letterers

Wonder Woman created by
William Moulton Marston

Dan DiDio
Senior VP-Executive Editor

Matt Idelson
Editor-original series

Nachie Castro
Associate Editor-original series

Anton Kawasaki
Editor-collected edition

Robbin Brosterman
Senior Art Director

Paul Levitz
President & Publisher

Georg Brewer
VP-Design & DC Direct Creative

Richard Bruning
Senior VP-Creative Director

Patrick Caldon
Executive VP-Finance & Operations

Chris Caramalis
VP-Finance

John Cunningham
VP-Marketing

Terri Cunningham
VP-Managing Editor

Alison Gill
VP-Manufacturing

Hank Kanalz
VP-General Manager, WildStorm

Jim Lee
Editorial Director-WildStorm

Paula Lowitt
Senior VP-Business & Legal Affairs

MaryEllen McLaughlin
VP-Advertising & Custom Publishing

John Nee
VP-Business Development

Gregory Noveck
Senior VP-Creative Affairs

Sue Pohja
VP-Book Trade Sales

Cheryl Rubin
Senior VP-Brand Management

Jeff Trojan
VP-Business Development, DC Direct

Bob Wayne
VP-Sales

Cover by Pete Woods

**WONDER WOMAN:
AMAZONS ATTACK!**

DC Comics, 1700 Broadway,
New York, NY 10019
A Warner Bros. Entertainment
Company
Printed in China. First Printing.

HC ISBN: 1-4012-1543-2
HC ISBN: 978-1-4012-1543-9
SC ISBN: 1-4012-1732-X
SC ISBN: 978-1-4012-1732-7

Cast of Characters

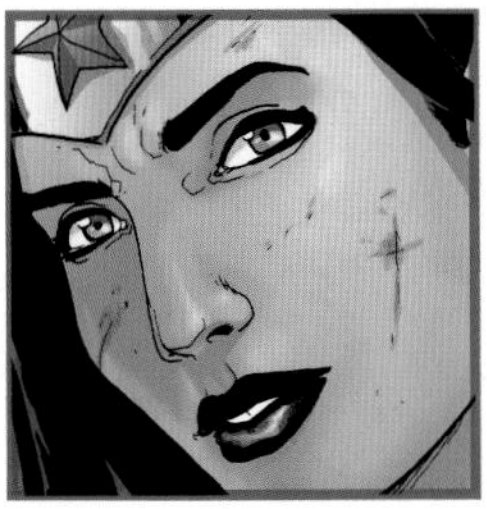

WONDER WOMAN

Born an Amazon princess, Diana was chosen to serve as her people's ambassador of peace in the World of Man. Armed with the lasso of truth and indestructible bracelets, she directs her gods-given abilities of strength and speed toward the betterment of mankind. But life has been difficult for Diana lately. In an act that would save the lives of millions, she was forced to kill a man — causing many to question and even fear her. After a year of soul-searching, she returned and adopted a secret "human" identity of Diana Prince — a special agent of the Department of Metahuman Affairs. She is also once again a member of the Justice League of America.

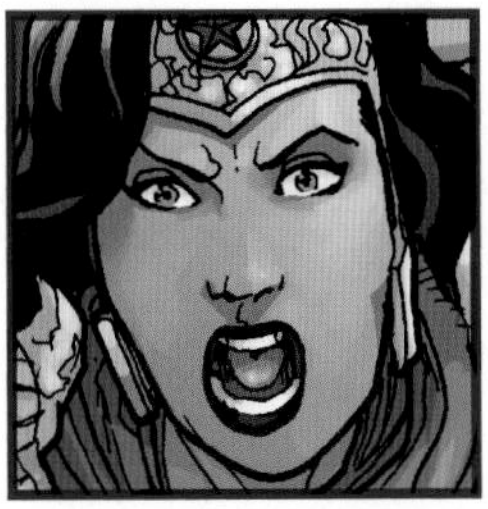

QUEEN HIPPOLYTA

The Queen of the Amazons and mother to Diana, Hippolyta was the strong but peaceful leader of the island of Themyscira. Very protective of her only daughter, Hippolyta put her life on the line many times in order to save her daughter from peril or harm. She ultimately made the difficult choice of allowing Diana to leave the island and be a protector in Man's World. During an interplanetary war, Hippolyta sacrificed herself to help save Earth — dying in Diana's arms.

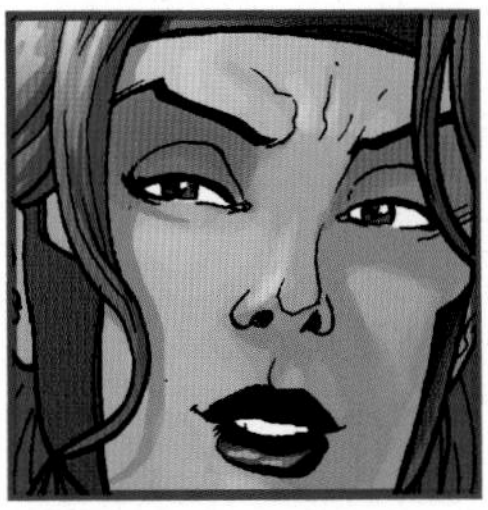

CIRCE

Daughter of Helios and Perseis, Circe is a powerful witch who can turn people into animals and control their minds, and those are merely the least of her amazing abilities. Circe has a long-standing hatred of Wonder Woman, as well as a complex history with the Amazons. She is responsible for giving immortality to the Amazon splinter group, the Bana-Mighdall — who in turn aided the witch during the War of the Gods, which caused the entire world to view the Amazons in a bad light.

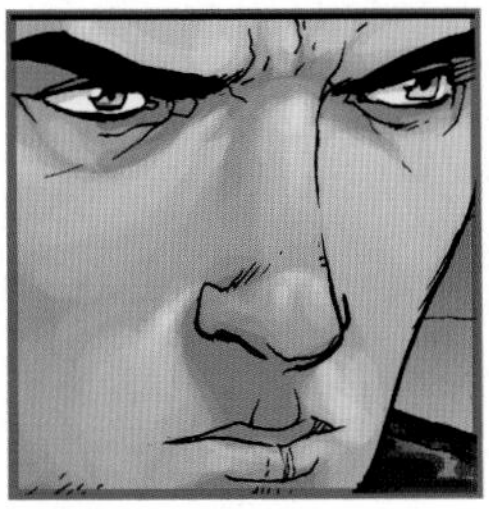

NEMESIS

Tom Tresser is a master of disguise who can instantly look like anyone else. Originally a vigilante, Tresser became an operative of the U.S. Government — most recently working for the Department of Metahuman Affairs, where his newest partner is Agent Diana Prince.

SARGE STEEL

Sarge Steel is currently in charge of Agents Diana Prince and Tom Tresser at the Department of Metahuman Affairs. Sarge has a mechanical left hand, and is known for his gruff personality. Recently it was revealed that the Shapeshifter known as Everyman, under order of Circe, has been impersonating Steel in order to instigate the events of an Amazon war.

WONDER GIRL & SUPERGIRL

As two of the most powerful teen heroes, Wonder Girl and Supergirl both have strong ties to the Amazons. Cassandra Sandsmark is the daughter of a human woman and the Greek God Zeus — who gave Cassie the abilities of flight, strength and speed that she uses as Wonder Girl. Kara Zor-El — who was rocketed to Earth and later trained in combat by the Amazons — is the cousin of Superman.

GRACE

Grace Choi is a 7-foot-tall woman with amazing strength and endurance. As a member of The Outsiders, she is a powerhouse to be reckoned with. Her past and the origins of her abilities are a mystery to her, but a big piece of the puzzle is about to be revealed…

THE JUSTICE LEAGUE OF AMERICA

The World's Greatest Super-Heroes are Earth's first line of defense against attacks by outside forces. In addition to Wonder Woman, the current JLA membership includes Superman, Batman, Black Canary (the League's chairwoman), Black Lightning, Green Lantern, Hawkgirl, Red Arrow, Vixen, and Red Tornado.

Chapter One

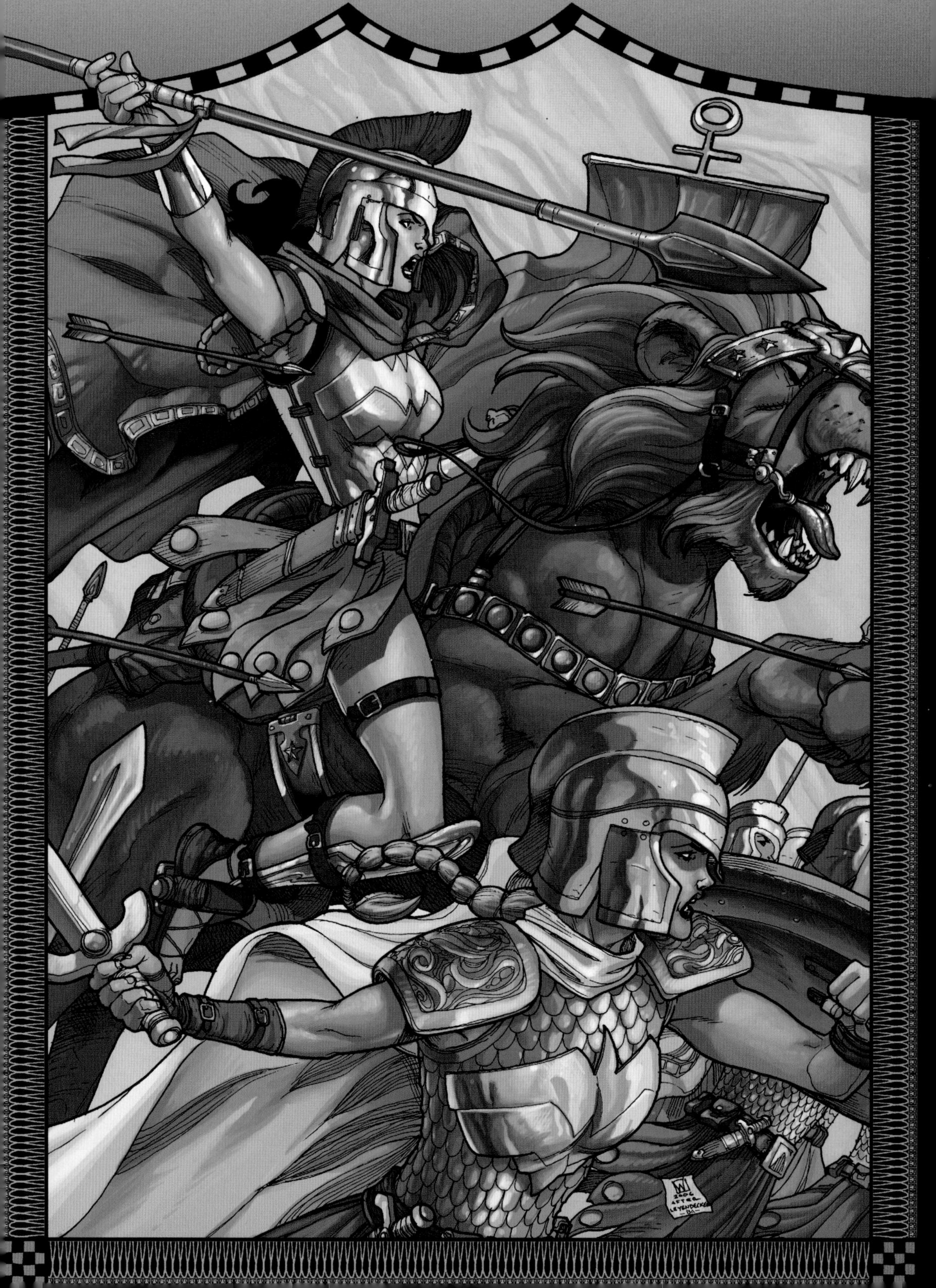

OUR STORY SO FAR...

The Department of Metahuman Affairs has been given orders to capture Wonder Woman by someone impersonating Sarge Steel. "Steel" demands to take the Amazon Princess into custody, but she goes along willingly — eager to resolve whatever misconceptions the government may have.

Deep within the otherwordly realm known as the Land of the Gods, on the shores of Themyscira — otherwise known as Paradise Island — a conjuration of dark magic is invoked, and a queen is reborn! The centuries-old enchantress known as Circe has brought Hippolyta back to life — but something isn't quite right with the leader of the Amazons.

Almost immediately, Hippolyta demands to know where her daughter is. Circe, knowing full well the ramifications of what she is about to say, informs the queen that her daughter Diana has been taken into custody by the United States government — and is being tortured in order to reveal the Amazons' secrets.

The news hits the reanimated Hippolyta hard and makes her Amazonian blood boil. Without hesitation she declares, "If it is a war that they want…it's a war that they'll get" — and prepares for the first strike against Washington, D.C.

Unknown to Hippolyta or Circe, Diana — with the help of Nemesis — has escaped custody…

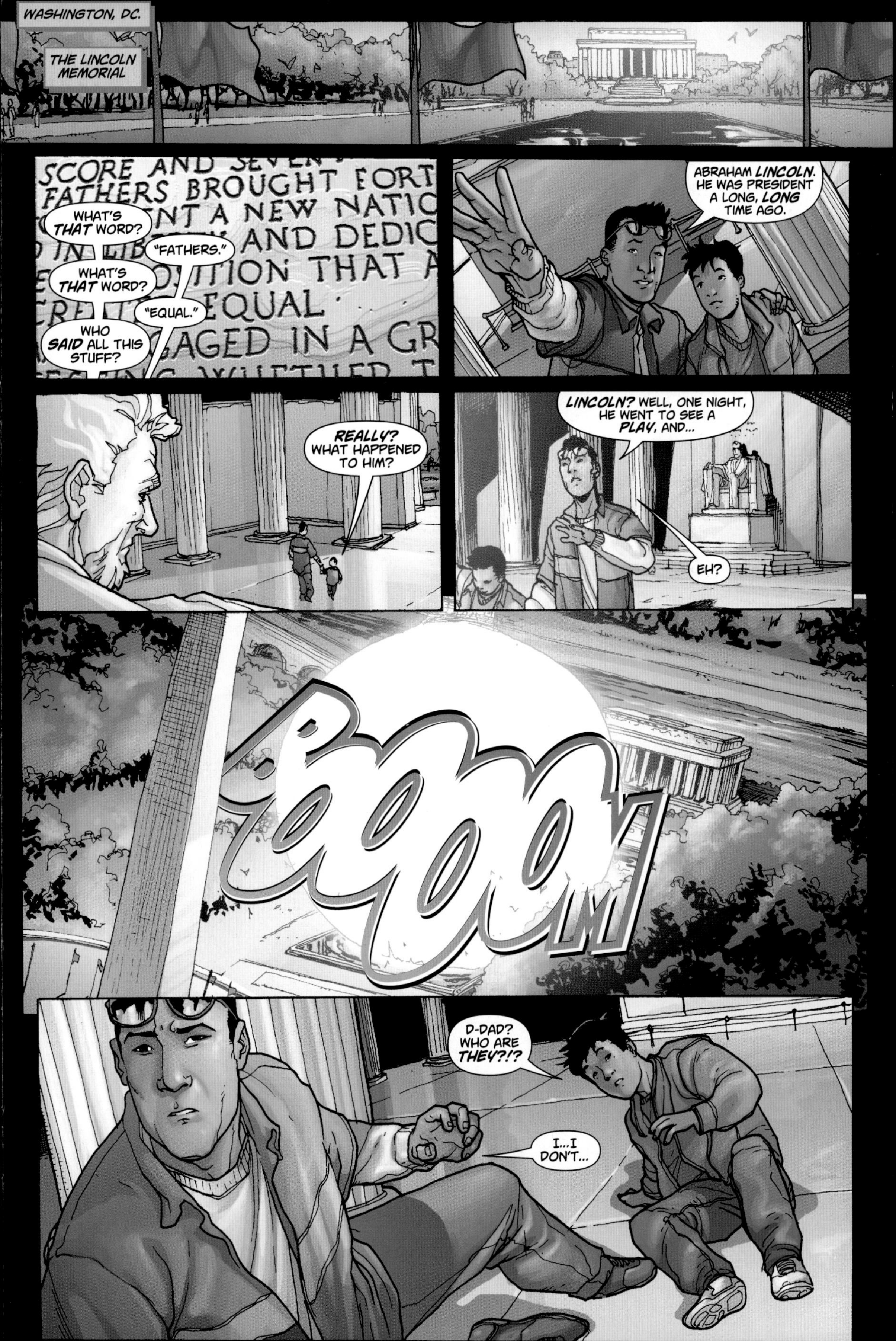
WASHINGTON, DC.
THE LINCOLN MEMORIAL
SCORE AND SEVEN
FATHERS BROUGHT FORT
A NEW NATIO
AND DEDIC
ITION THAT A
EQUAL
GAGED IN A GR
WHAT'S THAT WORD?
"FATHERS."
WHAT'S THAT WORD?
"EQUAL."
WHO SAID ALL THIS STUFF?
ABRAHAM LINCOLN. HE WAS PRESIDENT A LONG, LONG TIME AGO.
REALLY? WHAT HAPPENED TO HIM?
LINCOLN? WELL, ONE NIGHT, HE WENT TO SEE A PLAY, AND...
EH?
BOOOOM
D-DAD? WHO ARE THEY?!?
I...I DON'T...

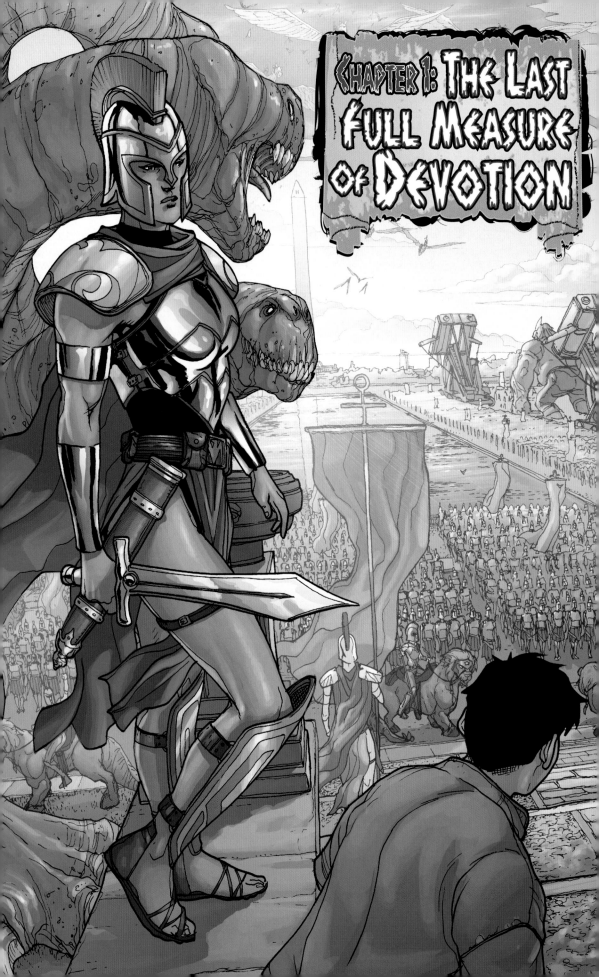

CHAPTER 1: THE LAST FULL MEASURE OF DEVOTION

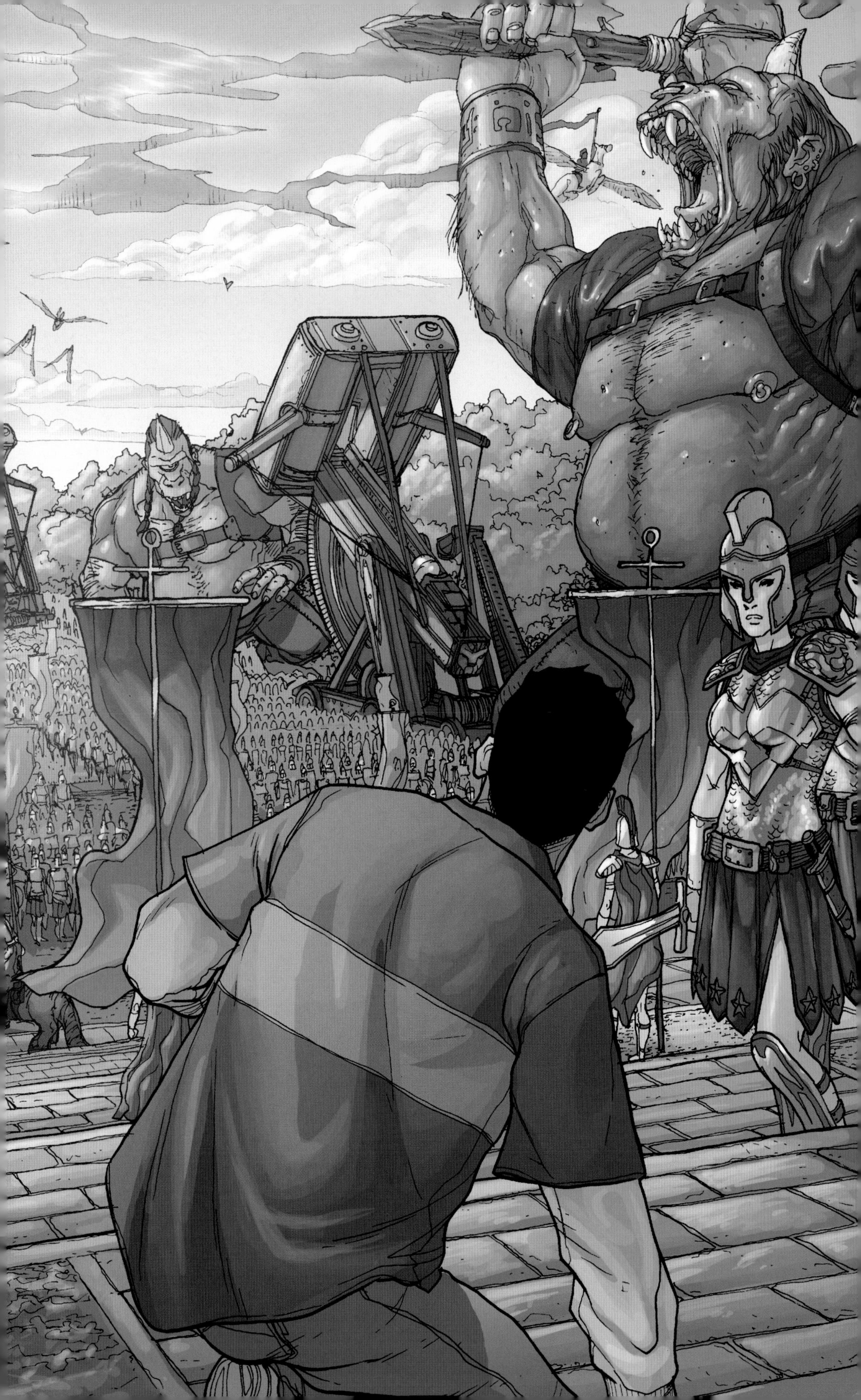

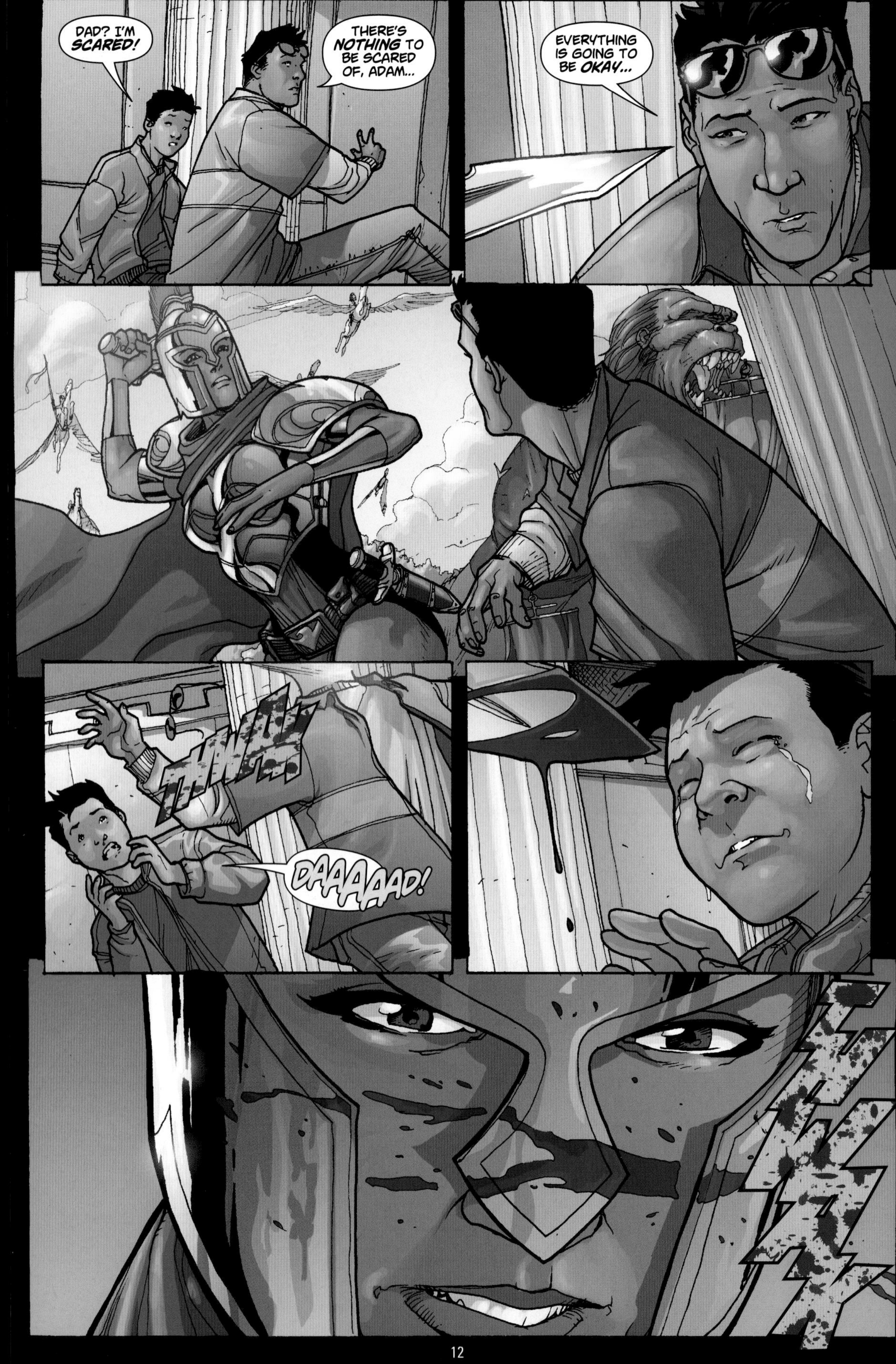
DAD? I'M SCARED!
THERE'S NOTHING TO BE SCARED OF, ADAM...
EVERYTHING IS GOING TO BE OKAY...
THWAK
DAAAAAAD!
THWAK

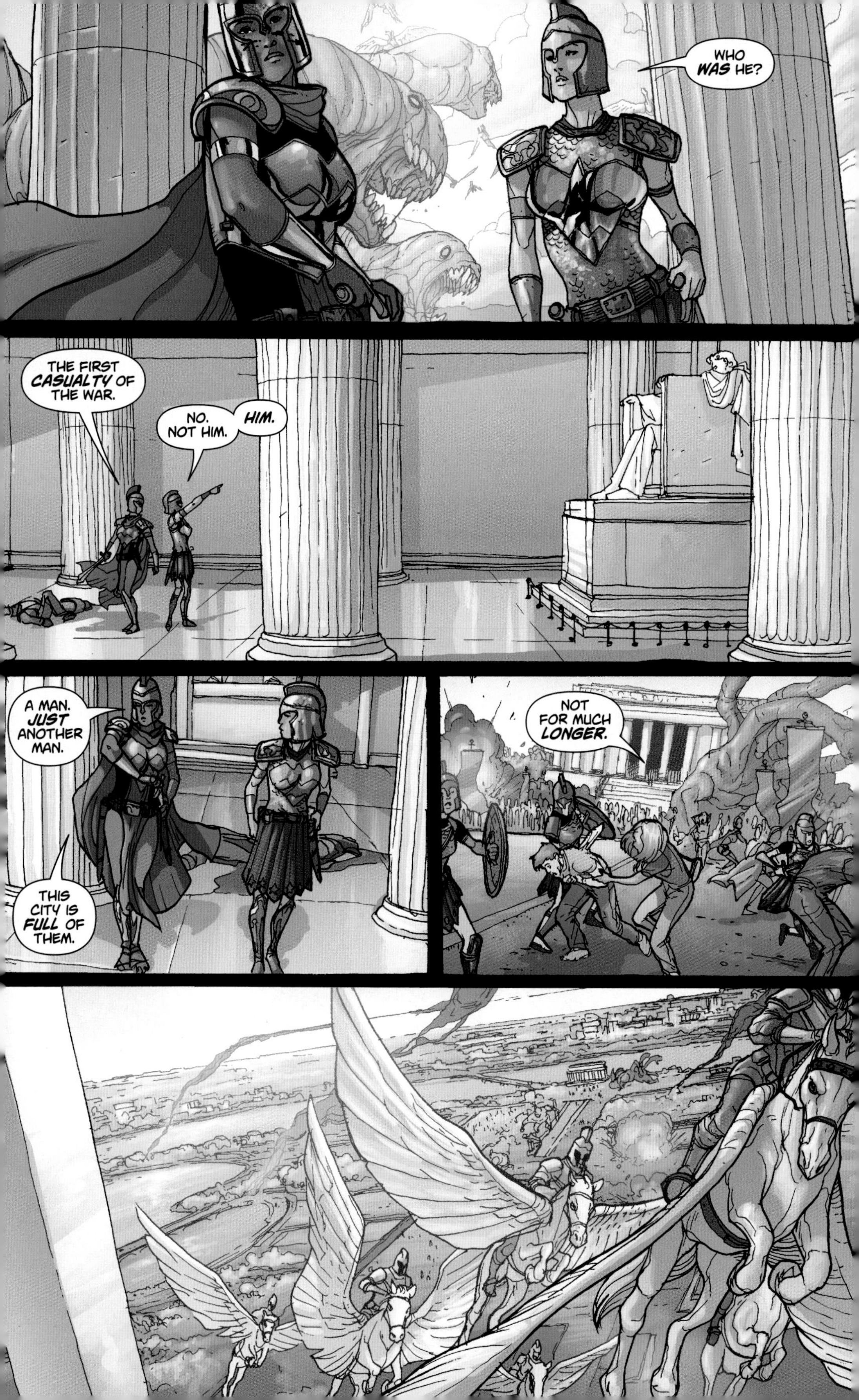
WHO WAS HE?
THE FIRST CASUALTY OF THE WAR.
NO. NOT HIM.
HIM.
A MAN. JUST ANOTHER MAN.
THIS CITY IS FULL OF THEM.
NOT FOR MUCH LONGER.

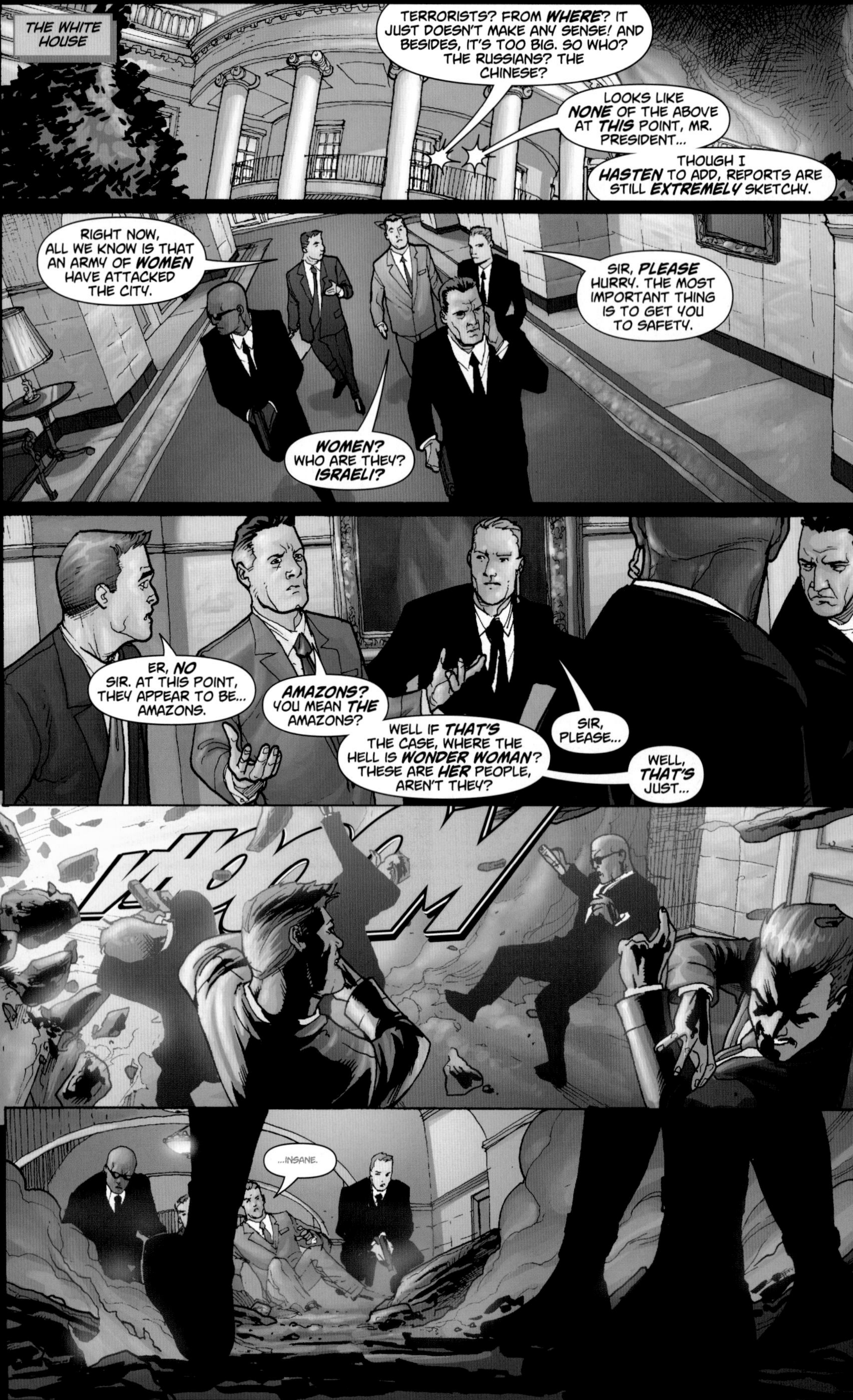
THE WHITE HOUSE
TERRORISTS? FROM WHERE? IT JUST DOESN'T MAKE ANY SENSE! AND BESIDES, IT'S TOO BIG. SO WHO? THE RUSSIANS? THE CHINESE?
LOOKS LIKE NONE OF THE ABOVE AT THIS POINT, MR. PRESIDENT...
THOUGH I HASTEN TO ADD, REPORTS ARE STILL EXTREMELY SKETCHY.
RIGHT NOW, ALL WE KNOW IS THAT AN ARMY OF WOMEN HAVE ATTACKED THE CITY.
SIR, PLEASE HURRY. THE MOST IMPORTANT THING IS TO GET YOU TO SAFETY.
WOMEN? WHO ARE THEY? ISRAELI?
ER, NO SIR. AT THIS POINT, THEY APPEAR TO BE... AMAZONS.
AMAZONS? YOU MEAN THE AMAZONS?
WELL IF THAT'S THE CASE, WHERE THE HELL IS WONDER WOMAN? THESE ARE HER PEOPLE, AREN'T THEY?
SIR, PLEASE...
WELL, THAT'S JUST...
...INSANE.

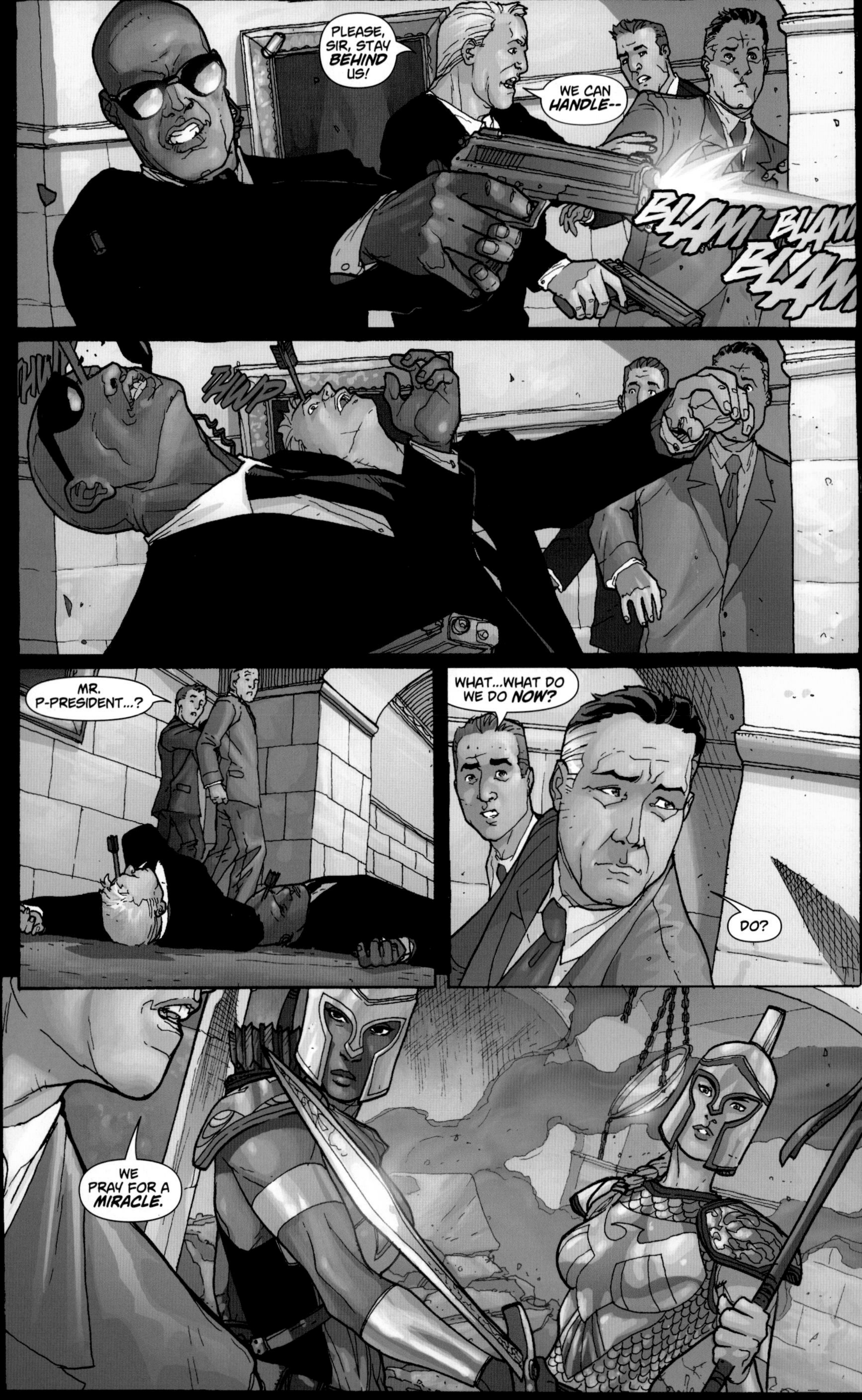
PLEASE, SIR, STAY BEHIND US!
WE CAN HANDLE--
BLAM BLAM BLAM
THWP
THWP
MR. P-PRESIDENT...?
WHAT...WHAT DO WE DO NOW?
DO?
WE PRAY FOR A MIRACLE.

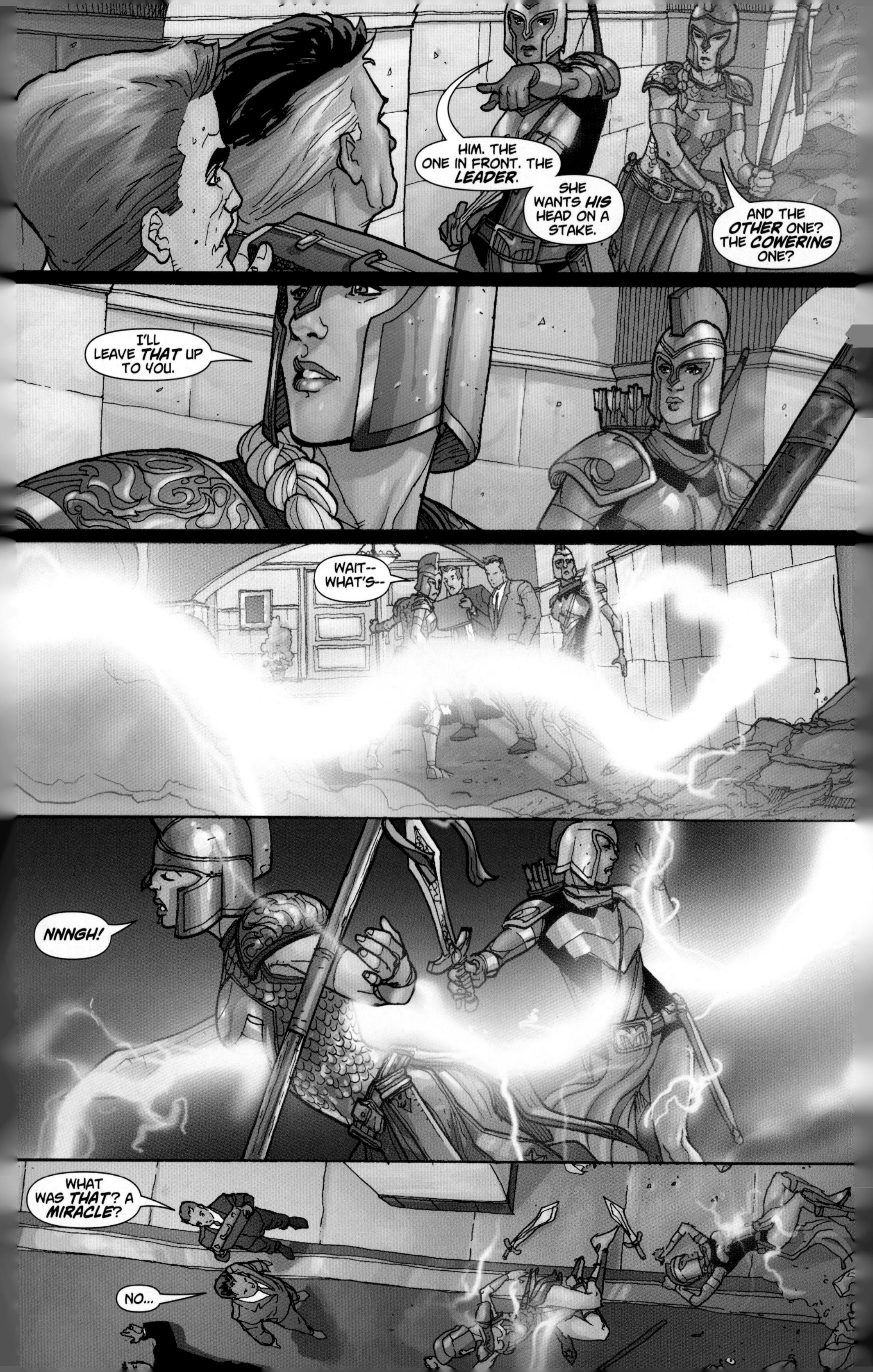
HIM. THE ONE IN FRONT. THE LEADER.
SHE WANTS HIS HEAD ON A STAKE.
AND THE OTHER ONE? THE COWERING ONE?
I'LL LEAVE THAT UP TO YOU.
WAIT-- WHAT'S--
NNNGH!
WHAT WAS THAT? A MIRACLE?
NO...

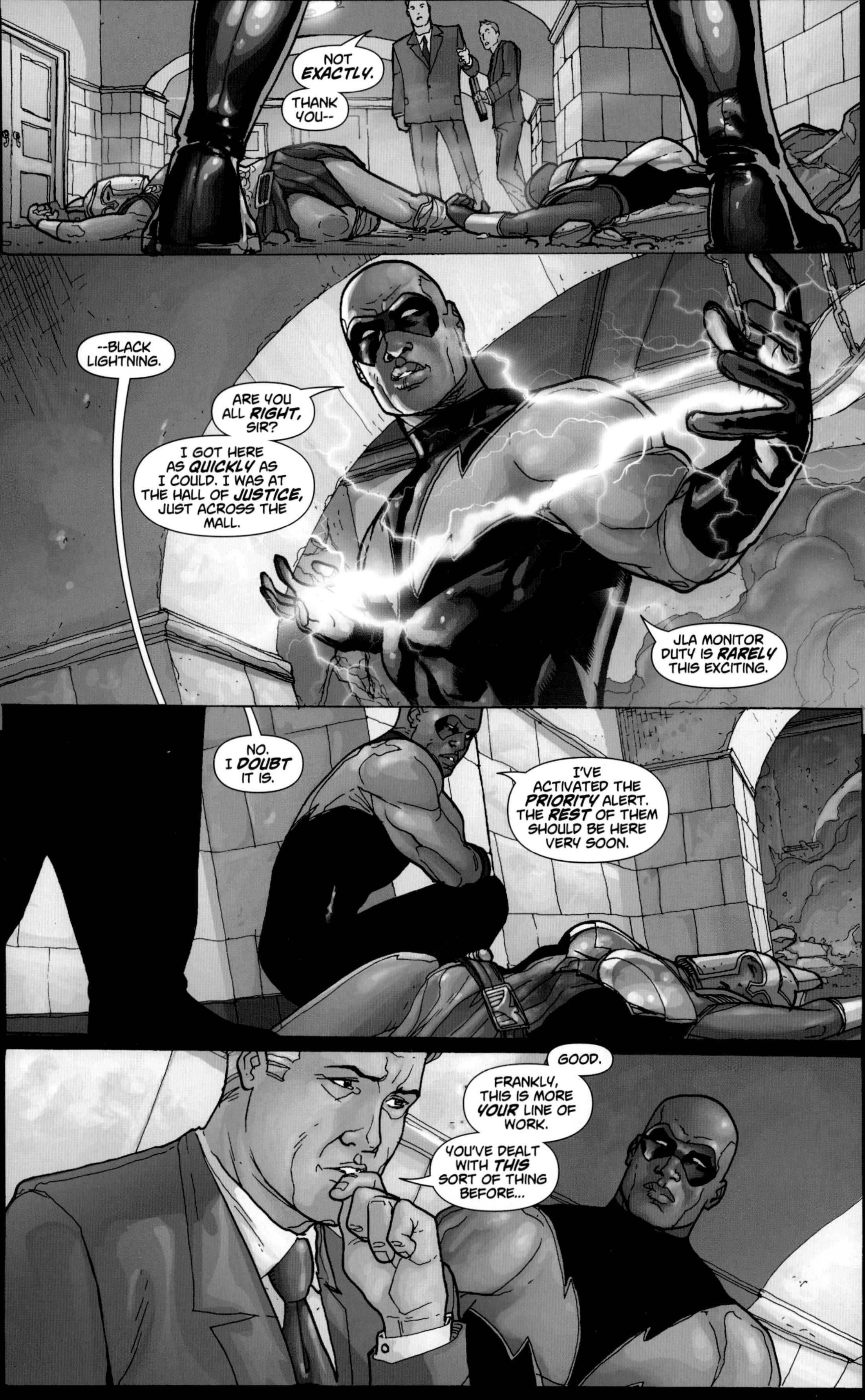
NOT EXACTLY.
THANK YOU--
--BLACK LIGHTNING.
ARE YOU ALL RIGHT, SIR?
I GOT HERE AS QUICKLY AS I COULD. I WAS AT THE HALL OF JUSTICE, JUST ACROSS THE MALL.
JLA MONITOR DUTY IS RARELY THIS EXCITING.
NO. I DOUBT IT IS.
I'VE ACTIVATED THE PRIORITY ALERT. THE REST OF THEM SHOULD BE HERE VERY SOON.
GOOD.
FRANKLY, THIS IS MORE YOUR LINE OF WORK.
YOU'VE DEALT WITH THIS SORT OF THING BEFORE...

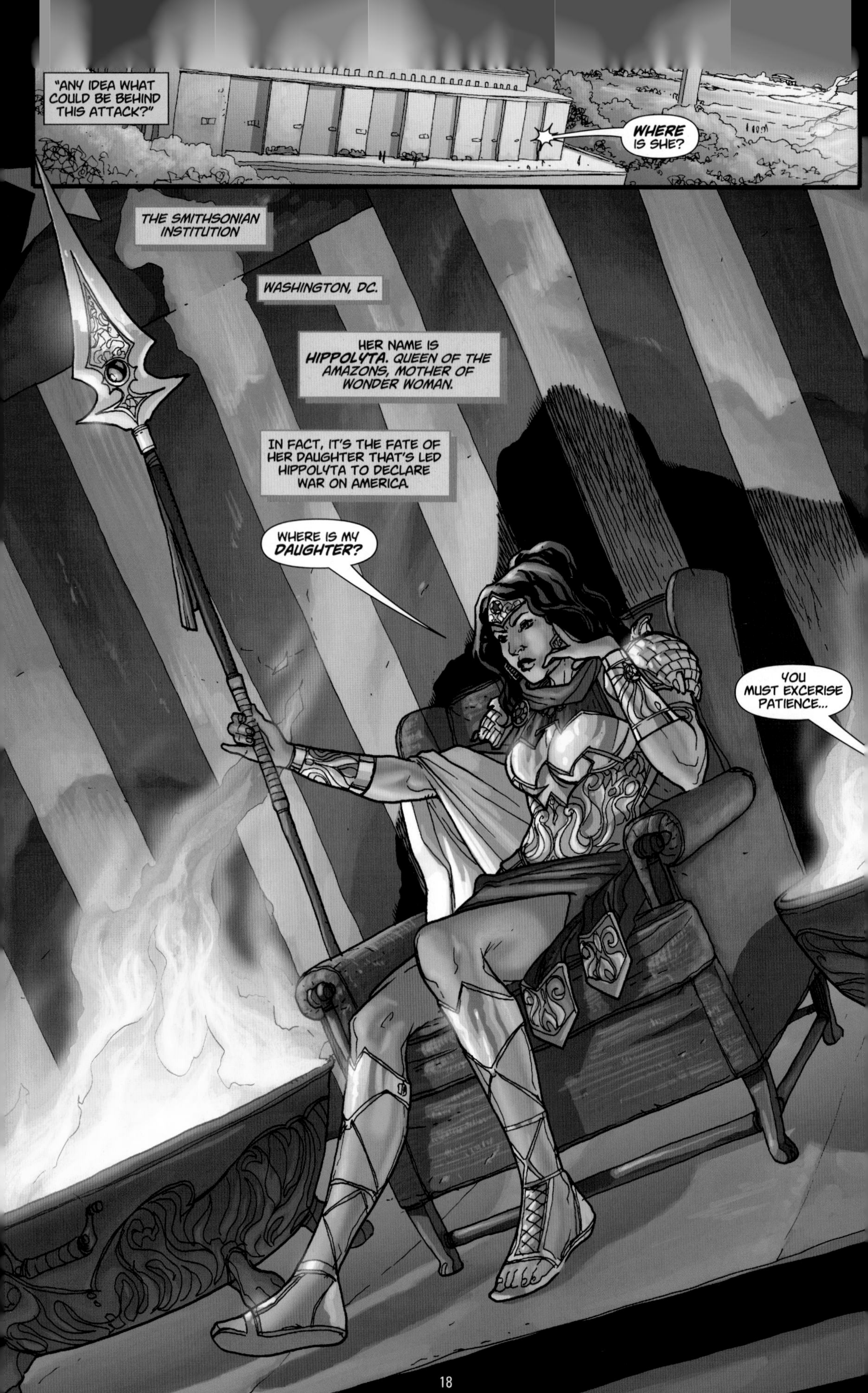
"ANY IDEA WHAT COULD BE BEHIND THIS ATTACK?"
WHERE IS SHE?
THE SMITHSONIAN INSTITUTION
WASHINGTON, DC.
HER NAME IS HIPPOLYTA. QUEEN OF THE AMAZONS, MOTHER OF WONDER WOMAN.
IN FACT, IT'S THE FATE OF HER DAUGHTER THAT'S LED HIPPOLYTA TO DECLARE WAR ON AMERICA.
WHERE IS MY DAUGHTER?
YOU MUST EXCERISE PATIENCE...

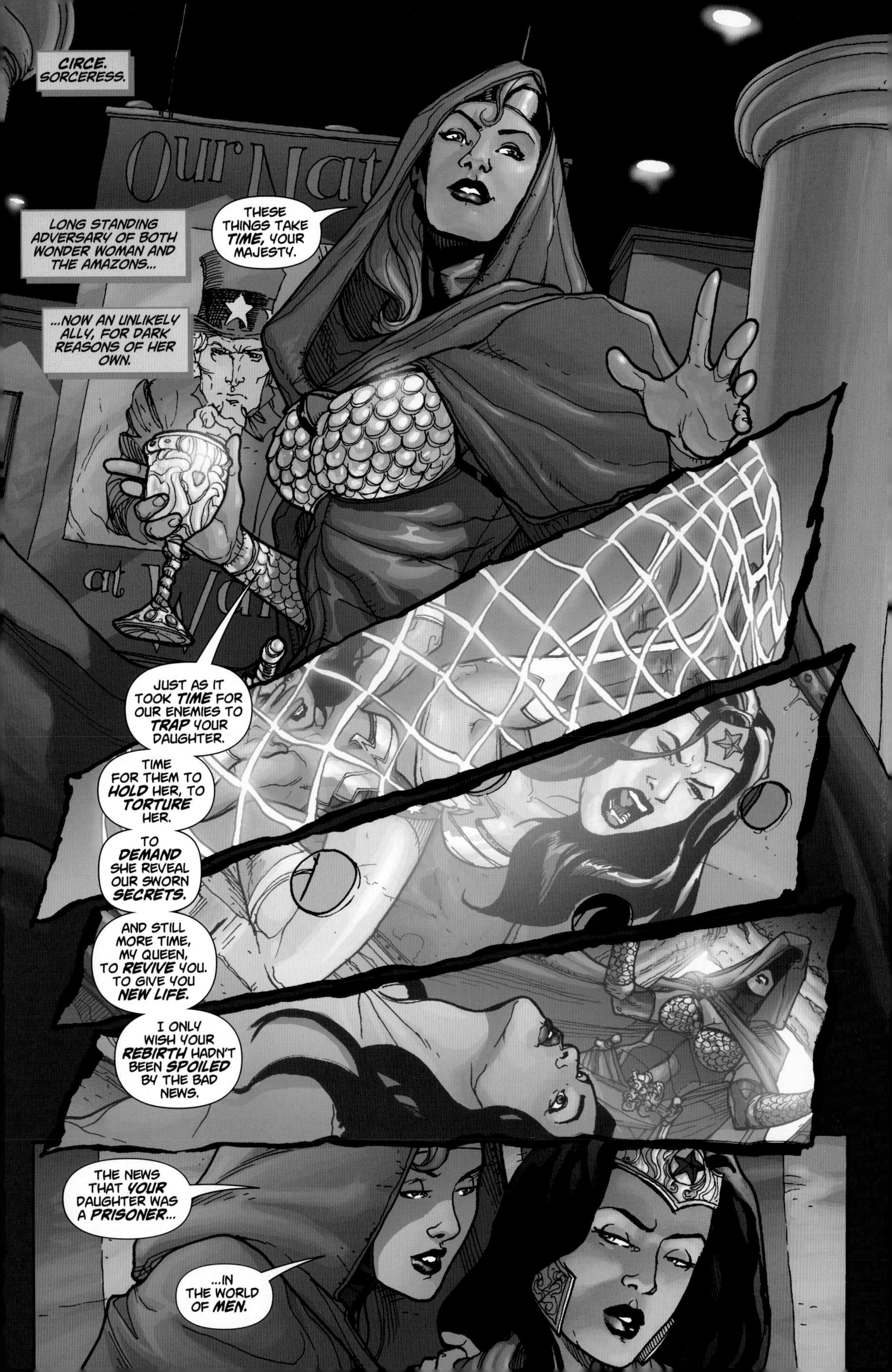
CIRCE. SORCERESS.
Our Nat
LONG STANDING ADVERSARY OF BOTH WONDER WOMAN AND THE AMAZONS...
THESE THINGS TAKE TIME, YOUR MAJESTY.
...NOW AN UNLIKELY ALLY, FOR DARK REASONS OF HER OWN.
at
JUST AS IT TOOK TIME FOR OUR ENEMIES TO TRAP YOUR DAUGHTER.
TIME FOR THEM TO HOLD HER, TO TORTURE HER.
TO DEMAND SHE REVEAL OUR SWORN SECRETS.
AND STILL MORE TIME, MY QUEEN, TO REVIVE YOU. TO GIVE YOU NEW LIFE.
I ONLY WISH YOUR REBIRTH HADN'T BEEN SPOILED BY THE BAD NEWS.
THE NEWS THAT YOUR DAUGHTER WAS A PRISONER...
...IN THE WORLD OF MEN.

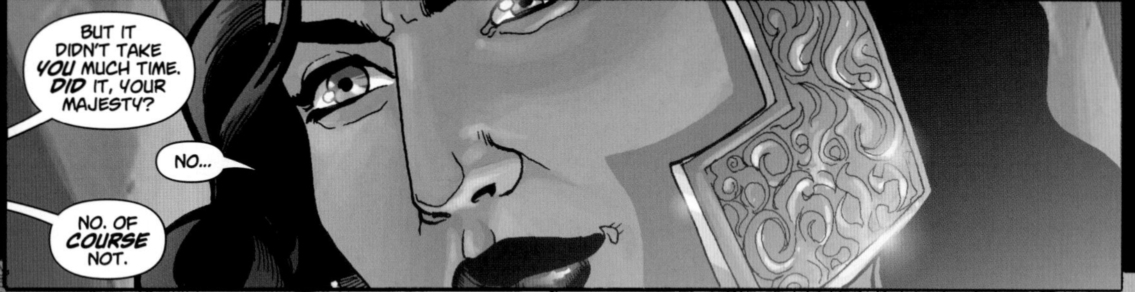
BUT IT DIDN'T TAKE *YOU* MUCH TIME. *DID* IT, YOUR MAJESTY?
NO...
NO. OF *COURSE* NOT.

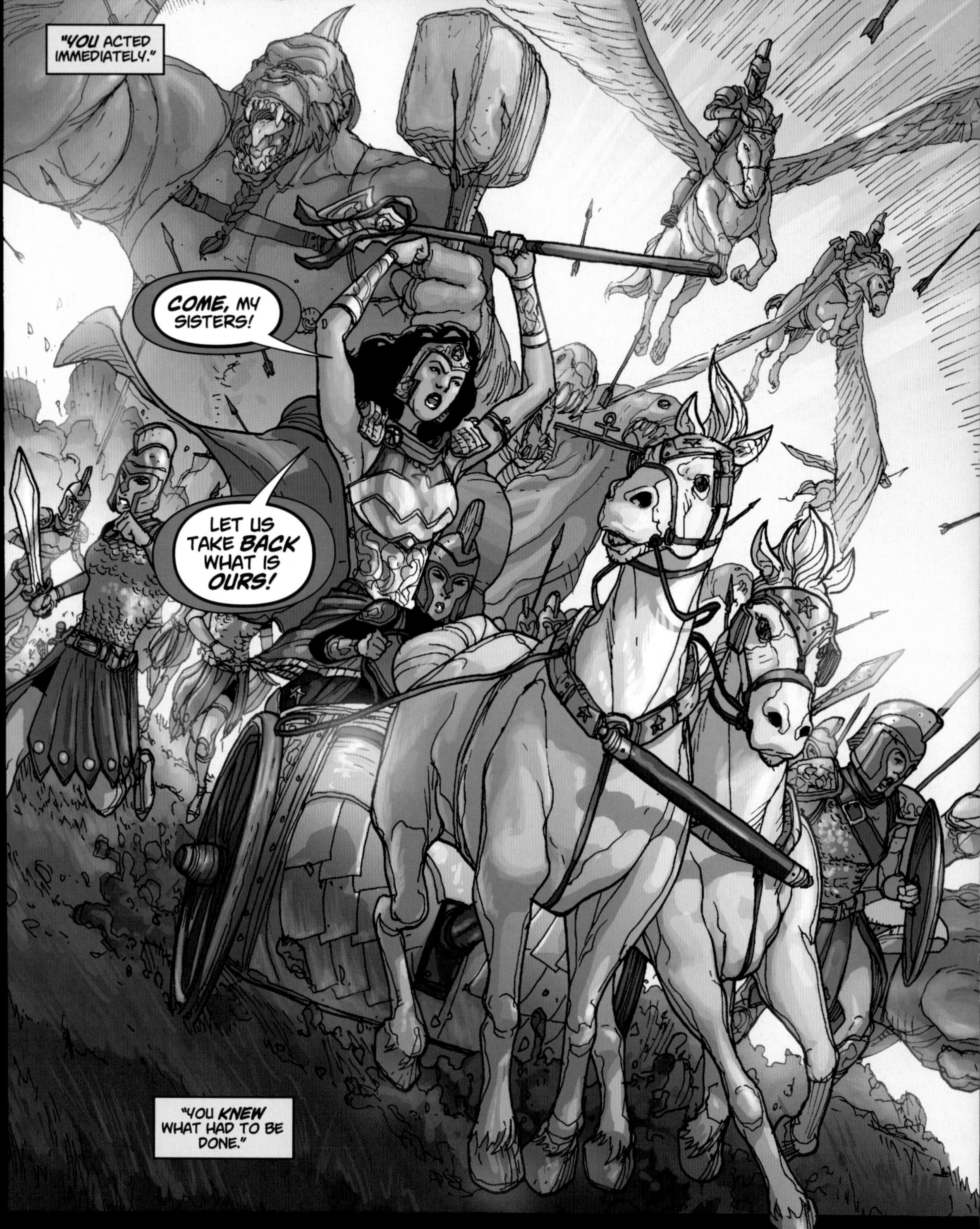
"*YOU* ACTED IMMEDIATELY."
COME, MY SISTERS!
LET US TAKE *BACK* WHAT IS *OURS!*
"YOU *KNEW* WHAT HAD TO BE DONE."

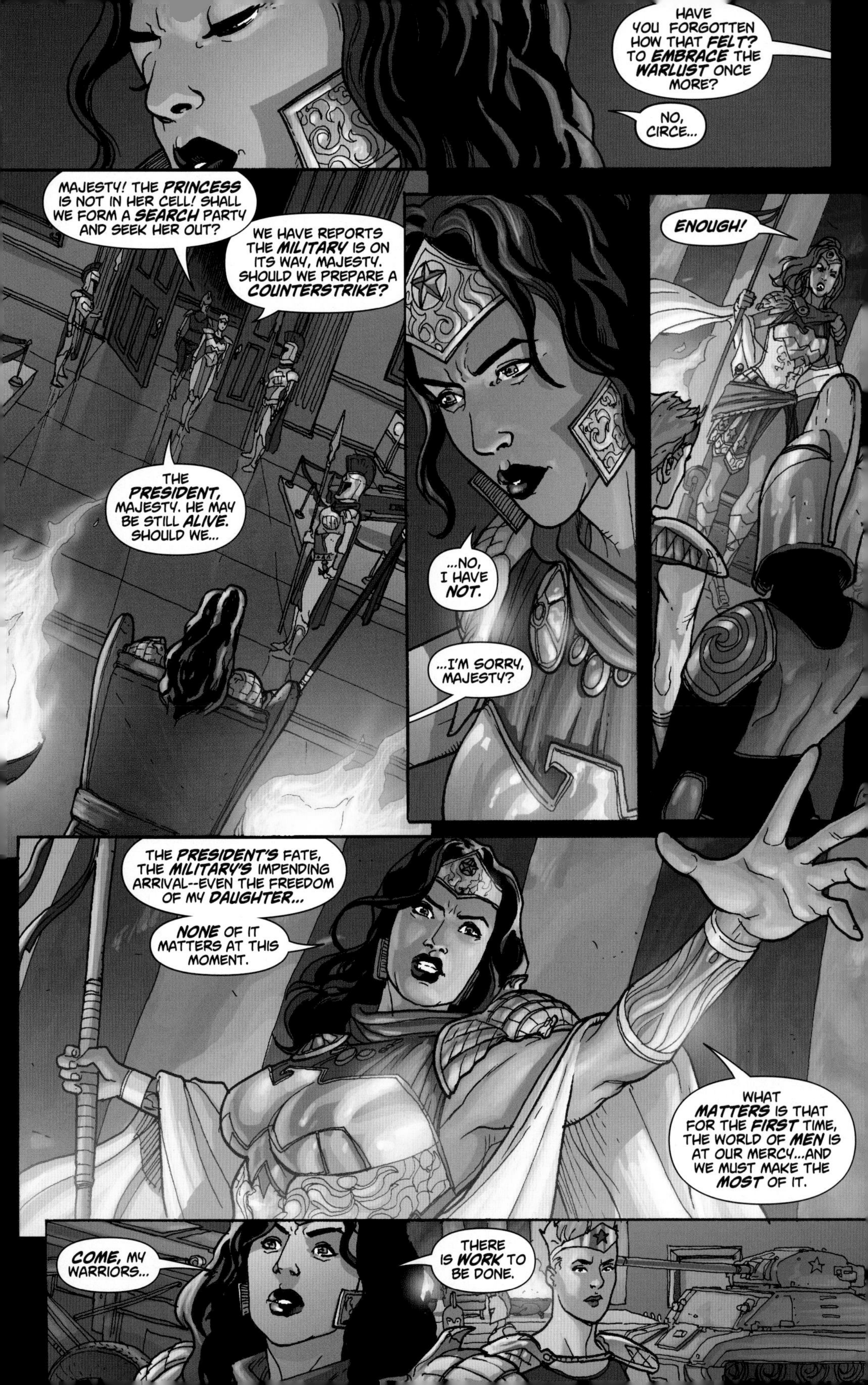
HAVE YOU FORGOTTEN HOW THAT FELT? TO EMBRACE THE WARLUST ONCE MORE?
NO, CIRCE...
MAJESTY! THE PRINCESS IS NOT IN HER CELL! SHALL WE FORM A SEARCH PARTY AND SEEK HER OUT?
WE HAVE REPORTS THE MILITARY IS ON ITS WAY, MAJESTY. SHOULD WE PREPARE A COUNTERSTRIKE?
THE PRESIDENT, MAJESTY. HE MAY BE STILL ALIVE. SHOULD WE...
...NO, I HAVE NOT.
...I'M SORRY, MAJESTY?
ENOUGH!
THE PRESIDENT'S FATE, THE MILITARY'S IMPENDING ARRIVAL--EVEN THE FREEDOM OF MY DAUGHTER...
NONE OF IT MATTERS AT THIS MOMENT.
WHAT MATTERS IS THAT FOR THE FIRST TIME, THE WORLD OF MEN IS AT OUR MERCY...AND WE MUST MAKE THE MOST OF IT.
COME, MY WARRIORS...
THERE IS WORK TO BE DONE.

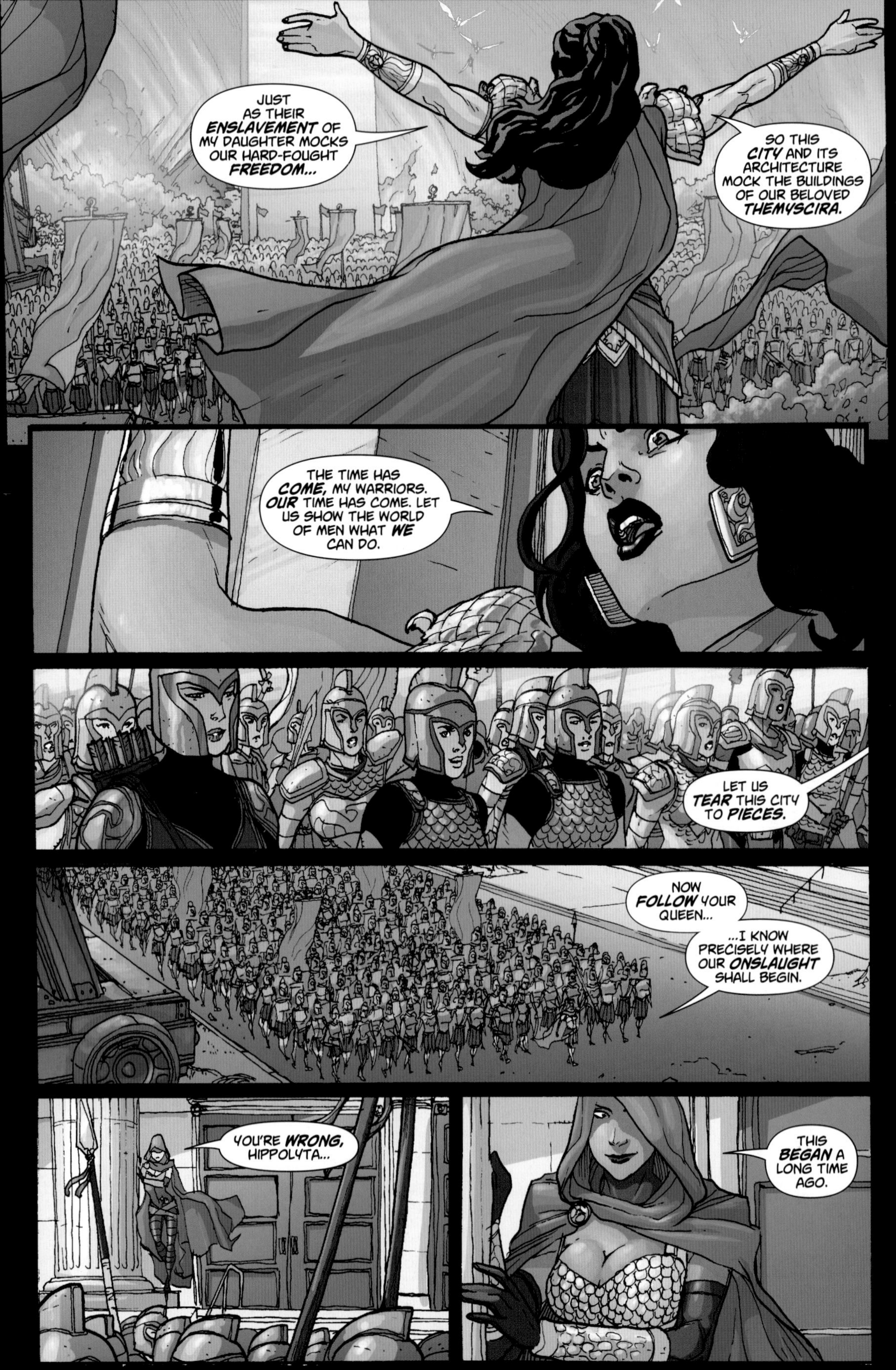
JUST AS THEIR ENSLAVEMENT OF MY DAUGHTER MOCKS OUR HARD-FOUGHT FREEDOM...
SO THIS CITY AND ITS ARCHITECTURE MOCK THE BUILDINGS OF OUR BELOVED THEMYSCIRA.
THE TIME HAS COME, MY WARRIORS. OUR TIME HAS COME. LET US SHOW THE WORLD OF MEN WHAT WE CAN DO.
LET US TEAR THIS CITY TO PIECES.
NOW FOLLOW YOUR QUEEN...
...I KNOW PRECISELY WHERE OUR ONSLAUGHT SHALL BEGIN.
YOU'RE WRONG, HIPPOLYTA...
THIS BEGAN A LONG TIME AGO.

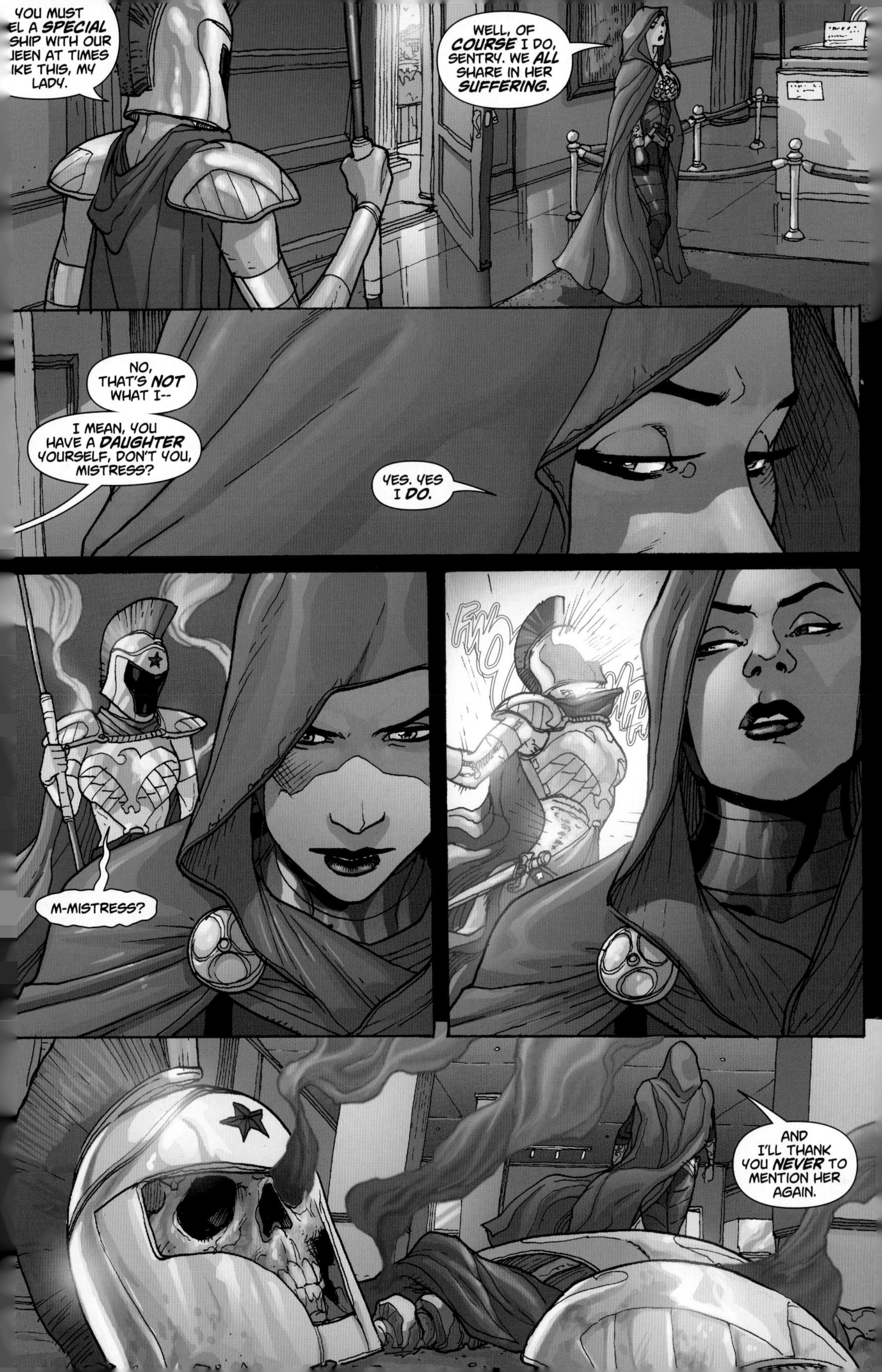

YOU MUST
EL A SPECIAL
SHIP WITH OUR
EEN AT TIMES
IKE THIS, MY
LADY.
WELL, OF COURSE I DO, SENTRY. WE ALL SHARE IN HER SUFFERING.
NO, THAT'S NOT WHAT I--
I MEAN, YOU HAVE A DAUGHTER YOURSELF, DON'T YOU, MISTRESS?
YES. YES I DO.
M-MISTRESS?
AND I'LL THANK YOU NEVER TO MENTION HER AGAIN.

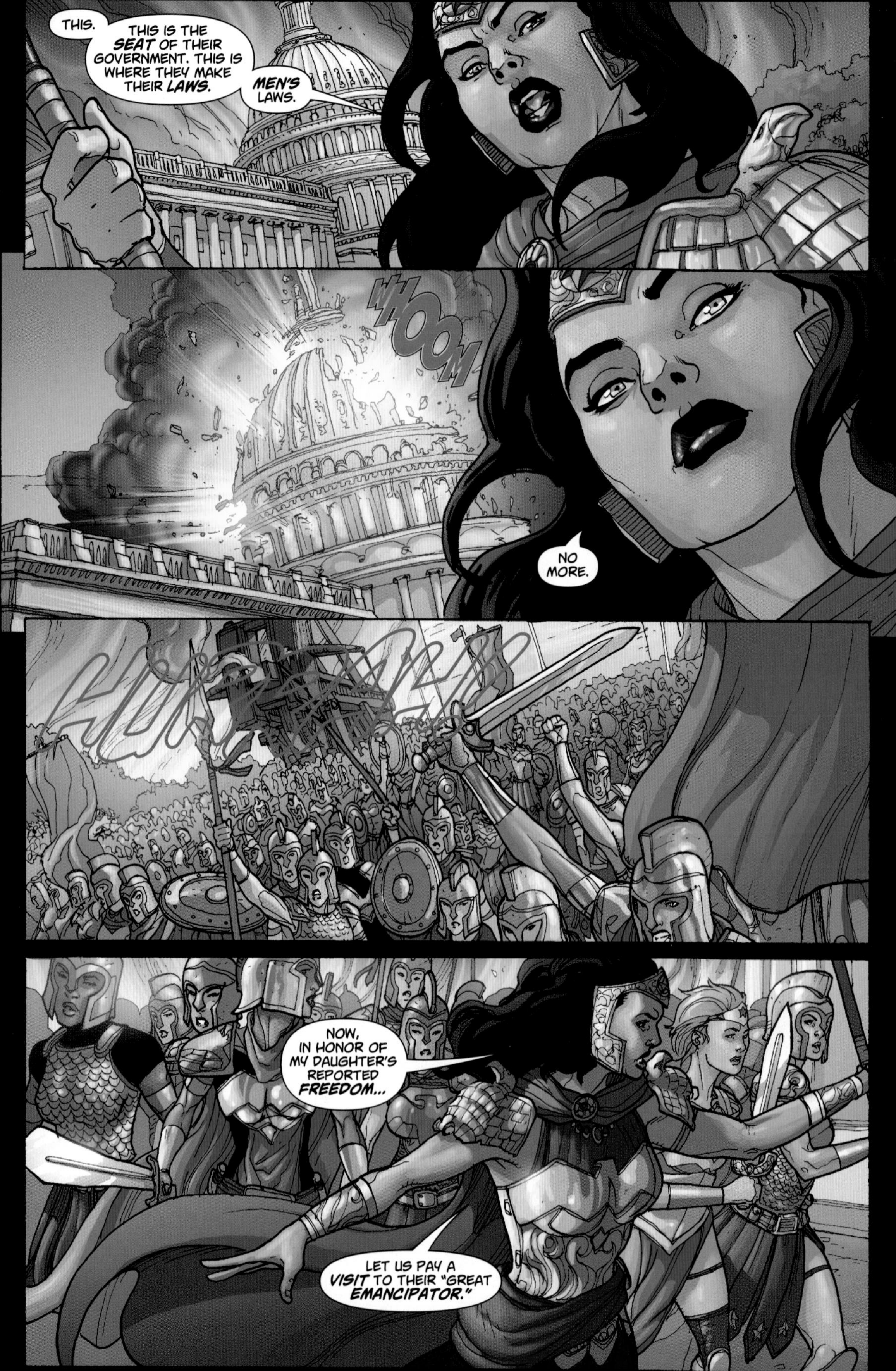
THIS.
THIS IS THE SEAT OF THEIR GOVERNMENT. THIS IS WHERE THEY MAKE THEIR LAWS.
MEN'S LAWS.
WHOOM
NO MORE.
NOW, IN HONOR OF MY DAUGHTER'S REPORTED FREEDOM...
LET US PAY A VISIT TO THEIR "GREAT EMANCIPATOR."

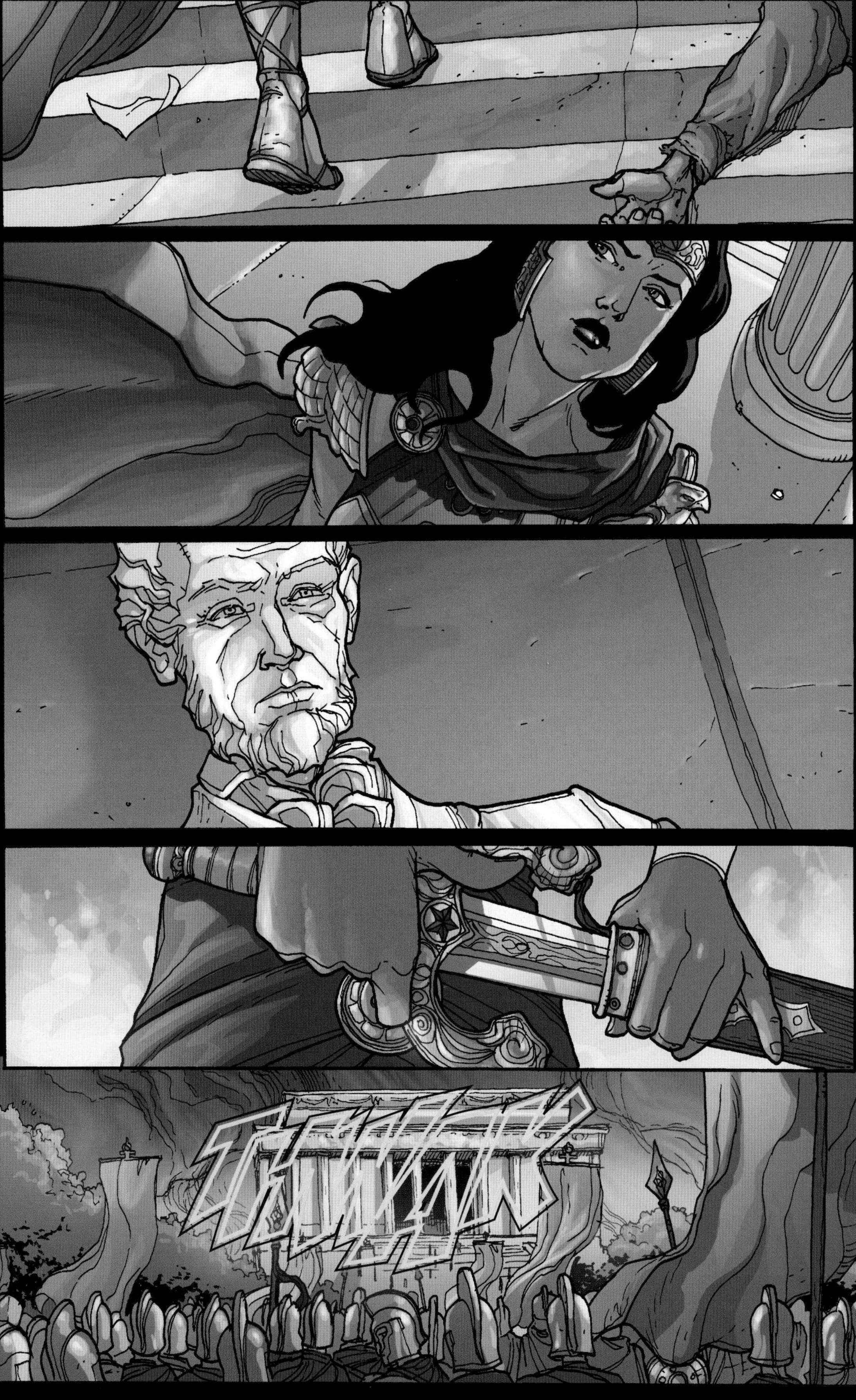
THWAK

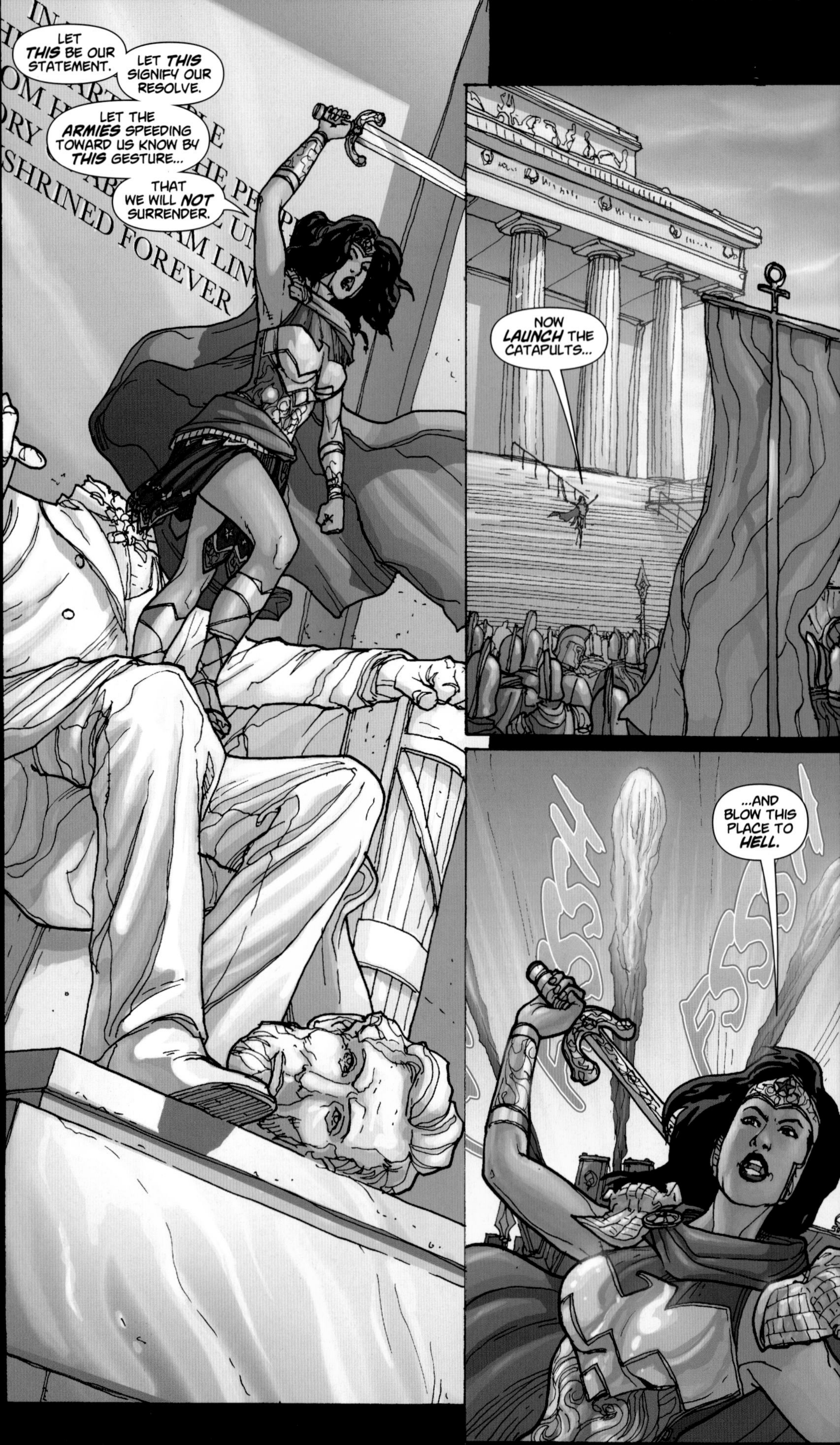
SHRINED FOREVER
LET THIS BE OUR STATEMENT.
LET THIS SIGNIFY OUR RESOLVE.
LET THE ARMIES SPEEDING TOWARD US KNOW BY THIS GESTURE...
THAT WE WILL NOT SURRENDER.
NOW LAUNCH THE CATAPULTS...
...AND BLOW THIS PLACE TO HELL.

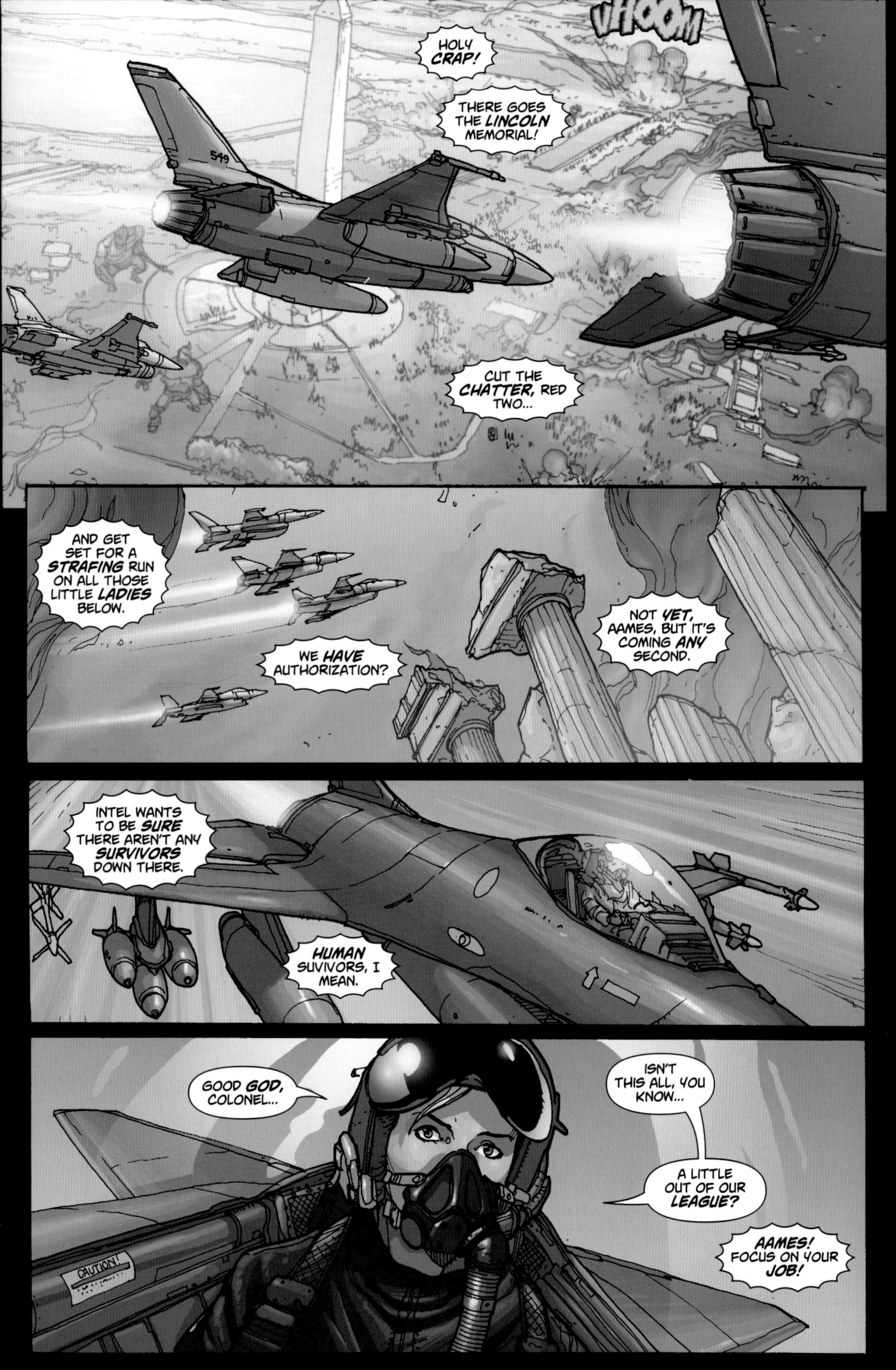
VHOOM
HOLY CRAP!
THERE GOES THE LINCOLN MEMORIAL!
CUT THE CHATTER, RED TWO...
AND GET SET FOR A STRAFING RUN ON ALL THOSE LITTLE LADIES BELOW.
WE HAVE AUTHORIZATION?
NOT YET, AAMES, BUT IT'S COMING ANY SECOND.
INTEL WANTS TO BE SURE THERE AREN'T ANY SURVIVORS DOWN THERE.
HUMAN SUVIVORS, I MEAN.
GOOD GOD, COLONEL...
ISN'T THIS ALL, YOU KNOW...
A LITTLE OUT OF OUR LEAGUE?
AAMES! FOCUS ON YOUR JOB!
CAUTION!

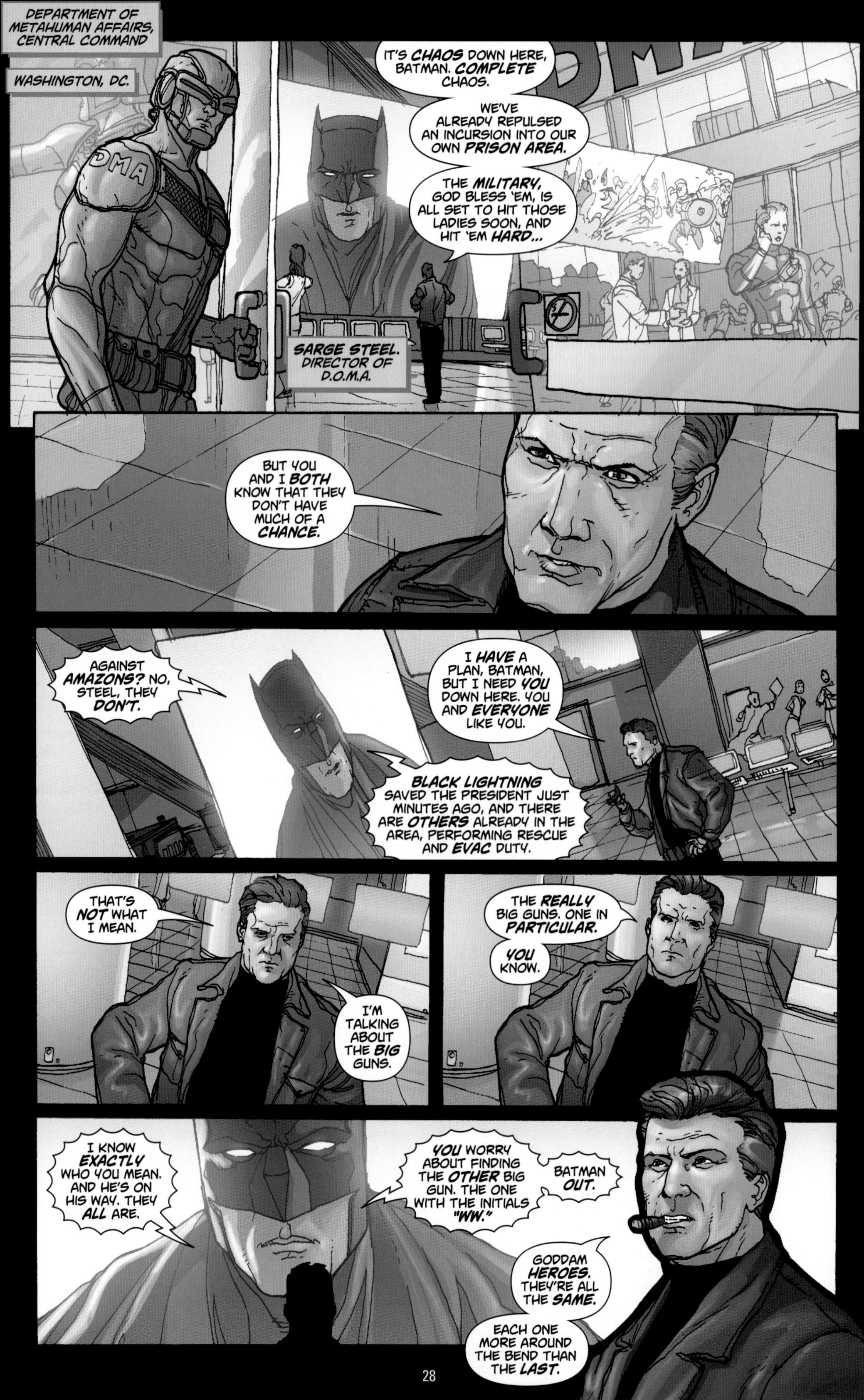
DEPARTMENT OF METAHUMAN AFFAIRS, CENTRAL COMMAND
WASHINGTON, DC.
IT'S CHAOS DOWN HERE, BATMAN. COMPLETE CHAOS.
WE'VE ALREADY REPULSED AN INCURSION INTO OUR OWN PRISON AREA.
THE MILITARY, GOD BLESS 'EM, IS ALL SET TO HIT THOSE LADIES SOON, AND HIT 'EM HARD...
SARGE STEEL. DIRECTOR OF D.O.M.A.
BUT YOU AND I BOTH KNOW THAT THEY DON'T HAVE MUCH OF A CHANCE.
AGAINST AMAZONS? NO, STEEL, THEY DON'T.
I HAVE A PLAN, BATMAN, BUT I NEED YOU DOWN HERE. YOU AND EVERYONE LIKE YOU.
BLACK LIGHTNING SAVED THE PRESIDENT JUST MINUTES AGO, AND THERE ARE OTHERS ALREADY IN THE AREA, PERFORMING RESCUE AND EVAC DUTY.
THAT'S NOT WHAT I MEAN.
I'M TALKING ABOUT THE BIG GUNS.
THE REALLY BIG GUNS. ONE IN PARTICULAR.
YOU KNOW.
I KNOW EXACTLY WHO YOU MEAN. AND HE'S ON HIS WAY. THEY ALL ARE.
YOU WORRY ABOUT FINDING THE OTHER BIG GUN. THE ONE WITH THE INITIALS "WW."
BATMAN OUT.
GODDAM HEROES. THEY'RE ALL THE SAME.
EACH ONE MORE AROUND THE BEND THAN THE LAST.

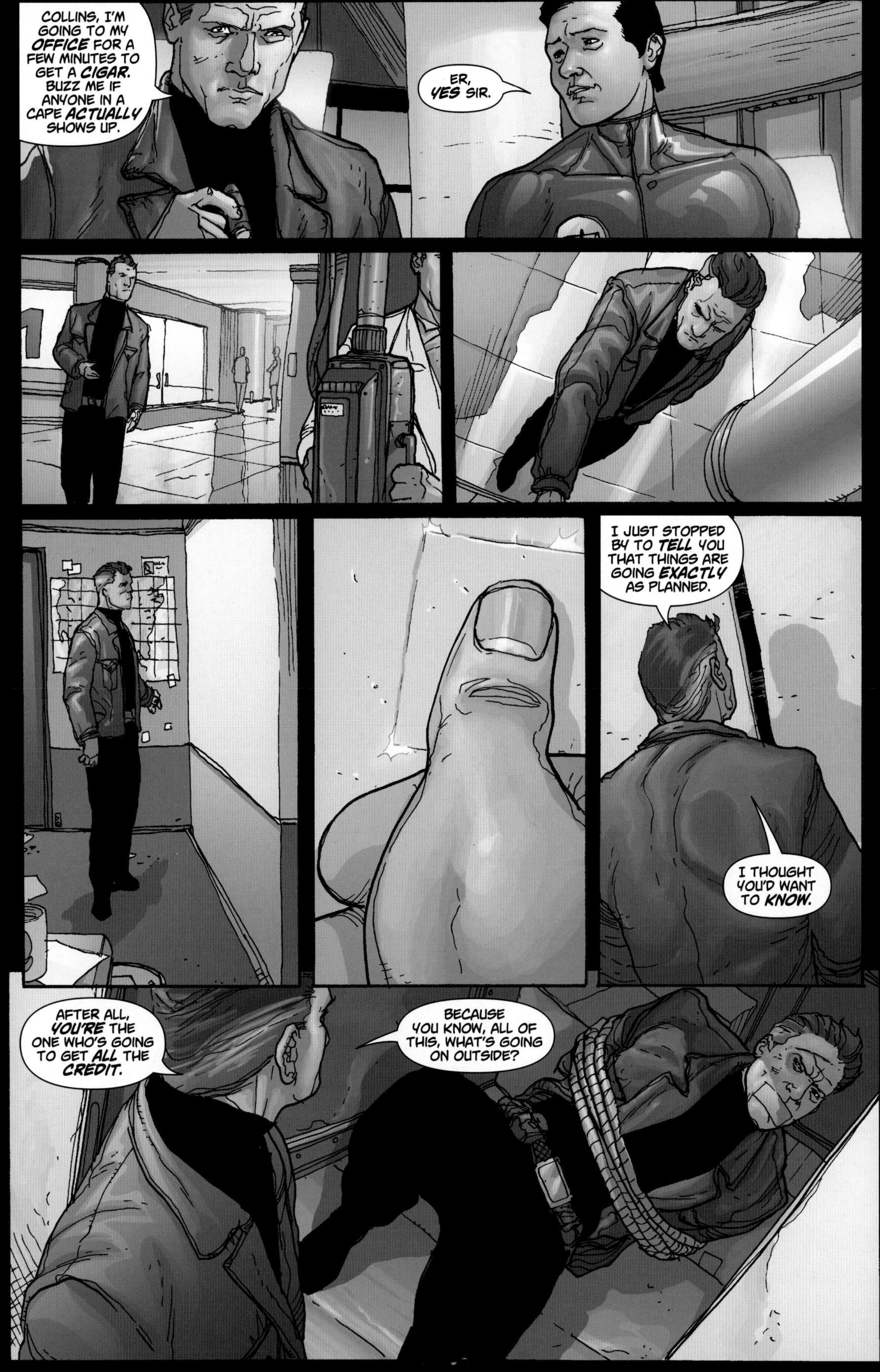
COLLINS, I'M GOING TO MY OFFICE FOR A FEW MINUTES TO GET A CIGAR. BUZZ ME IF ANYONE IN A CAPE ACTUALLY SHOWS UP.
ER, YES SIR.
I JUST STOPPED BY TO TELL YOU THAT THINGS ARE GOING EXACTLY AS PLANNED.
I THOUGHT YOU'D WANT TO KNOW.
AFTER ALL, YOU'RE THE ONE WHO'S GOING TO GET ALL THE CREDIT.
BECAUSE YOU KNOW, ALL OF THIS, WHAT'S GOING ON OUTSIDE?

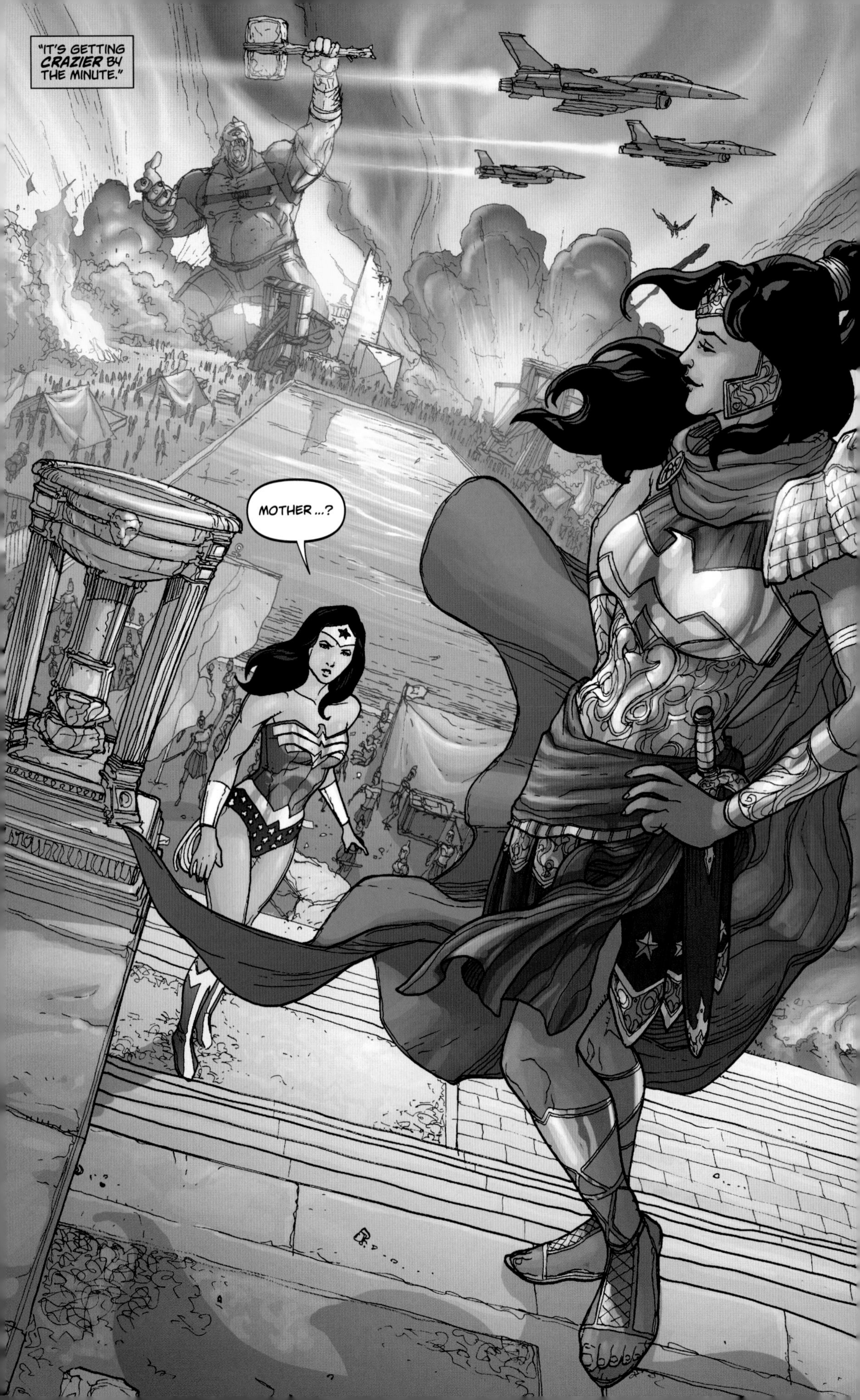
"IT'S GETTING CRAZIER BY THE MINUTE."
MOTHER...?

Chapter Two

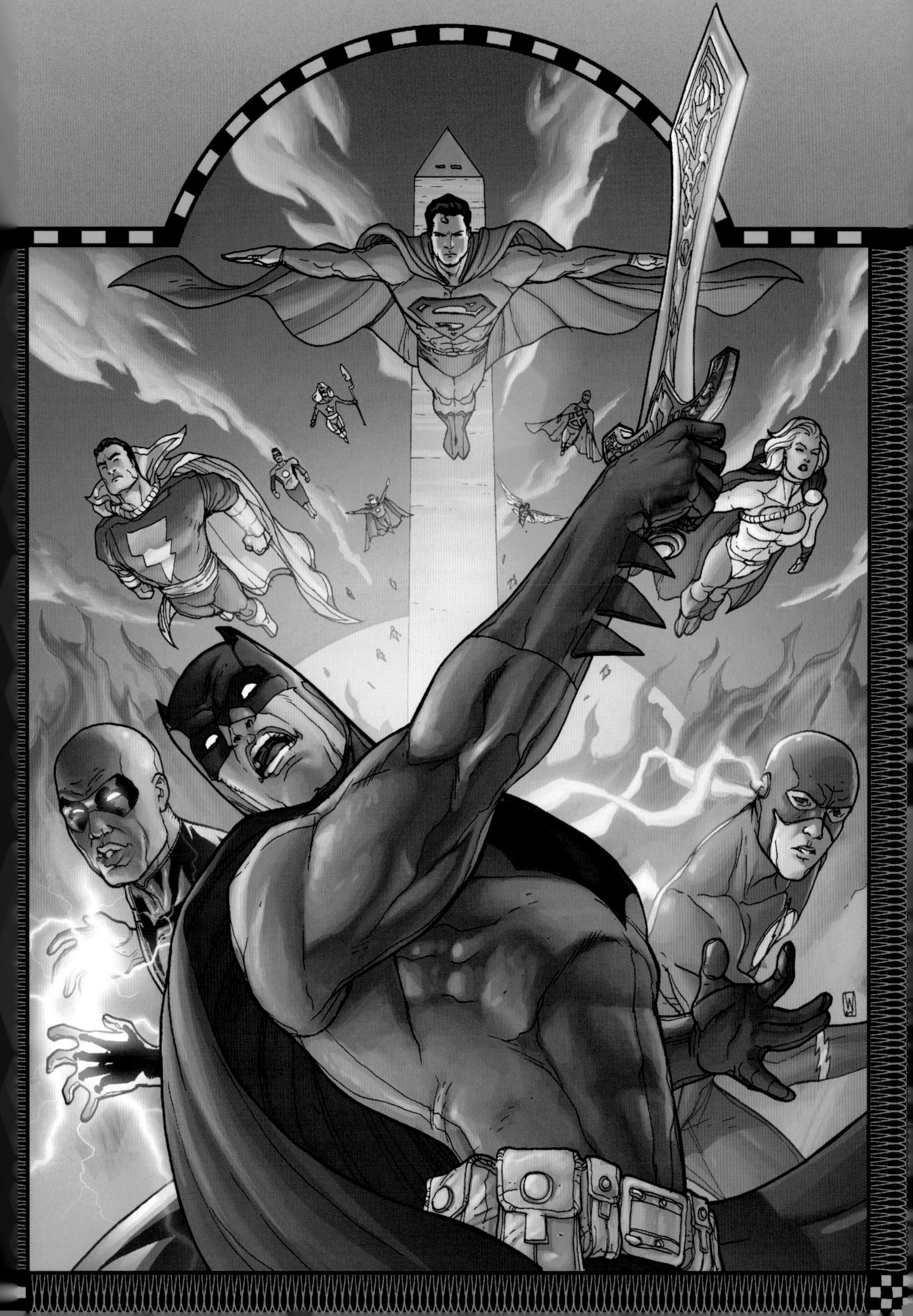

Diana comes face to face with her mother, but the reunion is bitter-sweet. When Diana confronts the Queen about her uncharacteristic attacks, she concludes that her mother must be under the control of the villainous witch Circe — for only black magic could explain why her once-peaceful mother could be launching an attack on mankind. Later, during a battle with Circe, Diana demands answers from the witch — who reveals her sinister plan of destroying the Amazons' home of Themyscira by launching nuclear missiles towards the island. When Hippolyta creeps up behind her and hears this, she impales the traitorous Circe with a spear — and the witch seemingly vanishes. Unfortunately Hippolyta's bloodlust is not dispelled, and mother and daughter remain locked in battle.

Meanwhile, the real Sarge Steel has been locked away in a vault, while his captor — the shapshifter known as Everyman — is now impersonating him. When Nemesis — a master of disguise himself — gets close to Everyman, he takes advantage of the ensuing chaos surrounding them and turns into a duplicate of Sarge Steel as well. With two fake Sarge Steels standing before them, the agents of the Department of Metahuman Affairs have no choice but to bring them both in and try to figure out who is who…

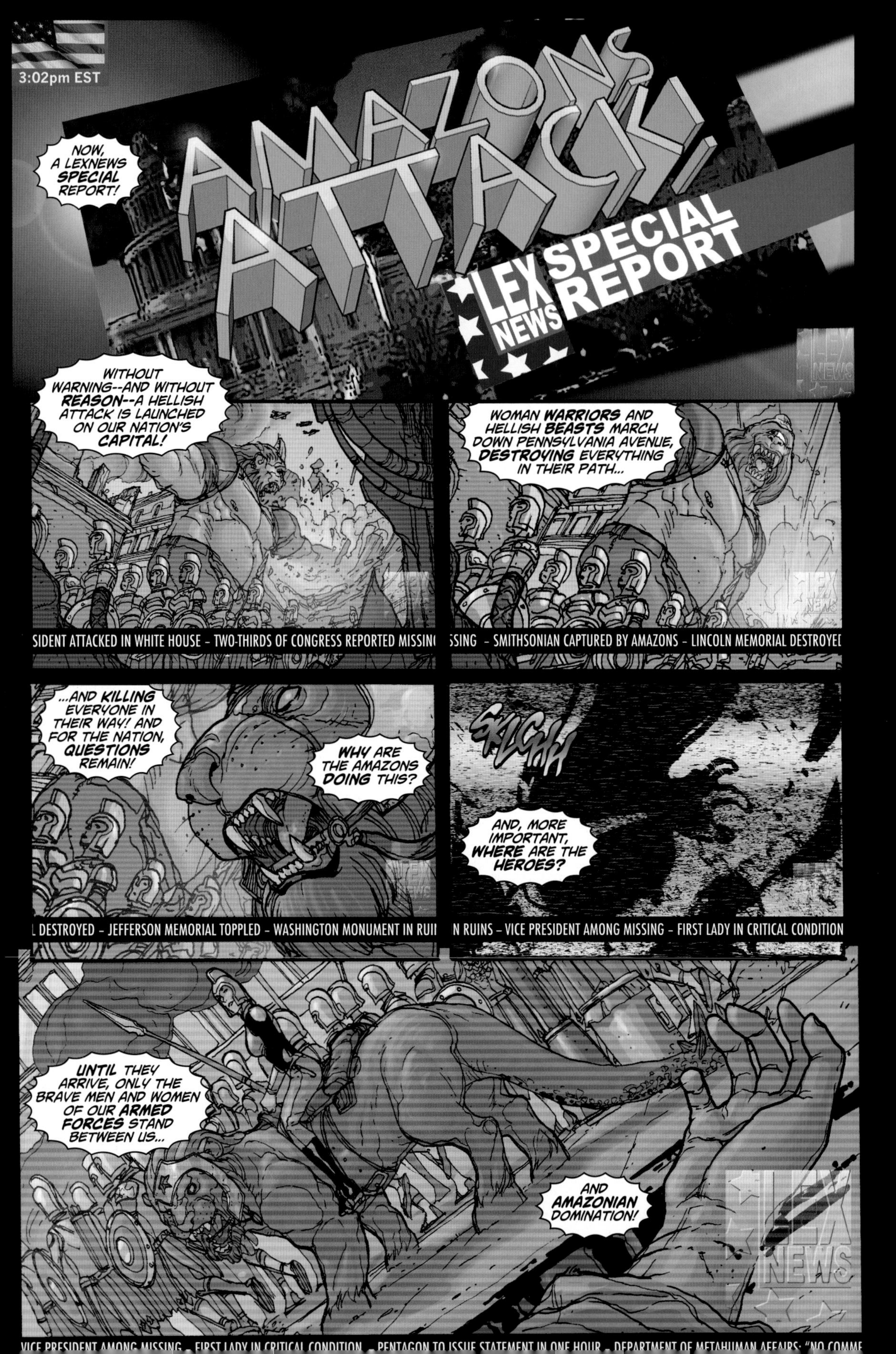
3:02pm EST
AMAZONS ATTACK!
NOW, A LEXNEWS SPECIAL REPORT!
LEX NEWS SPECIAL REPORT
WITHOUT WARNING--AND WITHOUT REASON--A HELLISH ATTACK IS LAUNCHED ON OUR NATION'S CAPITAL!
WOMAN WARRIORS AND HELLISH BEASTS MARCH DOWN PENNSYLVANIA AVENUE, DESTROYING EVERYTHING IN THEIR PATH...
SIDENT ATTACKED IN WHITE HOUSE - TWO-THIRDS OF CONGRESS REPORTED MISSING
SSING - SMITHSONIAN CAPTURED BY AMAZONS - LINCOLN MEMORIAL DESTROYED
...AND KILLING EVERYONE IN THEIR WAY! AND FOR THE NATION, QUESTIONS REMAIN!
WHY ARE THE AMAZONS DOING THIS?
SKLGHH
AND, MORE IMPORTANT, WHERE ARE THE HEROES?
L DESTROYED - JEFFERSON MEMORIAL TOPPLED - WASHINGTON MONUMENT IN RUI
N RUINS - VICE PRESIDENT AMONG MISSING - FIRST LADY IN CRITICAL CONDITION
UNTIL THEY ARRIVE, ONLY THE BRAVE MEN AND WOMEN OF OUR ARMED FORCES STAND BETWEEN US...
AND AMAZONIAN DOMINATION!
VICE PRESIDENT AMONG MISSING - FIRST LADY IN CRITICAL CONDITION - PENTAGON TO ISSUE STATEMENT IN ONE HOUR - DEPARTMENT OF METAHUMAN AFFAIRS: "NO COMME

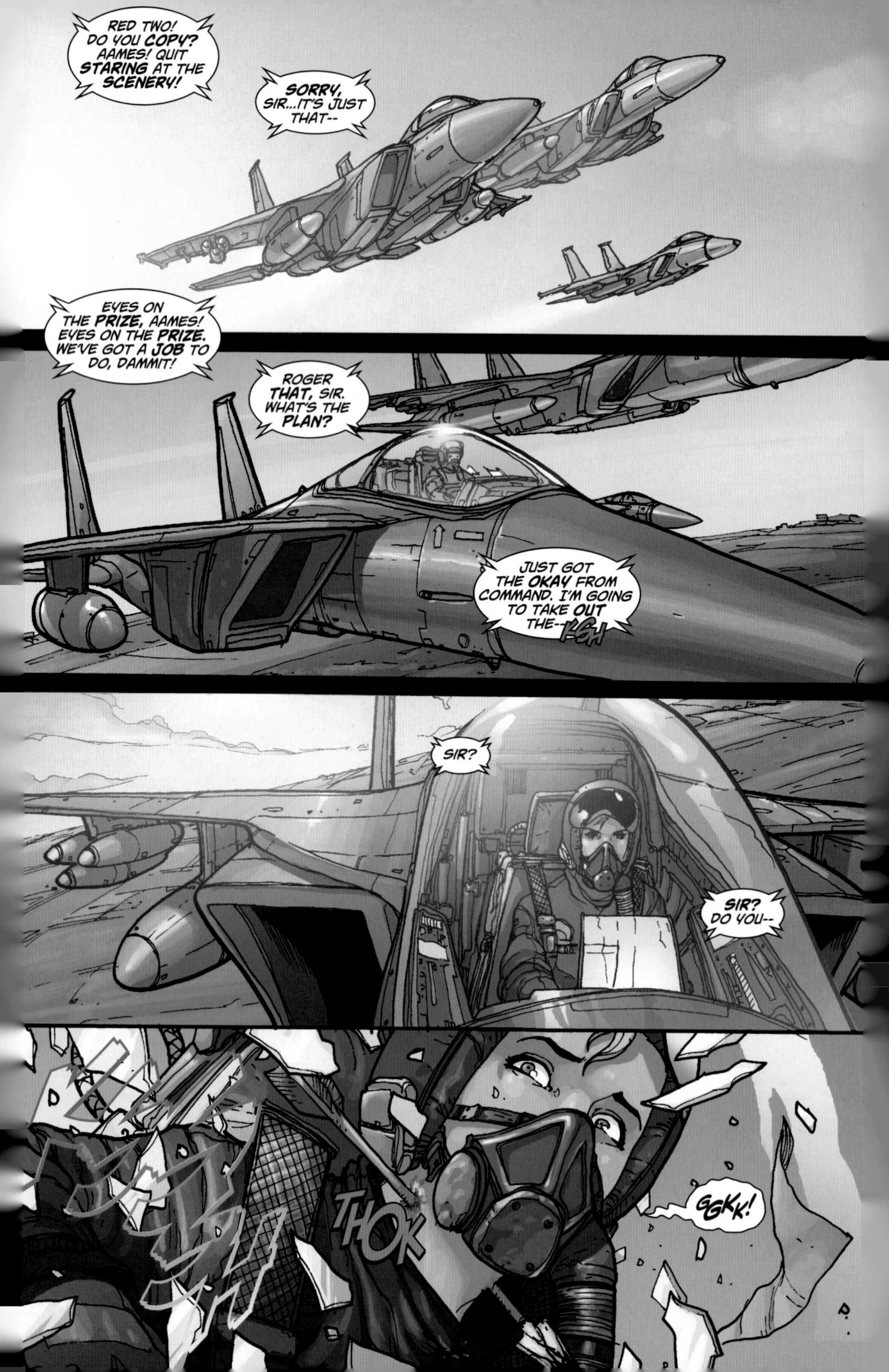
RED TWO! DO YOU COPY? AAMES! QUIT STARING AT THE SCENERY!
SORRY, SIR...IT'S JUST THAT--
EYES ON THE PRIZE, AAMES! EYES ON THE PRIZE. WE'VE GOT A JOB TO DO, DAMMIT!
ROGER THAT, SIR. WHAT'S THE PLAN?
JUST GOT THE OKAY FROM COMMAND. I'M GOING TO TAKE OUT THE--KGH
SIR?
SIR? DO YOU--
THOK
GGKK!

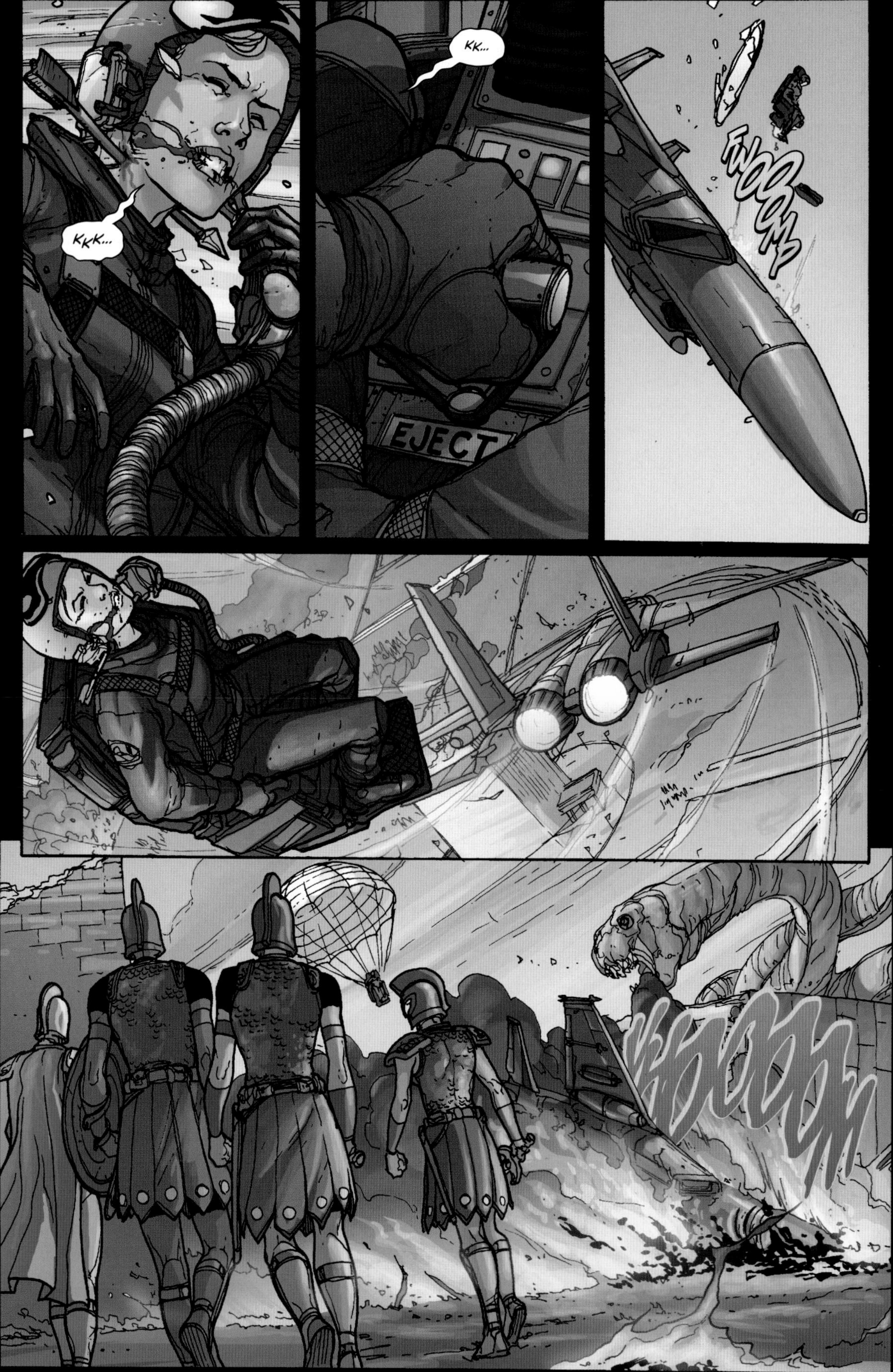
KKK...
KK...
FWOOOMP
KBOOOM

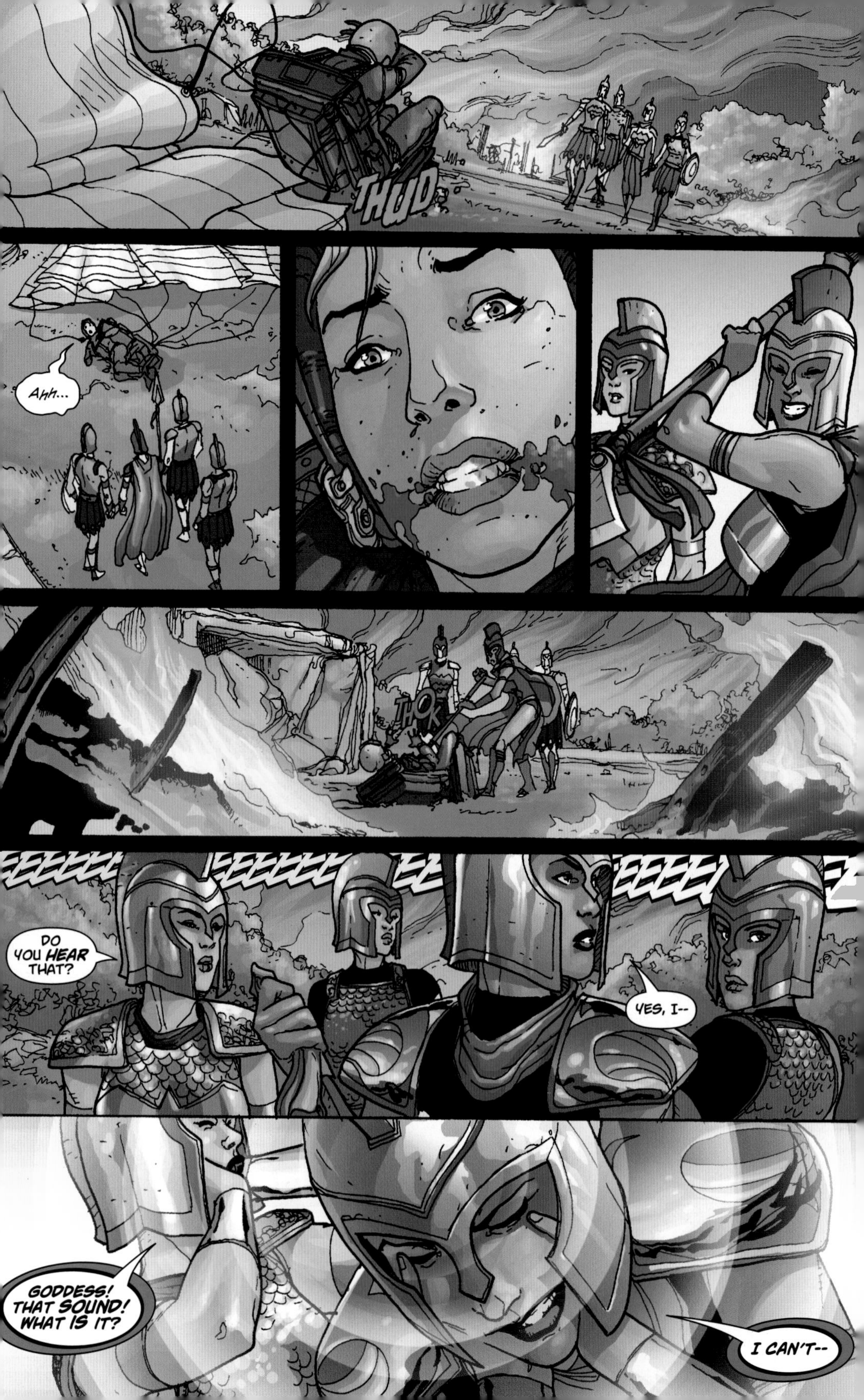
THUD
Ahh...
THOK
EEEEEEEEEEEEEEEEEEEEEEE
DO YOU HEAR THAT?
YES, I--
GODDESS! THAT SOUND! WHAT IS IT?
I CAN'T--

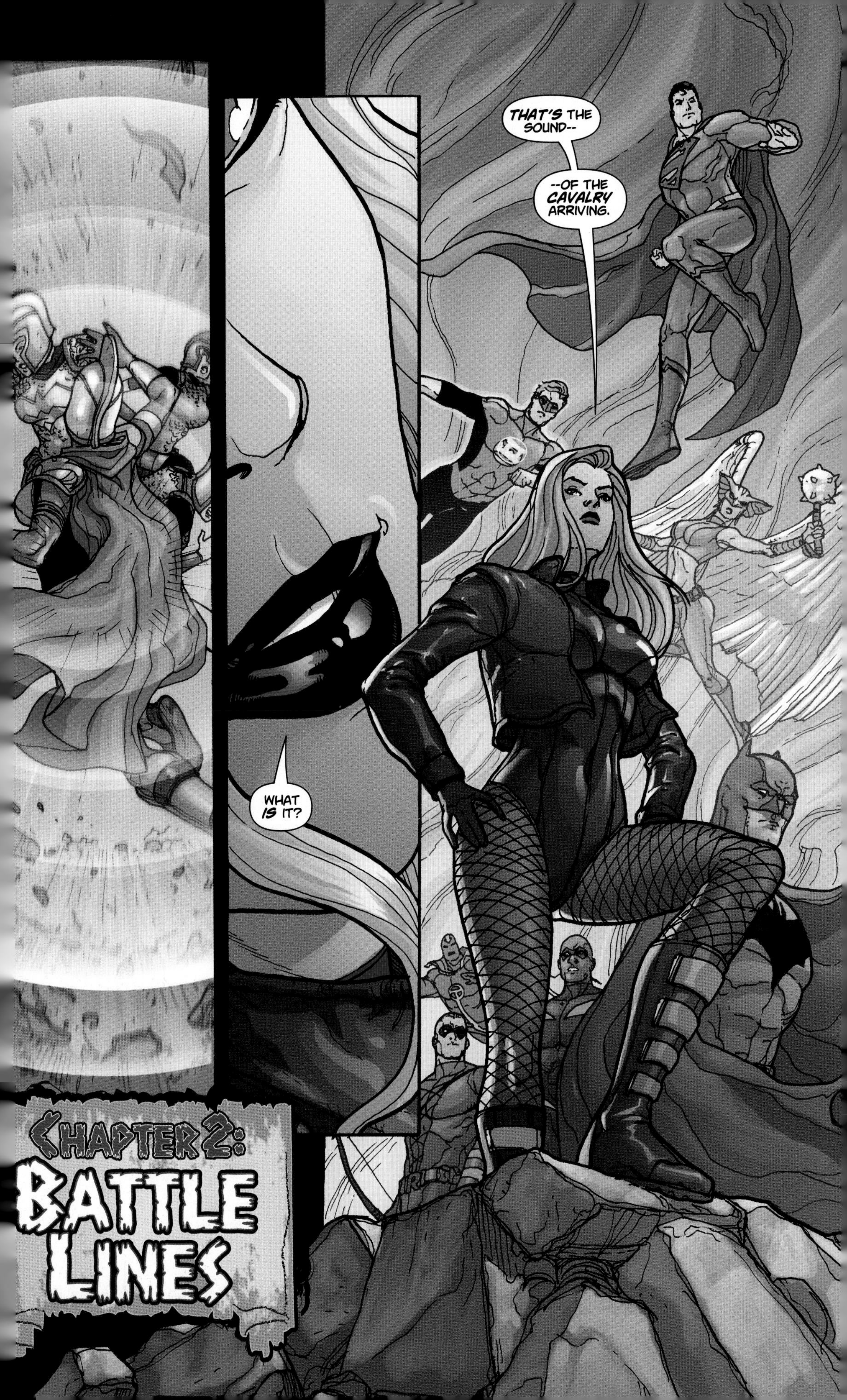
WHAT IS IT?
THAT'S THE SOUND--
--OF THE CAVALRY ARRIVING.
CHAPTER 2: BATTLE LINES

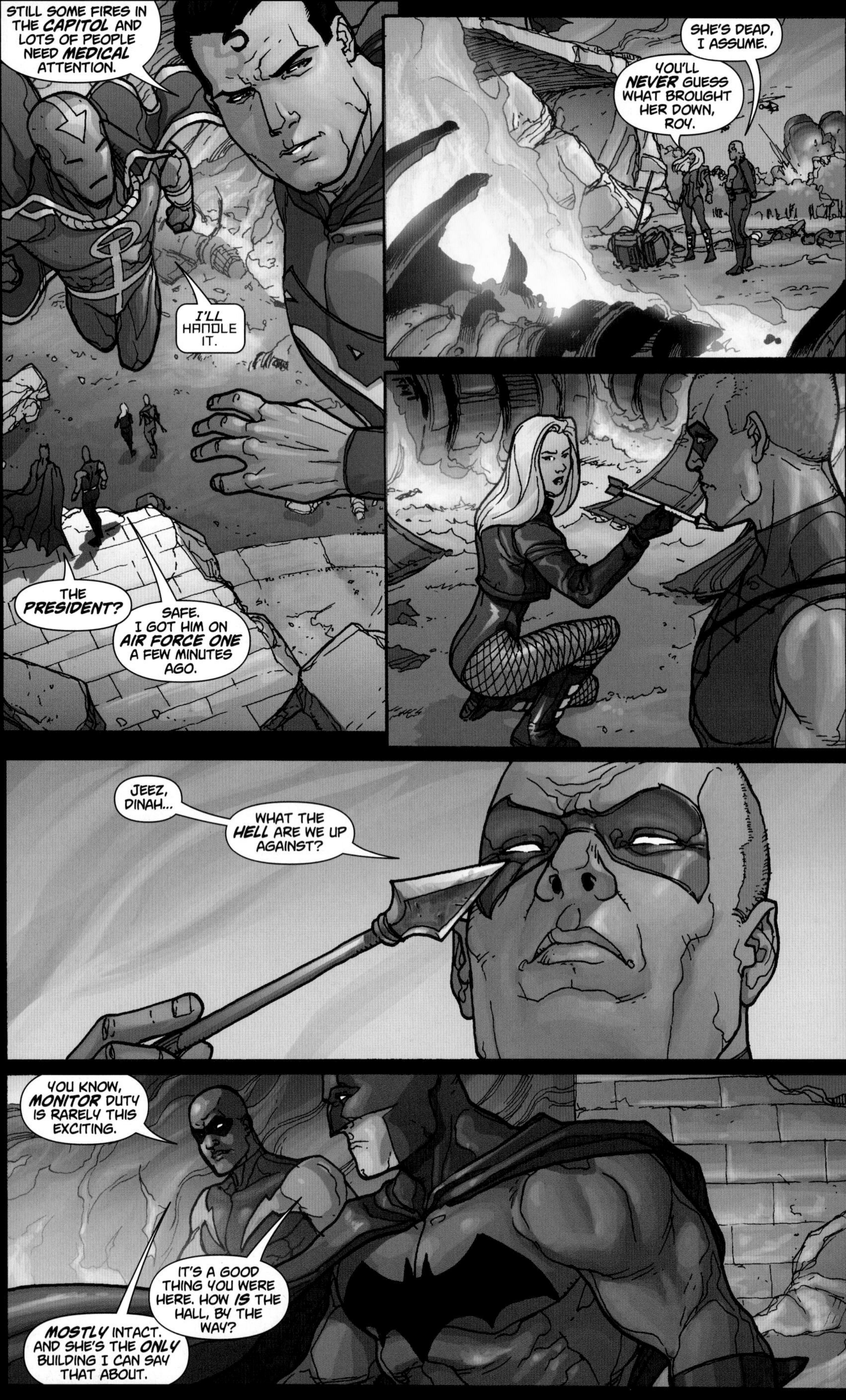

STILL SOME FIRES IN THE CAPITOL AND LOTS OF PEOPLE NEED MEDICAL ATTENTION.
I'LL HANDLE IT.
THE PRESIDENT?
SAFE. I GOT HIM ON AIR FORCE ONE A FEW MINUTES AGO.
SHE'S DEAD, I ASSUME.
YOU'LL NEVER GUESS WHAT BROUGHT HER DOWN, ROY.
JEEZ, DINAH...
WHAT THE HELL ARE WE UP AGAINST?
YOU KNOW, MONITOR DUTY IS RARELY THIS EXCITING.
IT'S A GOOD THING YOU WERE HERE. HOW IS THE HALL, BY THE WAY?
MOSTLY INTACT. AND SHE'S THE ONLY BUILDING I CAN SAY THAT ABOUT.

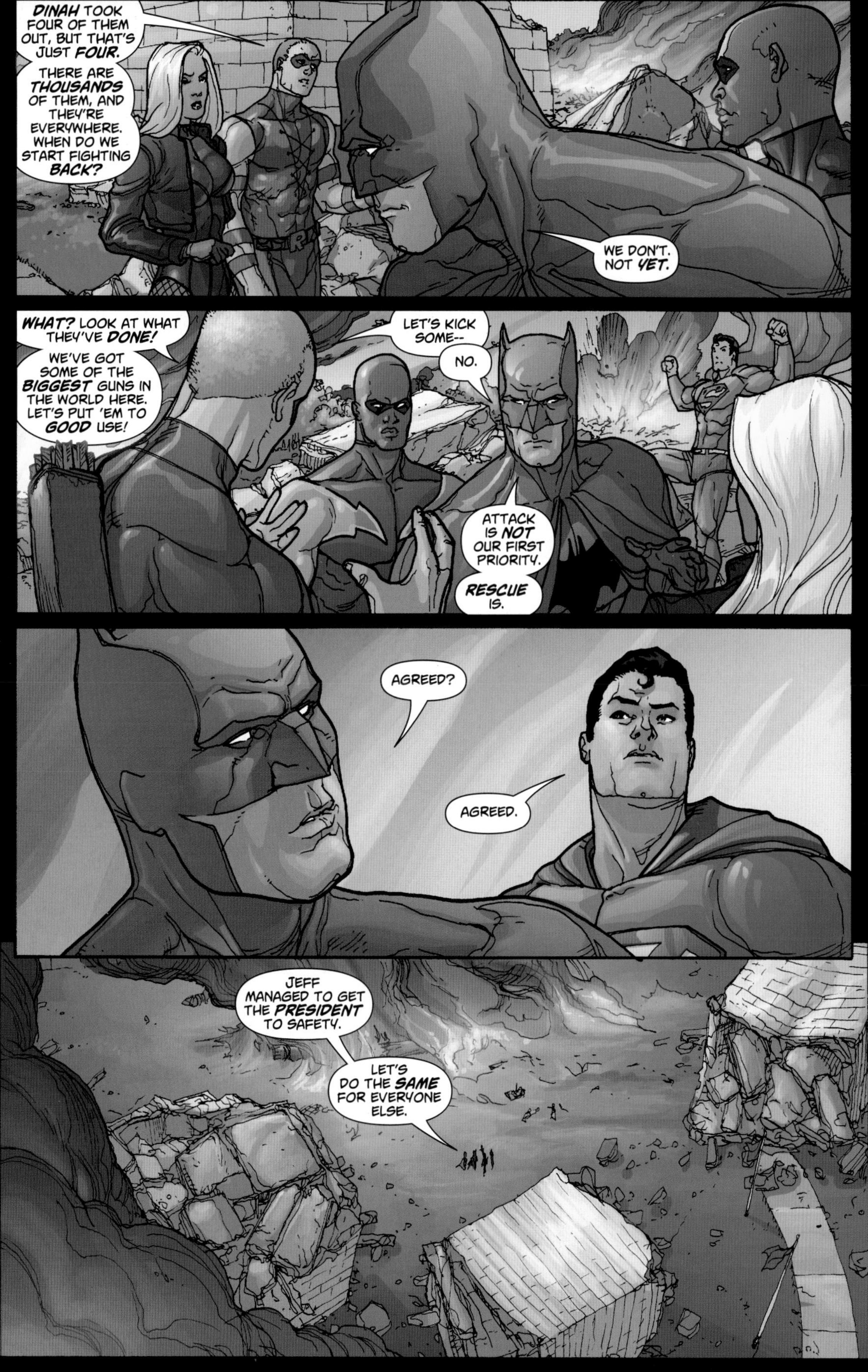
DINAH TOOK FOUR OF THEM OUT, BUT THAT'S JUST FOUR.
THERE ARE THOUSANDS OF THEM, AND THEY'RE EVERYWHERE. WHEN DO WE START FIGHTING BACK?
WE DON'T. NOT YET.
WHAT? LOOK AT WHAT THEY'VE DONE!
WE'VE GOT SOME OF THE BIGGEST GUNS IN THE WORLD HERE. LET'S PUT 'EM TO GOOD USE!
LET'S KICK SOME--
NO.
ATTACK IS NOT OUR FIRST PRIORITY.
RESCUE IS.
AGREED?
AGREED.
JEFF MANAGED TO GET THE PRESIDENT TO SAFETY.
LET'S DO THE SAME FOR EVERYONE ELSE.

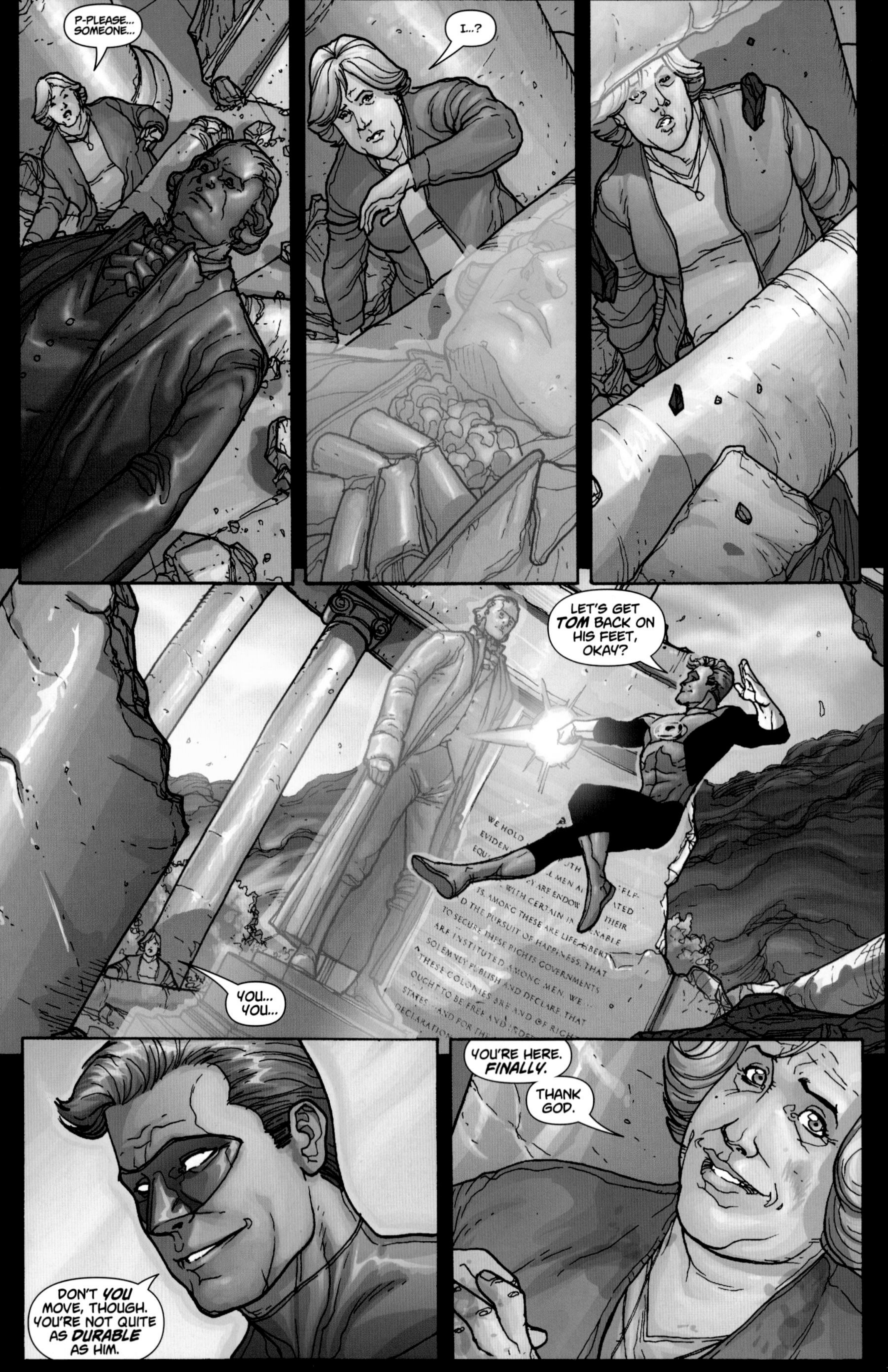
P-PLEASE... SOMEONE...
I...?
LET'S GET TOM BACK ON HIS FEET, OKAY?
YOU... YOU...
YOU'RE HERE. FINALLY.
THANK GOD.
DON'T YOU MOVE, THOUGH. YOU'RE NOT QUITE AS DURABLE AS HIM.

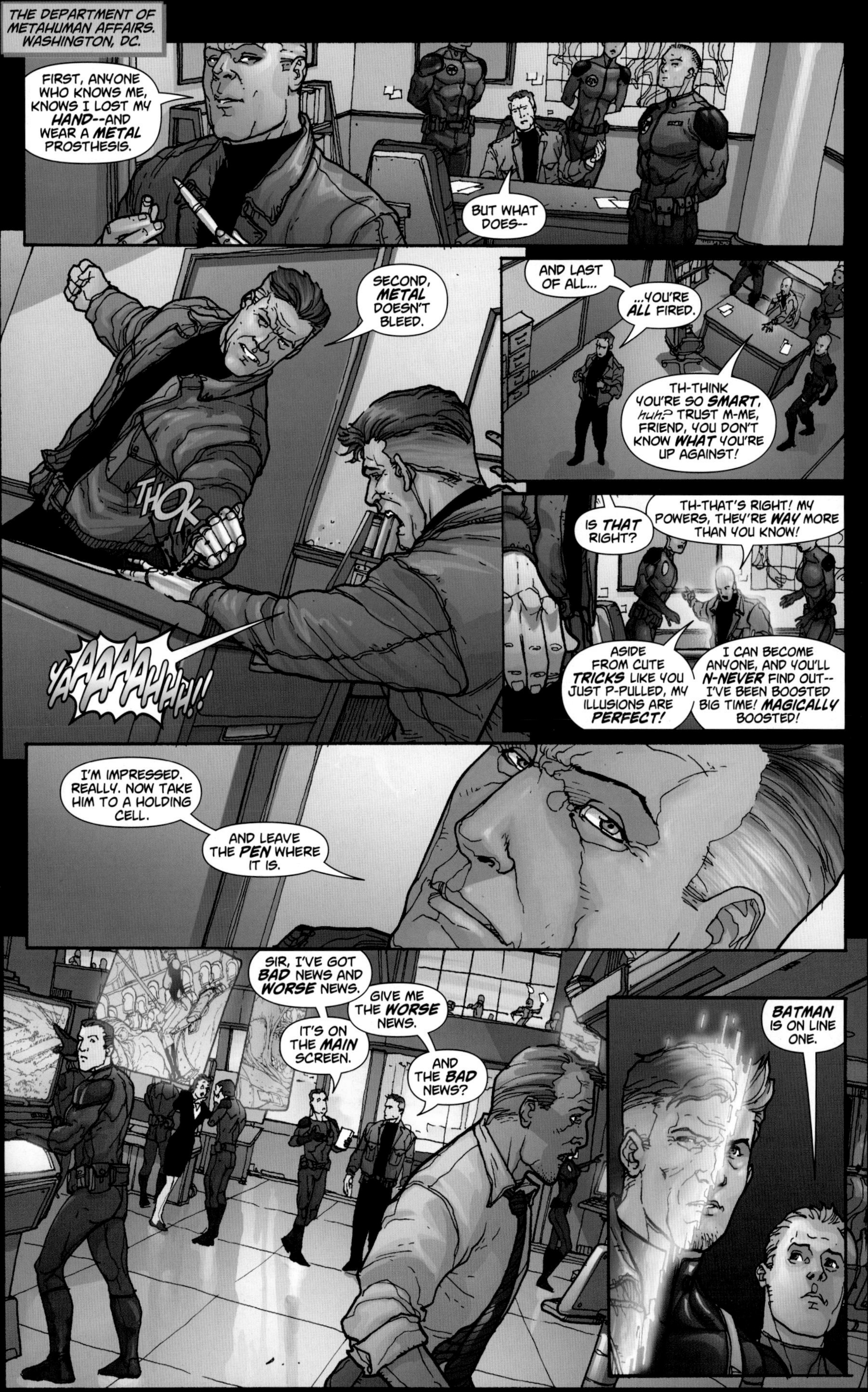
THE DEPARTMENT OF METAHUMAN AFFAIRS. WASHINGTON, DC.
FIRST, ANYONE WHO KNOWS ME, KNOWS I LOST MY HAND--AND WEAR A METAL PROSTHESIS.
BUT WHAT DOES--
SECOND, METAL DOESN'T BLEED.
THOK
YAAAAAHHH!!
AND LAST OF ALL...
...YOU'RE ALL FIRED.
TH-THINK YOU'RE SO SMART, huh? TRUST M-ME, FRIEND, YOU DON'T KNOW WHAT YOU'RE UP AGAINST!
IS THAT RIGHT?
TH-THAT'S RIGHT! MY POWERS, THEY'RE WAY MORE THAN YOU KNOW!
ASIDE FROM CUTE TRICKS LIKE YOU JUST P-PULLED, MY ILLUSIONS ARE PERFECT!
I CAN BECOME ANYONE, AND YOU'LL N-NEVER FIND OUT-- I'VE BEEN BOOSTED BIG TIME! MAGICALLY BOOSTED!
I'M IMPRESSED. REALLY. NOW TAKE HIM TO A HOLDING CELL.
AND LEAVE THE PEN WHERE IT IS.
SIR, I'VE GOT BAD NEWS AND WORSE NEWS.
GIVE ME THE WORSE NEWS.
IT'S ON THE MAIN SCREEN.
AND THE BAD NEWS?
BATMAN IS ON LINE ONE.

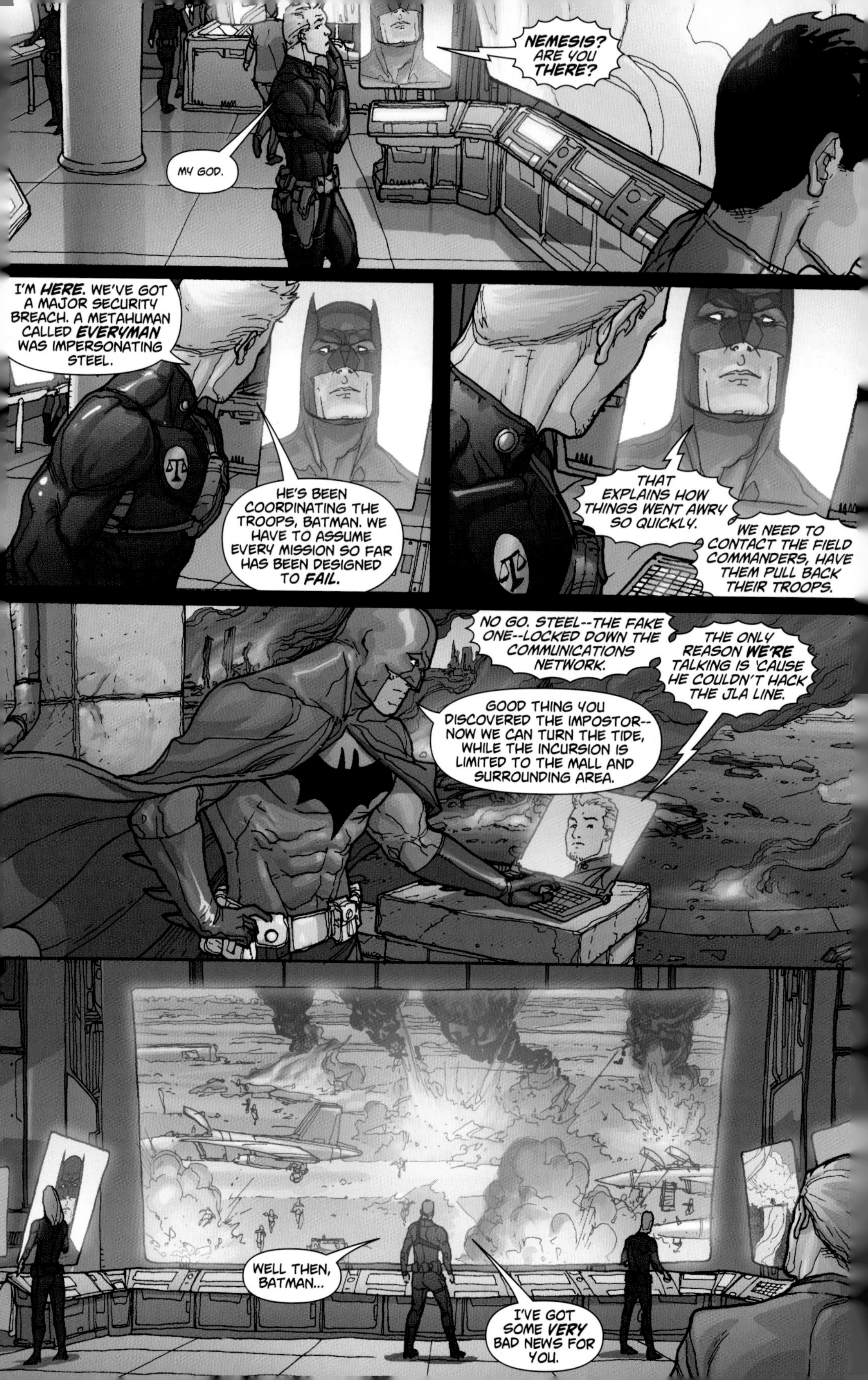
NEMESIS? ARE YOU THERE?
MY GOD.
I'M HERE. WE'VE GOT A MAJOR SECURITY BREACH. A METAHUMAN CALLED EVERYMAN WAS IMPERSONATING STEEL.
HE'S BEEN COORDINATING THE TROOPS, BATMAN. WE HAVE TO ASSUME EVERY MISSION SO FAR HAS BEEN DESIGNED TO FAIL.
THAT EXPLAINS HOW THINGS WENT AWRY SO QUICKLY.
WE NEED TO CONTACT THE FIELD COMMANDERS, HAVE THEM PULL BACK THEIR TROOPS.
NO GO. STEEL--THE FAKE ONE--LOCKED DOWN THE COMMUNICATIONS NETWORK.
THE ONLY REASON WE'RE TALKING IS 'CAUSE HE COULDN'T HACK THE JLA LINE.
GOOD THING YOU DISCOVERED THE IMPOSTOR--NOW WE CAN TURN THE TIDE, WHILE THE INCURSION IS LIMITED TO THE MALL AND SURROUNDING AREA.
WELL THEN, BATMAN...
I'VE GOT SOME VERY BAD NEWS FOR YOU.

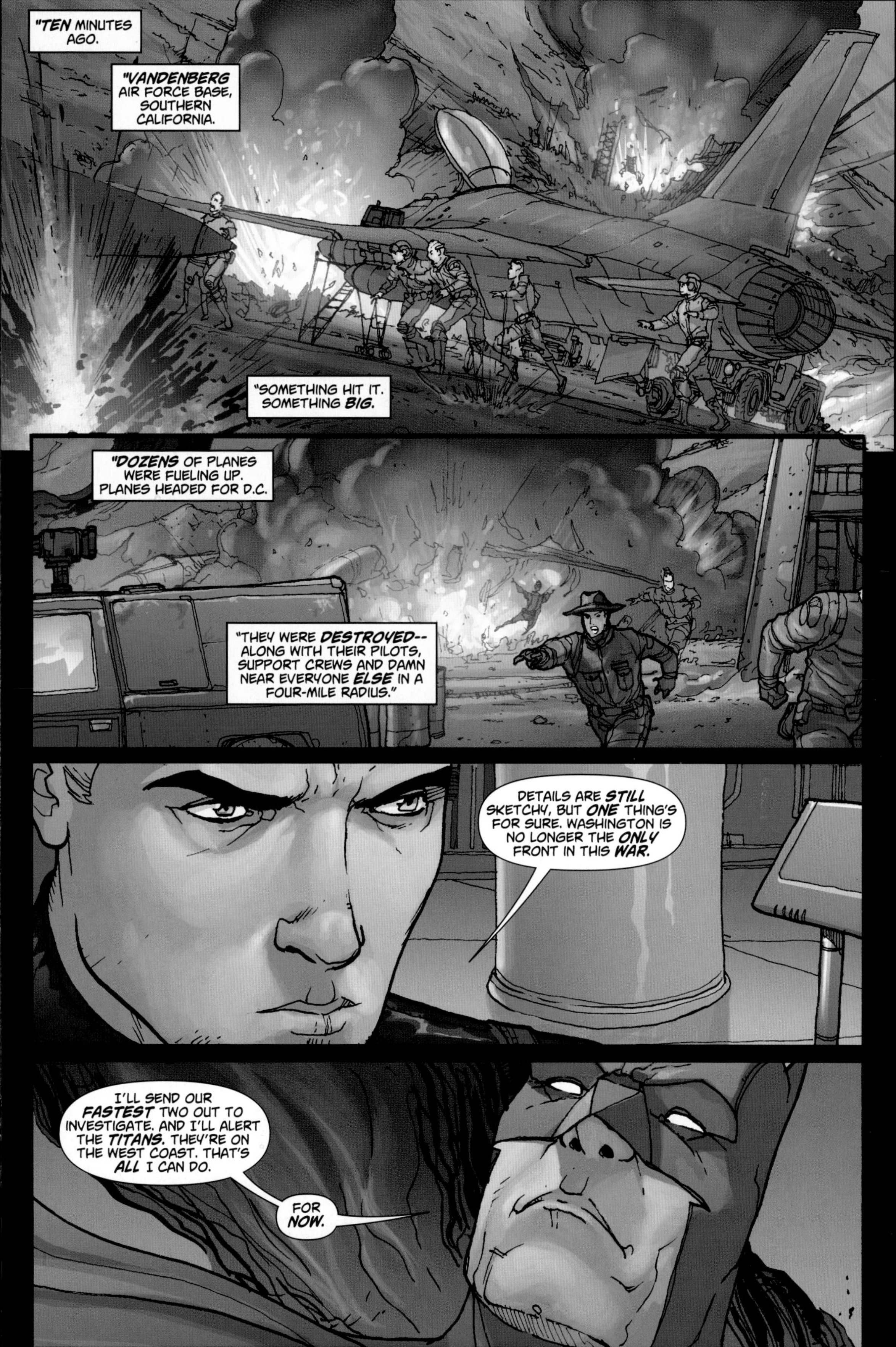
"TEN MINUTES AGO.
"VANDENBERG AIR FORCE BASE, SOUTHERN CALIFORNIA.
"SOMETHING HIT IT. SOMETHING BIG.
"DOZENS OF PLANES WERE FUELING UP. PLANES HEADED FOR D.C.
"THEY WERE DESTROYED--ALONG WITH THEIR PILOTS, SUPPORT CREWS AND DAMN NEAR EVERYONE ELSE IN A FOUR-MILE RADIUS."
DETAILS ARE STILL SKETCHY, BUT ONE THING'S FOR SURE. WASHINGTON IS NO LONGER THE ONLY FRONT IN THIS WAR.
I'LL SEND OUR FASTEST TWO OUT TO INVESTIGATE. AND I'LL ALERT THE TITANS. THEY'RE ON THE WEST COAST. THAT'S ALL I CAN DO.
FOR NOW.

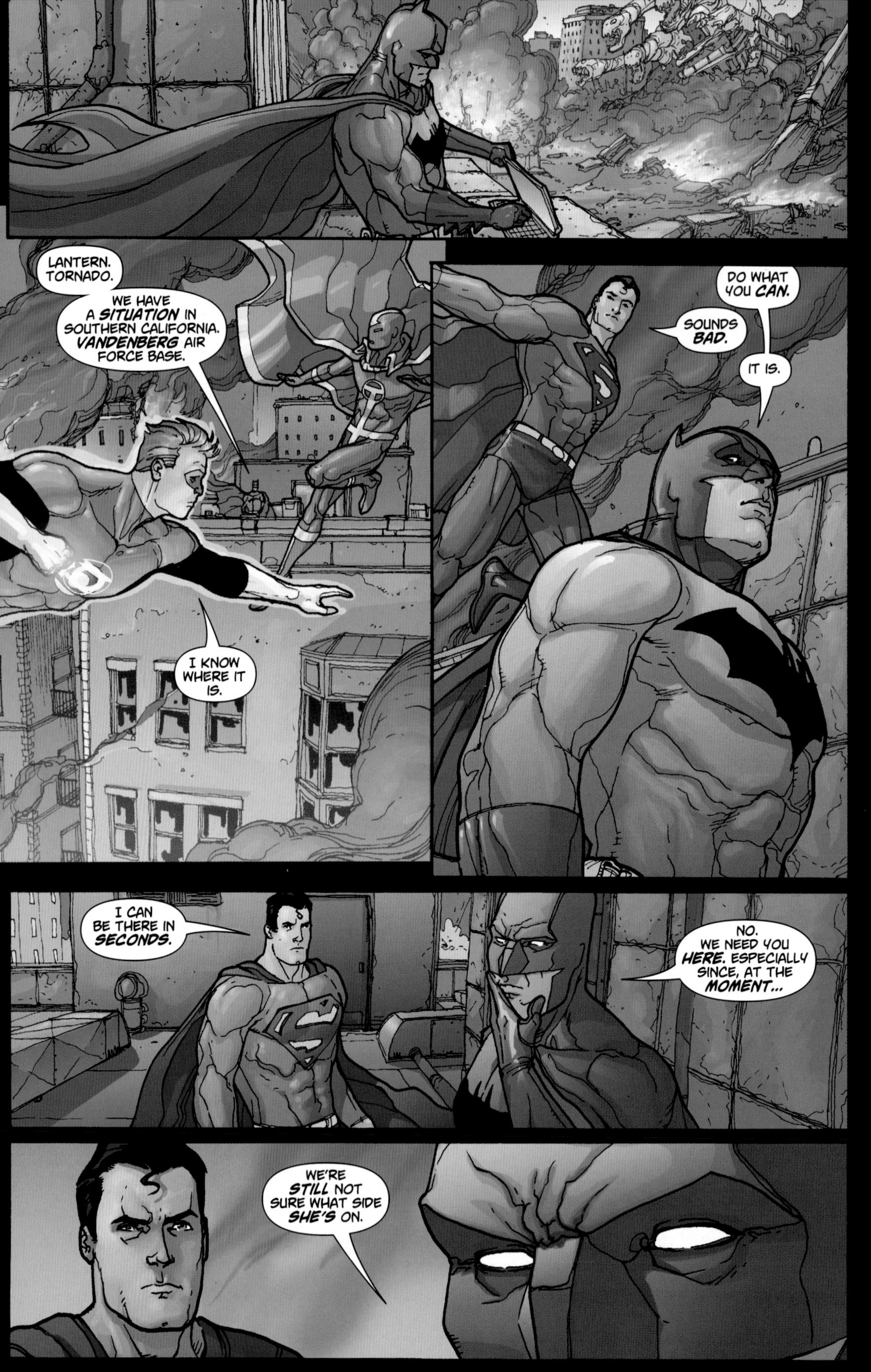
LANTERN. TORNADO.
WE HAVE A SITUATION IN SOUTHERN CALIFORNIA. VANDENBERG AIR FORCE BASE.
I KNOW WHERE IT IS.
SOUNDS BAD.
DO WHAT YOU CAN.
IT IS.
I CAN BE THERE IN SECONDS.
NO. WE NEED YOU HERE. ESPECIALLY SINCE, AT THE MOMENT...
WE'RE STILL NOT SURE WHAT SIDE SHE'S ON.

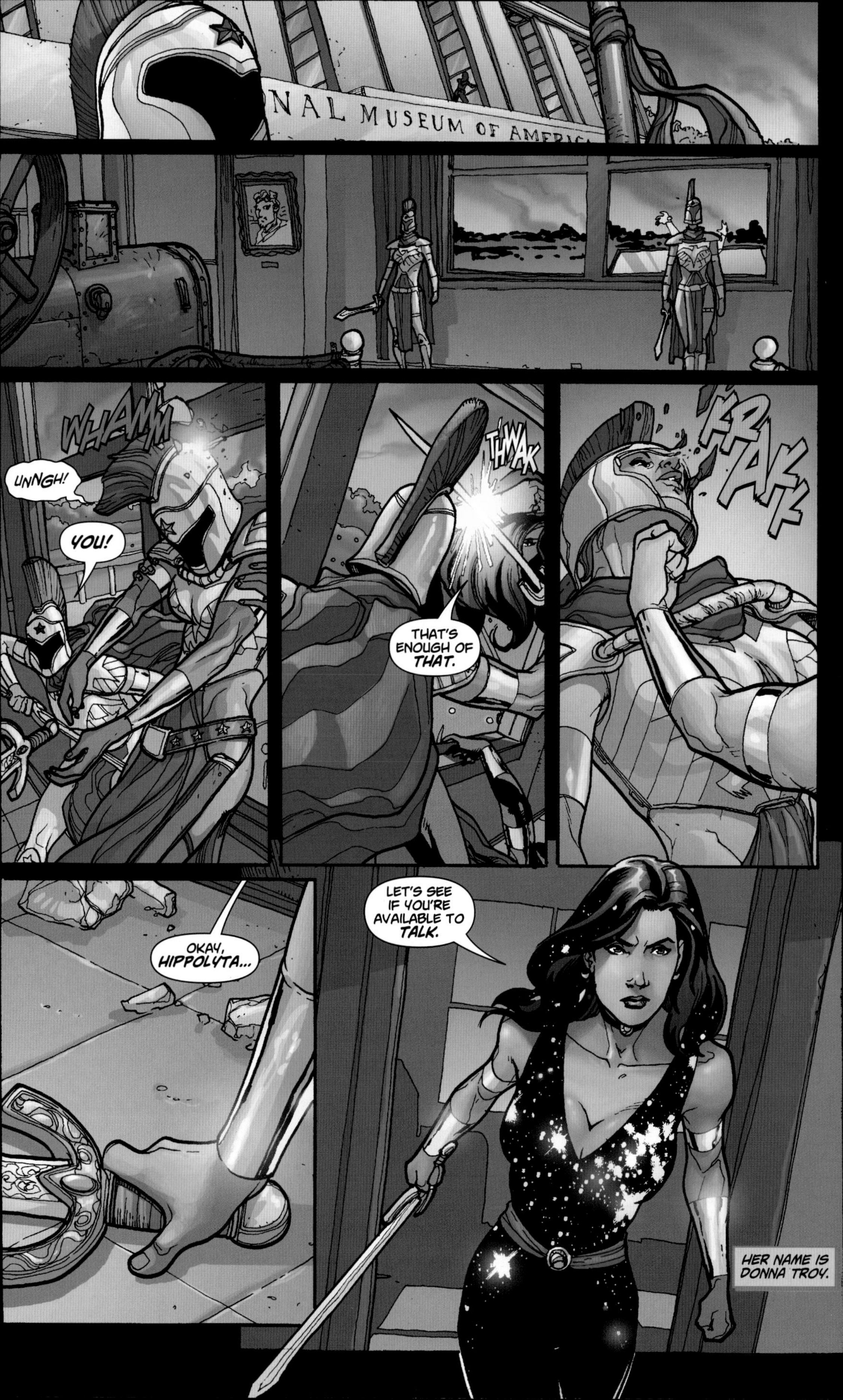
NAL MUSEUM OF AMERICA
WHAMM
UNNGH!
YOU!
THWAK
THAT'S ENOUGH OF THAT.
KRAK
OKAY, HIPPOLYTA...
LET'S SEE IF YOU'RE AVAILABLE TO TALK.
HER NAME IS DONNA TROY.

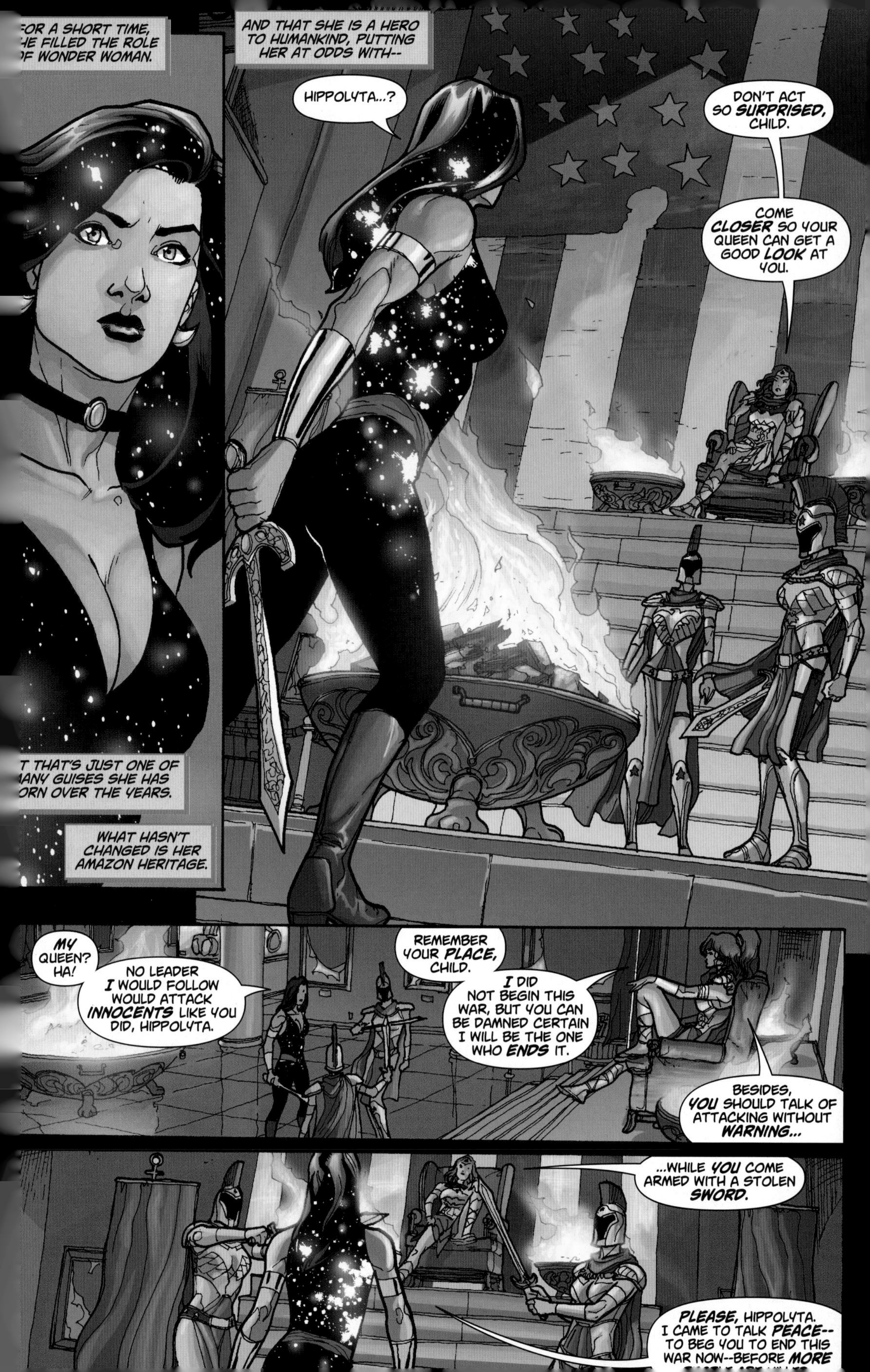
FOR A SHORT TIME, HE FILLED THE ROLE OF WONDER WOMAN.
AND THAT SHE IS A HERO TO HUMANKIND, PUTTING HER AT ODDS WITH--
HIPPOLYTA...?
DON'T ACT SO SURPRISED, CHILD.
COME CLOSER SO YOUR QUEEN CAN GET A GOOD LOOK AT YOU.
T THAT'S JUST ONE OF MANY GUISES SHE HAS ORN OVER THE YEARS.
WHAT HASN'T CHANGED IS HER AMAZON HERITAGE.
MY QUEEN? HA!
NO LEADER I WOULD FOLLOW WOULD ATTACK INNOCENTS LIKE YOU DID, HIPPOLYTA.
REMEMBER YOUR PLACE, CHILD.
I DID NOT BEGIN THIS WAR, BUT YOU CAN BE DAMNED CERTAIN I WILL BE THE ONE WHO ENDS IT.
BESIDES, YOU SHOULD TALK OF ATTACKING WITHOUT WARNING...
...WHILE YOU COME ARMED WITH A STOLEN SWORD.
PLEASE, HIPPOLYTA. I CAME TO TALK PEACE-- TO BEG YOU TO END THIS WAR NOW--BEFORE MORE

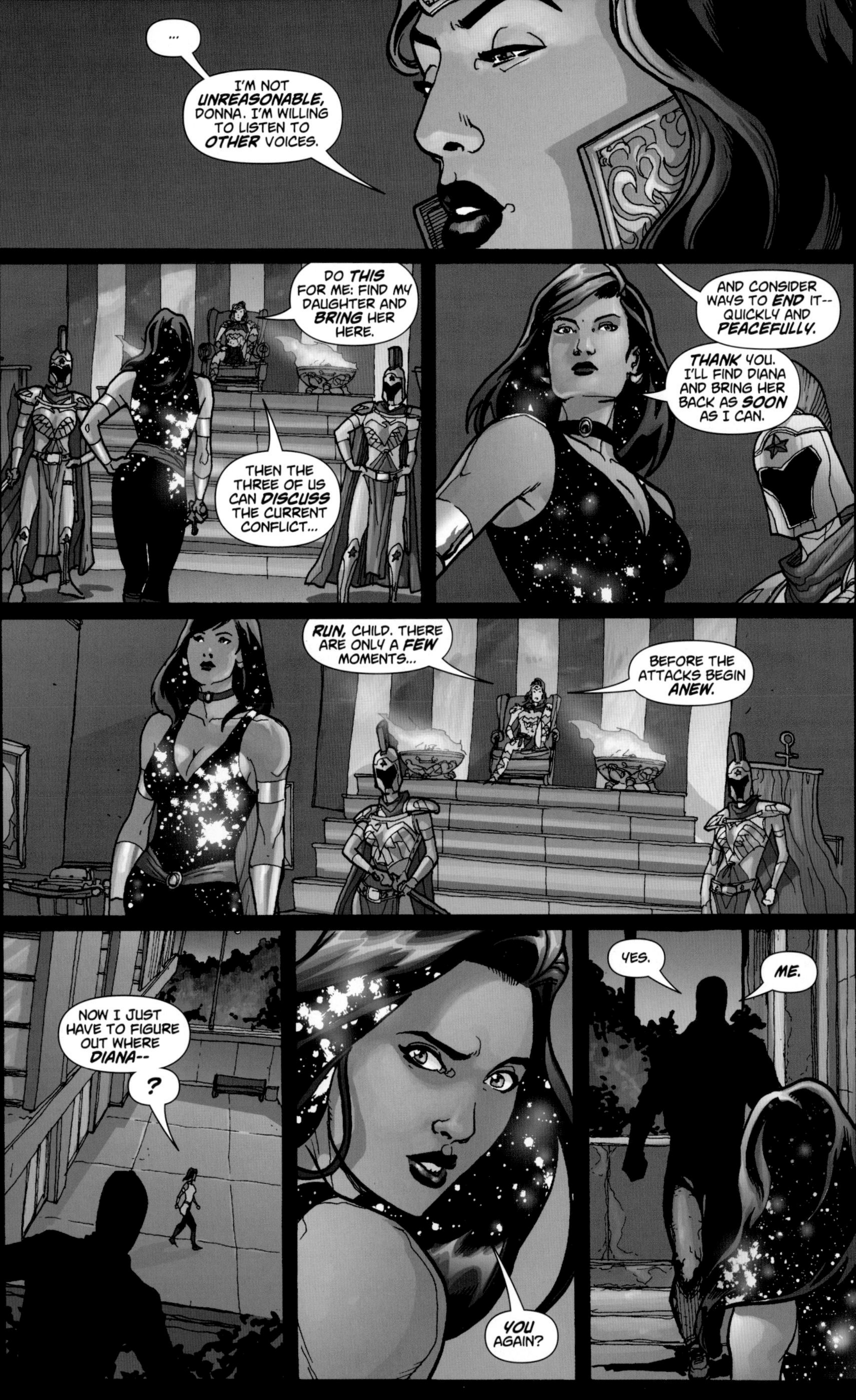
...
I'M NOT UNREASONABLE, DONNA. I'M WILLING TO LISTEN TO OTHER VOICES.
DO THIS FOR ME: FIND MY DAUGHTER AND BRING HER HERE.
THEN THE THREE OF US CAN DISCUSS THE CURRENT CONFLICT...
AND CONSIDER WAYS TO END IT-- QUICKLY AND PEACEFULLY.
THANK YOU. I'LL FIND DIANA AND BRING HER BACK AS SOON AS I CAN.
RUN, CHILD. THERE ARE ONLY A FEW MOMENTS...
BEFORE THE ATTACKS BEGIN ANEW.
NOW I JUST HAVE TO FIGURE OUT WHERE DIANA--
?
YOU AGAIN?
YES.
ME.

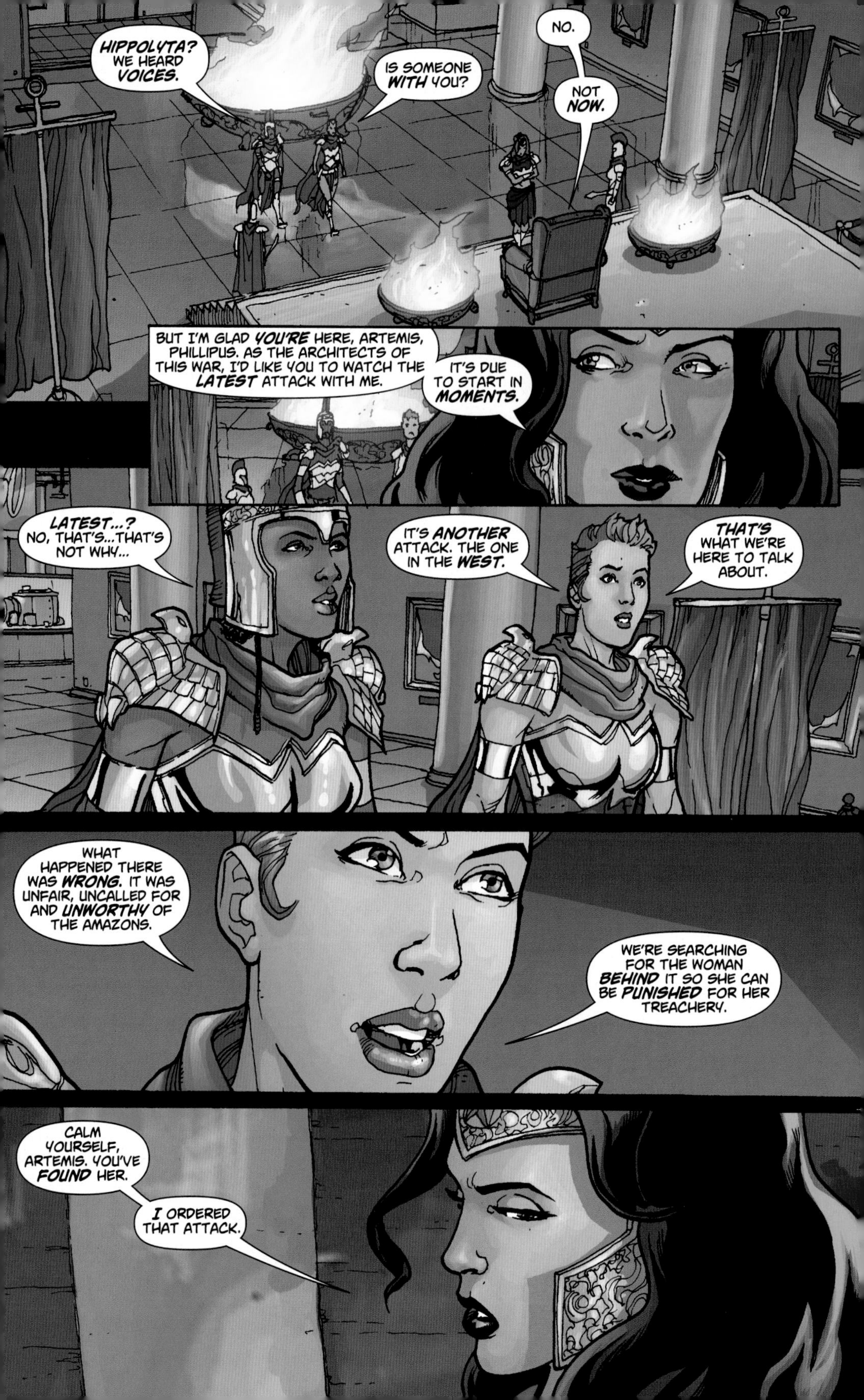
HIPPOLYTA? WE HEARD VOICES.
IS SOMEONE WITH YOU?
NO.
NOT NOW.
BUT I'M GLAD YOU'RE HERE, ARTEMIS, PHILLIPUS. AS THE ARCHITECTS OF THIS WAR, I'D LIKE YOU TO WATCH THE LATEST ATTACK WITH ME.
IT'S DUE TO START IN MOMENTS.
LATEST...? NO, THAT'S...THAT'S NOT WHY...
IT'S ANOTHER ATTACK. THE ONE IN THE WEST.
THAT'S WHAT WE'RE HERE TO TALK ABOUT.
WHAT HAPPENED THERE WAS WRONG. IT WAS UNFAIR, UNCALLED FOR AND UNWORTHY OF THE AMAZONS.
WE'RE SEARCHING FOR THE WOMAN BEHIND IT SO SHE CAN BE PUNISHED FOR HER TREACHERY.
CALM YOURSELF, ARTEMIS. YOU'VE FOUND HER.
I ORDERED THAT ATTACK.

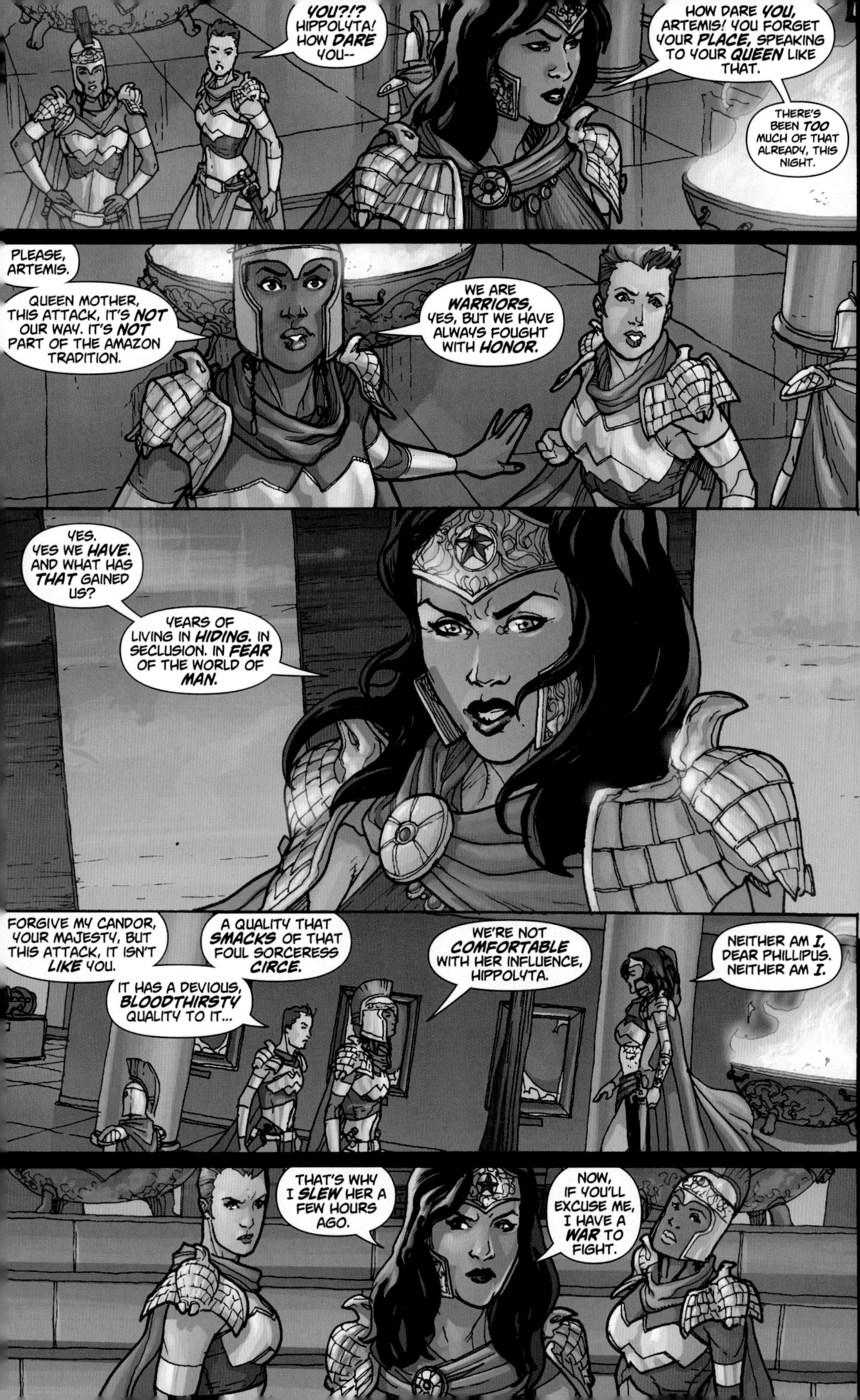
YOU?!? HIPPOLYTA! HOW DARE YOU--
HOW DARE YOU, ARTEMIS! YOU FORGET YOUR PLACE, SPEAKING TO YOUR QUEEN LIKE THAT.
THERE'S BEEN TOO MUCH OF THAT ALREADY, THIS NIGHT.
PLEASE, ARTEMIS.
QUEEN MOTHER, THIS ATTACK, IT'S NOT OUR WAY. IT'S NOT PART OF THE AMAZON TRADITION.
WE ARE WARRIORS, YES, BUT WE HAVE ALWAYS FOUGHT WITH HONOR.
YES. YES WE HAVE. AND WHAT HAS THAT GAINED US?
YEARS OF LIVING IN HIDING. IN SECLUSION. IN FEAR OF THE WORLD OF MAN.
FORGIVE MY CANDOR, YOUR MAJESTY, BUT THIS ATTACK, IT ISN'T LIKE YOU.
IT HAS A DEVIOUS, BLOODTHIRSTY QUALITY TO IT...
A QUALITY THAT SMACKS OF THAT FOUL SORCERESS CIRCE.
WE'RE NOT COMFORTABLE WITH HER INFLUENCE, HIPPOLYTA.
NEITHER AM I, DEAR PHILLIPUS. NEITHER AM I.
THAT'S WHY I SLEW HER A FEW HOURS AGO.
NOW, IF YOU'LL EXCUSE ME, I HAVE A WAR TO FIGHT.

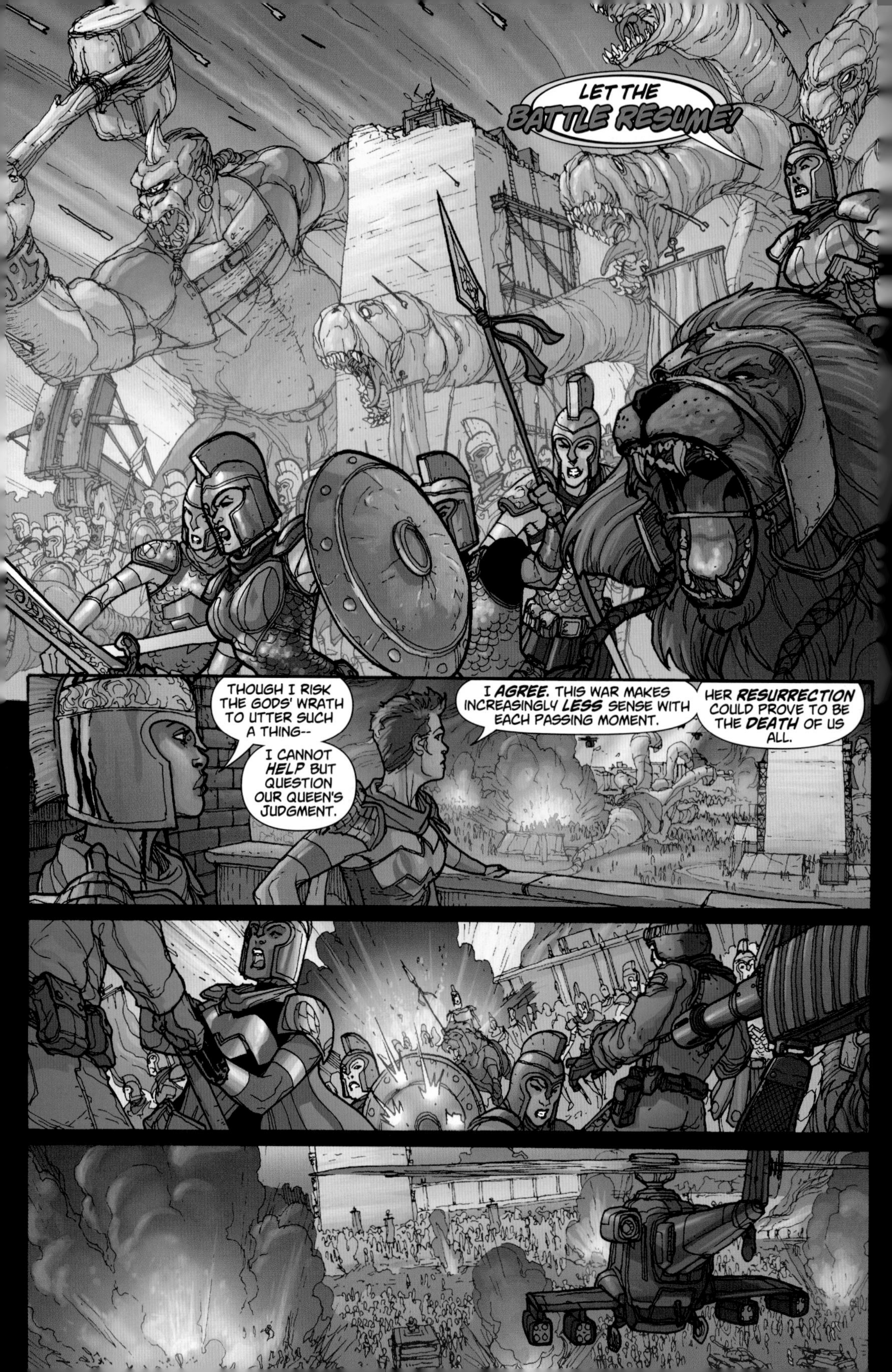
LET THE BATTLE RESUME!
THOUGH I RISK THE GODS' WRATH TO UTTER SUCH A THING--
I CANNOT HELP BUT QUESTION OUR QUEEN'S JUDGMENT.
I AGREE. THIS WAR MAKES INCREASINGLY LESS SENSE WITH EACH PASSING MOMENT.
HER RESURRECTION COULD PROVE TO BE THE DEATH OF US ALL.

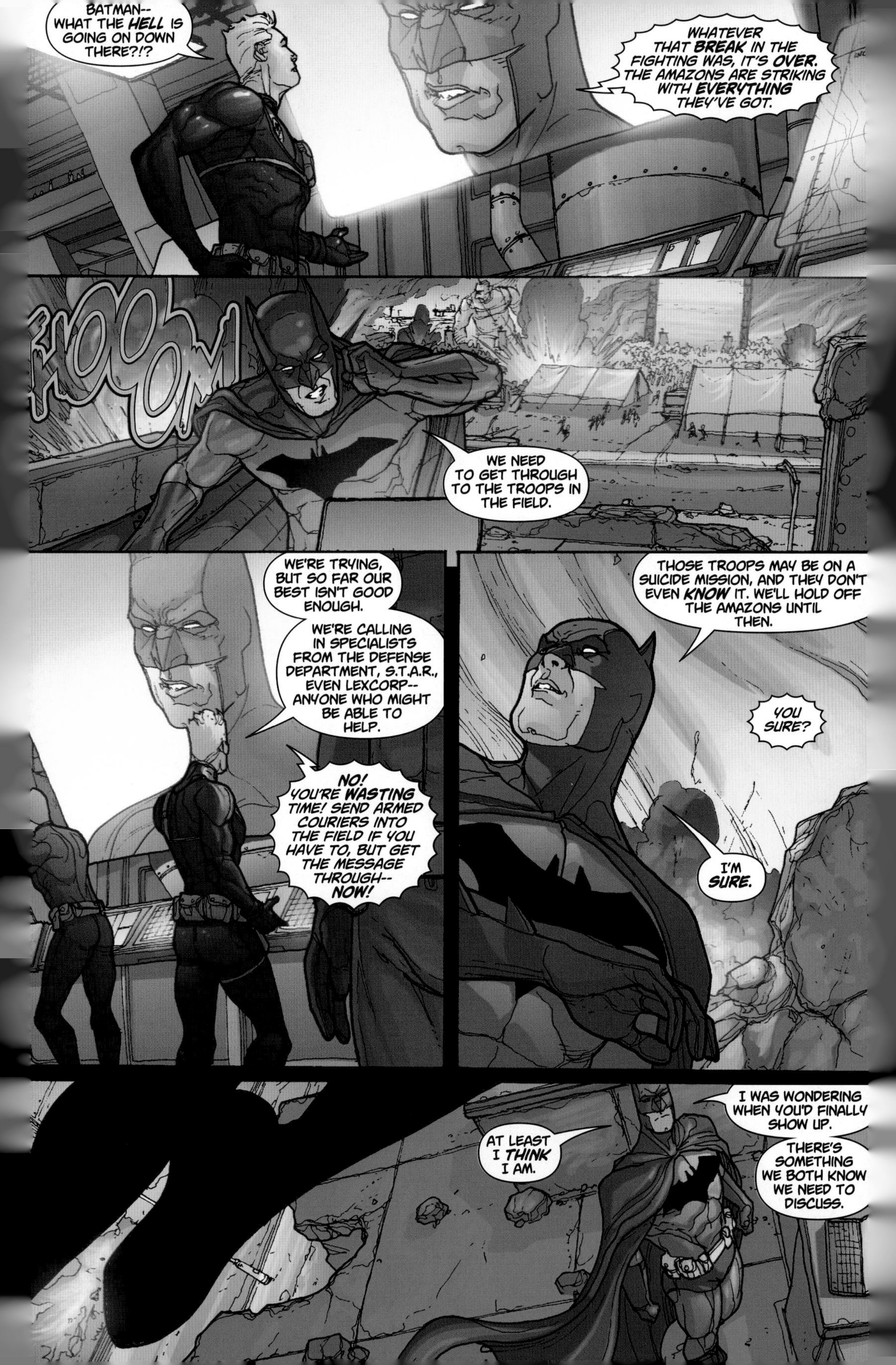
BATMAN-- WHAT THE HELL IS GOING ON DOWN THERE?!?
WHATEVER THAT BREAK IN THE FIGHTING WAS, IT'S OVER. THE AMAZONS ARE STRIKING WITH EVERYTHING THEY'VE GOT.
FOOOOM
WE NEED TO GET THROUGH TO THE TROOPS IN THE FIELD.
WE'RE TRYING, BUT SO FAR OUR BEST ISN'T GOOD ENOUGH.
WE'RE CALLING IN SPECIALISTS FROM THE DEFENSE DEPARTMENT, S.T.A.R., EVEN LEXCORP-- ANYONE WHO MIGHT BE ABLE TO HELP.
NO! YOU'RE WASTING TIME! SEND ARMED COURIERS INTO THE FIELD IF YOU HAVE TO, BUT GET THE MESSAGE THROUGH-- NOW!
THOSE TROOPS MAY BE ON A SUICIDE MISSION, AND THEY DON'T EVEN KNOW IT. WE'LL HOLD OFF THE AMAZONS UNTIL THEN.
YOU SURE?
I'M SURE.
AT LEAST I THINK I AM.
I WAS WONDERING WHEN YOU'D FINALLY SHOW UP.
THERE'S SOMETHING WE BOTH KNOW WE NEED TO DISCUSS.

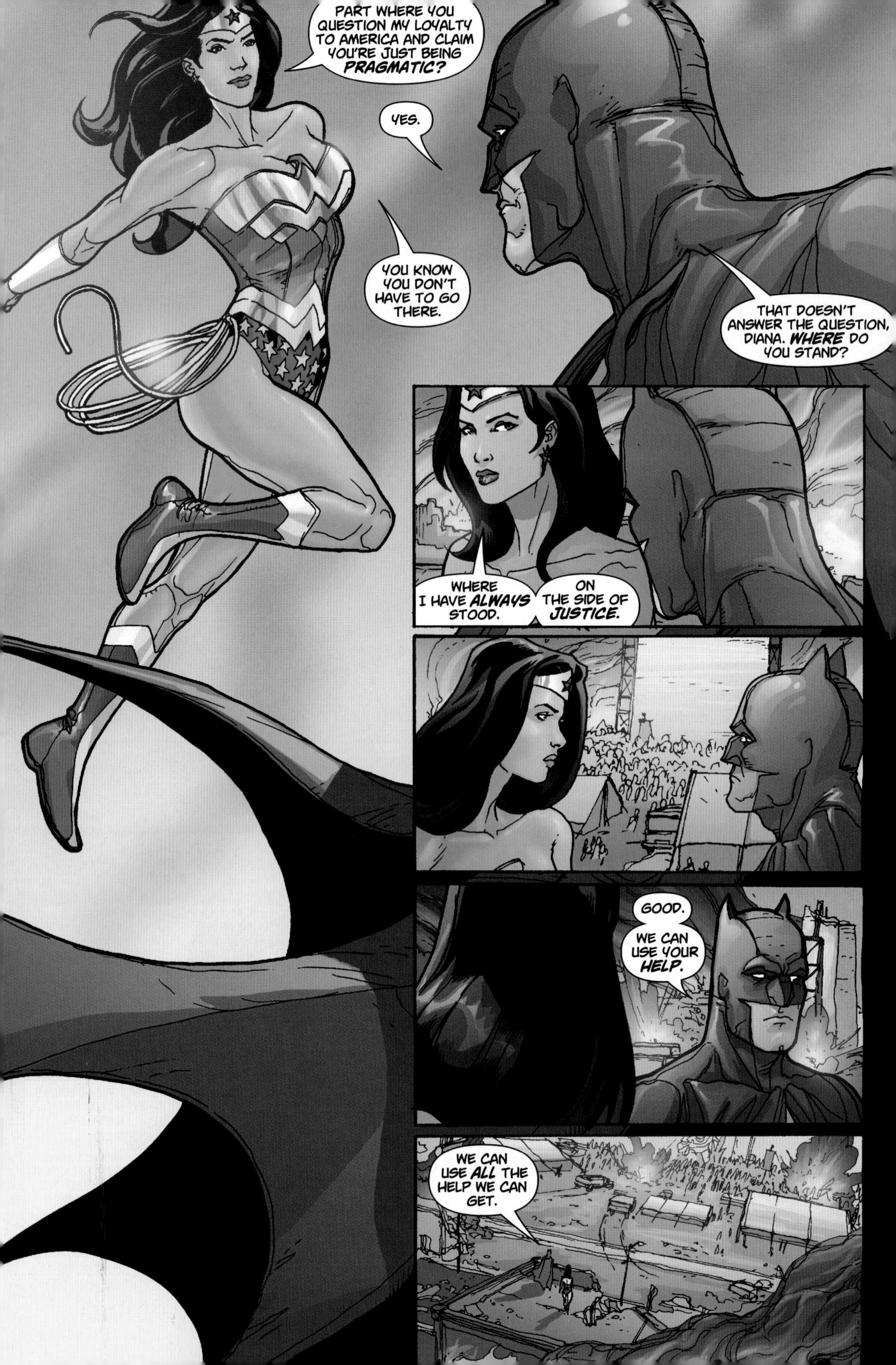
PART WHERE YOU QUESTION MY LOYALTY TO AMERICA AND CLAIM YOU'RE JUST BEING *PRAGMATIC?*
YES.
YOU KNOW YOU DON'T HAVE TO GO THERE.
THAT DOESN'T ANSWER THE QUESTION, DIANA. *WHERE* DO YOU STAND?
WHERE I HAVE *ALWAYS* STOOD.
ON THE SIDE OF *JUSTICE.*
GOOD.
WE CAN USE YOUR *HELP.*
WE CAN USE *ALL* THE HELP WE CAN GET.

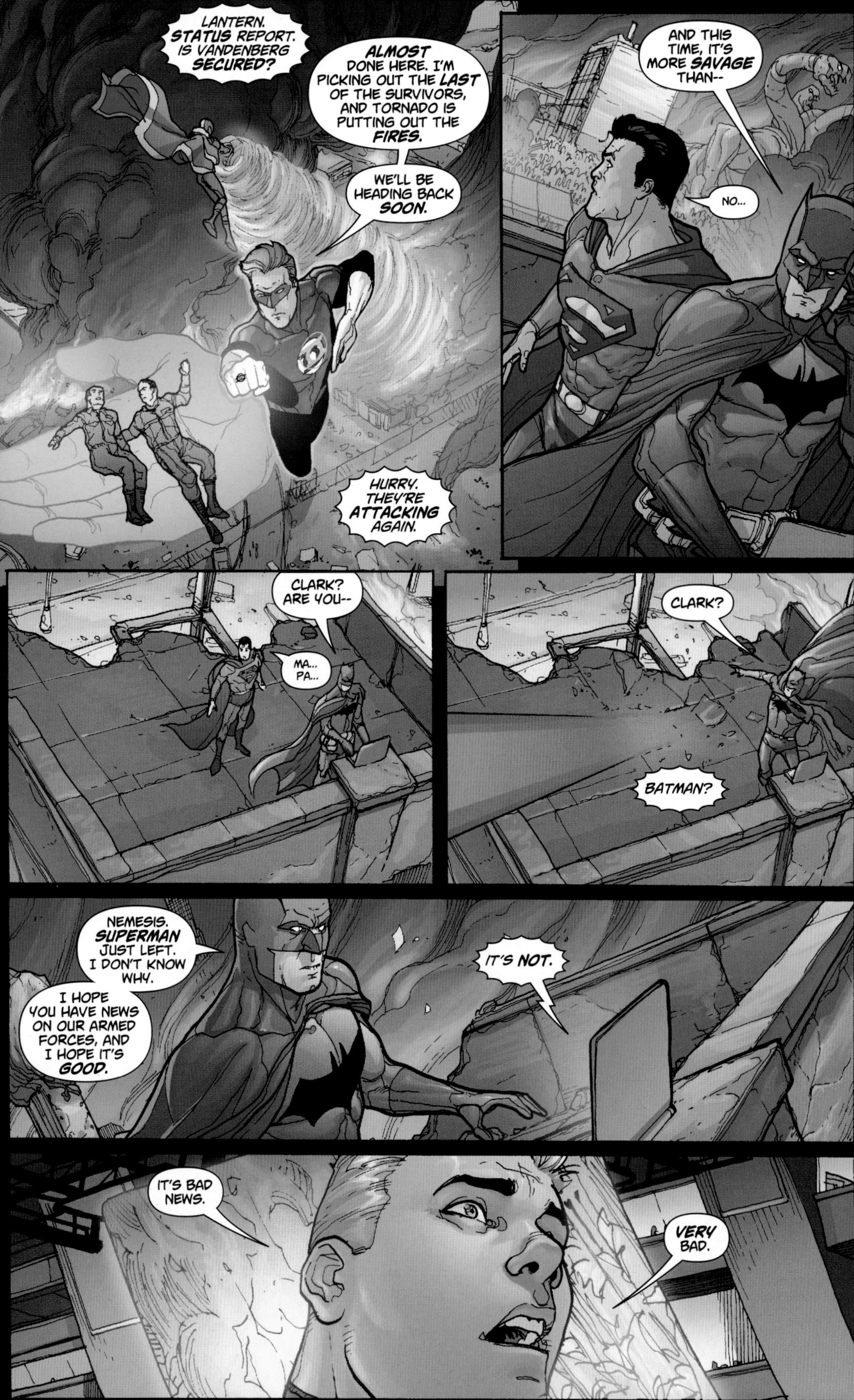
LANTERN. STATUS REPORT. IS VANDENBERG SECURED?
ALMOST DONE HERE. I'M PICKING OUT THE LAST OF THE SURVIVORS, AND TORNADO IS PUTTING OUT THE FIRES.
WE'LL BE HEADING BACK SOON.
HURRY. THEY'RE ATTACKING AGAIN.
AND THIS TIME, IT'S MORE SAVAGE THAN--
NO...
CLARK? ARE YOU--
MA... PA...
CLARK?
BATMAN?
NEMESIS. SUPERMAN JUST LEFT. I DON'T KNOW WHY.
I HOPE YOU HAVE NEWS ON OUR ARMED FORCES, AND I HOPE IT'S GOOD.
IT'S NOT.
IT'S BAD NEWS.
VERY BAD.

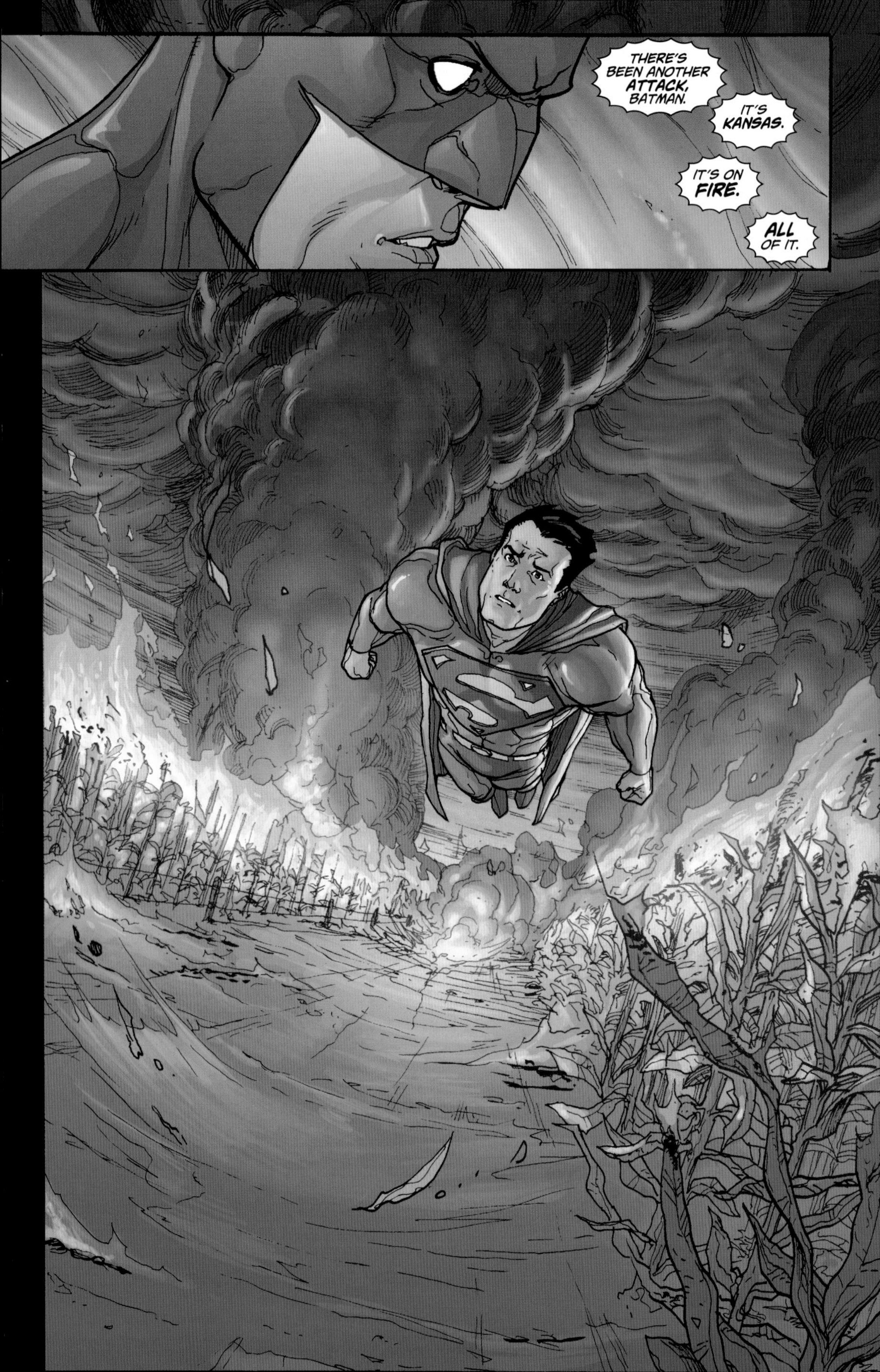
THERE'S BEEN ANOTHER ATTACK, BATMAN.
IT'S KANSAS.
IT'S ON FIRE.
ALL OF IT.

Chapter Three

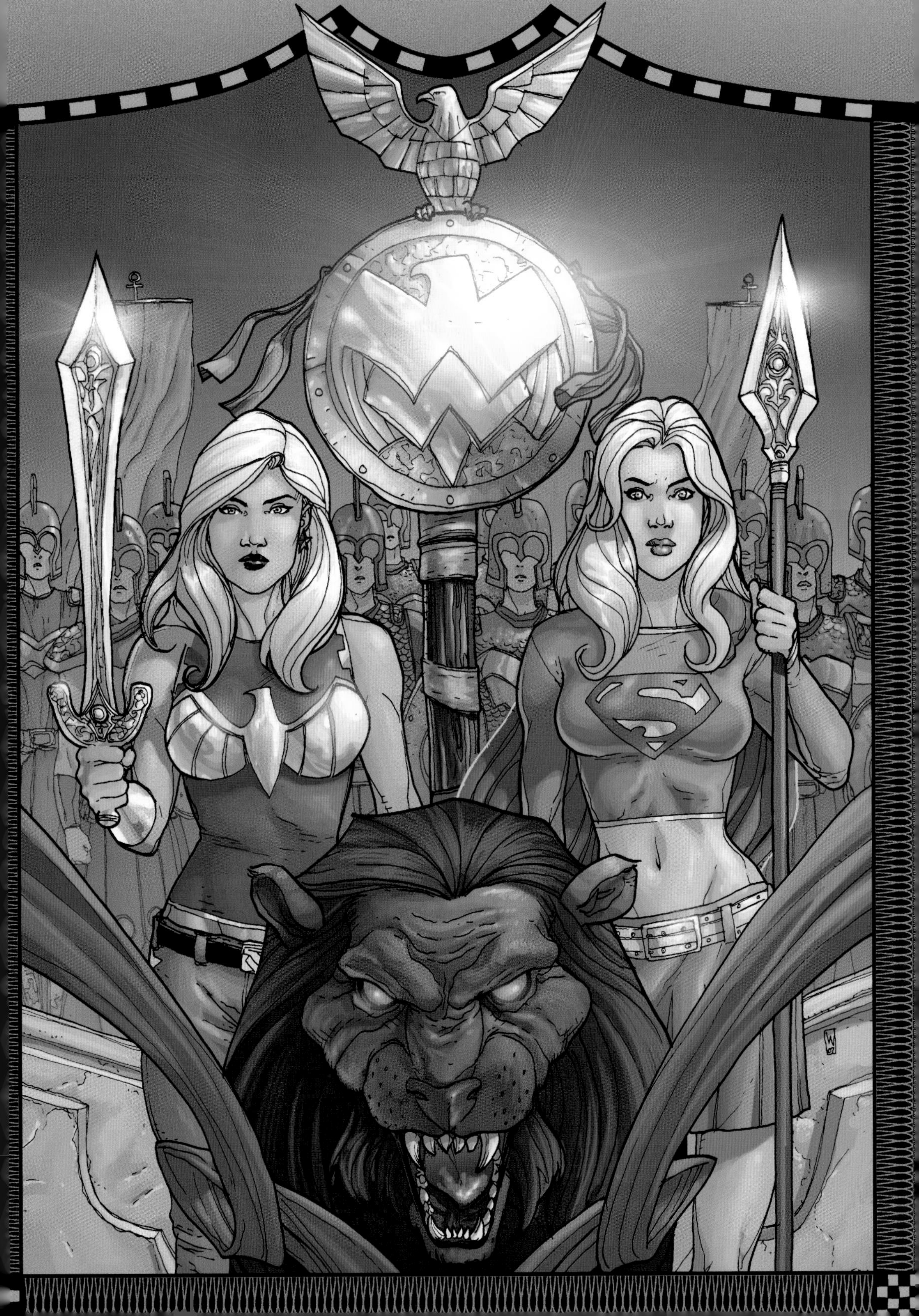

Donna Troy's search for Diana is interrupted when a figure from her recent past leads her into another conflict happening elsewhere — a turn of events which means that any sort of peace agreement between Hippolyta and Diana must now be put on hold.

Meanwhile, because the super-human government defense agents known as the Freedom Fighters are busy on a top-secret mission, the President of the United States is in a vulnerable position and is forced to take refuge aboard Air Force One and remain airborne to secure his safety.

And in the nation's capital, Wonder Woman and Hippolyta face off again — while Diana does everything in her power to stop the Amazons from releasing a deadly weapon upon mankind. When Nemesis intervenes, the "weapon" is inadvertently unleashed — a swarm of Stygian killer hornets, native to the island of Themyscira. Diana warns Nemesis that the bees are highly aggressive, and the venom in a single sting can kill within hours. But before other heroes such as Green Lantern and Superman fly in to handle the bees, Nemesis is stung twice — and is now mere hours from death.

Just after returning from a crisis of their own, the Teen Titans known as Wonder Girl and Supergirl are shocked to discover that the Amazons have declared war on humanity. As both have close ties to the Amazons, the girls are compelled to seek out Hippolyta to discover some means to end the war…

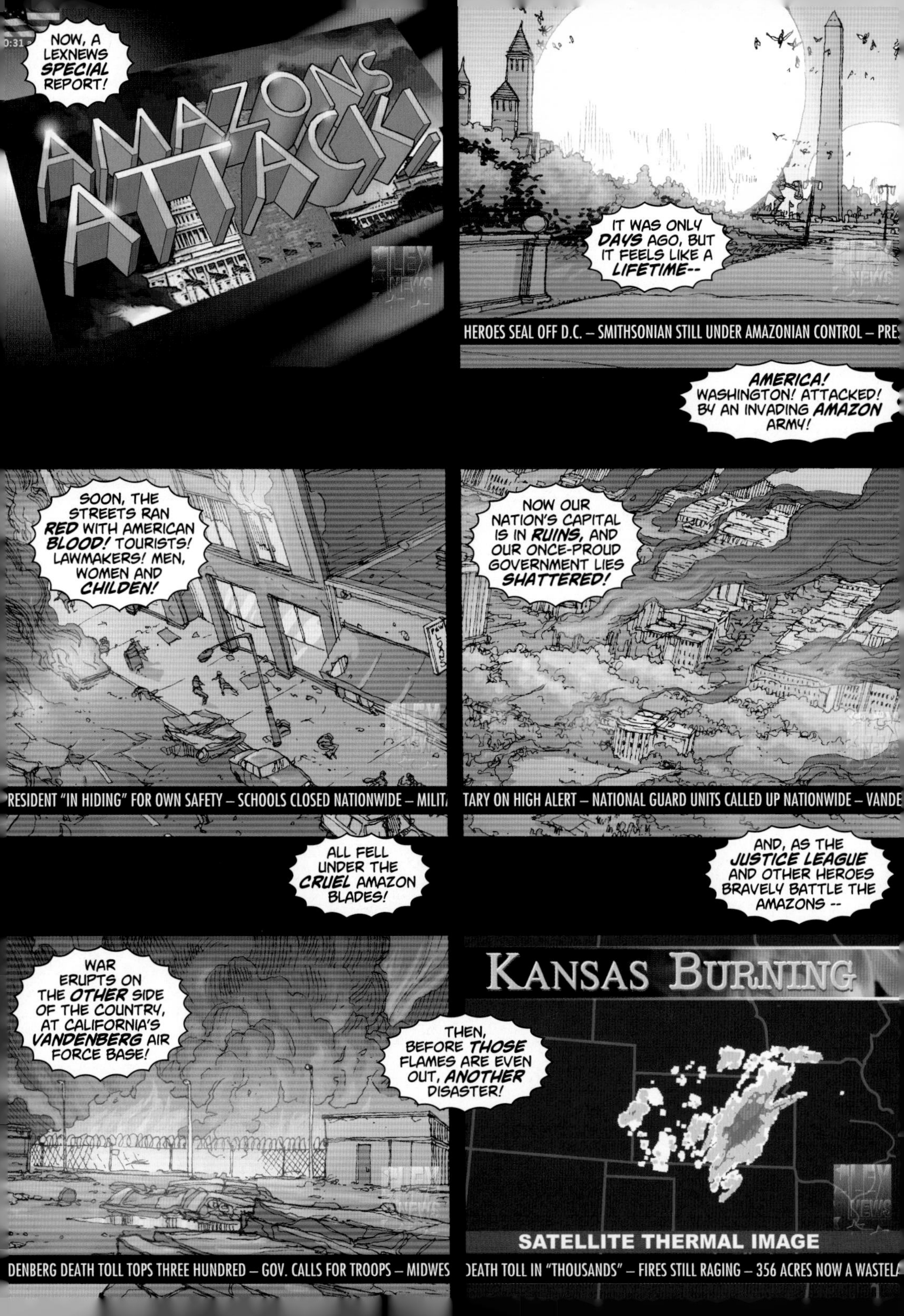
NOW, A LEXNEWS SPECIAL REPORT!
AMAZONS ATTACK!
IT WAS ONLY DAYS AGO, BUT IT FEELS LIKE A LIFETIME--
HEROES SEAL OFF D.C. – SMITHSONIAN STILL UNDER AMAZONIAN CONTROL – PRES
AMERICA! WASHINGTON! ATTACKED! BY AN INVADING AMAZON ARMY!
SOON, THE STREETS RAN RED WITH AMERICAN BLOOD! TOURISTS! LAWMAKERS! MEN, WOMEN AND CHILDEN!
PRESIDENT "IN HIDING" FOR OWN SAFETY – SCHOOLS CLOSED NATIONWIDE – MILIT
ALL FELL UNDER THE CRUEL AMAZON BLADES!
NOW OUR NATION'S CAPITAL IS IN RUINS, AND OUR ONCE-PROUD GOVERNMENT LIES SHATTERED!
TARY ON HIGH ALERT – NATIONAL GUARD UNITS CALLED UP NATIONWIDE – VANDE
AND, AS THE JUSTICE LEAGUE AND OTHER HEROES BRAVELY BATTLE THE AMAZONS --
WAR ERUPTS ON THE OTHER SIDE OF THE COUNTRY, AT CALIFORNIA'S VANDENBERG AIR FORCE BASE!
DENBERG DEATH TOLL TOPS THREE HUNDRED – GOV. CALLS FOR TROOPS – MIDWES
KANSAS BURNING
THEN, BEFORE THOSE FLAMES ARE EVEN OUT, ANOTHER DISASTER!
SATELLITE THERMAL IMAGE
DEATH TOLL IN "THOUSANDS" – FIRES STILL RAGING – 356 ACRES NOW A WASTELA

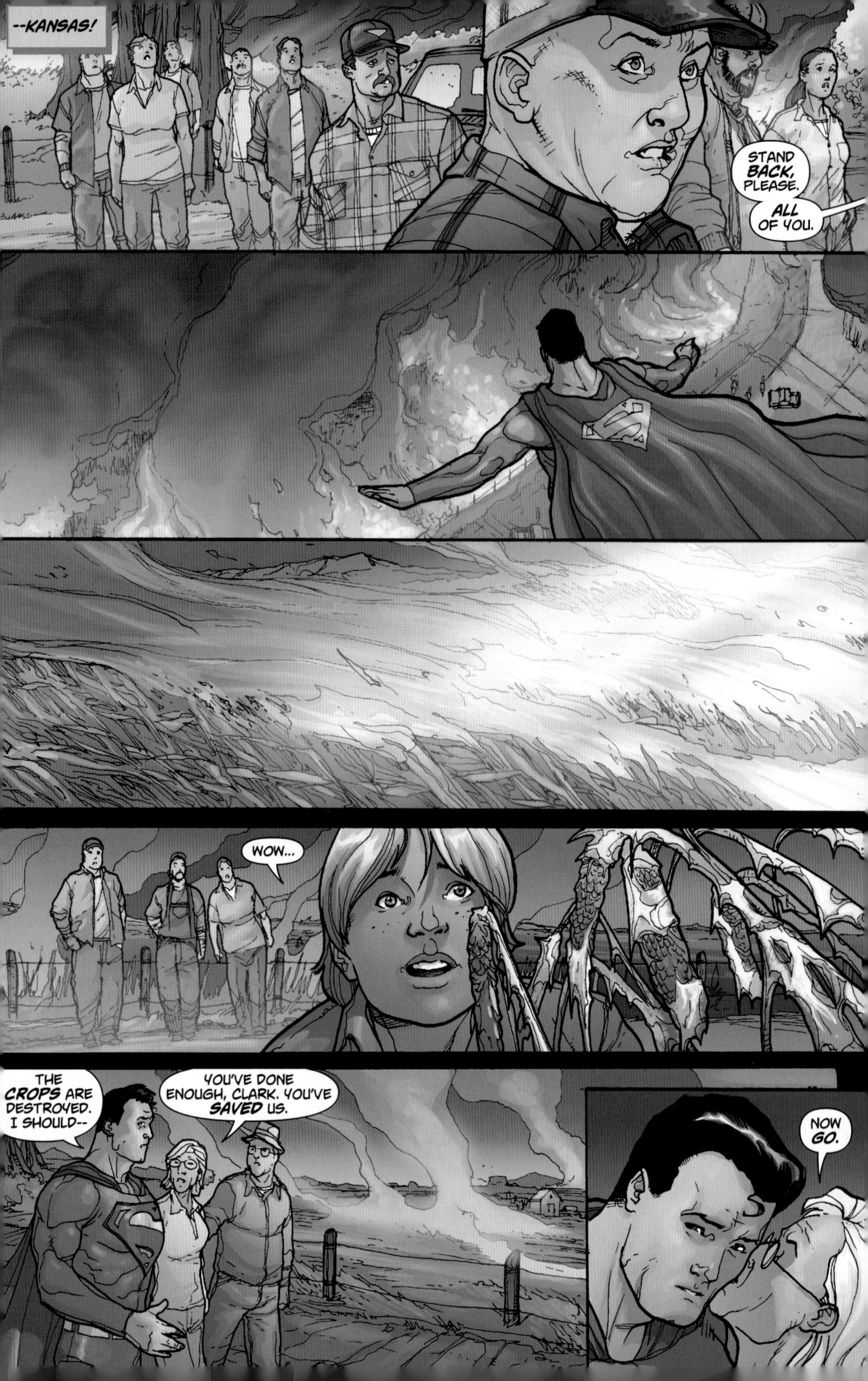
--KANSAS!
STAND BACK, PLEASE.
ALL OF YOU.
WOW...
THE CROPS ARE DESTROYED. I SHOULD--
YOU'VE DONE ENOUGH, CLARK. YOU'VE SAVED US.
NOW GO.

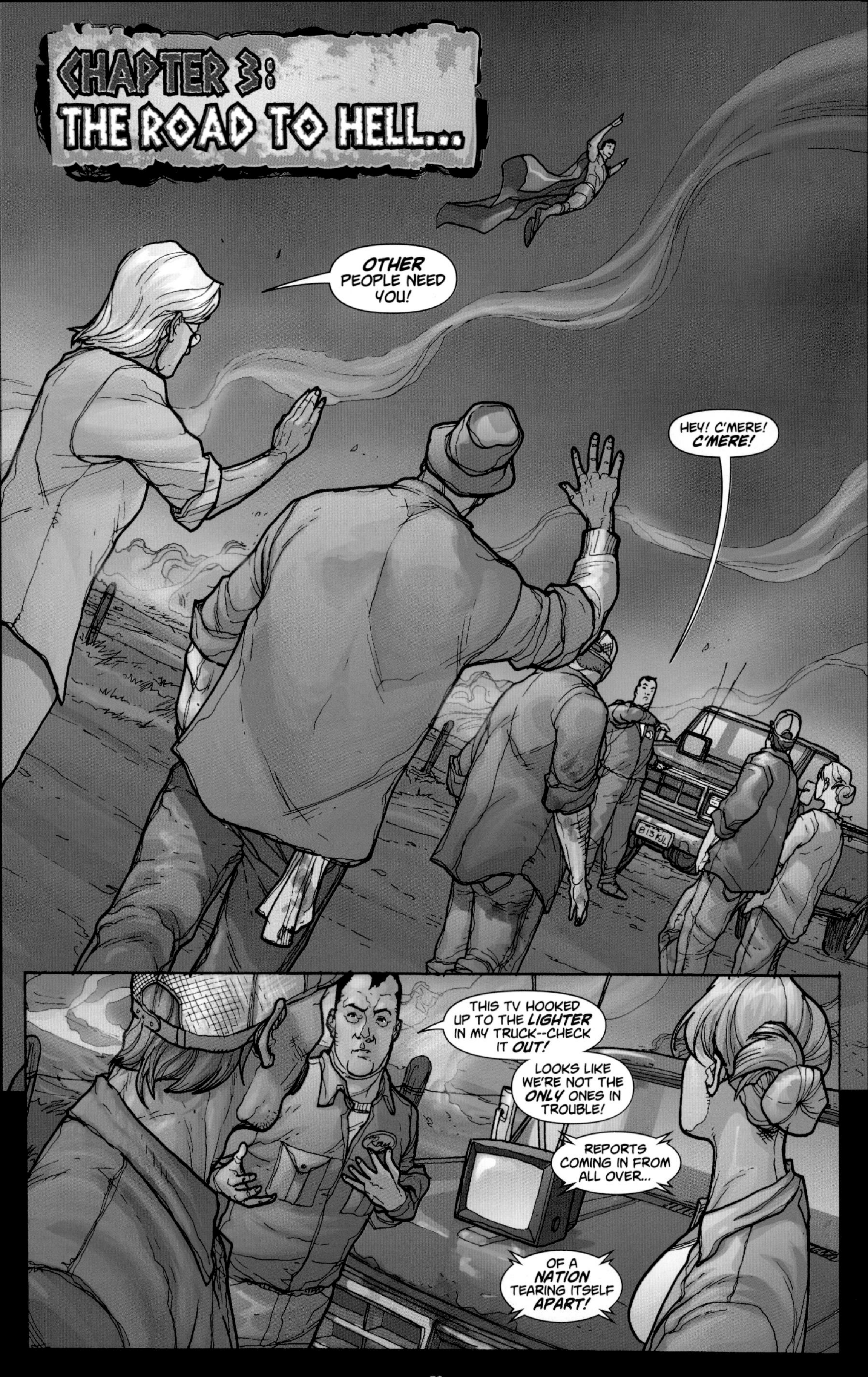
CHAPTER 3:
THE ROAD TO HELL...
OTHER PEOPLE NEED YOU!
HEY! C'MERE! C'MERE!
THIS TV HOOKED UP TO THE LIGHTER IN MY TRUCK--CHECK IT OUT!
LOOKS LIKE WE'RE NOT THE ONLY ONES IN TROUBLE!
REPORTS COMING IN FROM ALL OVER...
OF A NATION TEARING ITSELF APART!

TRAFFIC POURING OUT OF MANHATTAN AT A *STANDSTILL*--

--AS THOUSANDS ABANDON THEIR CARS, LEAVING *MASSIVE* TRAFFIC JAMS...

PRESIDENT "IN HIDING" FOR OWN SAFETY – SC̶ ̶MILIT̶

ALL FLIGHTS CANCELLED *NATIONWIDE.*

RIOTS AT O'HARE, L.A.X., SEA-TAC.

TARY ON HIGH ALERT – NATIONAL GUARD UNITS CALLED UP N̶

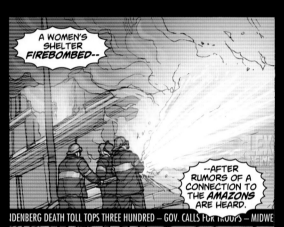

A WOMEN'S SHELTER *FIREBOMBED*--

--AFTER RUMORS OF A CONNECTION TO THE *AMAZONS* ARE HEARD.

̶DENBERG DEATH TOLL TOPS THREE HUNDRED – GOV. CALLS FOR TROOPS – MIDWE̶

AND *EVERY* HOUR, NEW REPORTS OF *MURDERS*, SUICIDES, ASSAULTS...

DEATH TOLL IN "THOUSANDS" – FIRES STILL RAGING – 356 ACRES NOW A WASTELA̶

AS AMERICA SLIPS CLOSER AND *CLOSER* TO--

WAIT--

I'VE *JUST* RECEIVED WORD THAT--

HEROES SEAL OFF D.C. – SMITHSONIAN STILL UNDER AMAZONIAN CONTRO̶

WE NOW BRING YOU A *LIVE* FEED FROM WASHINGTON--

WHO'S SHE?

IT'S *HER!* IT'S--

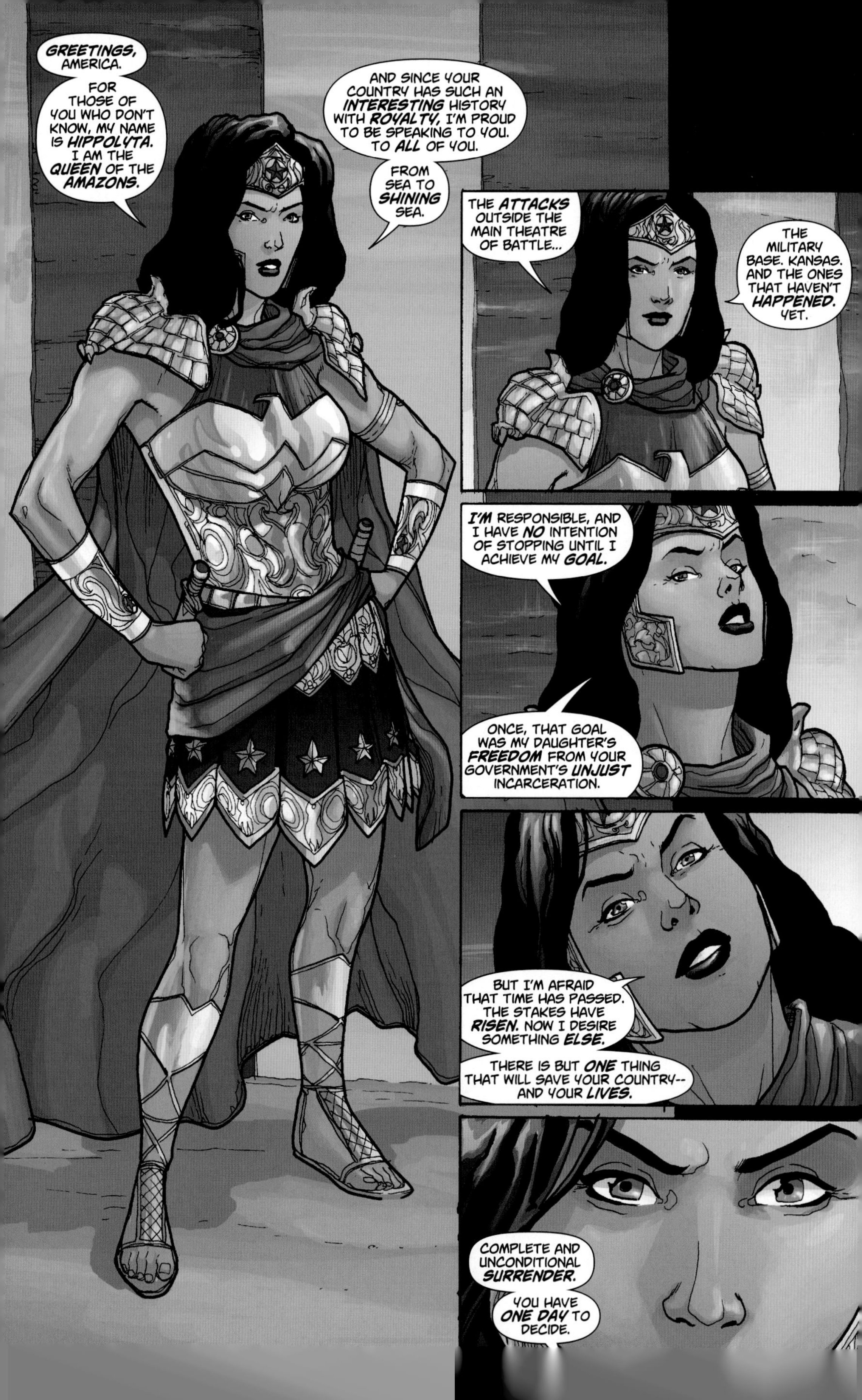
GREETINGS, AMERICA.
FOR THOSE OF YOU WHO DON'T KNOW, MY NAME IS HIPPOLYTA. I AM THE QUEEN OF THE AMAZONS.
AND SINCE YOUR COUNTRY HAS SUCH AN INTERESTING HISTORY WITH ROYALTY, I'M PROUD TO BE SPEAKING TO YOU. TO ALL OF YOU.
FROM SEA TO SHINING SEA.
THE ATTACKS OUTSIDE THE MAIN THEATRE OF BATTLE...
THE MILITARY BASE. KANSAS. AND THE ONES THAT HAVEN'T HAPPENED. YET.
I'M RESPONSIBLE, AND I HAVE NO INTENTION OF STOPPING UNTIL I ACHIEVE MY GOAL.
ONCE, THAT GOAL WAS MY DAUGHTER'S FREEDOM FROM YOUR GOVERNMENT'S UNJUST INCARCERATION.
BUT I'M AFRAID THAT TIME HAS PASSED. THE STAKES HAVE RISEN. NOW I DESIRE SOMETHING ELSE.
THERE IS BUT ONE THING THAT WILL SAVE YOUR COUNTRY-- AND YOUR LIVES.
COMPLETE AND UNCONDITIONAL SURRENDER.
YOU HAVE ONE DAY TO DECIDE.

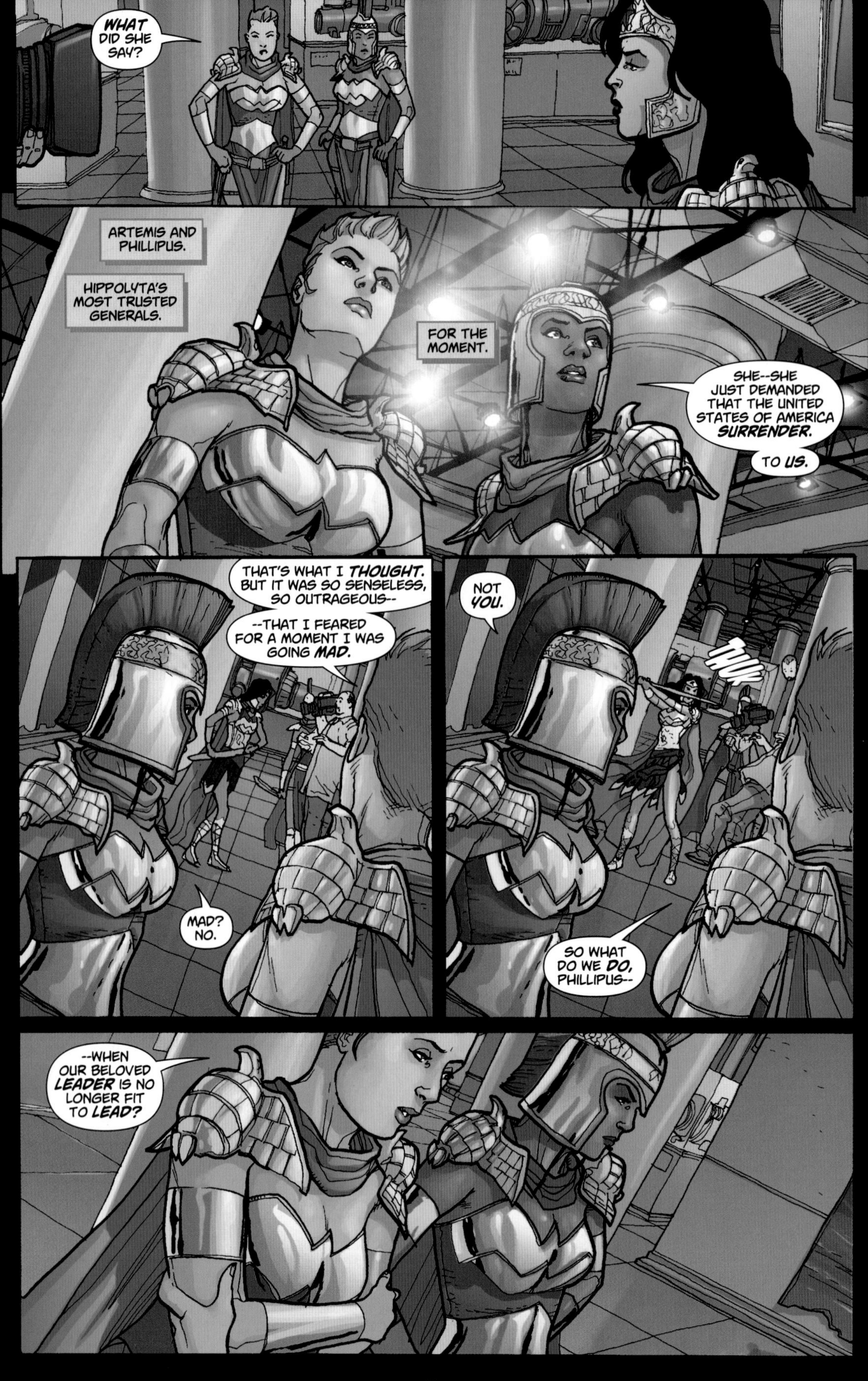
WHAT DID SHE SAY?
ARTEMIS AND PHILLIPUS.
HIPPOLYTA'S MOST TRUSTED GENERALS.
FOR THE MOMENT.
SHE--SHE JUST DEMANDED THAT THE UNITED STATES OF AMERICA SURRENDER.
TO US.
THAT'S WHAT I THOUGHT. BUT IT WAS SO SENSELESS, SO OUTRAGEOUS--
--THAT I FEARED FOR A MOMENT I WAS GOING MAD.
MAD? NO.
NOT YOU.
THUK
SO WHAT DO WE DO, PHILLIPUS--
--WHEN OUR BELOVED LEADER IS NO LONGER FIT TO LEAD?

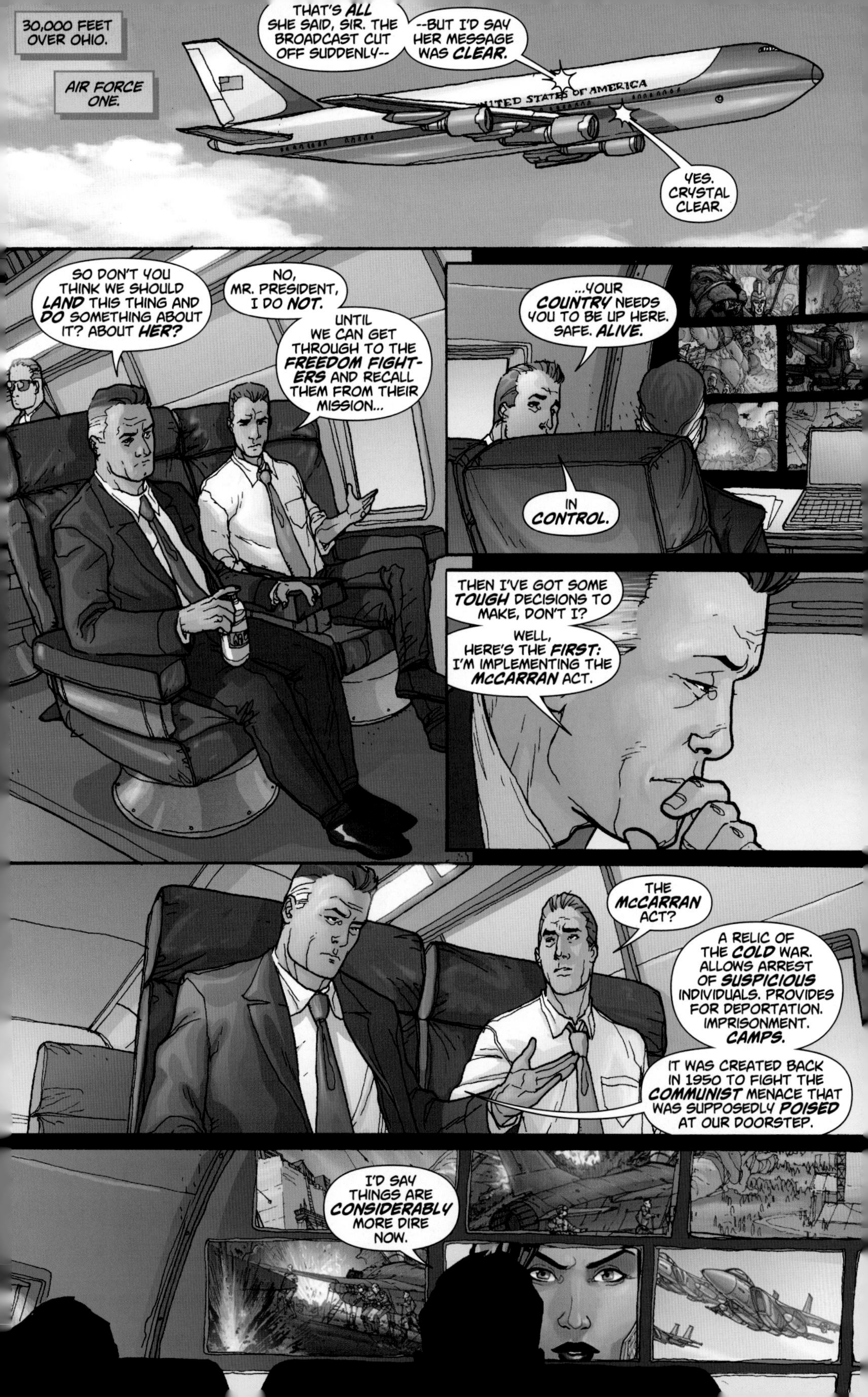
30,000 FEET OVER OHIO.
AIR FORCE ONE.
THAT'S ALL SHE SAID, SIR. THE BROADCAST CUT OFF SUDDENLY--
--BUT I'D SAY HER MESSAGE WAS CLEAR.
UNITED STATES OF AMERICA
YES. CRYSTAL CLEAR.
SO DON'T YOU THINK WE SHOULD LAND THIS THING AND DO SOMETHING ABOUT IT? ABOUT HER?
NO, MR. PRESIDENT, I DO NOT.
UNTIL WE CAN GET THROUGH TO THE FREEDOM FIGHTERS AND RECALL THEM FROM THEIR MISSION...
...YOUR COUNTRY NEEDS YOU TO BE UP HERE. SAFE. ALIVE.
IN CONTROL.
THEN I'VE GOT SOME TOUGH DECISIONS TO MAKE, DON'T I?
WELL, HERE'S THE FIRST: I'M IMPLEMENTING THE McCARRAN ACT.
THE McCARRAN ACT?
A RELIC OF THE COLD WAR. ALLOWS ARREST OF SUSPICIOUS INDIVIDUALS. PROVIDES FOR DEPORTATION. IMPRISONMENT. CAMPS.
IT WAS CREATED BACK IN 1950 TO FIGHT THE COMMUNIST MENACE THAT WAS SUPPOSEDLY POISED AT OUR DOORSTEP.
I'D SAY THINGS ARE CONSIDERABLY MORE DIRE NOW.

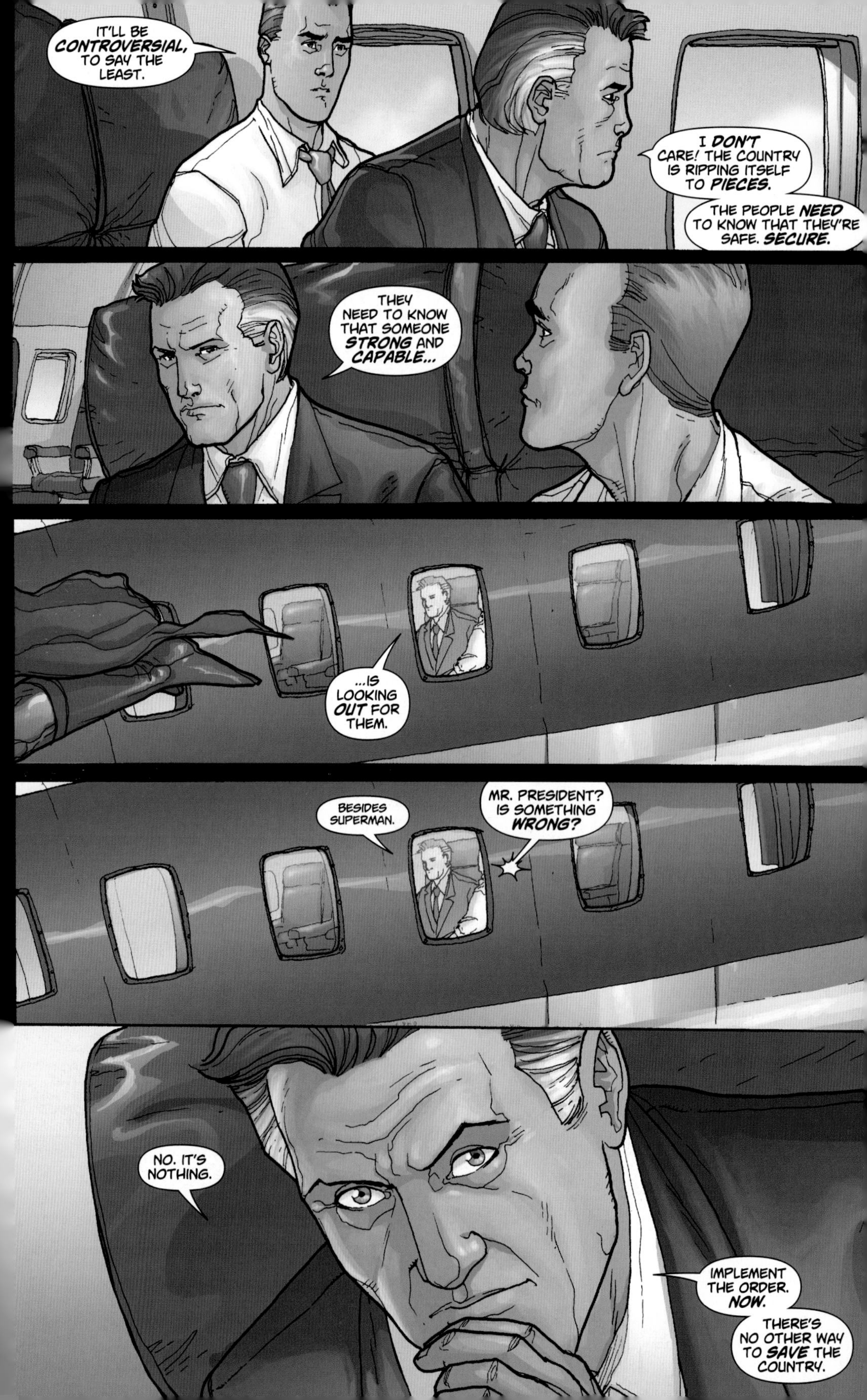
IT'LL BE CONTROVERSIAL, TO SAY THE LEAST.
I DON'T CARE! THE COUNTRY IS RIPPING ITSELF TO PIECES.
THE PEOPLE NEED TO KNOW THAT THEY'RE SAFE. SECURE.
THEY NEED TO KNOW THAT SOMEONE STRONG AND CAPABLE...
...IS LOOKING OUT FOR THEM.
BESIDES SUPERMAN.
MR. PRESIDENT? IS SOMETHING WRONG?
NO. IT'S NOTHING.
IMPLEMENT THE ORDER. NOW.
THERE'S NO OTHER WAY TO SAVE THE COUNTRY.

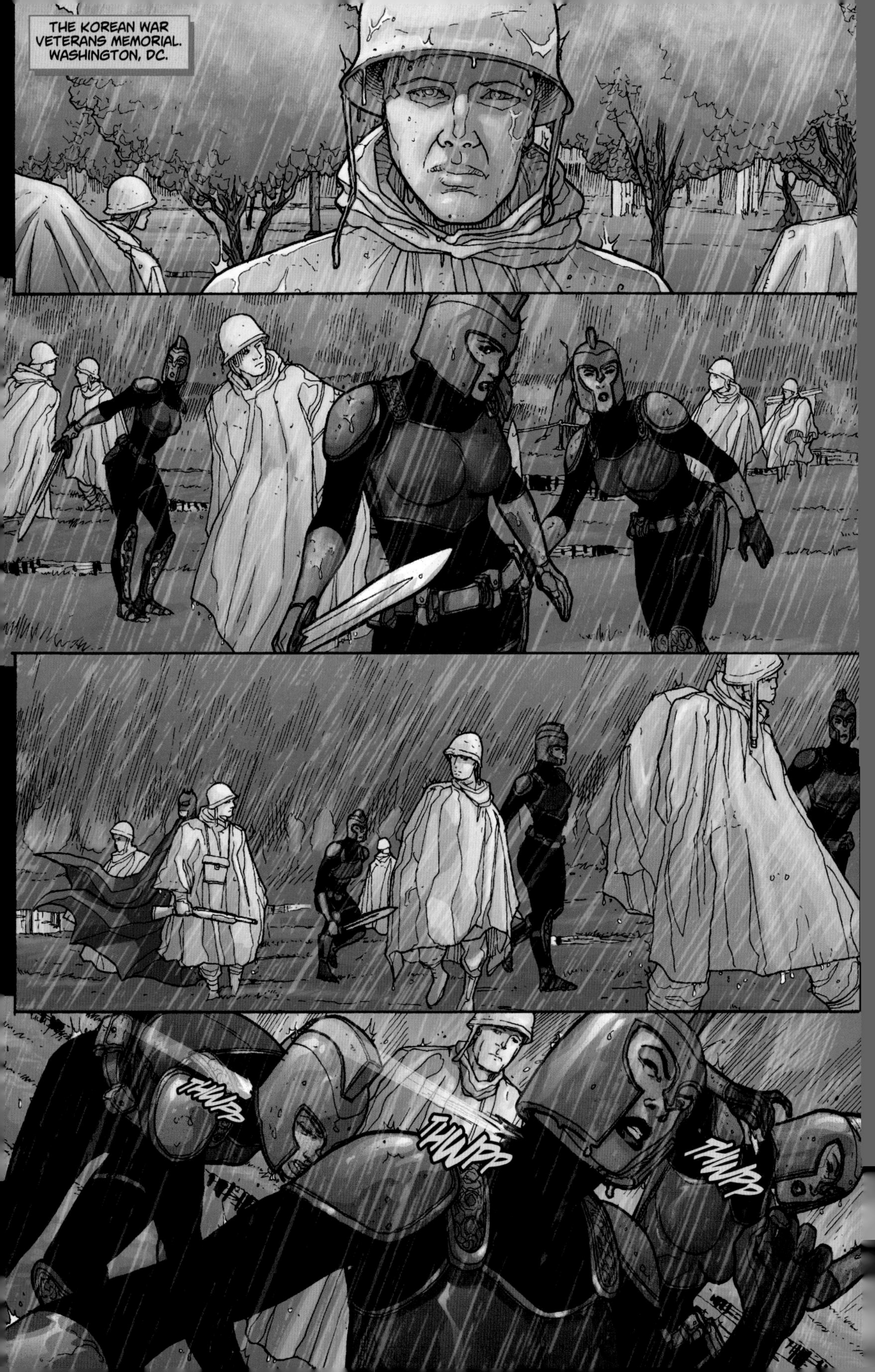
THE KOREAN WAR VETERANS MEMORIAL. WASHINGTON, DC.
THWPP
THWPP
THWPP

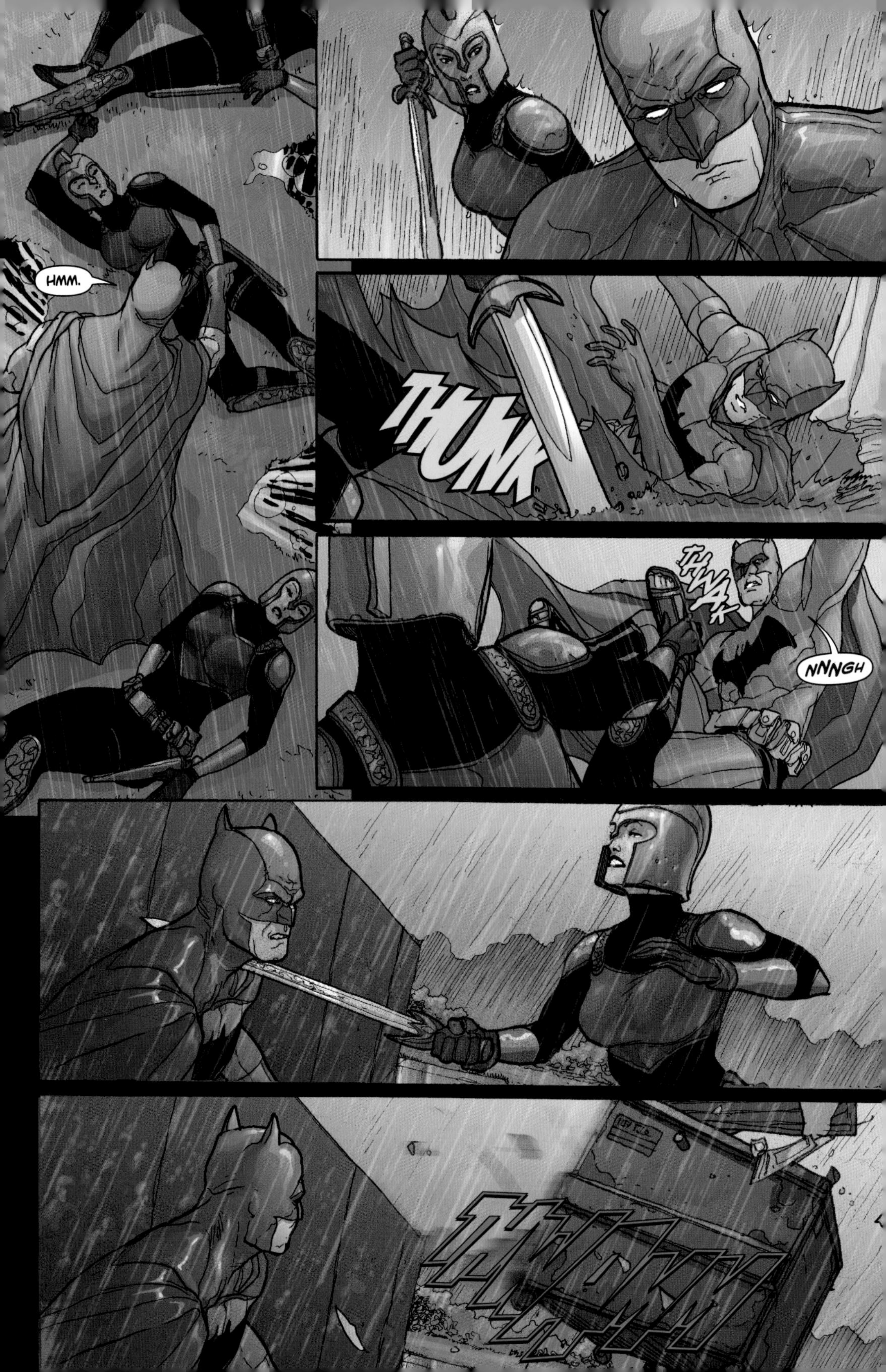
HMM.
THUNK
THWAK
NNNGH

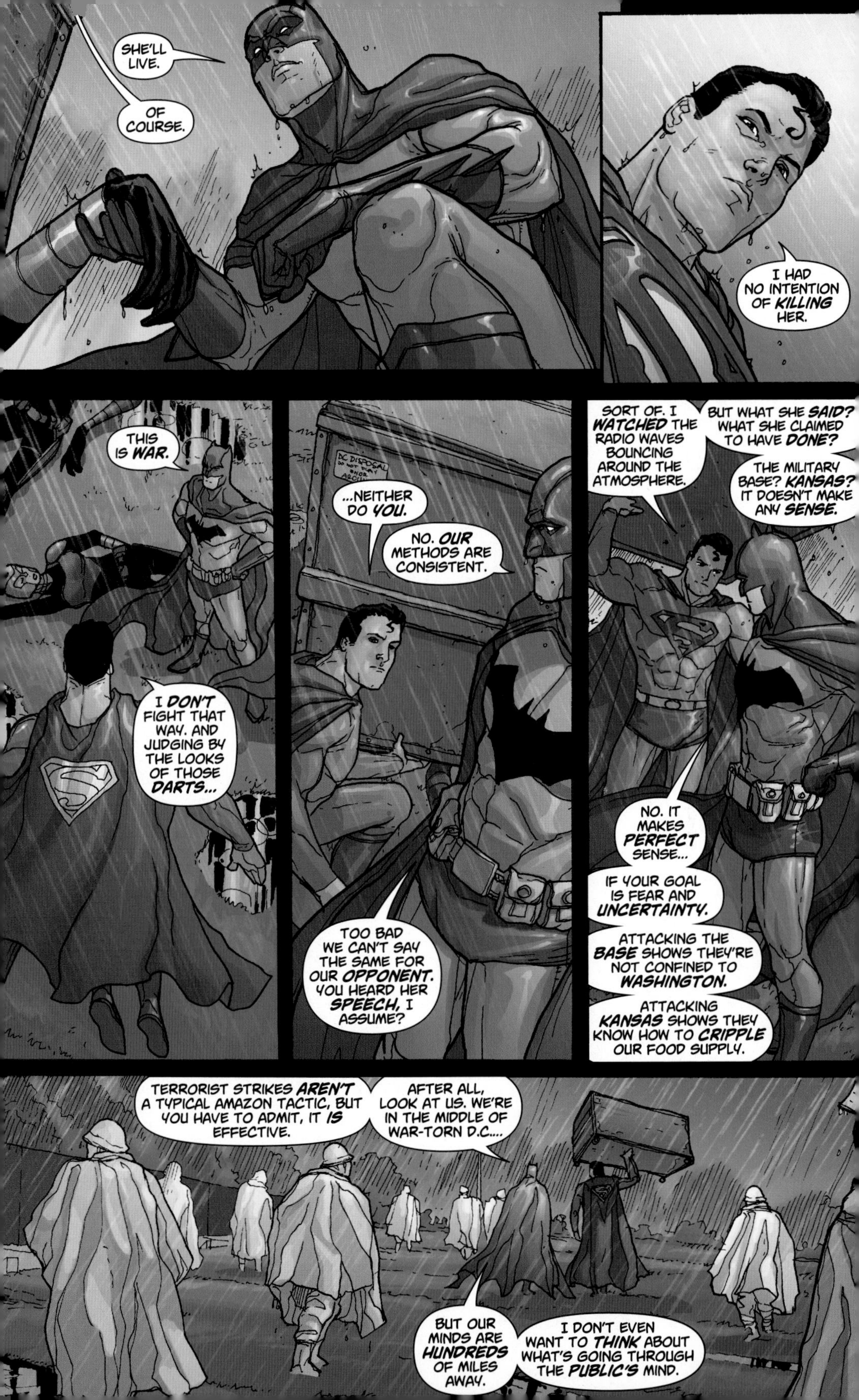
SHE'LL LIVE.
OF COURSE.
I HAD NO INTENTION OF KILLING HER.
THIS IS WAR.
I DON'T FIGHT THAT WAY. AND JUDGING BY THE LOOKS OF THOSE DARTS...
...NEITHER DO YOU.
NO. OUR METHODS ARE CONSISTENT.
TOO BAD WE CAN'T SAY THE SAME FOR OUR OPPONENT. YOU HEARD HER SPEECH, I ASSUME?
SORT OF. I WATCHED THE RADIO WAVES BOUNCING AROUND THE ATMOSPHERE.
BUT WHAT SHE SAID? WHAT SHE CLAIMED TO HAVE DONE?
THE MILITARY BASE? KANSAS? IT DOESN'T MAKE ANY SENSE.
NO. IT MAKES PERFECT SENSE...
IF YOUR GOAL IS FEAR AND UNCERTAINTY.
ATTACKING THE BASE SHOWS THEY'RE NOT CONFINED TO WASHINGTON.
ATTACKING KANSAS SHOWS THEY KNOW HOW TO CRIPPLE OUR FOOD SUPPLY.
TERRORIST STRIKES AREN'T A TYPICAL AMAZON TACTIC, BUT YOU HAVE TO ADMIT, IT IS EFFECTIVE.
AFTER ALL, LOOK AT US. WE'RE IN THE MIDDLE OF WAR-TORN D.C....
BUT OUR MINDS ARE HUNDREDS OF MILES AWAY.
I DON'T EVEN WANT TO THINK ABOUT WHAT'S GOING THROUGH THE PUBLIC'S MIND.

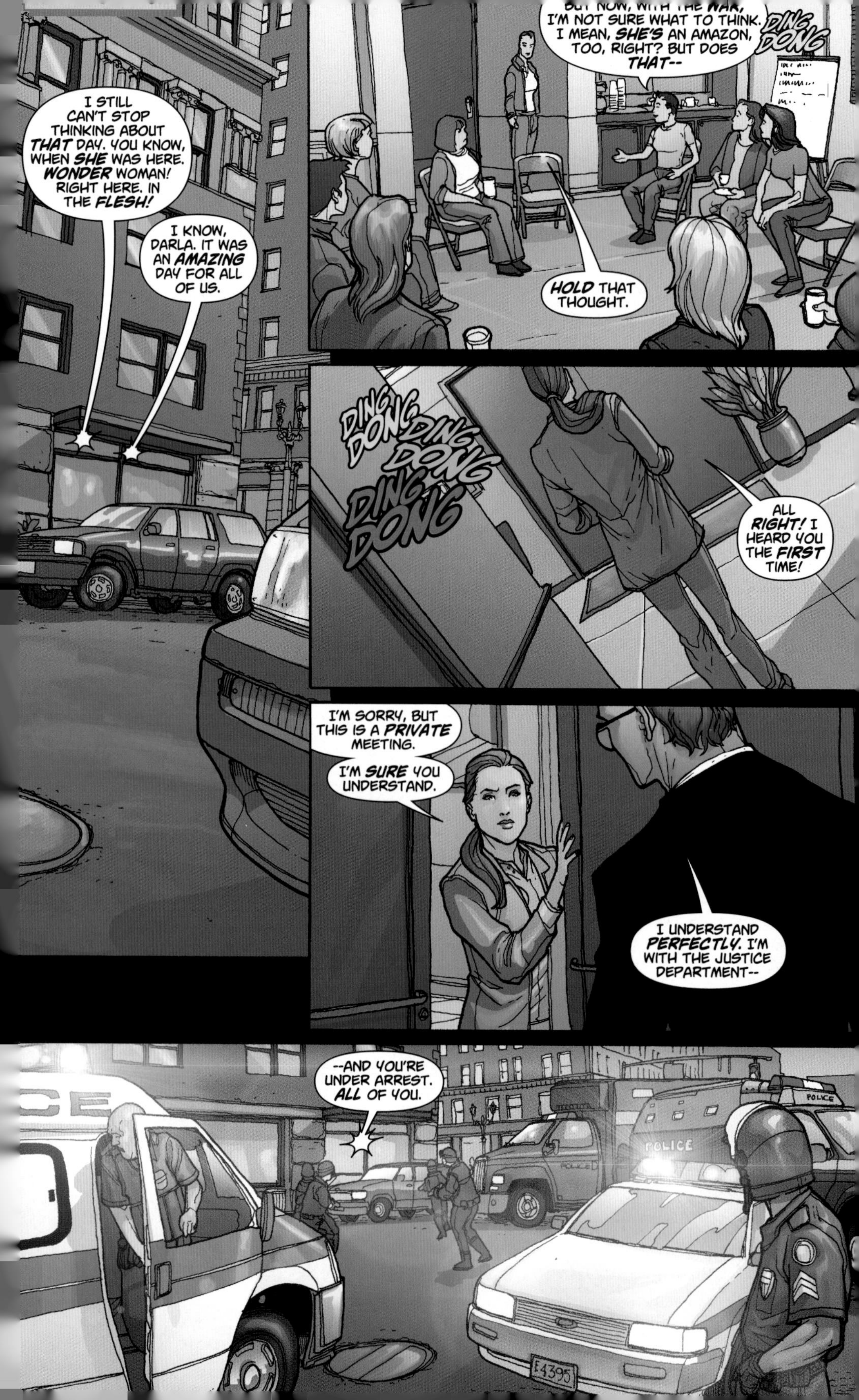
I STILL CAN'T STOP THINKING ABOUT THAT DAY. YOU KNOW, WHEN SHE WAS HERE. WONDER WOMAN! RIGHT HERE. IN THE FLESH!
I KNOW, DARLA. IT WAS AN AMAZING DAY FOR ALL OF US.
BUT NOW, WITH THE WAR, I'M NOT SURE WHAT TO THINK. I MEAN, SHE'S AN AMAZON, TOO, RIGHT? BUT DOES THAT--
DING DONG
HOLD THAT THOUGHT.
DING DONG DING DONG DING DONG
ALL RIGHT! I HEARD YOU THE FIRST TIME!
I'M SORRY, BUT THIS IS A PRIVATE MEETING.
I'M SURE YOU UNDERSTAND.
I UNDERSTAND PERFECTLY. I'M WITH THE JUSTICE DEPARTMENT--
--AND YOU'RE UNDER ARREST. ALL OF YOU.
POLICE
POLICE
E4395

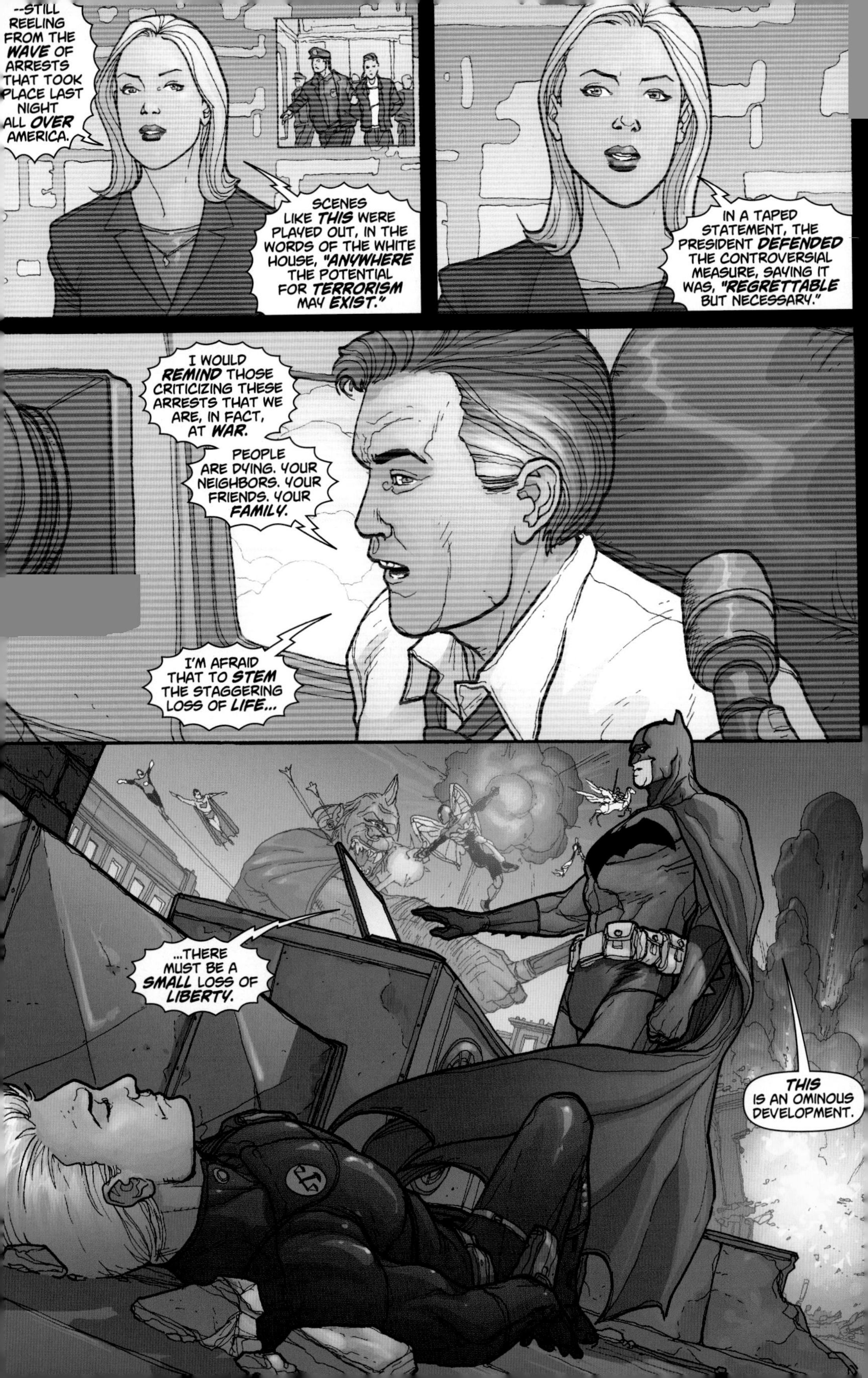
--STILL REELING FROM THE WAVE OF ARRESTS THAT TOOK PLACE LAST NIGHT ALL OVER AMERICA.
SCENES LIKE THIS WERE PLAYED OUT, IN THE WORDS OF THE WHITE HOUSE, "ANYWHERE THE POTENTIAL FOR TERRORISM MAY EXIST."
IN A TAPED STATEMENT, THE PRESIDENT DEFENDED THE CONTROVERSIAL MEASURE, SAYING IT WAS, "REGRETTABLE BUT NECESSARY."
I WOULD REMIND THOSE CRITICIZING THESE ARRESTS THAT WE ARE, IN FACT, AT WAR.
PEOPLE ARE DYING. YOUR NEIGHBORS. YOUR FRIENDS. YOUR FAMILY.
I'M AFRAID THAT TO STEM THE STAGGERING LOSS OF LIFE...
...THERE MUST BE A SMALL LOSS OF LIBERTY.
THIS IS AN OMINOUS DEVELOPMENT.

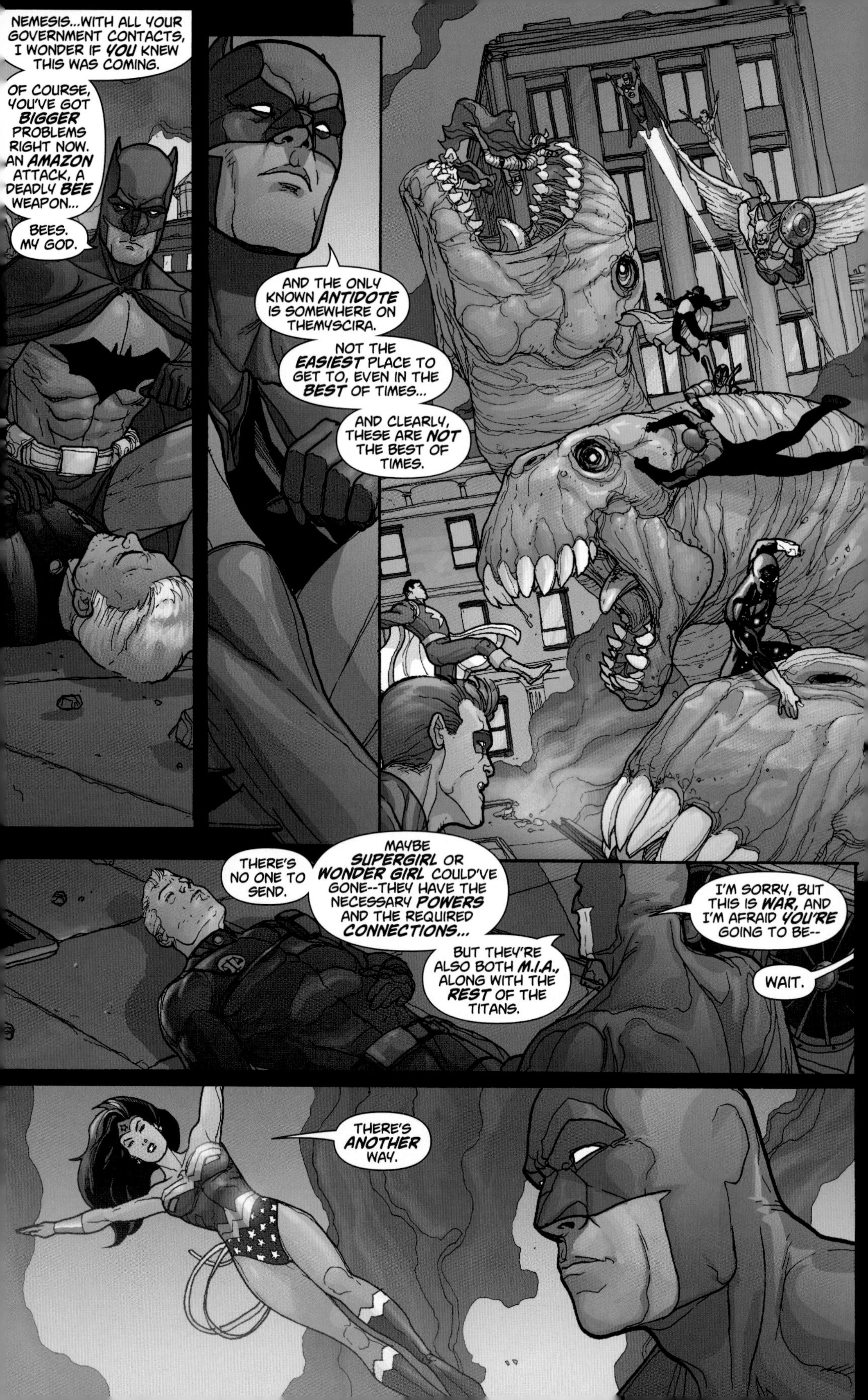
NEMESIS...WITH ALL YOUR GOVERNMENT CONTACTS, I WONDER IF YOU KNEW THIS WAS COMING.
OF COURSE, YOU'VE GOT BIGGER PROBLEMS RIGHT NOW. AN AMAZON ATTACK, A DEADLY BEE WEAPON...
BEES. MY GOD.
AND THE ONLY KNOWN ANTIDOTE IS SOMEWHERE ON THEMYSCIRA.
NOT THE EASIEST PLACE TO GET TO, EVEN IN THE BEST OF TIMES...
AND CLEARLY, THESE ARE NOT THE BEST OF TIMES.
THERE'S NO ONE TO SEND.
MAYBE SUPERGIRL OR WONDER GIRL COULD'VE GONE--THEY HAVE THE NECESSARY POWERS AND THE REQUIRED CONNECTIONS...
BUT THEY'RE ALSO BOTH M.I.A., ALONG WITH THE REST OF THE TITANS.
I'M SORRY, BUT THIS IS WAR, AND I'M AFRAID YOU'RE GOING TO BE--
WAIT.
THERE'S ANOTHER WAY.

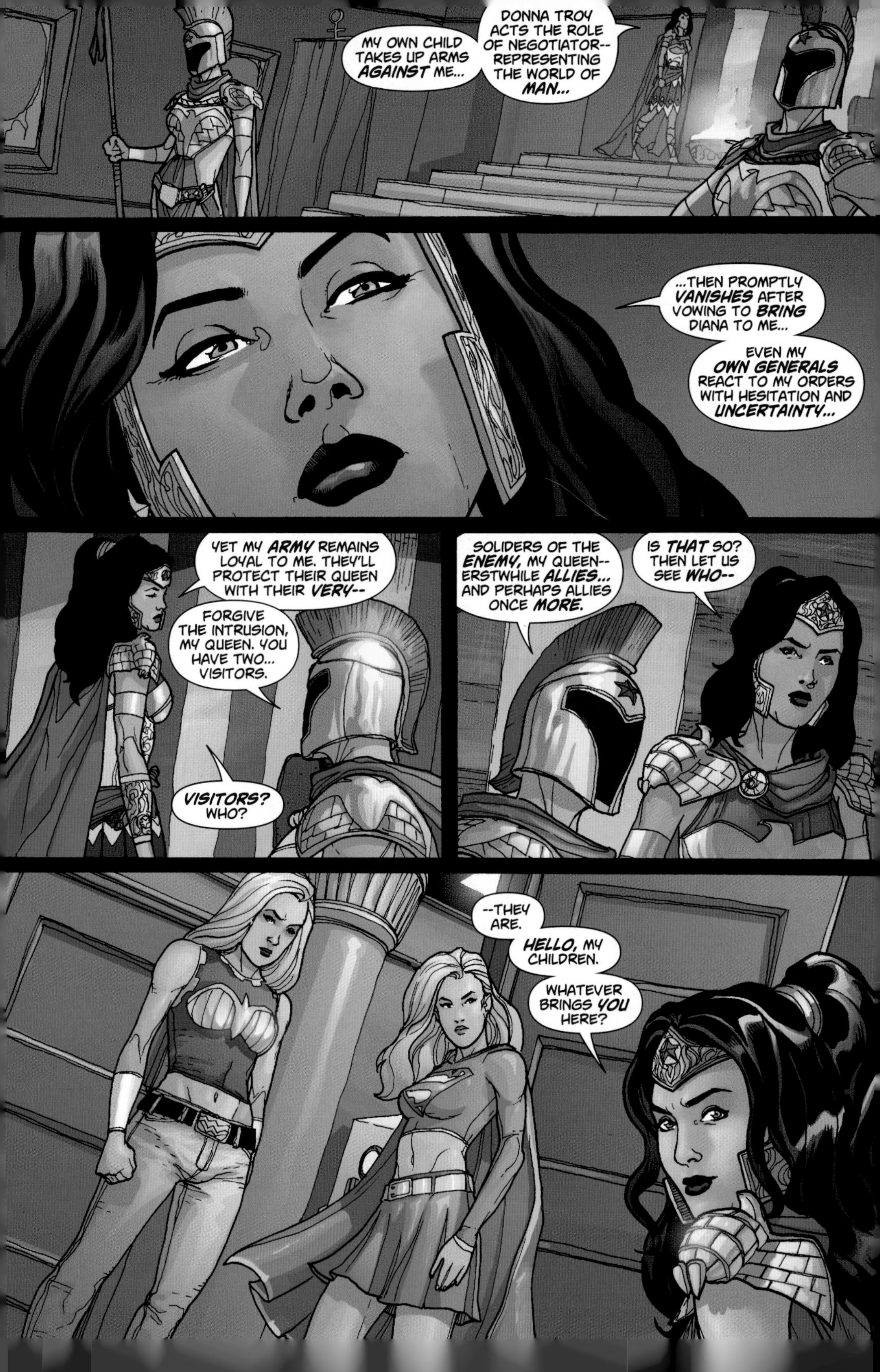
MY OWN CHILD TAKES UP ARMS AGAINST ME...
DONNA TROY ACTS THE ROLE OF NEGOTIATOR-- REPRESENTING THE WORLD OF MAN...
...THEN PROMPTLY VANISHES AFTER VOWING TO BRING DIANA TO ME...
EVEN MY OWN GENERALS REACT TO MY ORDERS WITH HESITATION AND UNCERTAINTY...
YET MY ARMY REMAINS LOYAL TO ME. THEY'LL PROTECT THEIR QUEEN WITH THEIR VERY--
FORGIVE THE INTRUSION, MY QUEEN. YOU HAVE TWO... VISITORS.
VISITORS? WHO?
SOLIDERS OF THE ENEMY, MY QUEEN-- ERSTWHILE ALLIES... AND PERHAPS ALLIES ONCE MORE.
IS THAT SO? THEN LET US SEE WHO--
--THEY ARE.
HELLO, MY CHILDREN.
WHATEVER BRINGS YOU HERE?

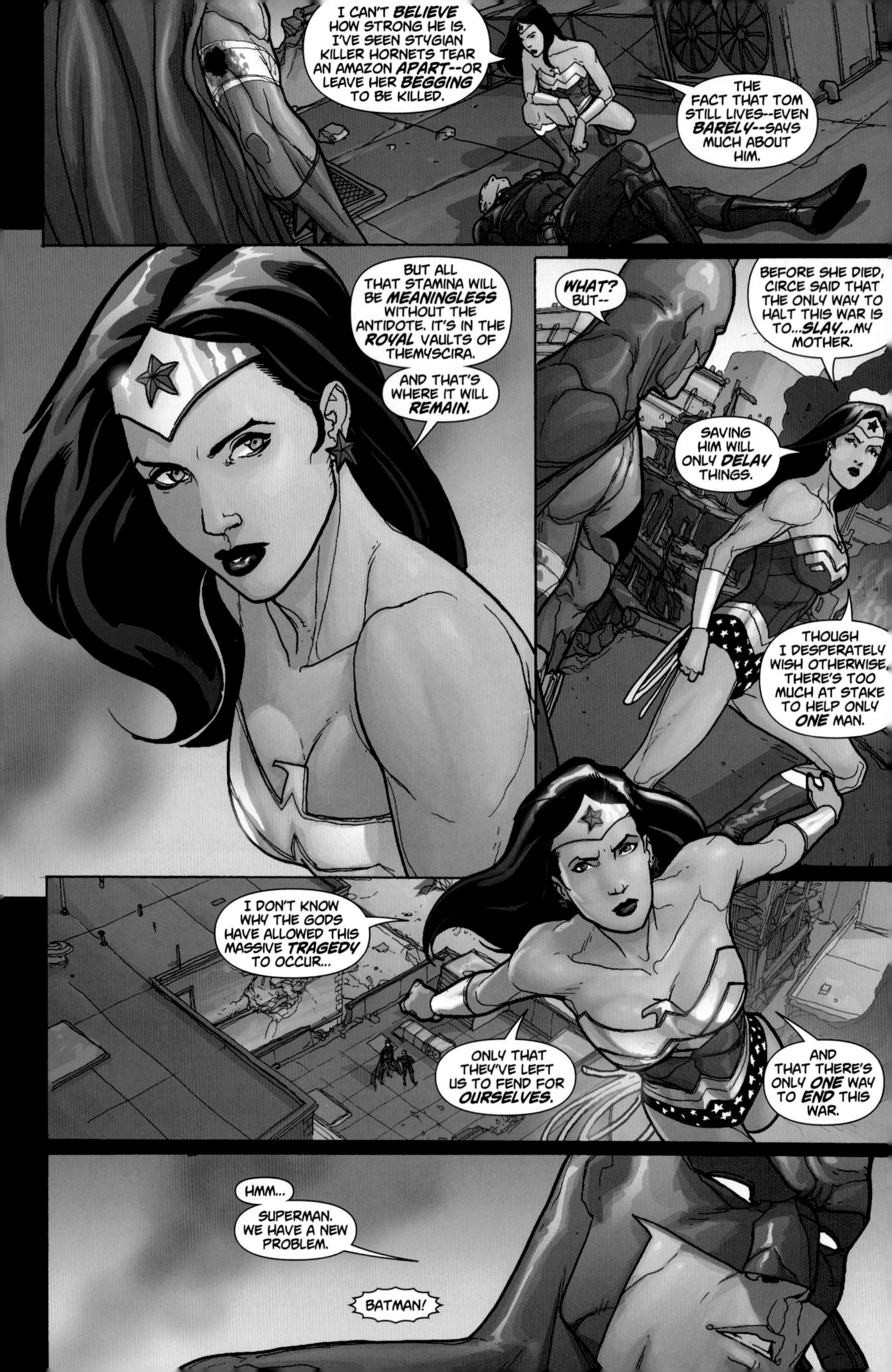
I CAN'T **BELIEVE** HOW STRONG HE IS. I'VE SEEN STYGIAN KILLER HORNETS TEAR AN AMAZON **APART**--OR LEAVE HER **BEGGING** TO BE KILLED.
THE FACT THAT TOM STILL LIVES--EVEN **BARELY**--SAYS MUCH ABOUT HIM.
BUT ALL THAT STAMINA WILL BE **MEANINGLESS** WITHOUT THE ANTIDOTE. IT'S IN THE **ROYAL** VAULTS OF THEMYSCIRA.
AND THAT'S WHERE IT WILL **REMAIN.**
WHAT? BUT--
BEFORE SHE DIED, CIRCE SAID THAT THE ONLY WAY TO HALT THIS WAR IS TO...**SLAY...**MY MOTHER.
SAVING HIM WILL ONLY **DELAY** THINGS.
THOUGH I DESPERATELY WISH OTHERWISE, THERE'S TOO MUCH AT STAKE TO HELP ONLY **ONE** MAN.
I DON'T KNOW WHY THE GODS HAVE ALLOWED THIS MASSIVE **TRAGEDY** TO OCCUR...
ONLY THAT THEY'VE LEFT US TO FEND FOR **OURSELVES.**
AND THAT THERE'S ONLY **ONE** WAY TO **END** THIS WAR.
HMM...
SUPERMAN. WE HAVE A NEW PROBLEM.
BATMAN!

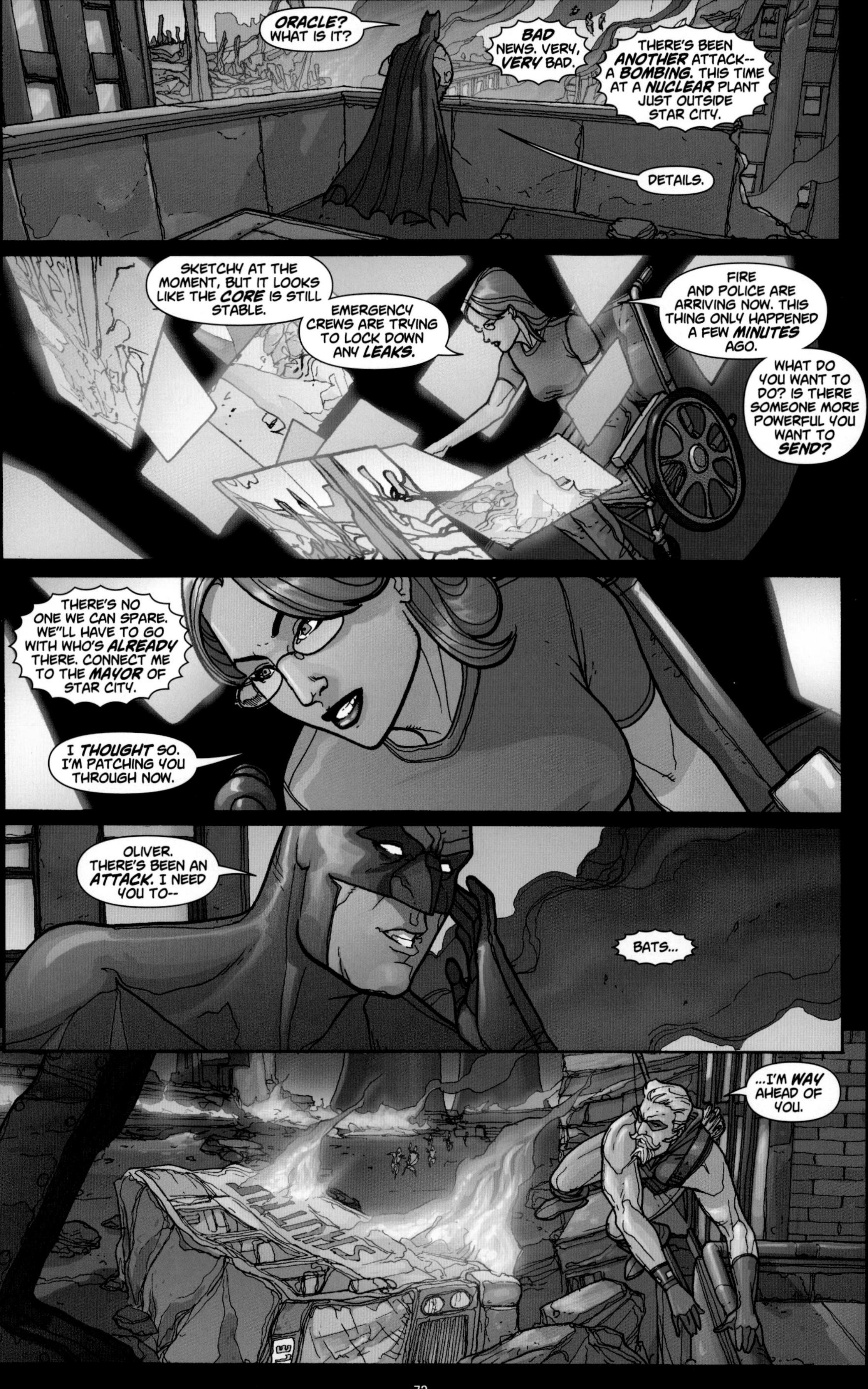

ORACLE? WHAT IS IT?
BAD NEWS. VERY, VERY BAD.
THERE'S BEEN ANOTHER ATTACK-- A BOMBING. THIS TIME AT A NUCLEAR PLANT JUST OUTSIDE STAR CITY.
DETAILS.
SKETCHY AT THE MOMENT, BUT IT LOOKS LIKE THE CORE IS STILL STABLE.
EMERGENCY CREWS ARE TRYING TO LOCK DOWN ANY LEAKS.
FIRE AND POLICE ARE ARRIVING NOW. THIS THING ONLY HAPPENED A FEW MINUTES AGO.
WHAT DO YOU WANT TO DO? IS THERE SOMEONE MORE POWERFUL YOU WANT TO SEND?
THERE'S NO ONE WE CAN SPARE. WE'LL HAVE TO GO WITH WHO'S ALREADY THERE. CONNECT ME TO THE MAYOR OF STAR CITY.
I THOUGHT SO. I'M PATCHING YOU THROUGH NOW.
OLIVER. THERE'S BEEN AN ATTACK. I NEED YOU TO--
BATS...
...I'M WAY AHEAD OF YOU.

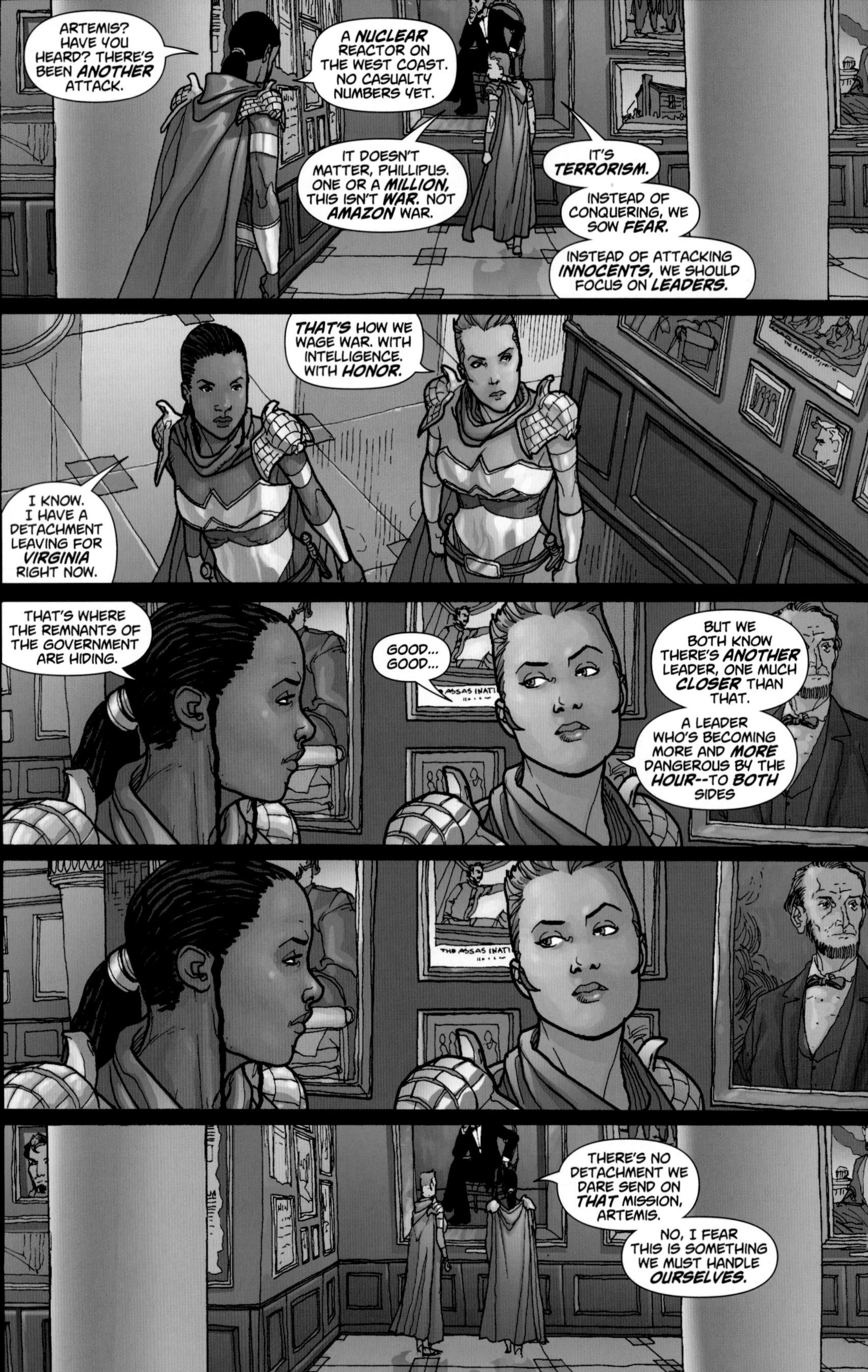

ARTEMIS? HAVE YOU HEARD? THERE'S BEEN ANOTHER ATTACK.
A NUCLEAR REACTOR ON THE WEST COAST. NO CASUALTY NUMBERS YET.
IT DOESN'T MATTER, PHILLIPUS. ONE OR A MILLION, THIS ISN'T WAR. NOT AMAZON WAR.
IT'S TERRORISM.
INSTEAD OF CONQUERING, WE SOW FEAR.
INSTEAD OF ATTACKING INNOCENTS, WE SHOULD FOCUS ON LEADERS.
THAT'S HOW WE WAGE WAR. WITH INTELLIGENCE. WITH HONOR.
I KNOW. I HAVE A DETACHMENT LEAVING FOR VIRGINIA RIGHT NOW.
THAT'S WHERE THE REMNANTS OF THE GOVERNMENT ARE HIDING.
GOOD... GOOD...
BUT WE BOTH KNOW THERE'S ANOTHER LEADER, ONE MUCH CLOSER THAN THAT.
A LEADER WHO'S BECOMING MORE AND MORE DANGEROUS BY THE HOUR--TO BOTH SIDES
THERE'S NO DETACHMENT WE DARE SEND ON THAT MISSION, ARTEMIS.
NO, I FEAR THIS IS SOMETHING WE MUST HANDLE OURSELVES.

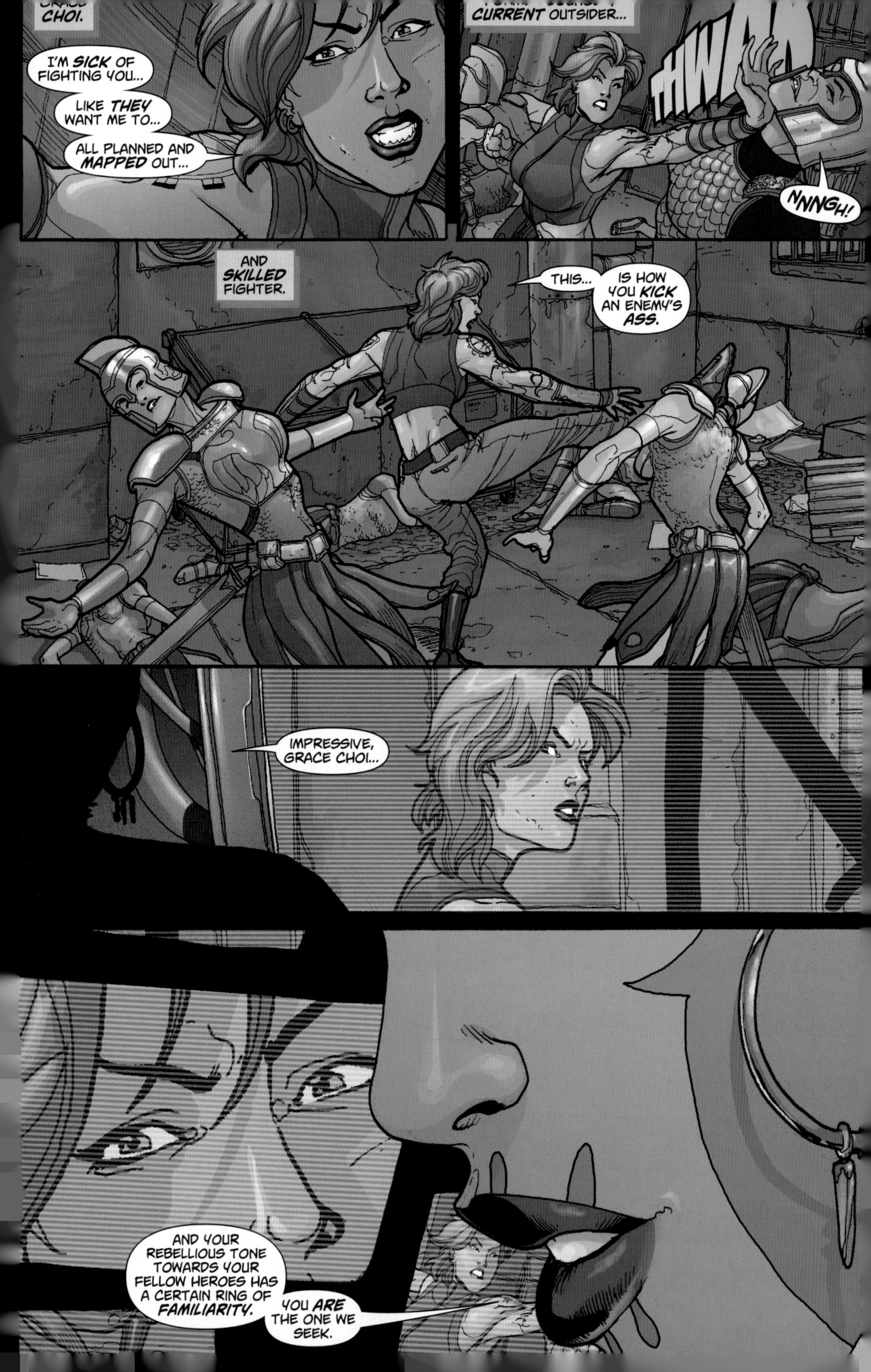
CHOI.
I'M SICK OF FIGHTING YOU...
LIKE THEY WANT ME TO...
ALL PLANNED AND MAPPED OUT...
CURRENT OUTSIDER...
NNNGH!
AND SKILLED FIGHTER.
THIS...
IS HOW YOU KICK AN ENEMY'S ASS.
IMPRESSIVE, GRACE CHOI...
AND YOUR REBELLIOUS TONE TOWARDS YOUR FELLOW HEROES HAS A CERTAIN RING OF FAMILIARITY.
YOU ARE THE ONE WE SEEK.

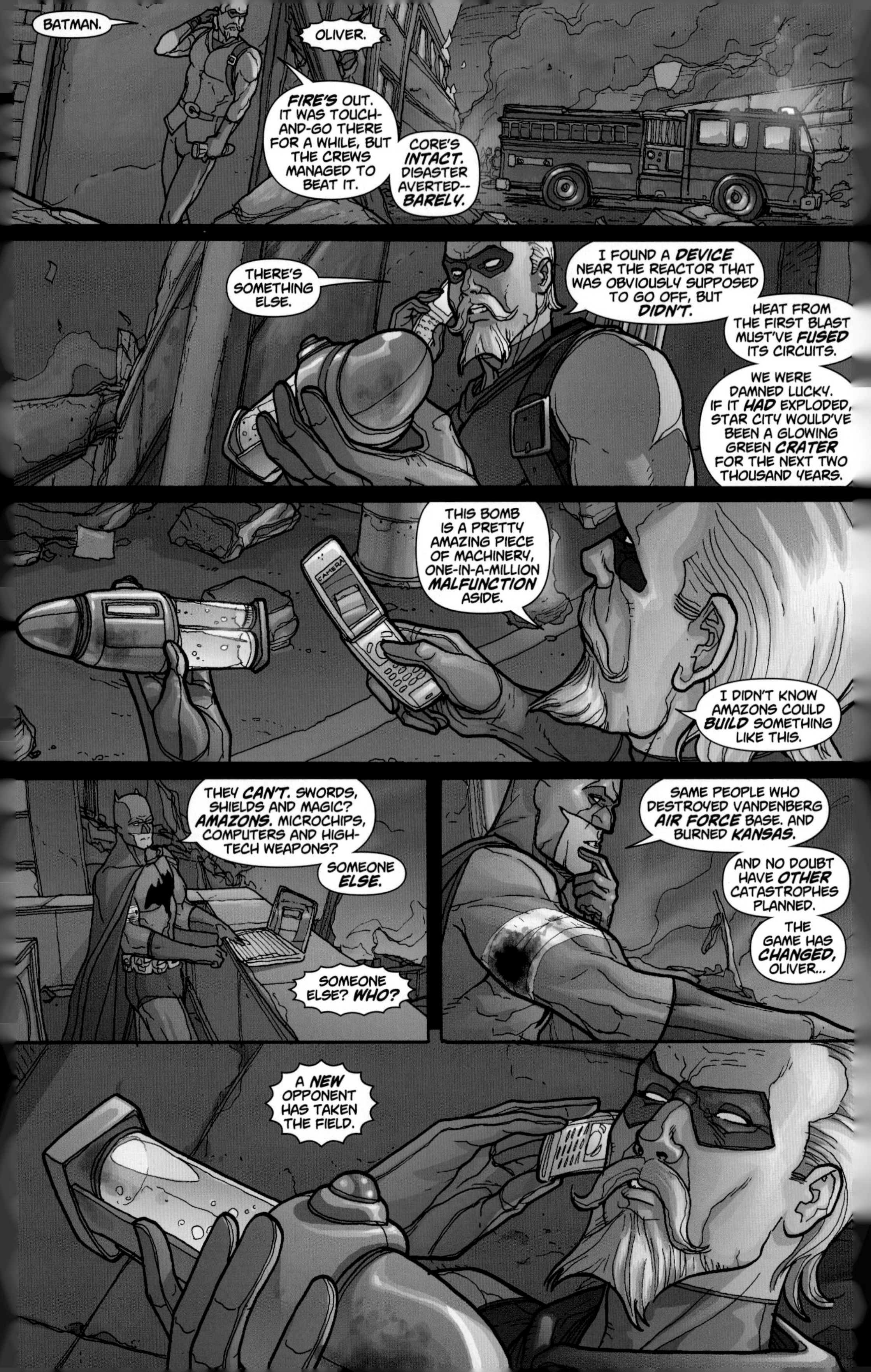
BATMAN.
OLIVER.
FIRE'S OUT. IT WAS TOUCH-AND-GO THERE FOR A WHILE, BUT THE CREWS MANAGED TO BEAT IT.
CORE'S INTACT. DISASTER AVERTED-- BARELY.
THERE'S SOMETHING ELSE.
I FOUND A DEVICE NEAR THE REACTOR THAT WAS OBVIOUSLY SUPPOSED TO GO OFF, BUT DIDN'T.
HEAT FROM THE FIRST BLAST MUST'VE FUSED ITS CIRCUITS.
WE WERE DAMNED LUCKY. IF IT HAD EXPLODED, STAR CITY WOULD'VE BEEN A GLOWING GREEN CRATER FOR THE NEXT TWO THOUSAND YEARS.
THIS BOMB IS A PRETTY AMAZING PIECE OF MACHINERY, ONE-IN-A-MILLION MALFUNCTION ASIDE.
CAMERA
I DIDN'T KNOW AMAZONS COULD BUILD SOMETHING LIKE THIS.
THEY CAN'T. SWORDS, SHIELDS AND MAGIC? AMAZONS. MICROCHIPS, COMPUTERS AND HIGH-TECH WEAPONS?
SOMEONE ELSE.
SOMEONE ELSE? WHO?
SAME PEOPLE WHO DESTROYED VANDENBERG AIR FORCE BASE. AND BURNED KANSAS.
AND NO DOUBT HAVE OTHER CATASTROPHES PLANNED.
THE GAME HAS CHANGED, OLIVER...
A NEW OPPONENT HAS TAKEN THE FIELD.

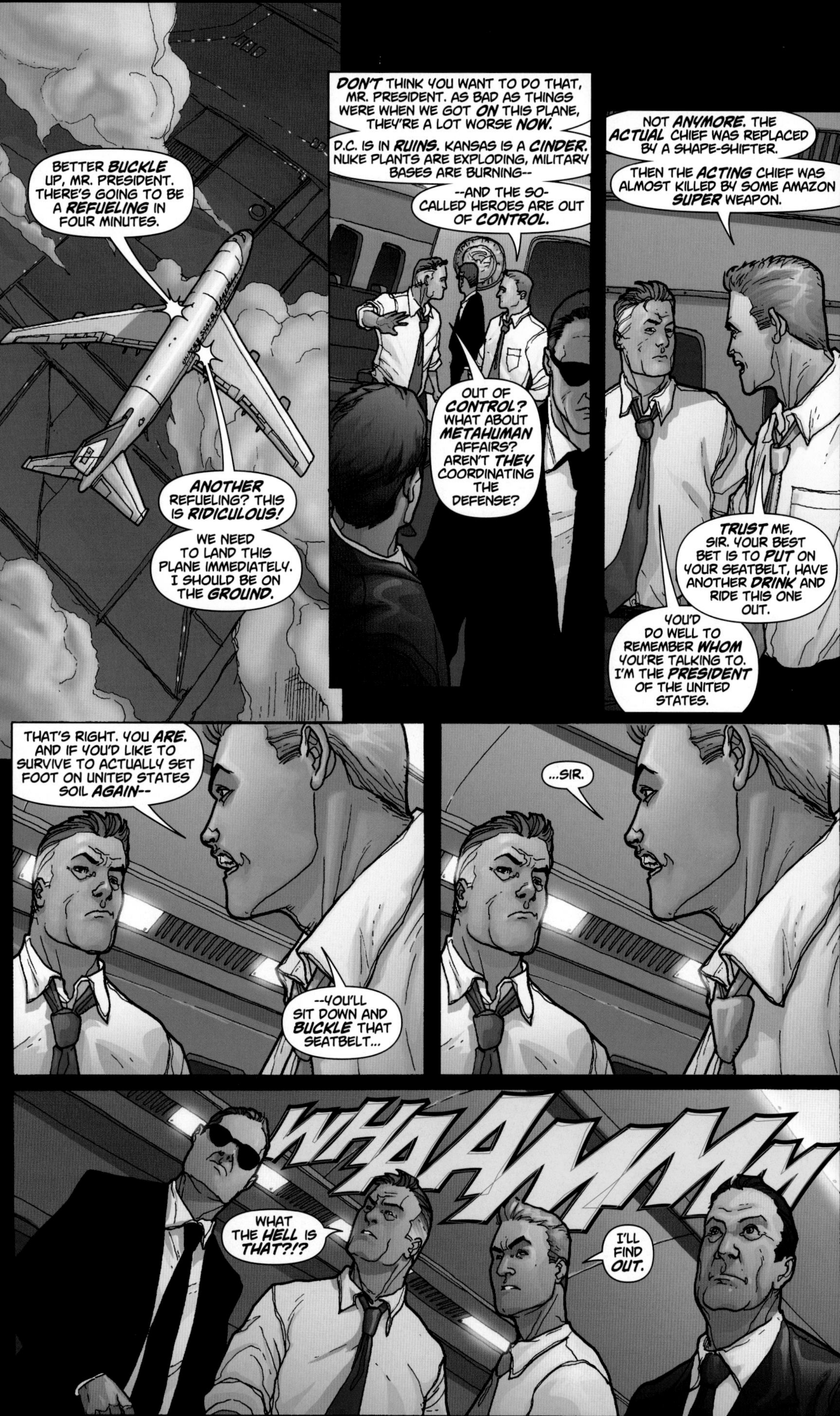
BETTER BUCKLE UP, MR. PRESIDENT. THERE'S GOING TO BE A REFUELING IN FOUR MINUTES.
ANOTHER REFUELING? THIS IS RIDICULOUS!
WE NEED TO LAND THIS PLANE IMMEDIATELY. I SHOULD BE ON THE GROUND.
DON'T THINK YOU WANT TO DO THAT, MR. PRESIDENT. AS BAD AS THINGS WERE WHEN WE GOT ON THIS PLANE, THEY'RE A LOT WORSE NOW.
D.C. IS IN RUINS. KANSAS IS A CINDER. NUKE PLANTS ARE EXPLODING, MILITARY BASES ARE BURNING--
--AND THE SO-CALLED HEROES ARE OUT OF CONTROL.
OUT OF CONTROL? WHAT ABOUT METAHUMAN AFFAIRS? AREN'T THEY COORDINATING THE DEFENSE?
NOT ANYMORE. THE ACTUAL CHIEF WAS REPLACED BY A SHAPE-SHIFTER.
THEN THE ACTING CHIEF WAS ALMOST KILLED BY SOME AMAZON SUPER WEAPON.
TRUST ME, SIR. YOUR BEST BET IS TO PUT ON YOUR SEATBELT, HAVE ANOTHER DRINK AND RIDE THIS ONE OUT.
YOU'D DO WELL TO REMEMBER WHOM YOU'RE TALKING TO. I'M THE PRESIDENT OF THE UNITED STATES.
THAT'S RIGHT. YOU ARE. AND IF YOU'D LIKE TO SURVIVE TO ACTUALLY SET FOOT ON UNITED STATES SOIL AGAIN--
--YOU'LL SIT DOWN AND BUCKLE THAT SEATBELT...
...SIR.
WHAMMM
WHAT THE HELL IS THAT?!?
I'LL FIND OUT.

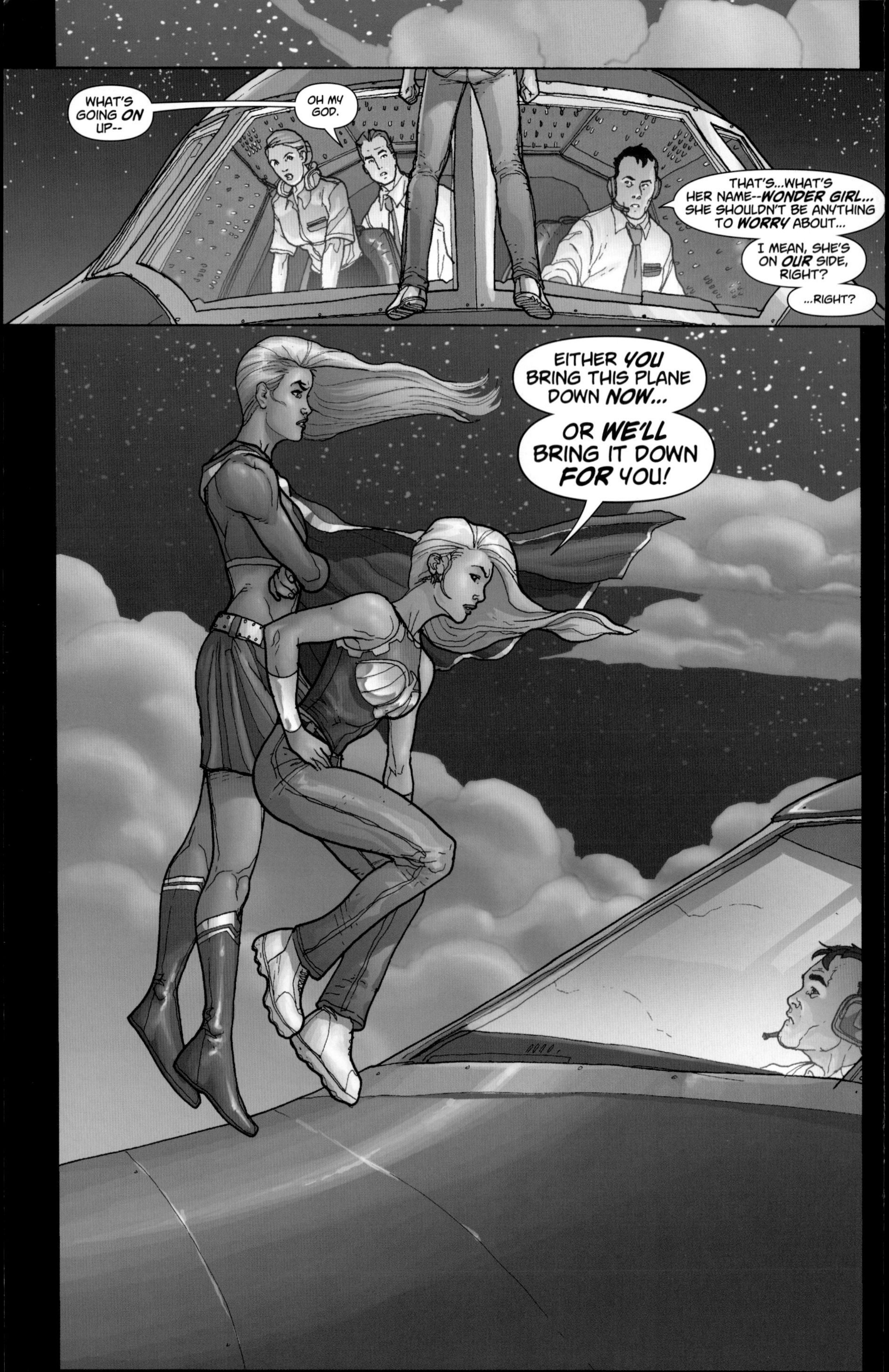
WHAT'S GOING ON UP--
OH MY GOD.
THAT'S...WHAT'S HER NAME--WONDER GIRL... SHE SHOULDN'T BE ANYTHING TO WORRY ABOUT...
I MEAN, SHE'S ON OUR SIDE, RIGHT?
...RIGHT?
EITHER YOU BRING THIS PLANE DOWN NOW...
OR WE'LL BRING IT DOWN FOR YOU!

Chapter Four

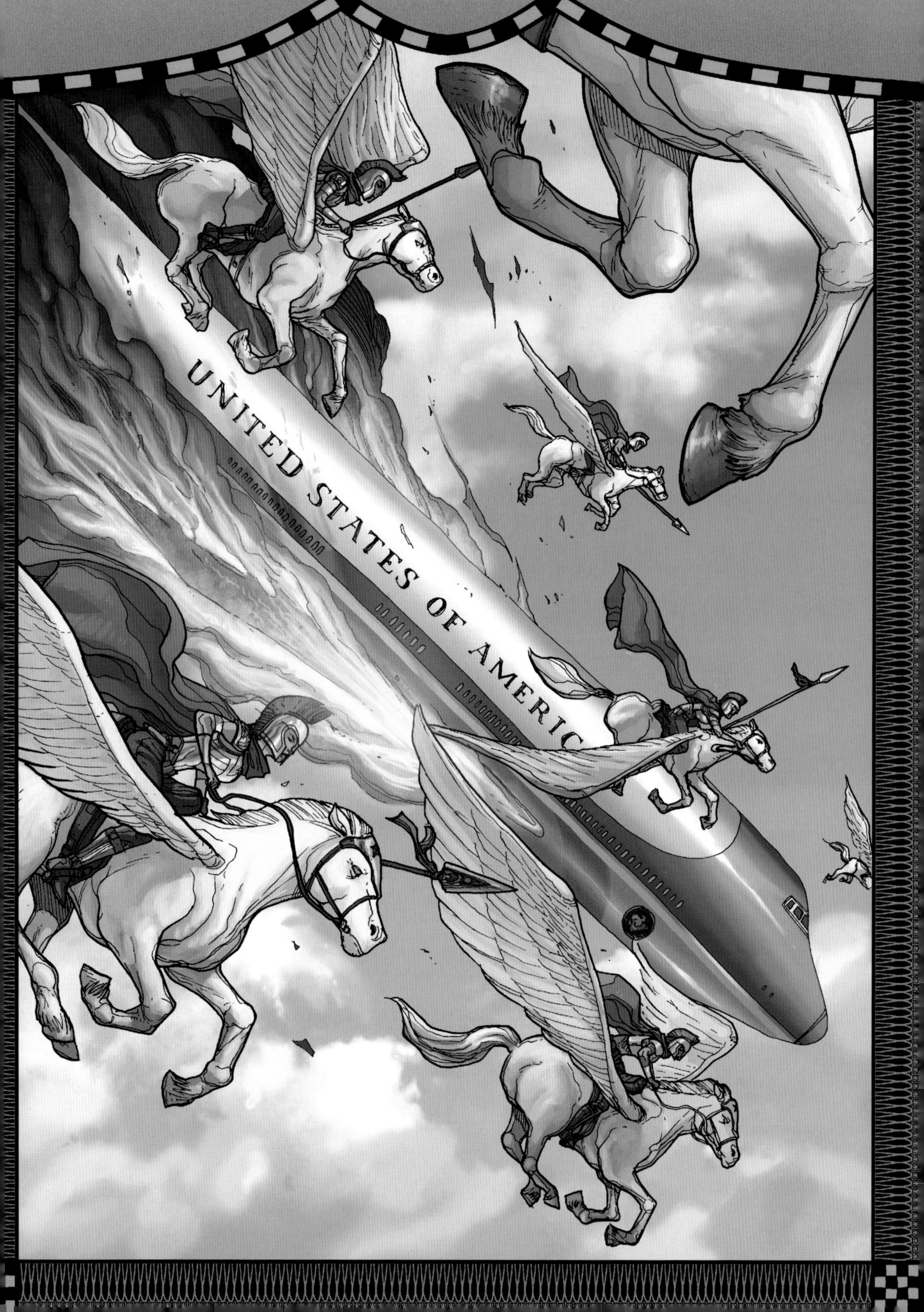
UNITED STATES OF AMERIC

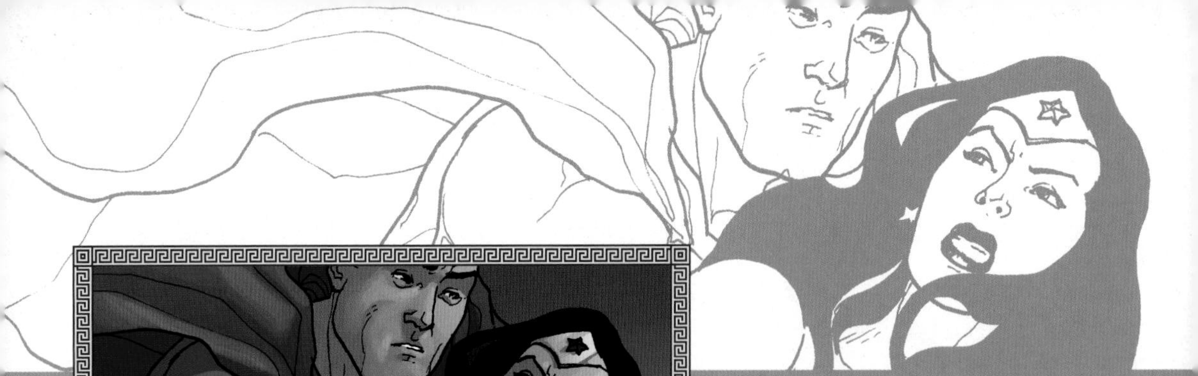

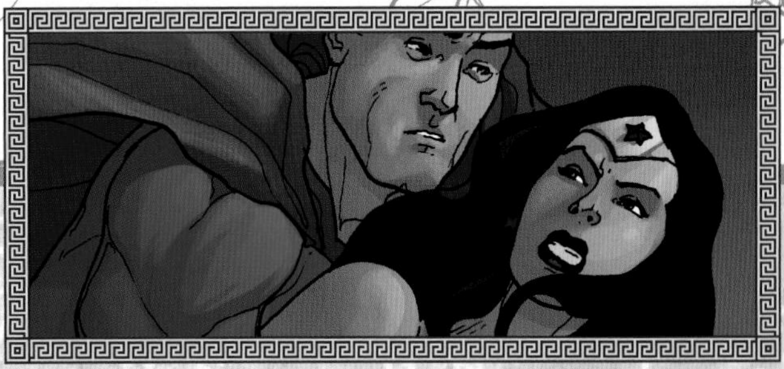

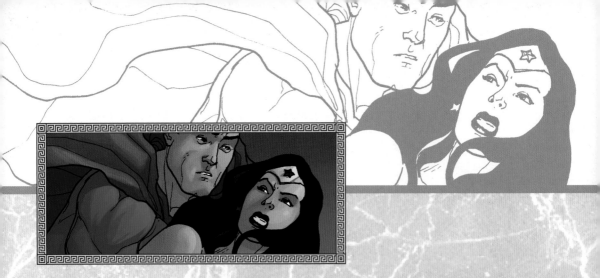

In the midst of her battle with her mother in the nation's capital, Diana recounts the time that the Queen asked her if she would ever die for the humans her mother sent her out to protect — and she reiterates that her answer remains *yes.* Then she asks Hippolyta a question of her own, while handing her mother a dagger that she directs towards her own throat: "Would *you* kill me to win?"

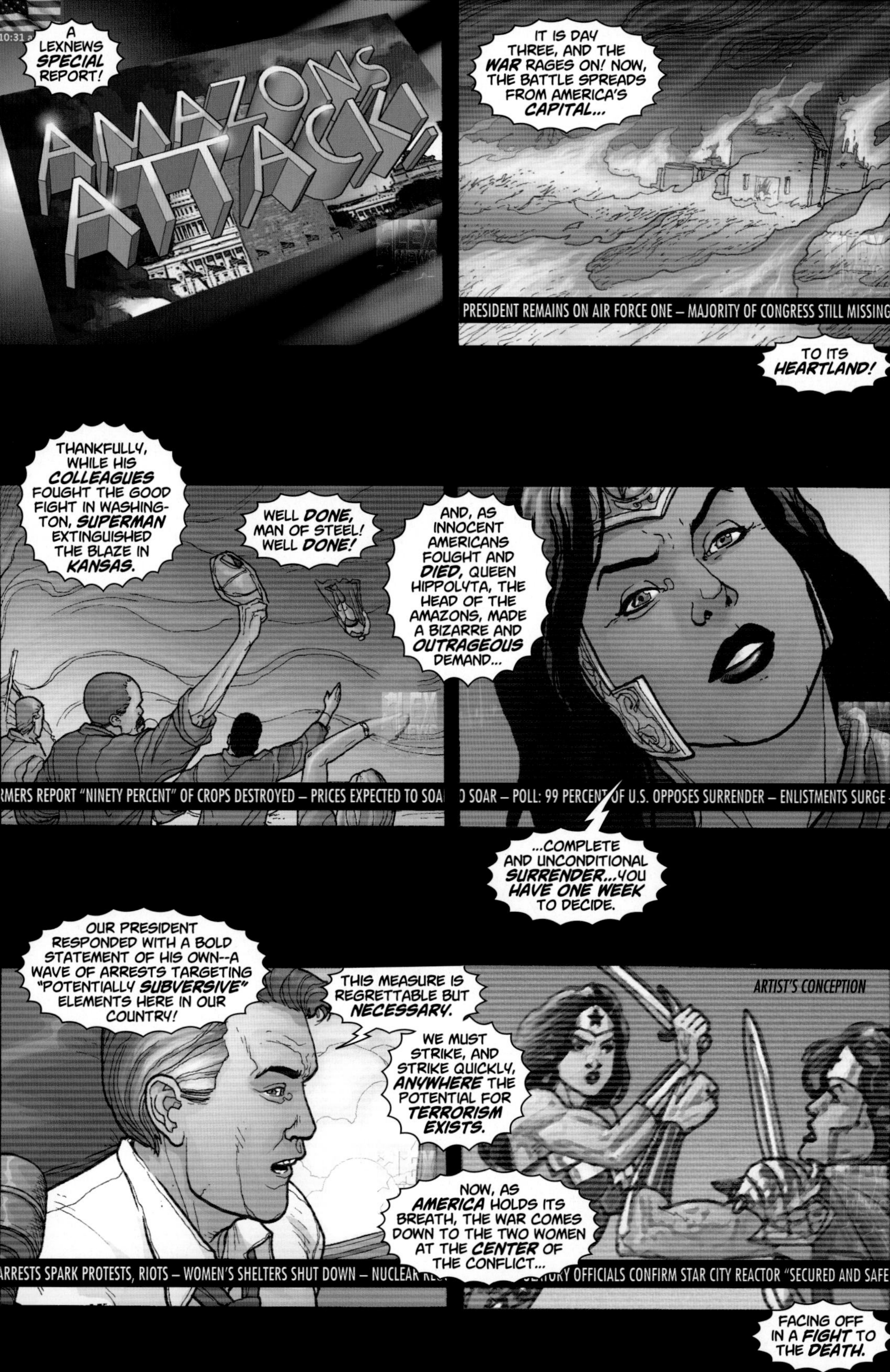
10:31
A LEXNEWS SPECIAL REPORT!
AMAZONS ATTACK!
IT IS DAY THREE, AND THE WAR RAGES ON! NOW, THE BATTLE SPREADS FROM AMERICA'S CAPITAL...
PRESIDENT REMAINS ON AIR FORCE ONE – MAJORITY OF CONGRESS STILL MISSING
TO ITS HEARTLAND!
THANKFULLY, WHILE HIS COLLEAGUES FOUGHT THE GOOD FIGHT IN WASHING-TON, SUPERMAN EXTINGUISHED THE BLAZE IN KANSAS.
WELL DONE, MAN OF STEEL! WELL DONE!
AND, AS INNOCENT AMERICANS FOUGHT AND DIED, QUEEN HIPPOLYTA, THE HEAD OF THE AMAZONS, MADE A BIZARRE AND OUTRAGEOUS DEMAND...
RMERS REPORT "NINETY PERCENT" OF CROPS DESTROYED – PRICES EXPECTED TO SOA
SOAR – POLL: 99 PERCENT OF U.S. OPPOSES SURRENDER – ENLISTMENTS SURGE
...COMPLETE AND UNCONDITIONAL SURRENDER...YOU HAVE ONE WEEK TO DECIDE.
OUR PRESIDENT RESPONDED WITH A BOLD STATEMENT OF HIS OWN--A WAVE OF ARRESTS TARGETING "POTENTIALLY SUBVERSIVE" ELEMENTS HERE IN OUR COUNTRY!
THIS MEASURE IS REGRETTABLE BUT NECESSARY.
WE MUST STRIKE, AND STRIKE QUICKLY, ANYWHERE THE POTENTIAL FOR TERRORISM EXISTS.
ARTIST'S CONCEPTION
NOW, AS AMERICA HOLDS ITS BREATH, THE WAR COMES DOWN TO THE TWO WOMEN AT THE CENTER OF THE CONFLICT...
ARRESTS SPARK PROTESTS, RIOTS – WOMEN'S SHELTERS SHUT DOWN – NUCLEAR
OFFICIALS CONFIRM STAR CITY REACTOR "SECURED AND SAFE
FACING OFF IN A FIGHT TO THE DEATH.

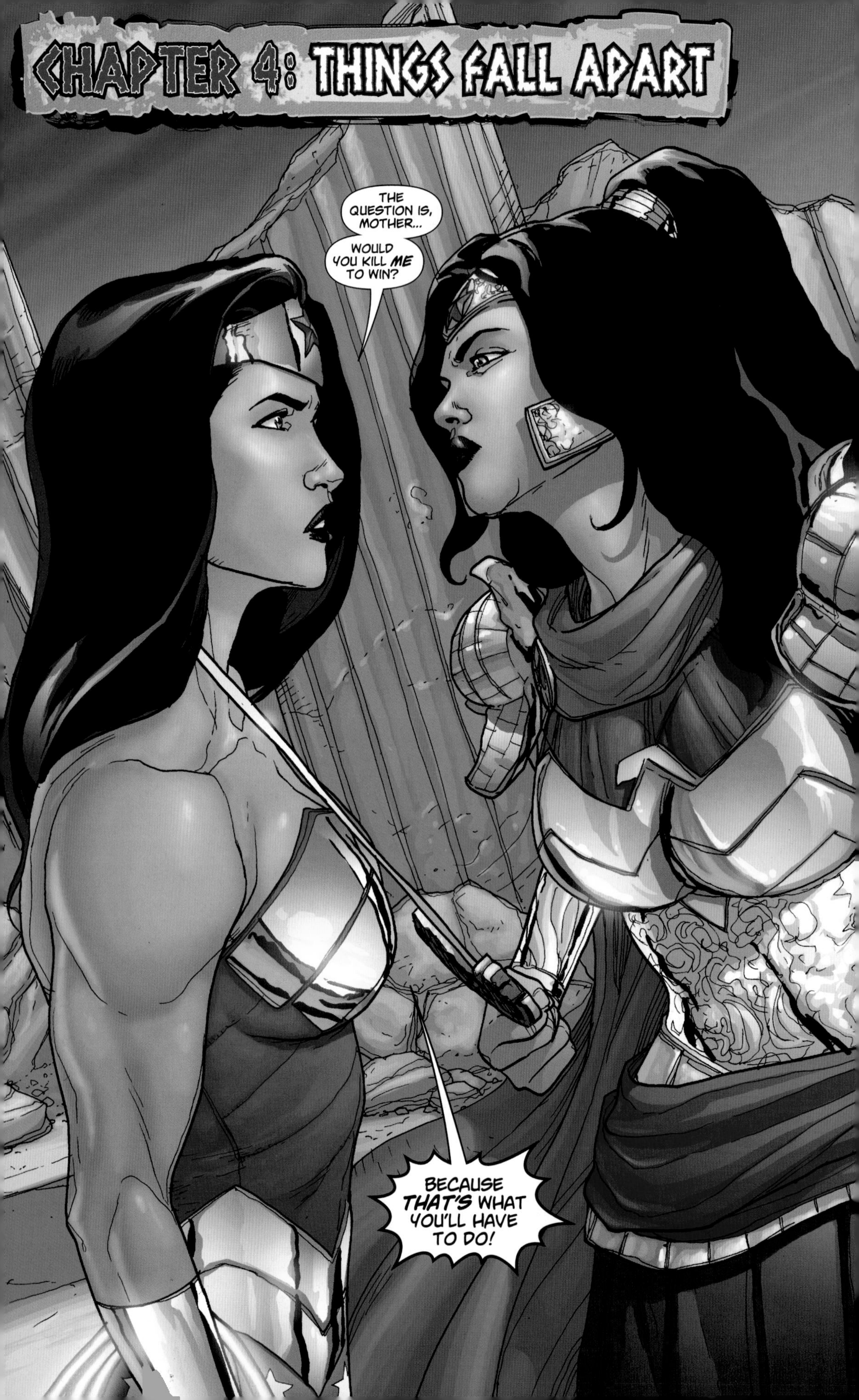
CHAPTER 4: THINGS FALL APART
THE QUESTION IS, MOTHER...
WOULD YOU KILL ME TO WIN?
BECAUSE THAT'S WHAT YOU'LL HAVE TO DO!

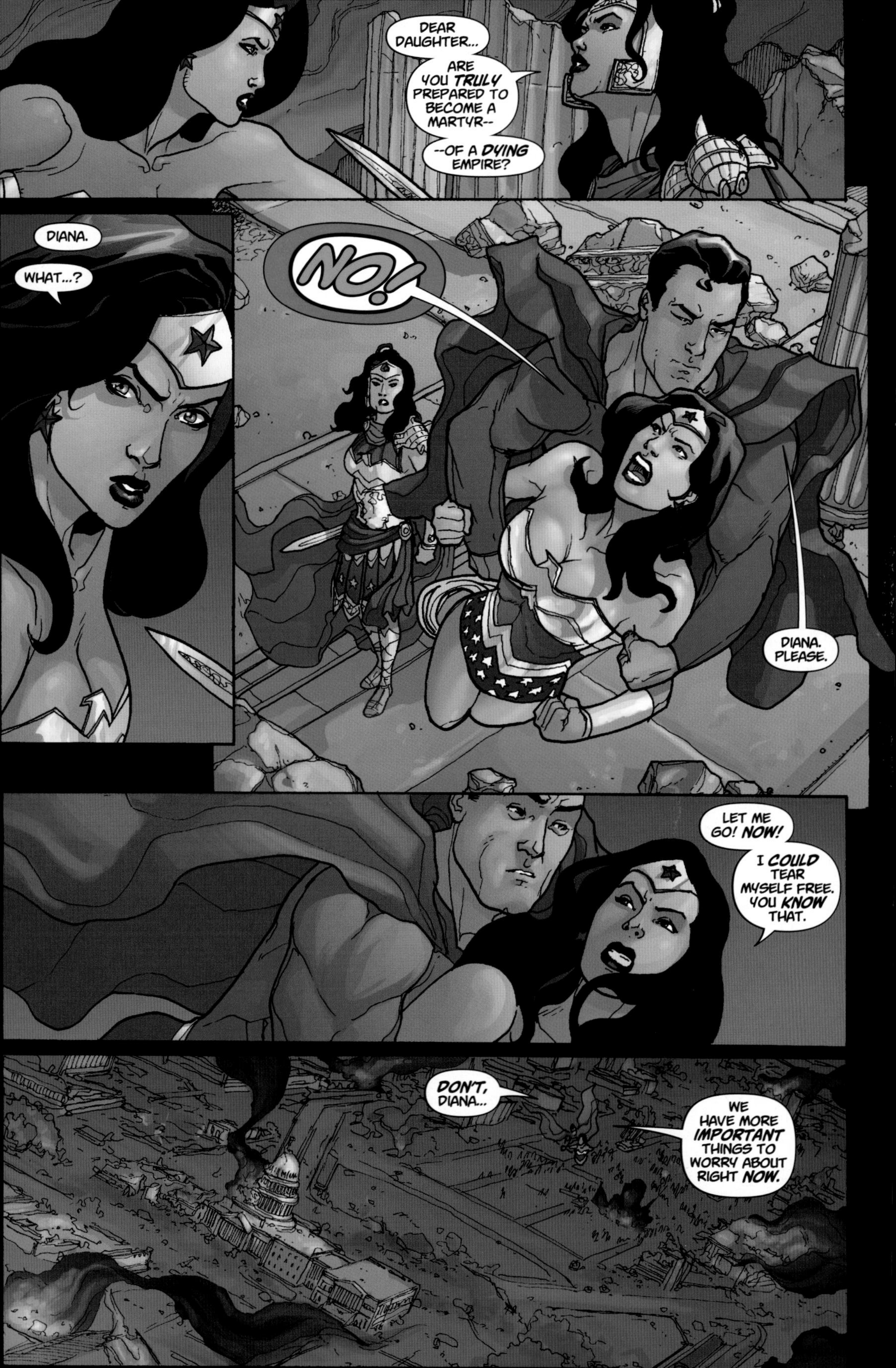
DEAR DAUGHTER...
ARE YOU TRULY PREPARED TO BECOME A MARTYR--
--OF A DYING EMPIRE?
DIANA.
WHAT...?
NO!
DIANA. PLEASE.
LET ME GO! NOW!
I COULD TEAR MYSELF FREE. YOU KNOW THAT.
DON'T, DIANA...
WE HAVE MORE IMPORTANT THINGS TO WORRY ABOUT RIGHT NOW.

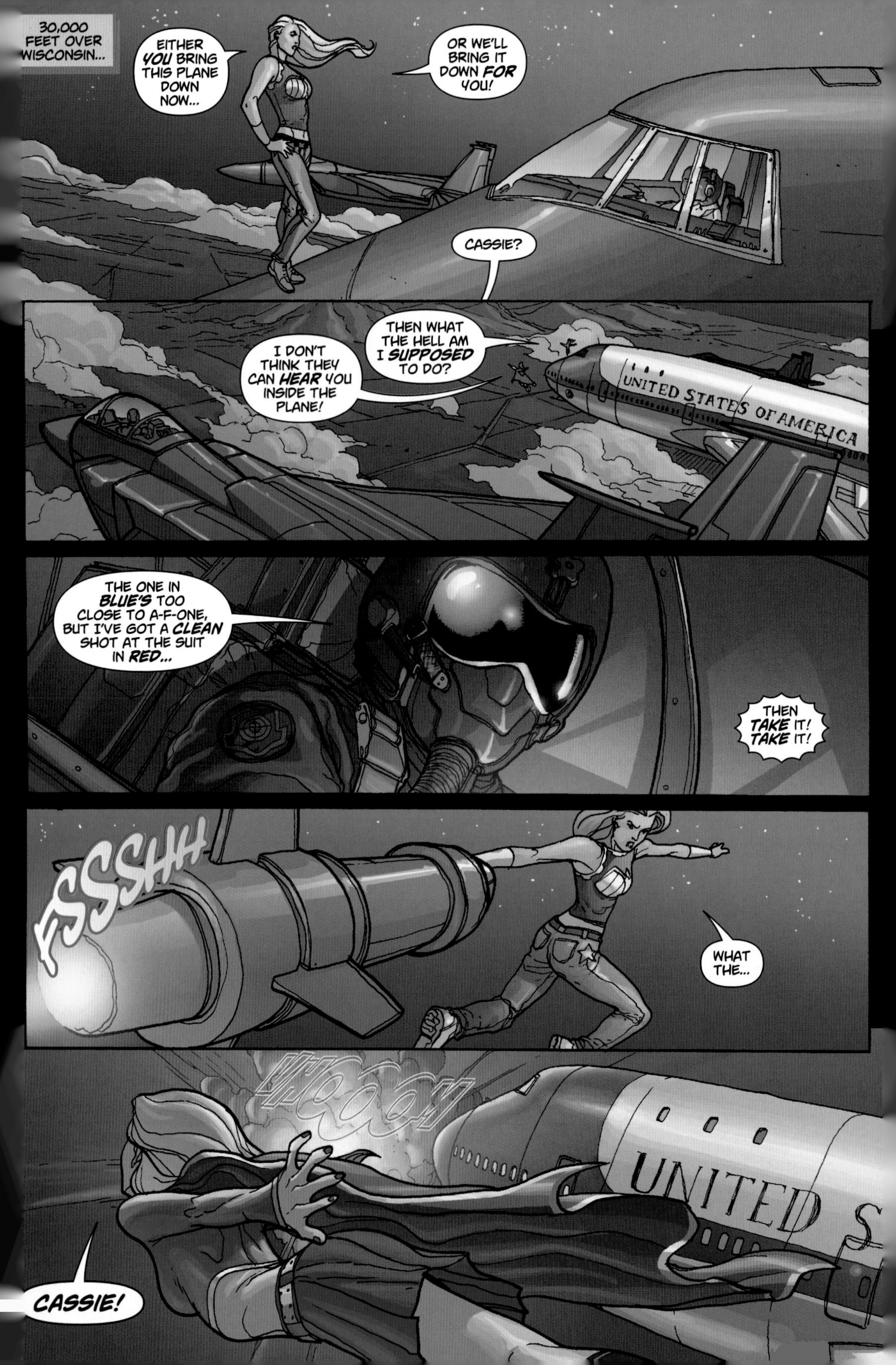
30,000 FEET OVER WISCONSIN...
EITHER YOU BRING THIS PLANE DOWN NOW...
OR WE'LL BRING IT DOWN FOR YOU!
CASSIE?
THEN WHAT THE HELL AM I SUPPOSED TO DO?
I DON'T THINK THEY CAN HEAR YOU INSIDE THE PLANE!
UNITED STATES OF AMERICA
THE ONE IN BLUE'S TOO CLOSE TO A-F-ONE, BUT I'VE GOT A CLEAN SHOT AT THE SUIT IN RED...
THEN TAKE IT! TAKE IT!
FSSHH
WHAT THE...
UNITED S
CASSIE!

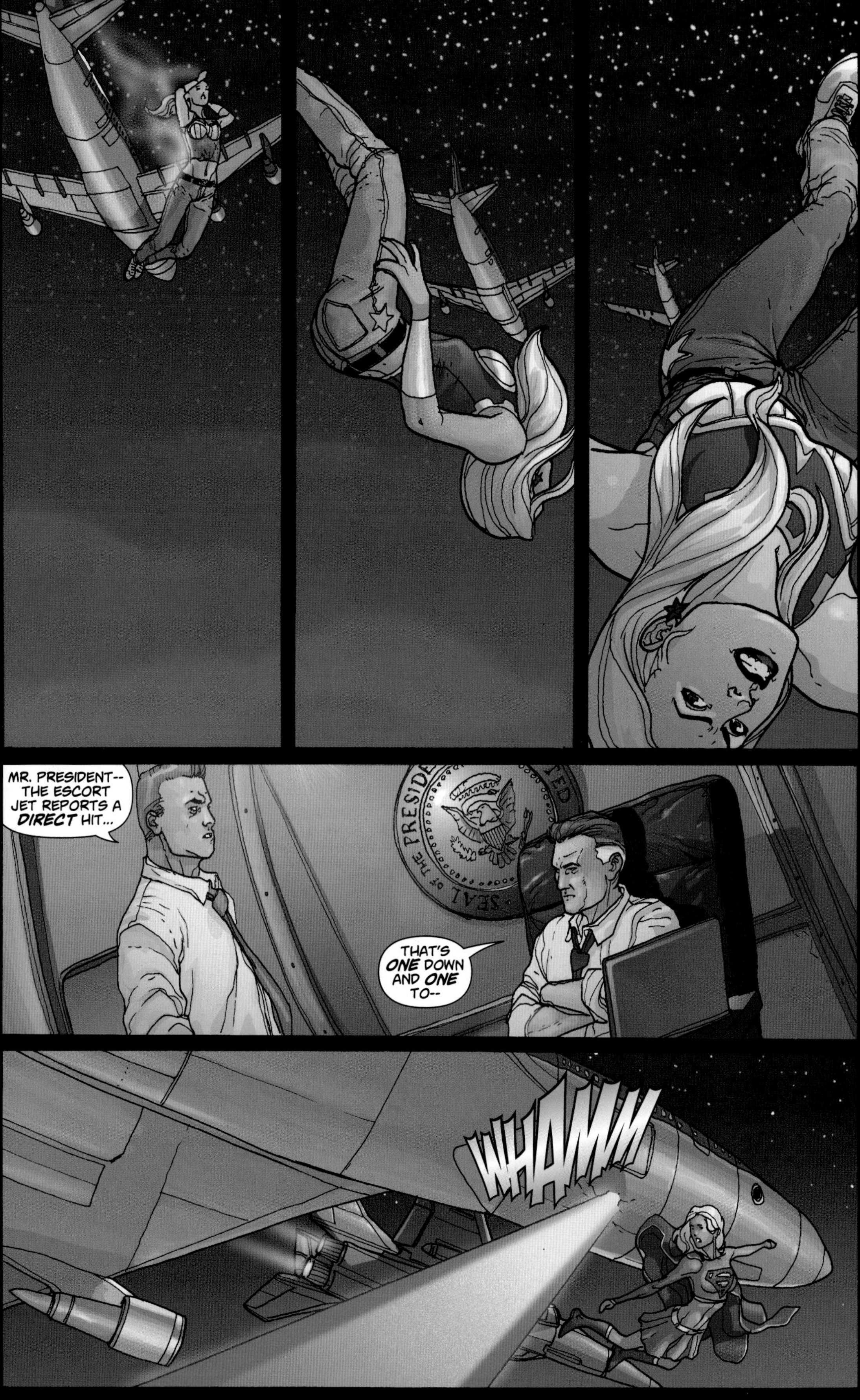
MR. PRESIDENT-- THE ESCORT JET REPORTS A *DIRECT* HIT...
THAT'S *ONE* DOWN AND *ONE* TO--
WHAMM

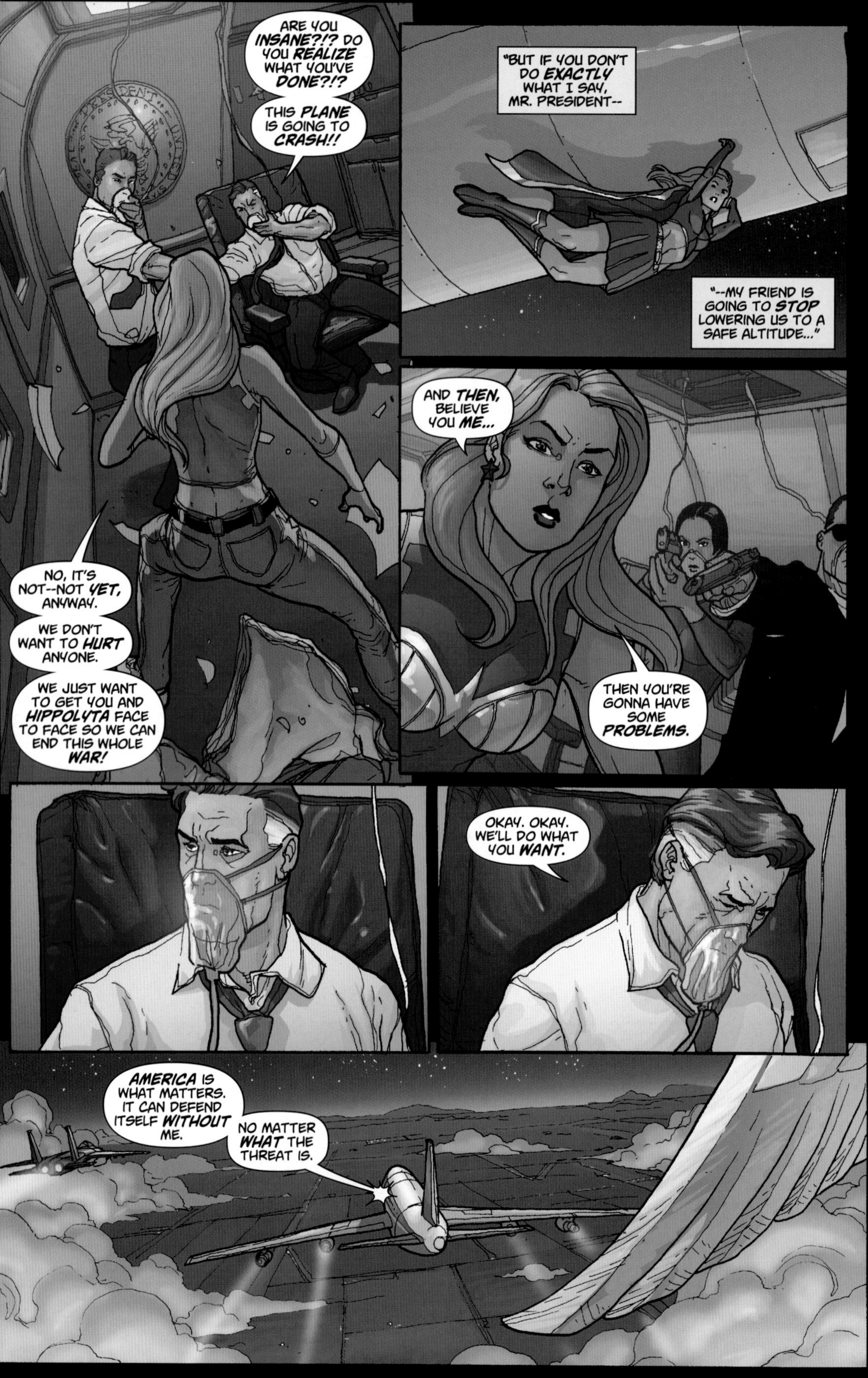
ARE YOU INSANE?!? DO YOU REALIZE WHAT YOU'VE DONE?!?
THIS PLANE IS GOING TO CRASH!!
NO, IT'S NOT--NOT YET, ANYWAY.
WE DON'T WANT TO HURT ANYONE.
WE JUST WANT TO GET YOU AND HIPPOLYTA FACE TO FACE SO WE CAN END THIS WHOLE WAR!
"BUT IF YOU DON'T DO EXACTLY WHAT I SAY, MR. PRESIDENT--
"--MY FRIEND IS GOING TO STOP LOWERING US TO A SAFE ALTITUDE..."
AND THEN, BELIEVE YOU ME...
THEN YOU'RE GONNA HAVE SOME PROBLEMS.
OKAY. OKAY. WE'LL DO WHAT YOU WANT.
AMERICA IS WHAT MATTERS. IT CAN DEFEND ITSELF WITHOUT ME.
NO MATTER WHAT THE THREAT IS.

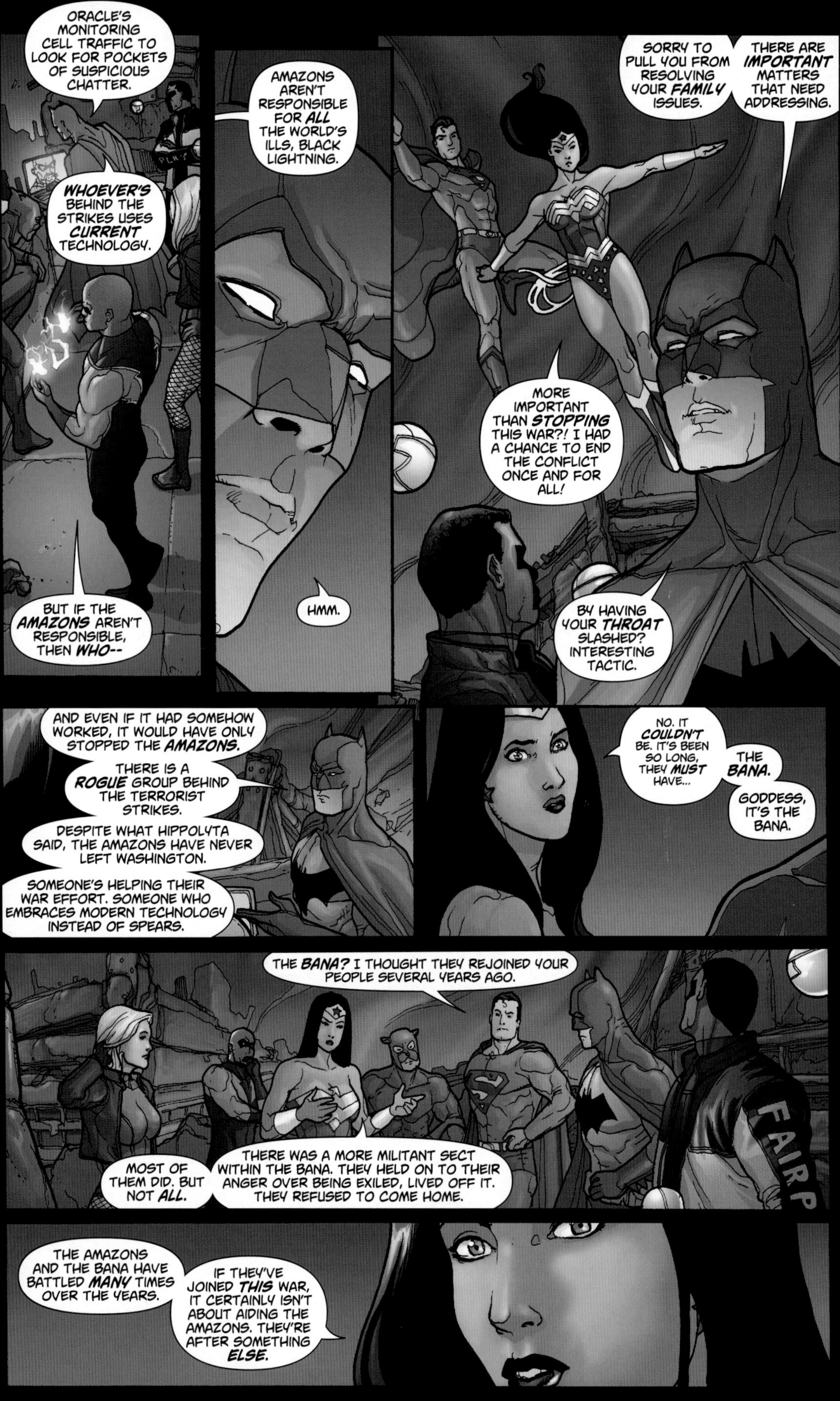
ORACLE'S MONITORING CELL TRAFFIC TO LOOK FOR POCKETS OF SUSPICIOUS CHATTER.
WHOEVER'S BEHIND THE STRIKES USES CURRENT TECHNOLOGY.
BUT IF THE AMAZONS AREN'T RESPONSIBLE, THEN WHO--
AMAZONS AREN'T RESPONSIBLE FOR ALL THE WORLD'S ILLS, BLACK LIGHTNING.
HMM.
SORRY TO PULL YOU FROM RESOLVING YOUR FAMILY ISSUES.
THERE ARE IMPORTANT MATTERS THAT NEED ADDRESSING.
MORE IMPORTANT THAN STOPPING THIS WAR?! I HAD A CHANCE TO END THE CONFLICT ONCE AND FOR ALL!
BY HAVING YOUR THROAT SLASHED? INTERESTING TACTIC.
AND EVEN IF IT HAD SOMEHOW WORKED, IT WOULD HAVE ONLY STOPPED THE AMAZONS.
THERE IS A ROGUE GROUP BEHIND THE TERRORIST STRIKES.
DESPITE WHAT HIPPOLYTA SAID, THE AMAZONS HAVE NEVER LEFT WASHINGTON.
SOMEONE'S HELPING THEIR WAR EFFORT. SOMEONE WHO EMBRACES MODERN TECHNOLOGY INSTEAD OF SPEARS.
NO. IT COULDN'T BE. IT'S BEEN SO LONG, THEY MUST HAVE...
THE BANA.
GODDESS, IT'S THE BANA.
THE BANA? I THOUGHT THEY REJOINED YOUR PEOPLE SEVERAL YEARS AGO.
MOST OF THEM DID. BUT NOT ALL.
THERE WAS A MORE MILITANT SECT WITHIN THE BANA. THEY HELD ON TO THEIR ANGER OVER BEING EXILED, LIVED OFF IT. THEY REFUSED TO COME HOME.
THE AMAZONS AND THE BANA HAVE BATTLED MANY TIMES OVER THE YEARS.
IF THEY'VE JOINED THIS WAR, IT CERTAINLY ISN'T ABOUT AIDING THE AMAZONS. THEY'RE AFTER SOMETHING ELSE.

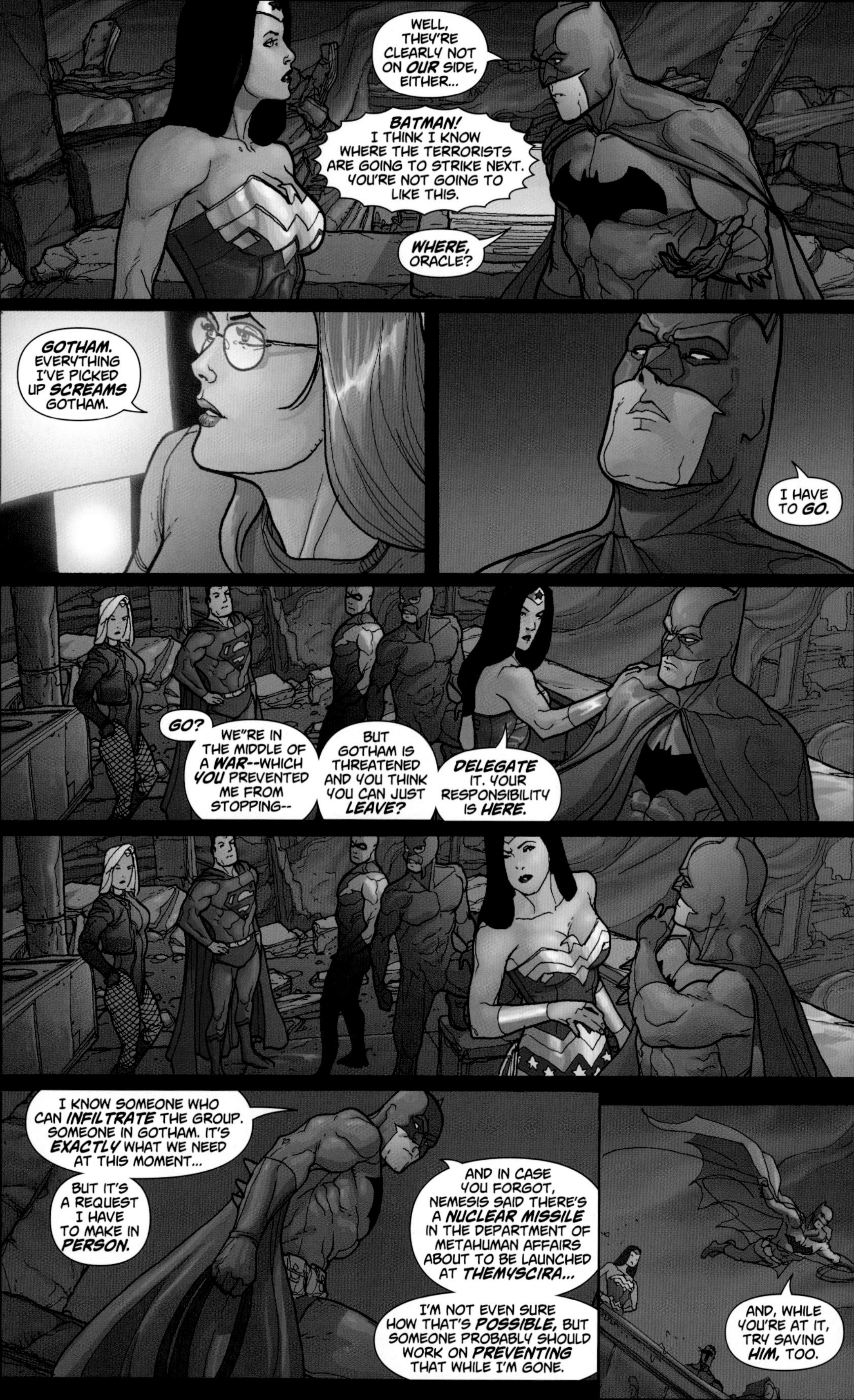

WELL, THEY'RE CLEARLY NOT ON OUR SIDE, EITHER...
BATMAN! I THINK I KNOW WHERE THE TERRORISTS ARE GOING TO STRIKE NEXT. YOU'RE NOT GOING TO LIKE THIS.
WHERE, ORACLE?
GOTHAM. EVERYTHING I'VE PICKED UP SCREAMS GOTHAM.
I HAVE TO GO.
GO?
WE"RE IN THE MIDDLE OF A WAR--WHICH YOU PREVENTED ME FROM STOPPING--
BUT GOTHAM IS THREATENED AND YOU THINK YOU CAN JUST LEAVE?
DELEGATE IT. YOUR RESPONSIBILITY IS HERE.
I KNOW SOMEONE WHO CAN INFILTRATE THE GROUP. SOMEONE IN GOTHAM. IT'S EXACTLY WHAT WE NEED AT THIS MOMENT...
BUT IT'S A REQUEST I HAVE TO MAKE IN PERSON.
AND IN CASE YOU FORGOT, NEMESIS SAID THERE'S A NUCLEAR MISSILE IN THE DEPARTMENT OF METAHUMAN AFFAIRS ABOUT TO BE LAUNCHED AT THEMYSCIRA...
I'M NOT EVEN SURE HOW THAT'S POSSIBLE, BUT SOMEONE PROBABLY SHOULD WORK ON PREVENTING THAT WHILE I'M GONE.
AND, WHILE YOU'RE AT IT, TRY SAVING HIM, TOO.

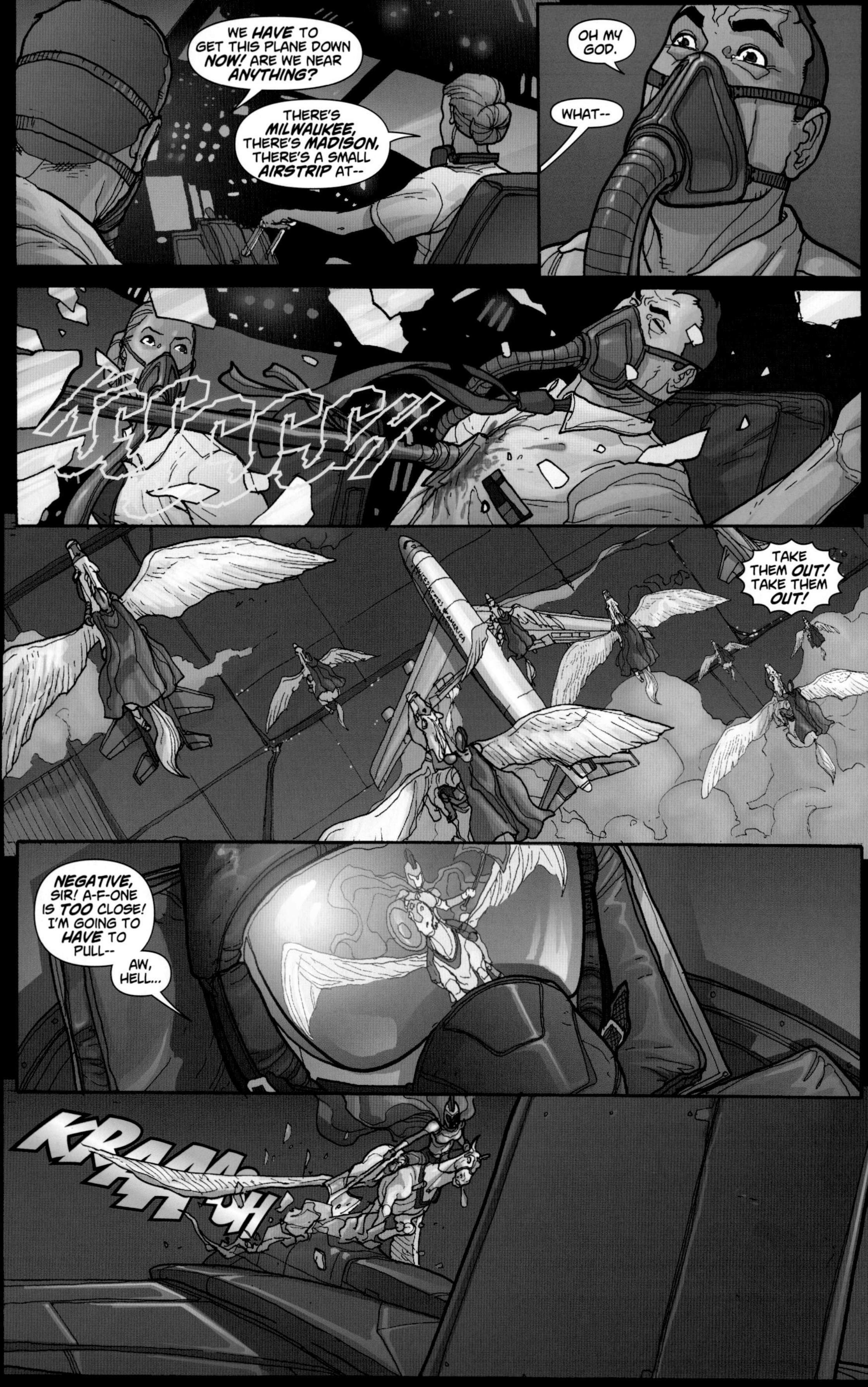
WE HAVE TO GET THIS PLANE DOWN NOW! ARE WE NEAR ANYTHING?
THERE'S MILWAUKEE, THERE'S MADISON, THERE'S A SMALL AIRSTRIP AT--
OH MY GOD.
WHAT--
TAKE THEM OUT! TAKE THEM OUT!
NEGATIVE, SIR! A-F-ONE IS TOO CLOSE! I'M GOING TO HAVE TO PULL--
AW, HELL...

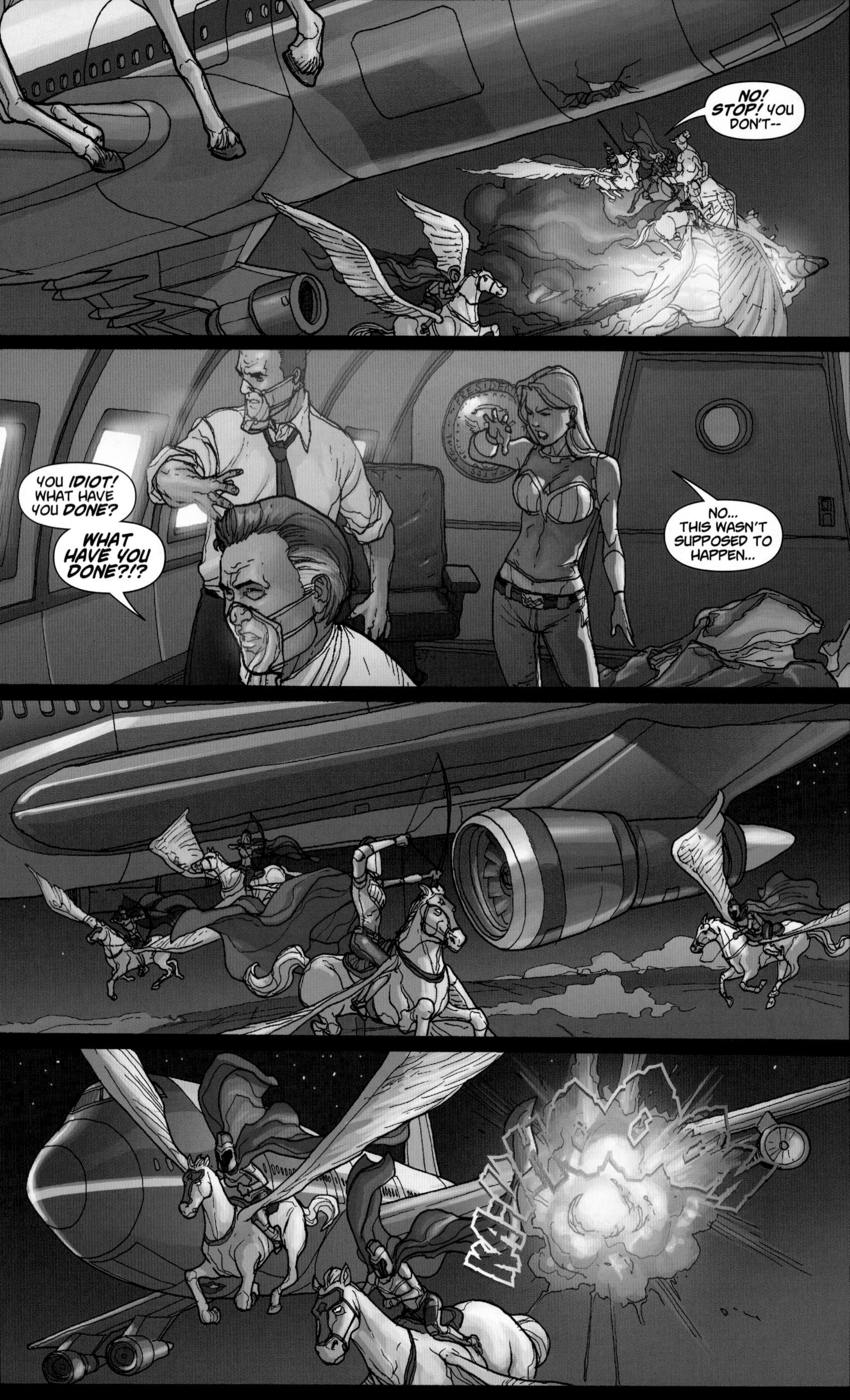
NO! STOP! YOU DON'T--
YOU IDIOT! WHAT HAVE YOU DONE?
WHAT HAVE YOU DONE?!?
NO... THIS WASN'T SUPPOSED TO HAPPEN...

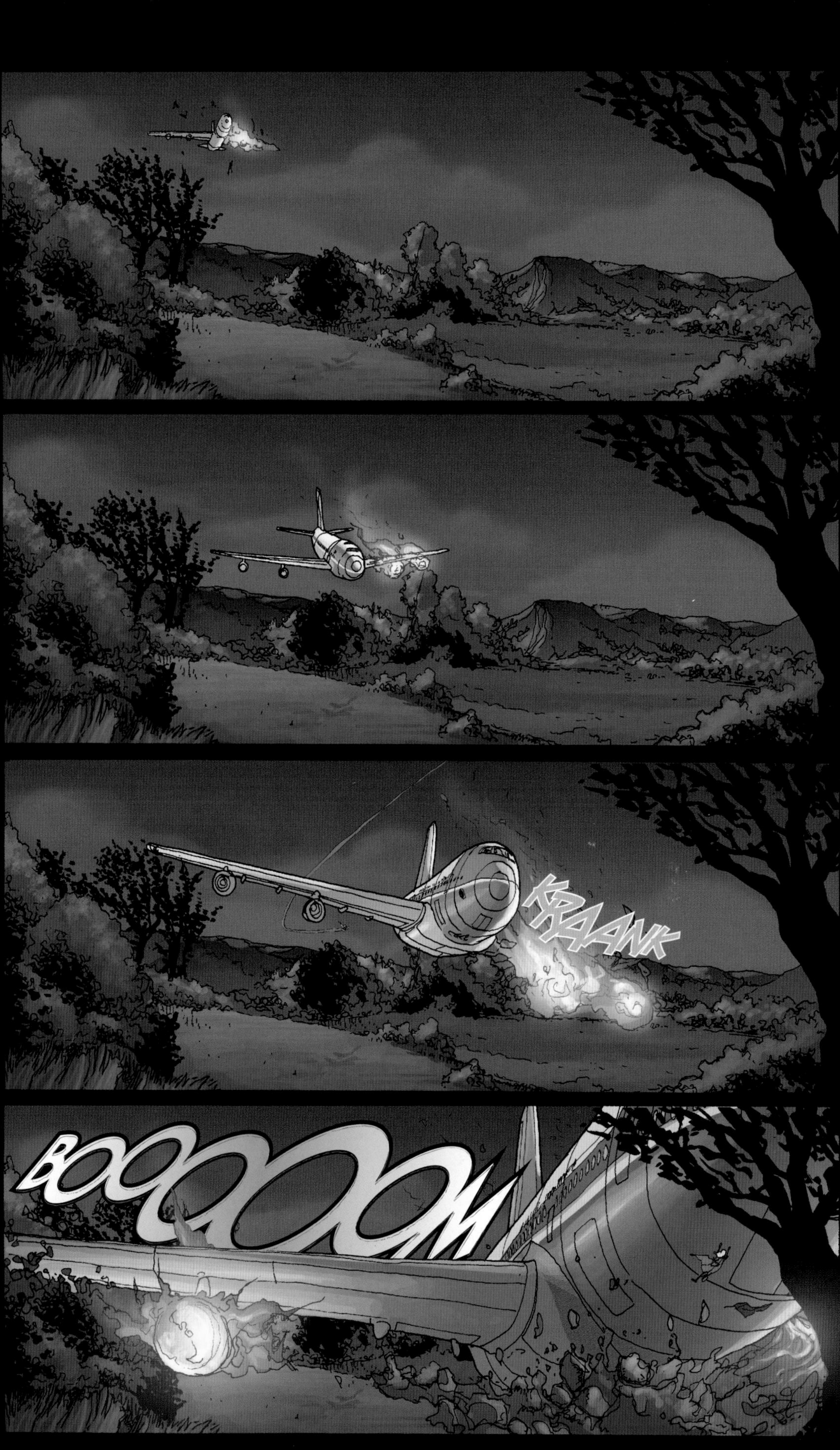
KRAANK
BOOOOOM

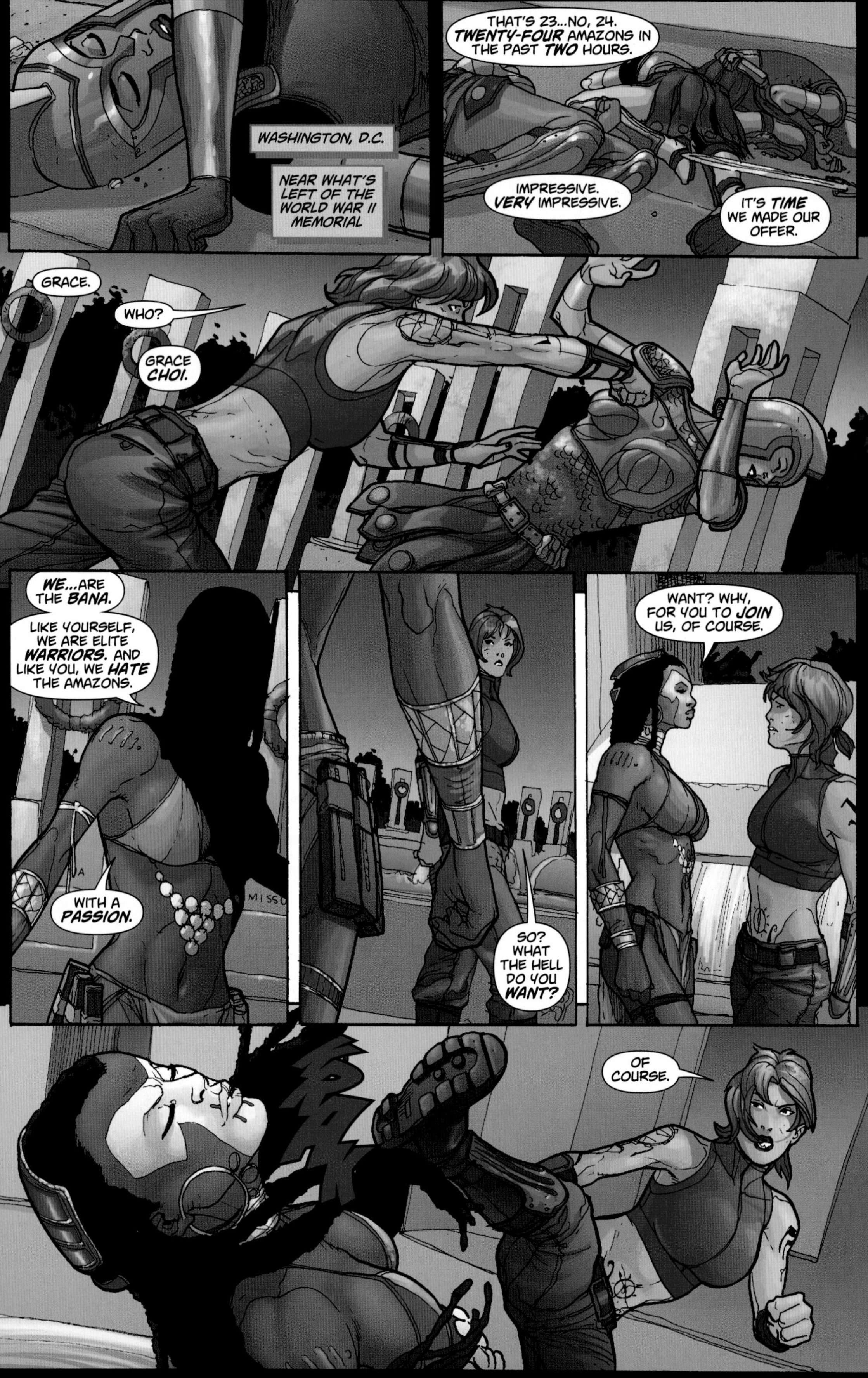
WASHINGTON, D.C.
NEAR WHAT'S LEFT OF THE WORLD WAR II MEMORIAL
THAT'S 23...NO, 24. TWENTY-FOUR AMAZONS IN THE PAST TWO HOURS.
IMPRESSIVE. VERY IMPRESSIVE.
IT'S TIME WE MADE OUR OFFER.
GRACE.
WHO?
GRACE CHOI.
WE...ARE THE BANA.
LIKE YOURSELF, WE ARE ELITE WARRIORS. AND LIKE YOU, WE HATE THE AMAZONS.
WITH A PASSION.
SO? WHAT THE HELL DO YOU WANT?
WANT? WHY, FOR YOU TO JOIN US, OF COURSE.
OF COURSE.

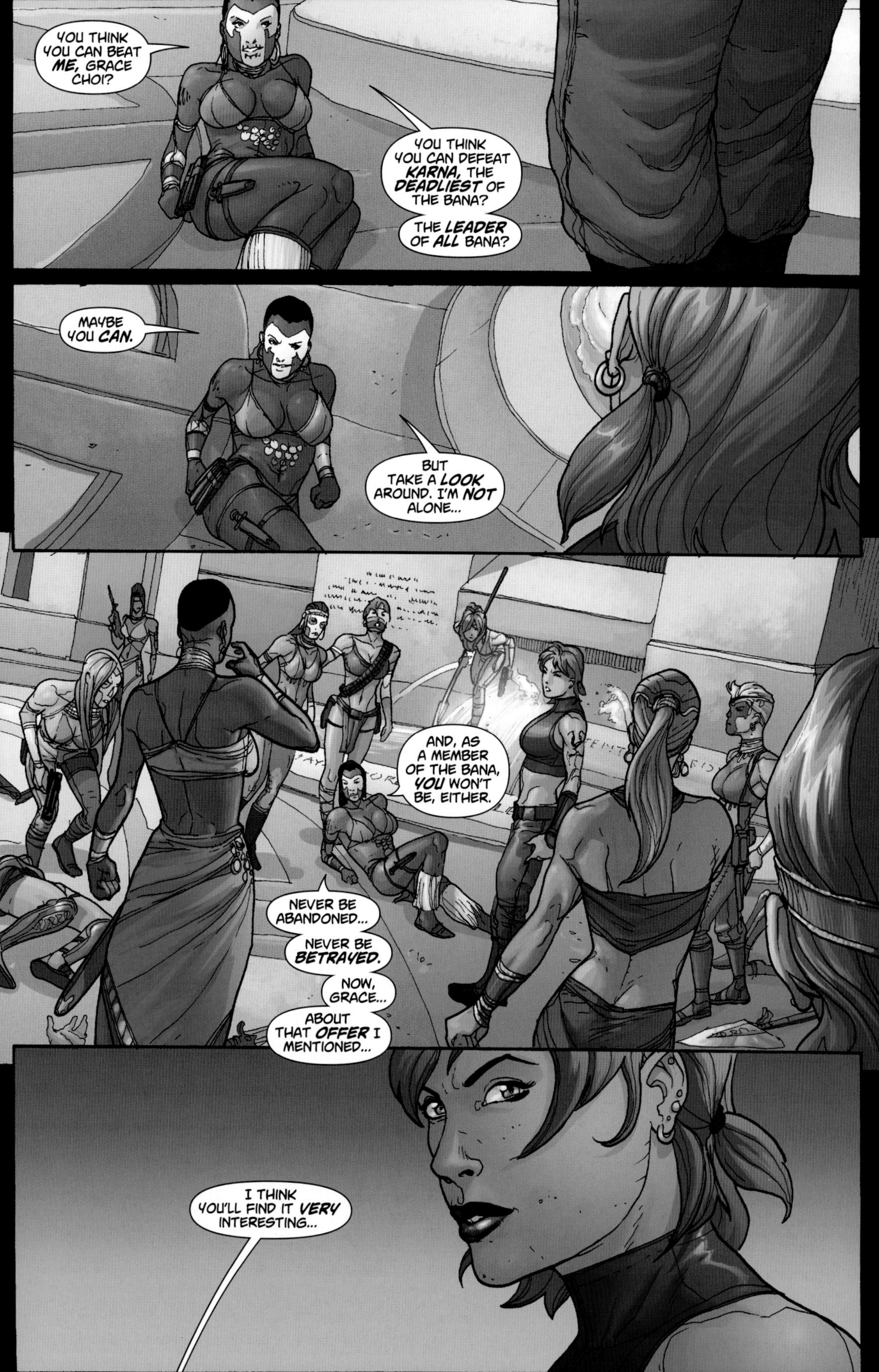
YOU THINK YOU CAN BEAT ME, GRACE CHOI?
YOU THINK YOU CAN DEFEAT KARNA, THE DEADLIEST OF THE BANA?
THE LEADER OF ALL BANA?
MAYBE YOU CAN.
BUT TAKE A LOOK AROUND. I'M NOT ALONE...
AND, AS A MEMBER OF THE BANA, YOU WON'T BE, EITHER.
NEVER BE ABANDONED...
NEVER BE BETRAYED.
NOW, GRACE...
ABOUT THAT OFFER I MENTIONED...
I THINK YOU'LL FIND IT VERY INTERESTING...

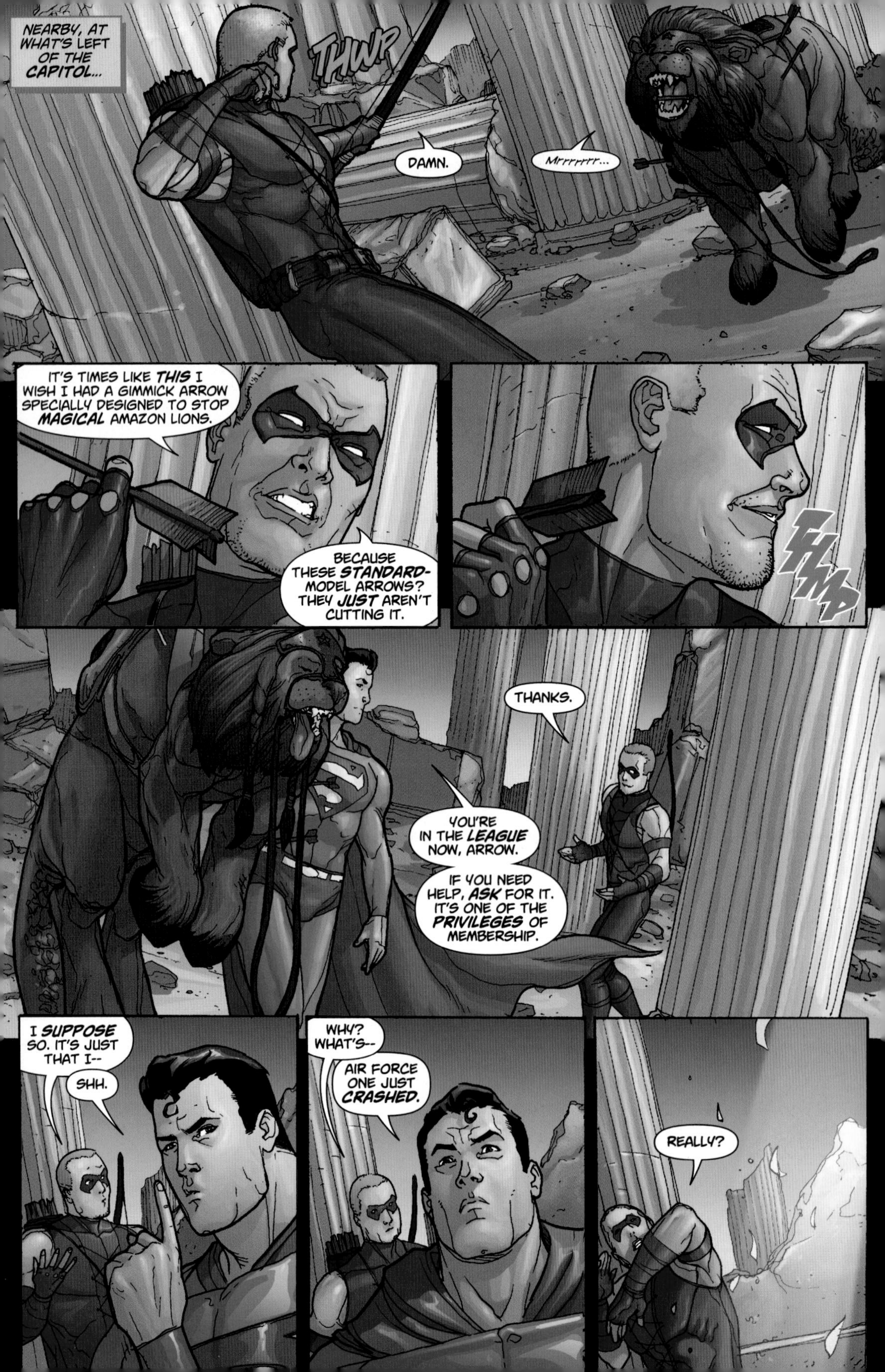
NEARBY, AT WHAT'S LEFT OF THE CAPITOL...
THWP
DAMN.
Mrrrrrrr...
IT'S TIMES LIKE THIS I WISH I HAD A GIMMICK ARROW SPECIALLY DESIGNED TO STOP MAGICAL AMAZON LIONS.
BECAUSE THESE STANDARD-MODEL ARROWS? THEY JUST AREN'T CUTTING IT.
THMP
THANKS.
YOU'RE IN THE LEAGUE NOW, ARROW.
IF YOU NEED HELP, ASK FOR IT. IT'S ONE OF THE PRIVILEGES OF MEMBERSHIP.
I SUPPOSE SO. IT'S JUST THAT I--
SHH.
WHY? WHAT'S--
AIR FORCE ONE JUST CRASHED.
REALLY?

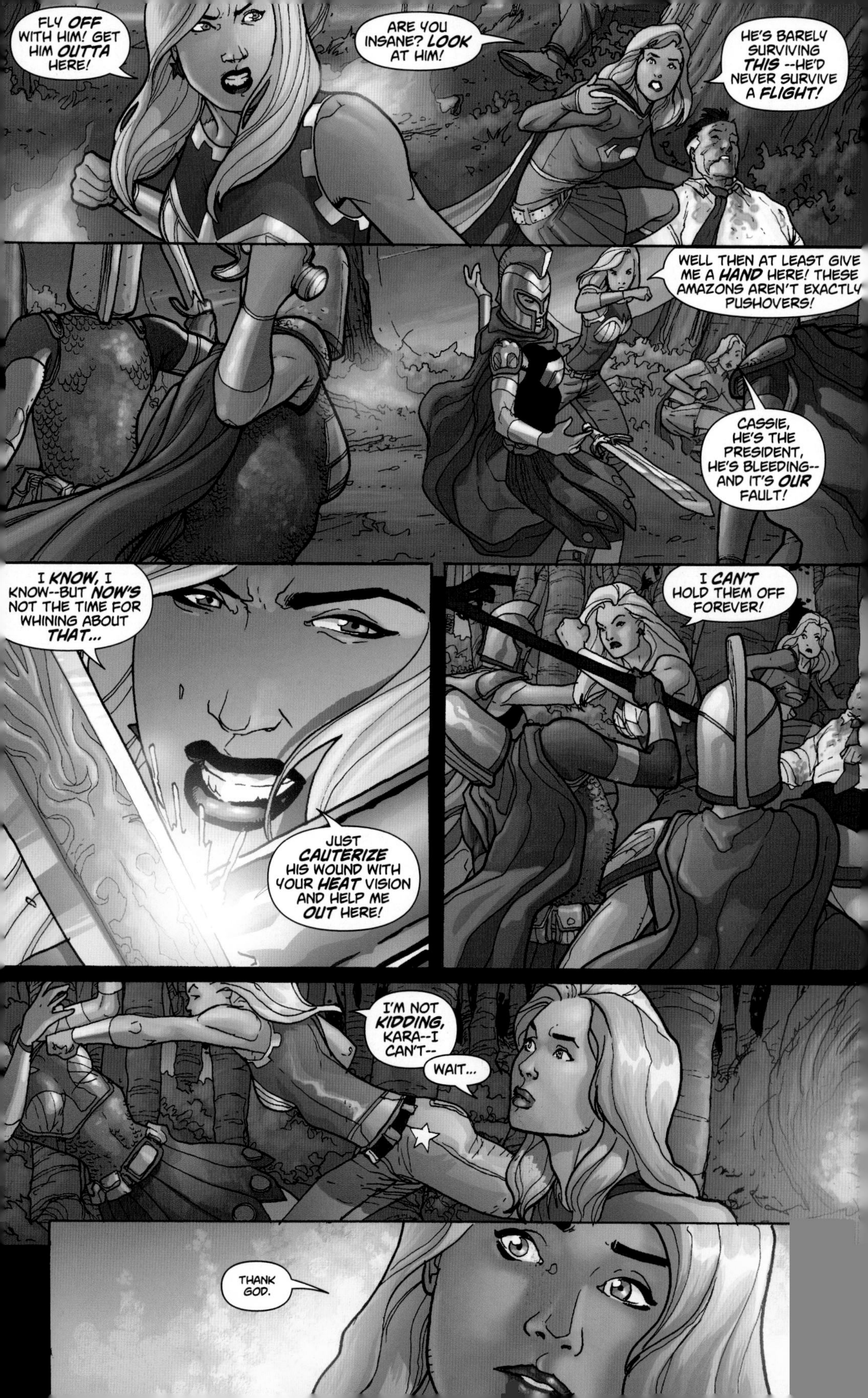
FLY OFF WITH HIM! GET HIM OUTTA HERE!
ARE YOU INSANE? LOOK AT HIM!
HE'S BARELY SURVIVING THIS --HE'D NEVER SURVIVE A FLIGHT!
WELL THEN AT LEAST GIVE ME A HAND HERE! THESE AMAZONS AREN'T EXACTLY PUSHOVERS!
CASSIE, HE'S THE PRESIDENT, HE'S BLEEDING-- AND IT'S OUR FAULT!
I KNOW, I KNOW--BUT NOW'S NOT THE TIME FOR WHINING ABOUT THAT...
JUST CAUTERIZE HIS WOUND WITH YOUR HEAT VISION AND HELP ME OUT HERE!
I CAN'T HOLD THEM OFF FOREVER!
I'M NOT KIDDING, KARA--I CAN'T--
WAIT...
THANK GOD.

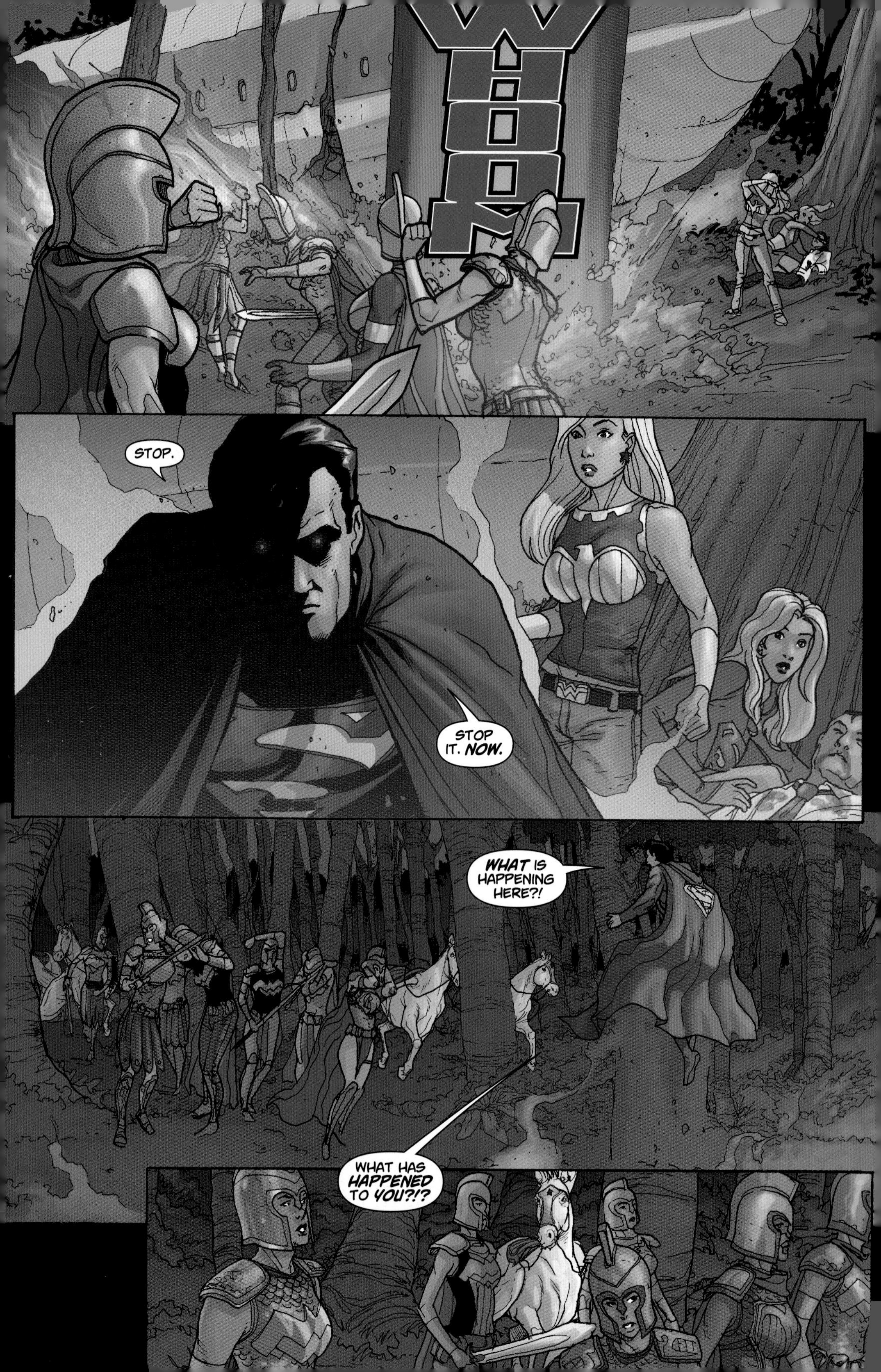
WHOOM
STOP.
STOP IT. NOW.
WHAT IS HAPPENING HERE?!
WHAT HAS HAPPENED TO YOU?!?

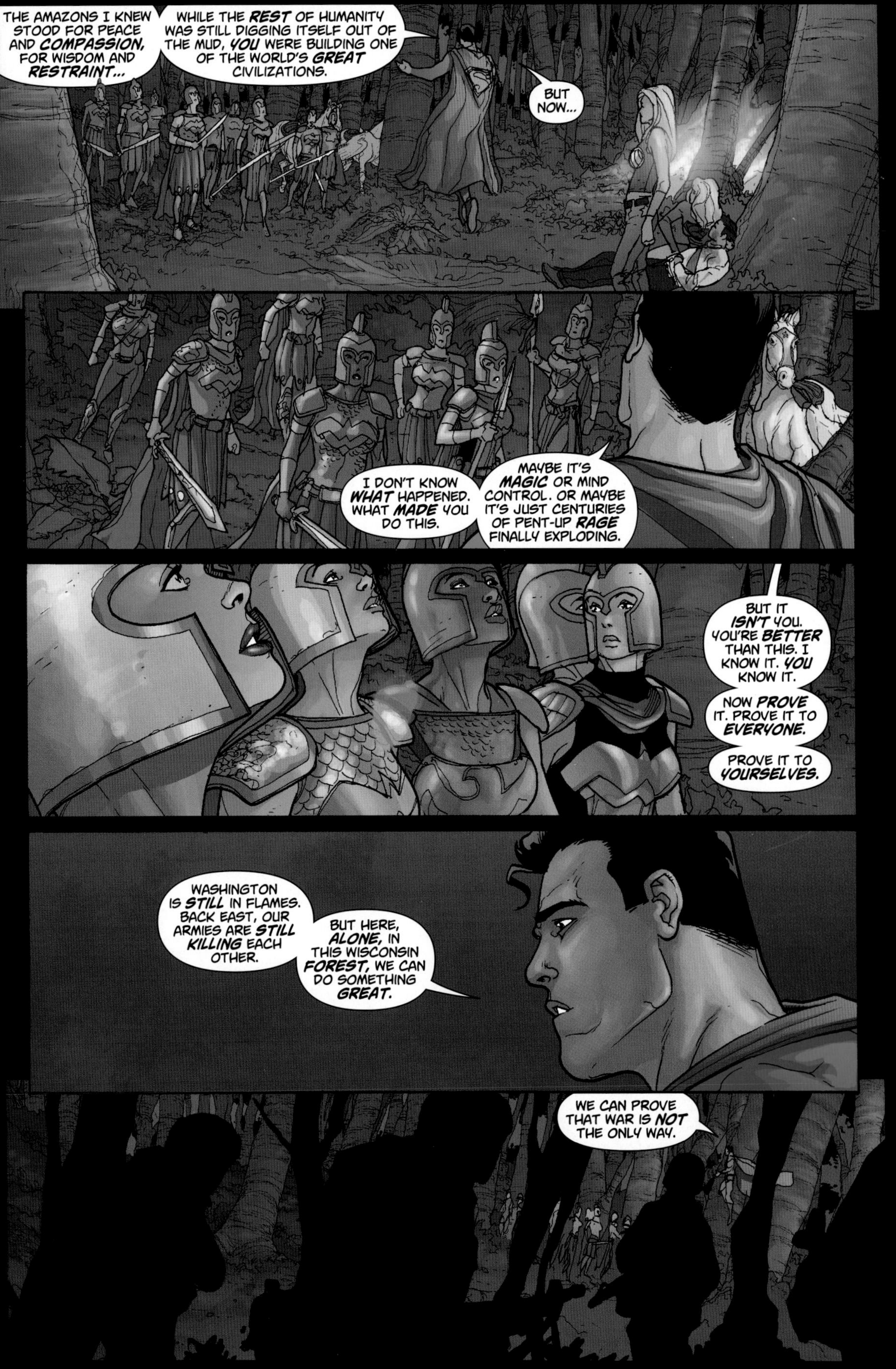
THE AMAZONS I KNEW STOOD FOR PEACE AND COMPASSION, FOR WISDOM AND RESTRAINT...
WHILE THE REST OF HUMANITY WAS STILL DIGGING ITSELF OUT OF THE MUD, YOU WERE BUILDING ONE OF THE WORLD'S GREAT CIVILIZATIONS.
BUT NOW...
I DON'T KNOW WHAT HAPPENED. WHAT MADE YOU DO THIS.
MAYBE IT'S MAGIC OR MIND CONTROL. OR MAYBE IT'S JUST CENTURIES OF PENT-UP RAGE FINALLY EXPLODING.
BUT IT ISN'T YOU. YOU'RE BETTER THAN THIS. I KNOW IT. YOU KNOW IT.
NOW PROVE IT. PROVE IT TO EVERYONE.
PROVE IT TO YOURSELVES.
WASHINGTON IS STILL IN FLAMES. BACK EAST, OUR ARMIES ARE STILL KILLING EACH OTHER.
BUT HERE, ALONE, IN THIS WISCONSIN FOREST, WE CAN DO SOMETHING GREAT.
WE CAN PROVE THAT WAR IS NOT THE ONLY WAY.

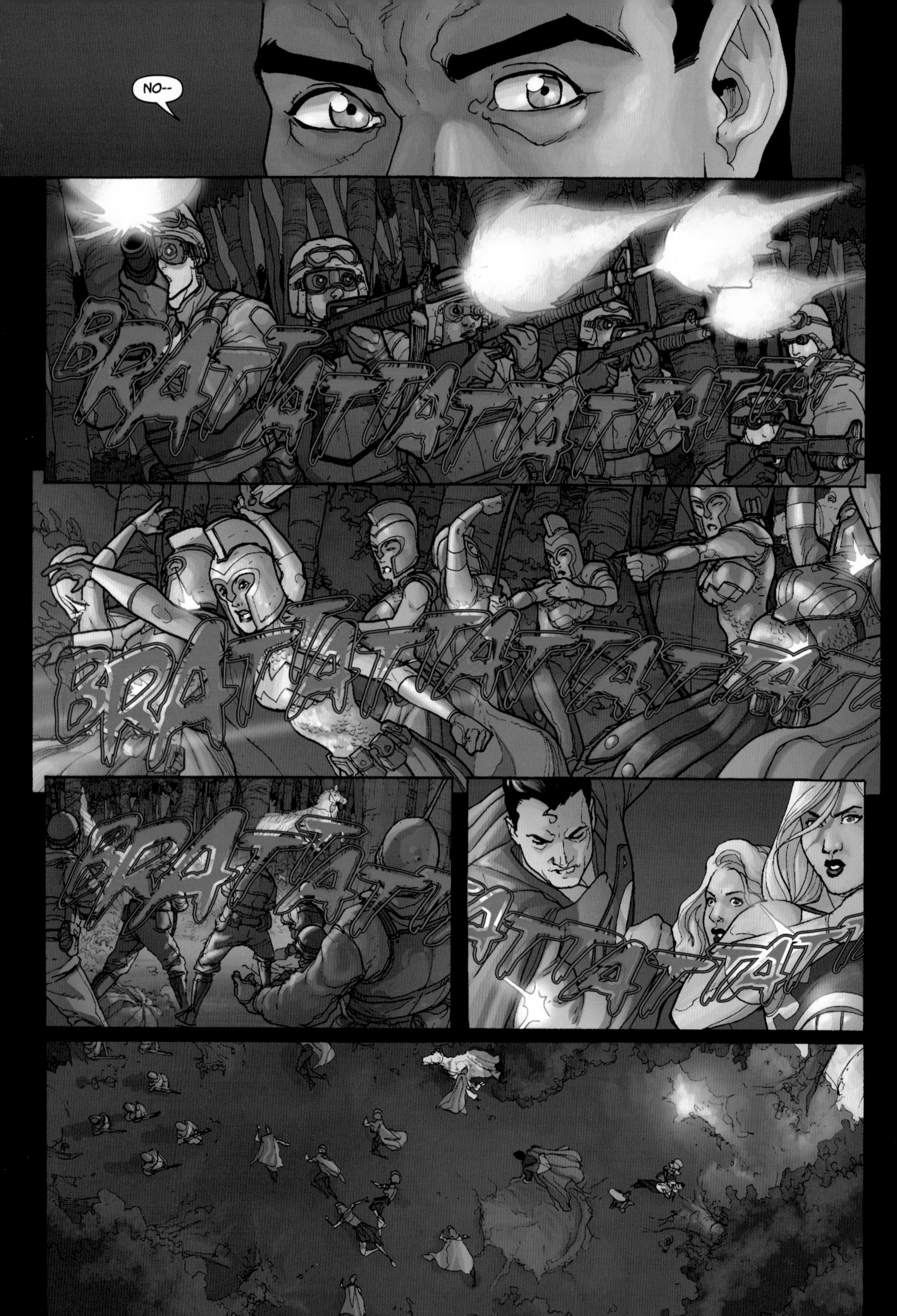
NO--

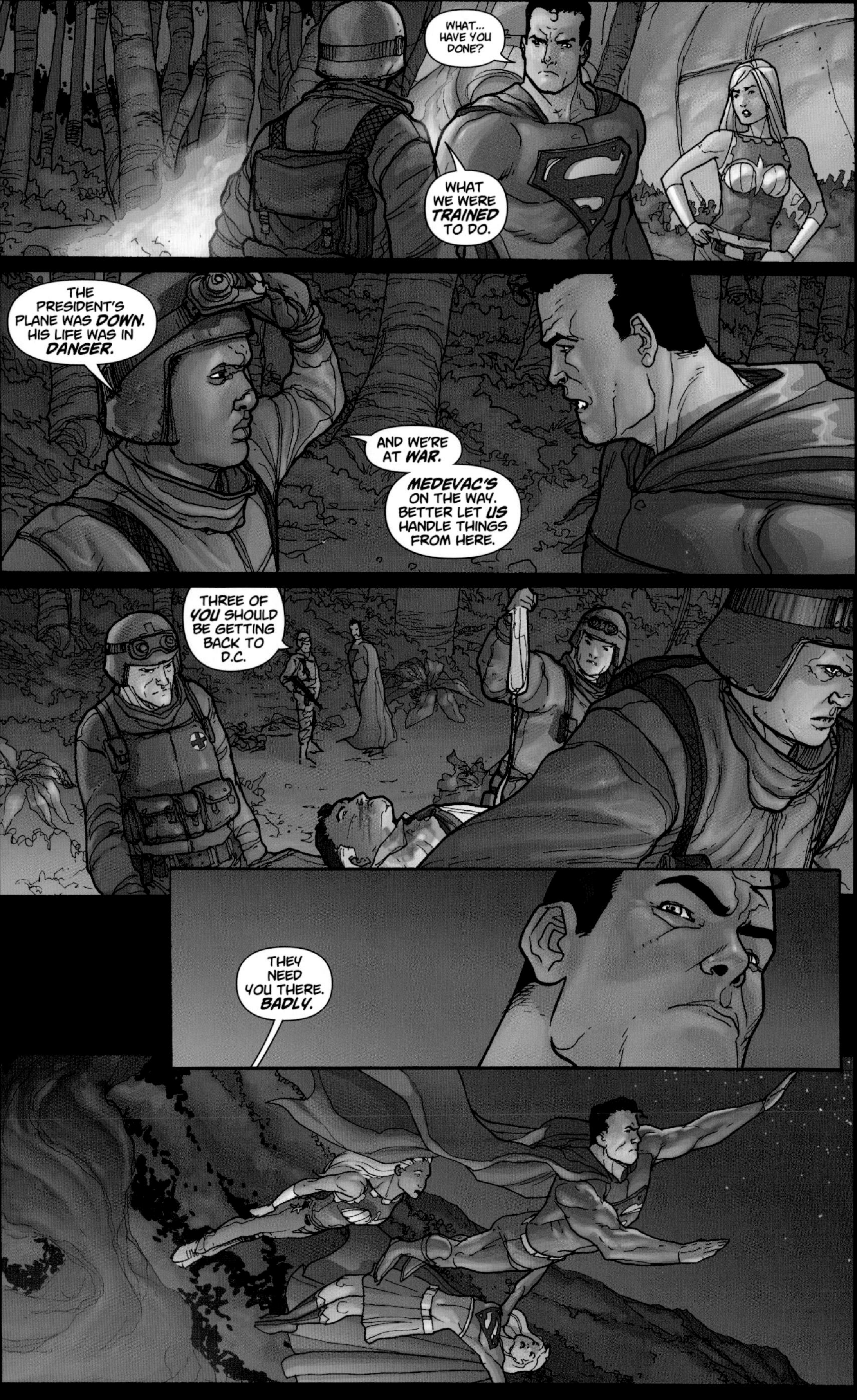
WHAT... HAVE YOU DONE?
WHAT WE WERE TRAINED TO DO.
THE PRESIDENT'S PLANE WAS DOWN. HIS LIFE WAS IN DANGER.
AND WE'RE AT WAR.
MEDEVAC'S ON THE WAY. BETTER LET US HANDLE THINGS FROM HERE.
THREE OF YOU SHOULD BE GETTING BACK TO D.C.
THEY NEED YOU THERE. BADLY.

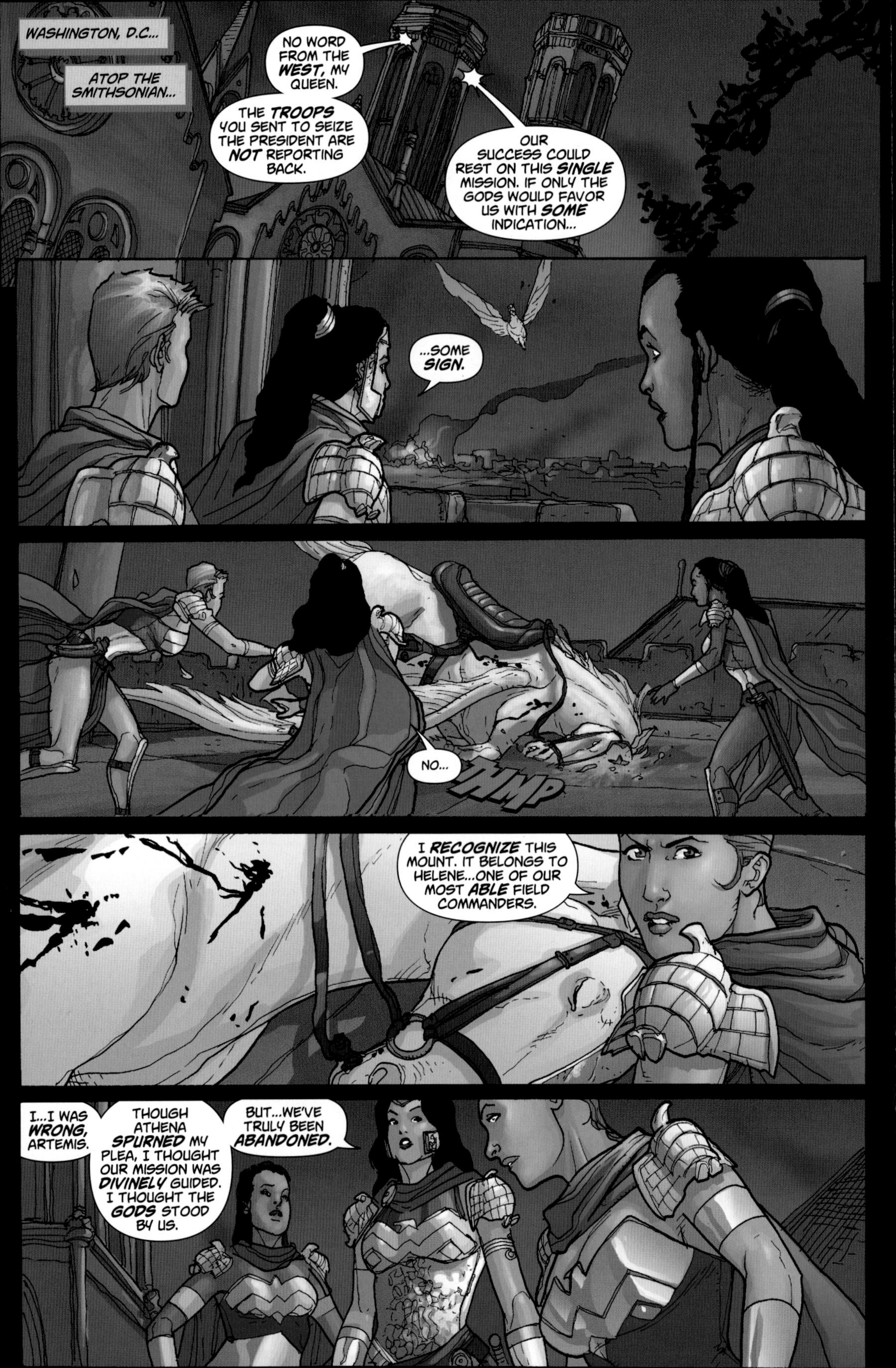
WASHINGTON, D.C...
ATOP THE SMITHSONIAN...
NO WORD FROM THE WEST, MY QUEEN.
THE TROOPS YOU SENT TO SEIZE THE PRESIDENT ARE NOT REPORTING BACK.
OUR SUCCESS COULD REST ON THIS SINGLE MISSION. IF ONLY THE GODS WOULD FAVOR US WITH SOME INDICATION...
...SOME SIGN.
NO...
THMP
I RECOGNIZE THIS MOUNT. IT BELONGS TO HELENE...ONE OF OUR MOST ABLE FIELD COMMANDERS.
I...I WAS WRONG, ARTEMIS.
THOUGH ATHENA SPURNED MY PLEA, I THOUGHT OUR MISSION WAS DIVINELY GUIDED. I THOUGHT THE GODS STOOD BY US.
BUT...WE'VE TRULY BEEN ABANDONED.

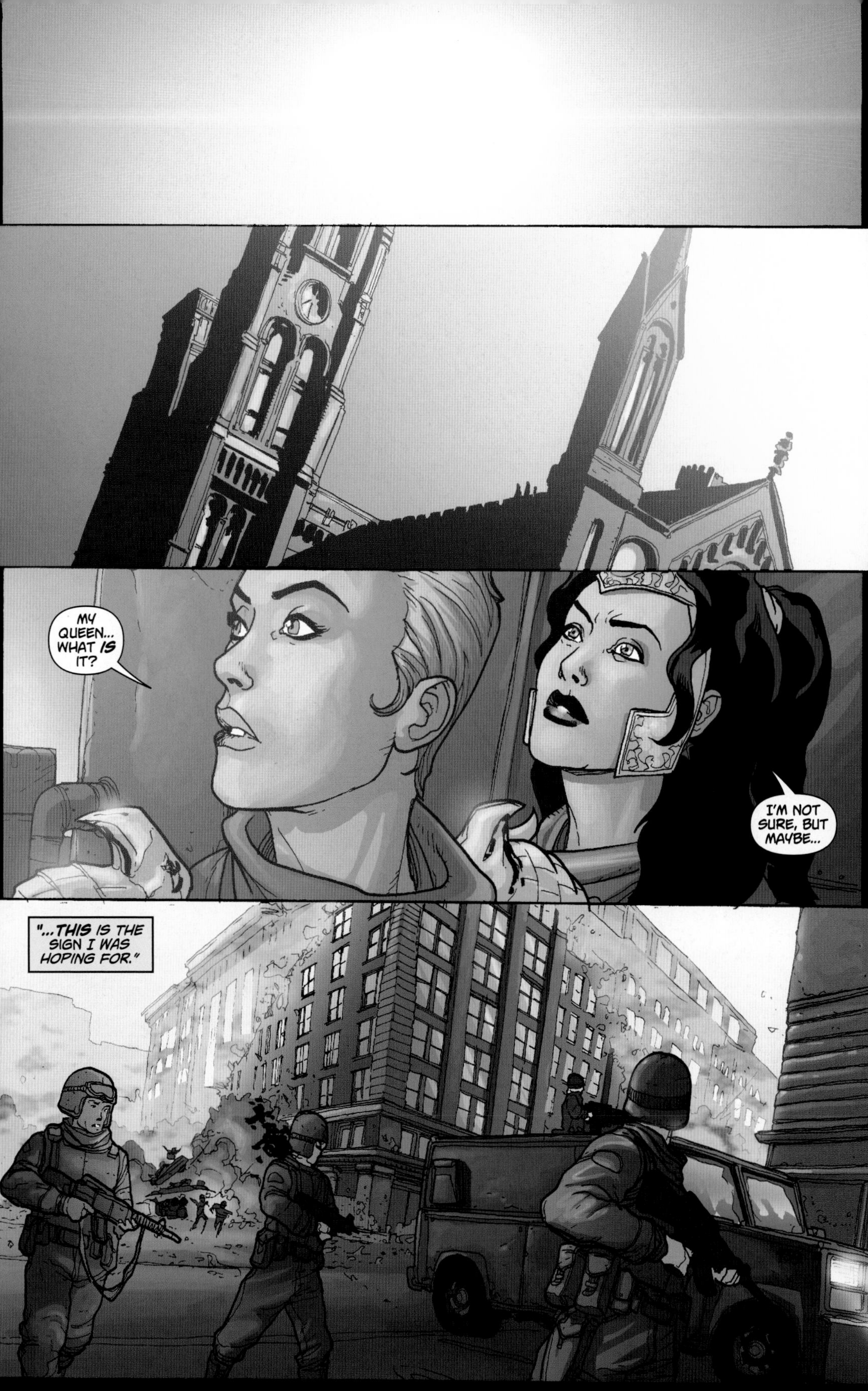
MY QUEEN... WHAT IS IT?
I'M NOT SURE, BUT MAYBE...
"...THIS IS THE SIGN I WAS HOPING FOR."

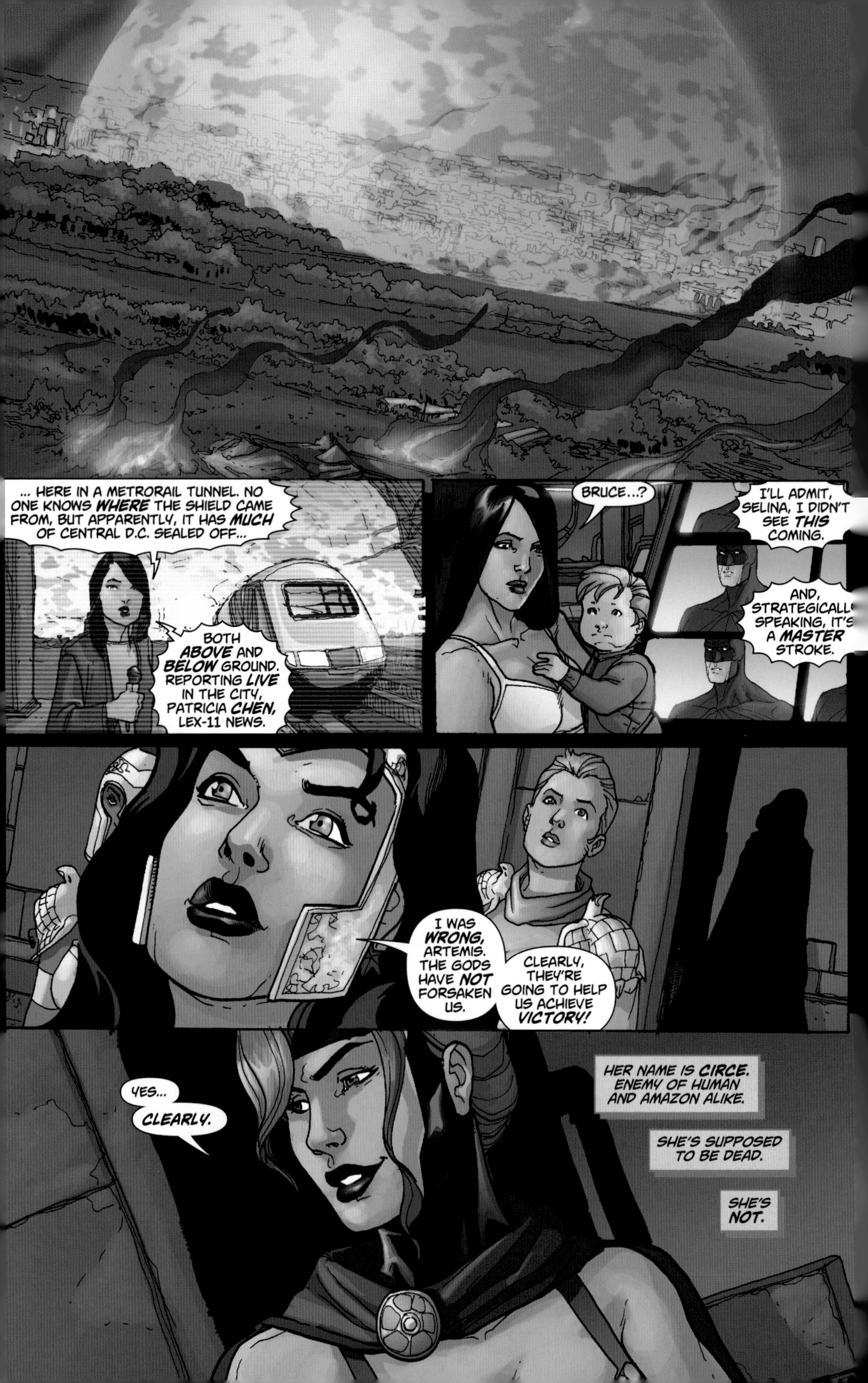
... HERE IN A METROPAIL TUNNEL. NO ONE KNOWS WHERE THE SHIELD CAME FROM, BUT APPARENTLY, IT HAS MUCH OF CENTRAL D.C. SEALED OFF...
BOTH ABOVE AND BELOW GROUND. REPORTING LIVE IN THE CITY, PATRICIA CHEN, LEX-11 NEWS.
BRUCE...?
I'LL ADMIT, SELINA, I DIDN'T SEE THIS COMING.
AND, STRATEGICALL SPEAKING, IT'S A MASTER STROKE.
I WAS WRONG, ARTEMIS. THE GODS HAVE NOT FORSAKEN US.
CLEARLY, THEY'RE GOING TO HELP US ACHIEVE VICTORY!
YES...
CLEARLY.
HER NAME IS CIRCE. ENEMY OF HUMAN AND AMAZON ALIKE.
SHE'S SUPPOSED TO BE DEAD.
SHE'S NOT.

Chapter Five

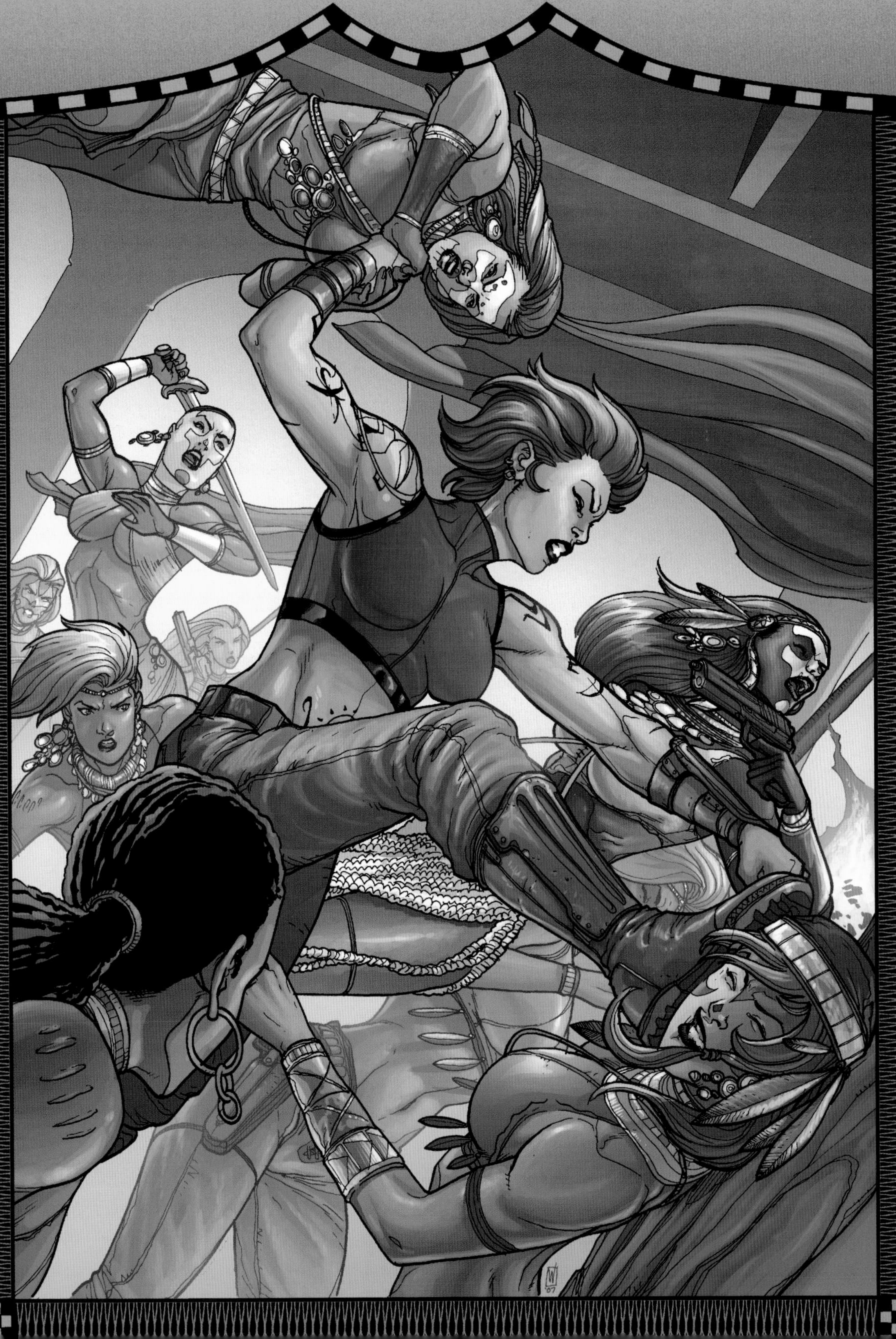

In Gotham City, Batman enlists the help of Catwoman in dealing with a splinter group of the Amazons — the Bana-Mighdall. The high-tech warriors plan a terrorist strike, which Catwoman thwarts — leaving the Dark Knight free to fight the war where he is most needed.

Meanwhile, Wonder Woman returns to Themyscira to recover the antidote for Nemesis's bee sting. While there, Circe's nuclear missile attack is finally launched upon the island, and Wonder Woman must stop it alone. During her attempt to defuse and redirect the missile, Diana calls upon Athena and asks why the Goddess of Wisdom has allowed this war to continue, and why she has forsaken her once favored island of Themyscira. Athena finally appears, destroying the missile — but reminds Wonder Woman that she is also the Goddess of War and Strategy, and she alone decides when to interfere with the affairs of man. With a wave of her mighty hand, she sends the Amazon Princess back to the battlefront, to see the war to its bitter end.

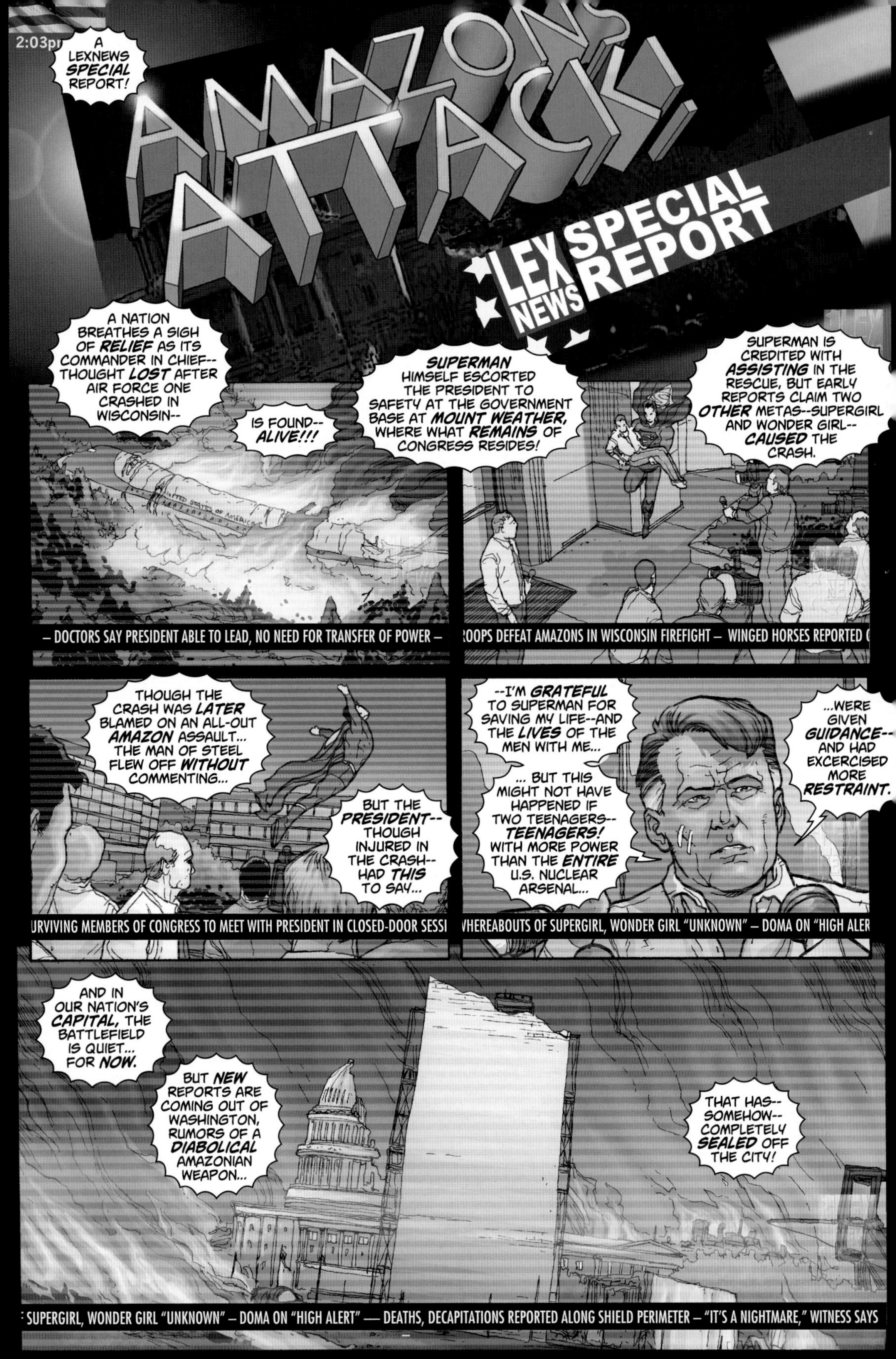
2:03p
A LEXNEWS SPECIAL REPORT!
AMAZONS ATTACK!
LEX NEWS SPECIAL REPORT
A NATION BREATHES A SIGH OF RELIEF AS ITS COMMANDER IN CHIEF--THOUGHT LOST AFTER AIR FORCE ONE CRASHED IN WISCONSIN--
IS FOUND--ALIVE!!!
SUPERMAN HIMSELF ESCORTED THE PRESIDENT TO SAFETY AT THE GOVERNMENT BASE AT MOUNT WEATHER, WHERE WHAT REMAINS OF CONGRESS RESIDES!
SUPERMAN IS CREDITED WITH ASSISTING IN THE RESCUE, BUT EARLY REPORTS CLAIM TWO OTHER METAS--SUPERGIRL AND WONDER GIRL--CAUSED THE CRASH.
UNITED STATES OF AMERICA
– DOCTORS SAY PRESIDENT ABLE TO LEAD, NO NEED FOR TRANSFER OF POWER –
ROOPS DEFEAT AMAZONS IN WISCONSIN FIREFIGHT – WINGED HORSES REPORTED
THOUGH THE CRASH WAS LATER BLAMED ON AN ALL-OUT AMAZON ASSAULT... THE MAN OF STEEL FLEW OFF WITHOUT COMMENTING...
BUT THE PRESIDENT--THOUGH INJURED IN THE CRASH--HAD THIS TO SAY...
--I'M GRATEFUL TO SUPERMAN FOR SAVING MY LIFE--AND THE LIVES OF THE MEN WITH ME...
... BUT THIS MIGHT NOT HAVE HAPPENED IF TWO TEENAGERS--TEENAGERS! WITH MORE POWER THAN THE ENTIRE U.S. NUCLEAR ARSENAL...
...WERE GIVEN GUIDANCE--AND HAD EXCERCISED MORE RESTRAINT.
URVIVING MEMBERS OF CONGRESS TO MEET WITH PRESIDENT IN CLOSED-DOOR SESSI
VHEREABOUTS OF SUPERGIRL, WONDER GIRL "UNKNOWN" – DOMA ON "HIGH ALER
AND IN OUR NATION'S CAPITAL, THE BATTLEFIELD IS QUIET... FOR NOW.
BUT NEW REPORTS ARE COMING OUT OF WASHINGTON, RUMORS OF A DIABOLICAL AMAZONIAN WEAPON...
THAT HAS--SOMEHOW--COMPLETELY SEALED OFF THE CITY!
F SUPERGIRL, WONDER GIRL "UNKNOWN" – DOMA ON "HIGH ALERT" — DEATHS, DECAPITATIONS REPORTED ALONG SHIELD PERIMETER – "IT'S A NIGHTMARE," WITNESS SAYS

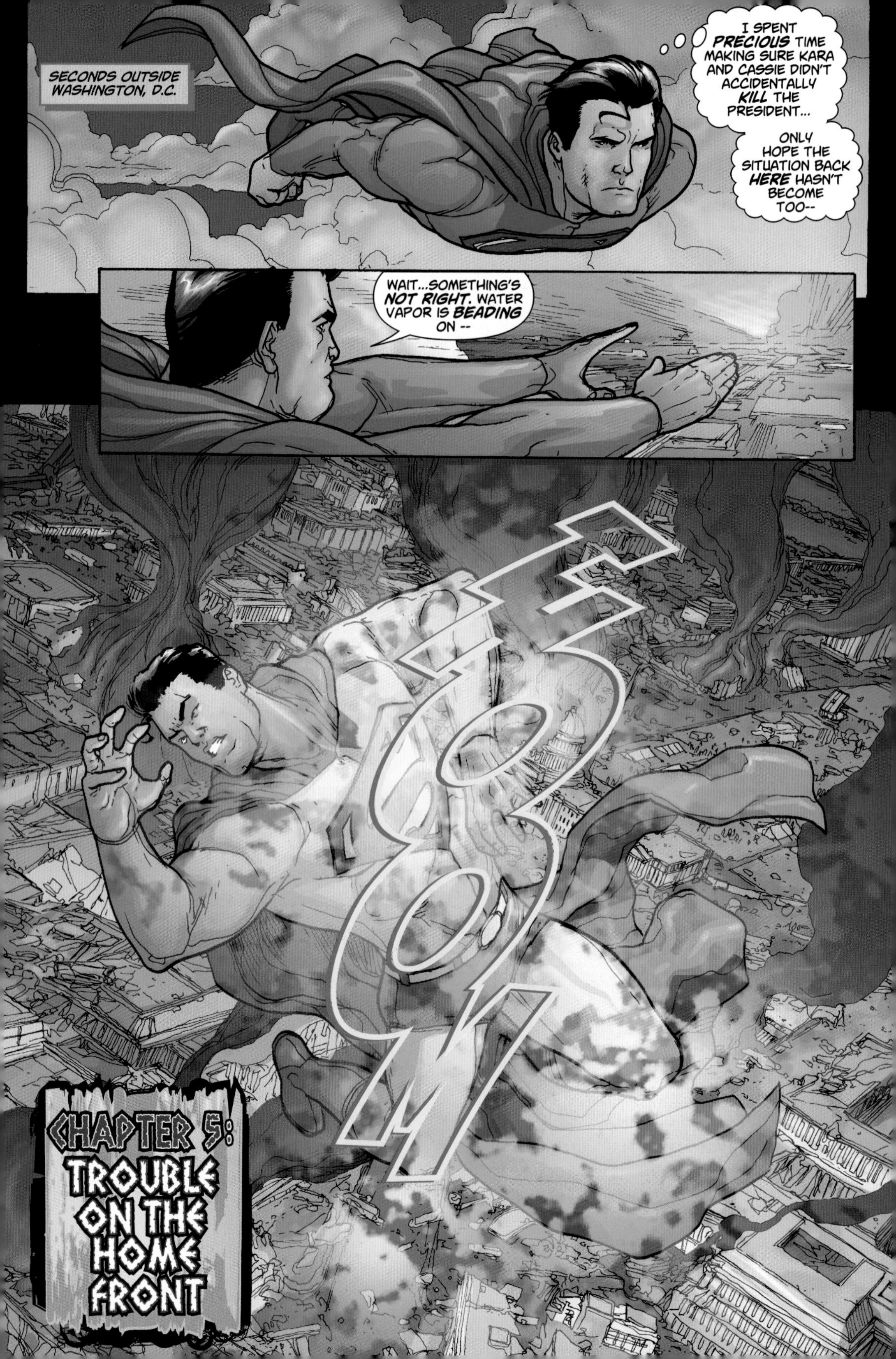
SECONDS OUTSIDE WASHINGTON, D.C.
I SPENT PRECIOUS TIME MAKING SURE KARA AND CASSIE DIDN'T ACCIDENTALLY KILL THE PRESIDENT...
ONLY HOPE THE SITUATION BACK HERE HASN'T BECOME TOO--
WAIT...SOMETHING'S NOT RIGHT. WATER VAPOR IS BEADING ON --
FOOOM
CHAPTER 5:
TROUBLE ON THE HOME FRONT

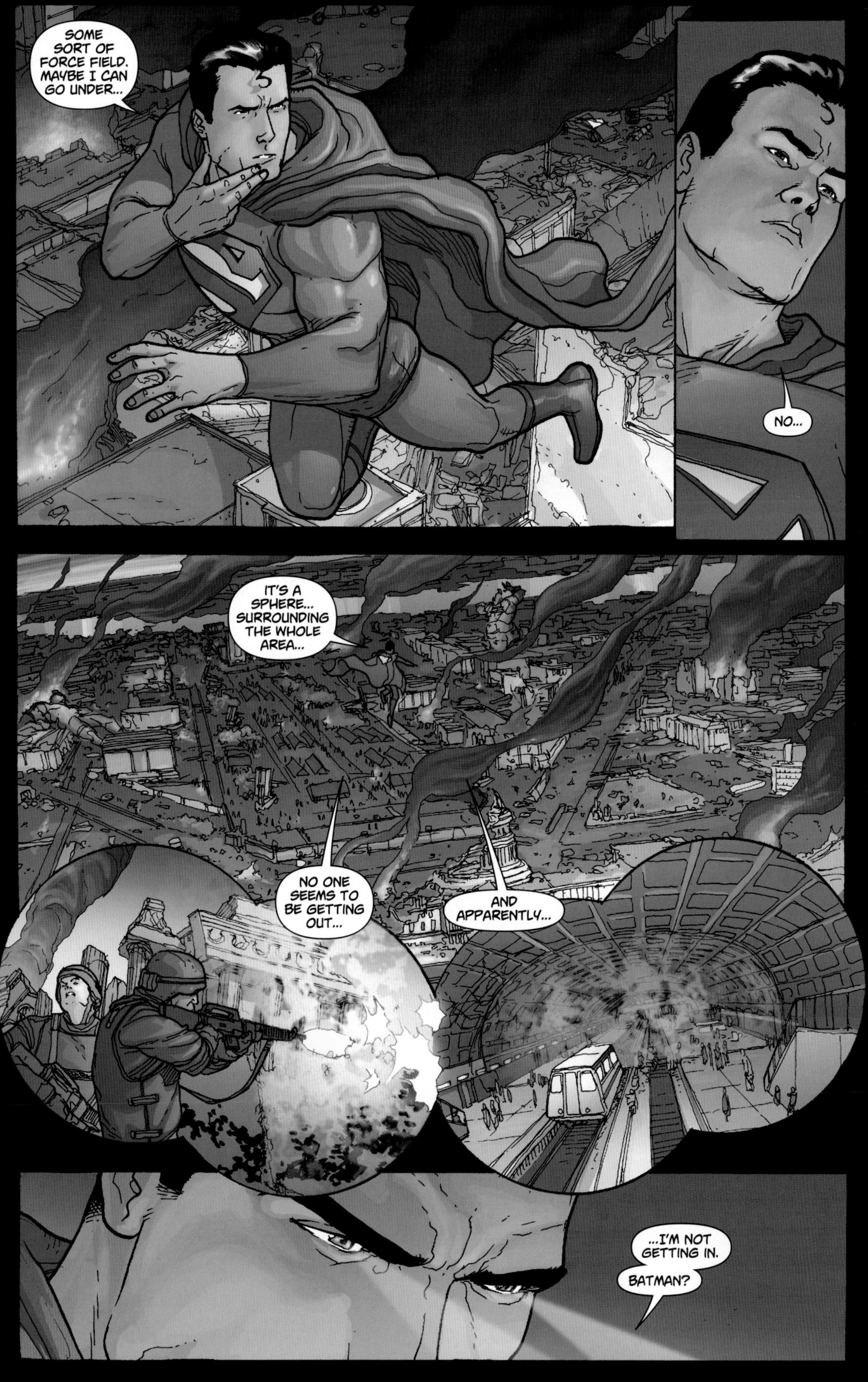
SOME SORT OF FORCE FIELD. MAYBE I CAN GO UNDER...
NO...
IT'S A SPHERE... SURROUNDING THE WHOLE AREA...
NO ONE SEEMS TO BE GETTING OUT...
AND APPARENTLY...
...I'M NOT GETTING IN.
BATMAN?

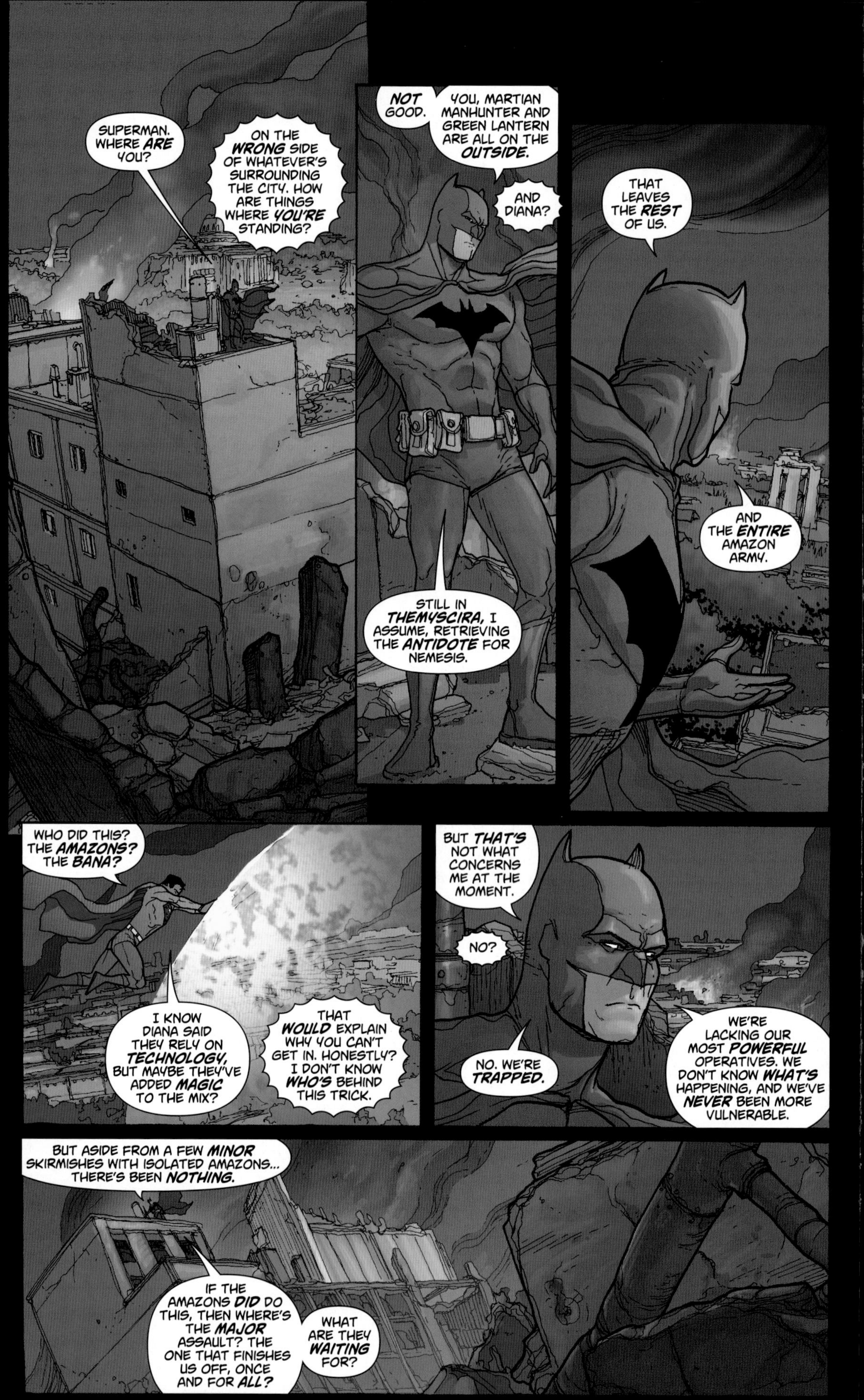
SUPERMAN. WHERE ARE YOU?
ON THE WRONG SIDE OF WHATEVER'S SURROUNDING THE CITY. HOW ARE THINGS WHERE YOU'RE STANDING?
NOT GOOD.
YOU, MARTIAN MANHUNTER AND GREEN LANTERN ARE ALL ON THE OUTSIDE.
AND DIANA?
STILL IN THEMYSCIRA, I ASSUME, RETRIEVING THE ANTIDOTE FOR NEMESIS.
THAT LEAVES THE REST OF US.
AND THE ENTIRE AMAZON ARMY.
WHO DID THIS? THE AMAZONS? THE BANA?
I KNOW DIANA SAID THEY RELY ON TECHNOLOGY, BUT MAYBE THEY'VE ADDED MAGIC TO THE MIX?
THAT WOULD EXPLAIN WHY YOU CAN'T GET IN. HONESTLY? I DON'T KNOW WHO'S BEHIND THIS TRICK.
BUT THAT'S NOT WHAT CONCERNS ME AT THE MOMENT.
NO?
NO. WE'RE TRAPPED.
WE'RE LACKING OUR MOST POWERFUL OPERATIVES. WE DON'T KNOW WHAT'S HAPPENING, AND WE'VE NEVER BEEN MORE VULNERABLE.
BUT ASIDE FROM A FEW MINOR SKIRMISHES WITH ISOLATED AMAZONS... THERE'S BEEN NOTHING.
IF THE AMAZONS DID DO THIS, THEN WHERE'S THE MAJOR ASSAULT? THE ONE THAT FINISHES US OFF, ONCE AND FOR ALL?
WHAT ARE THEY WAITING FOR?

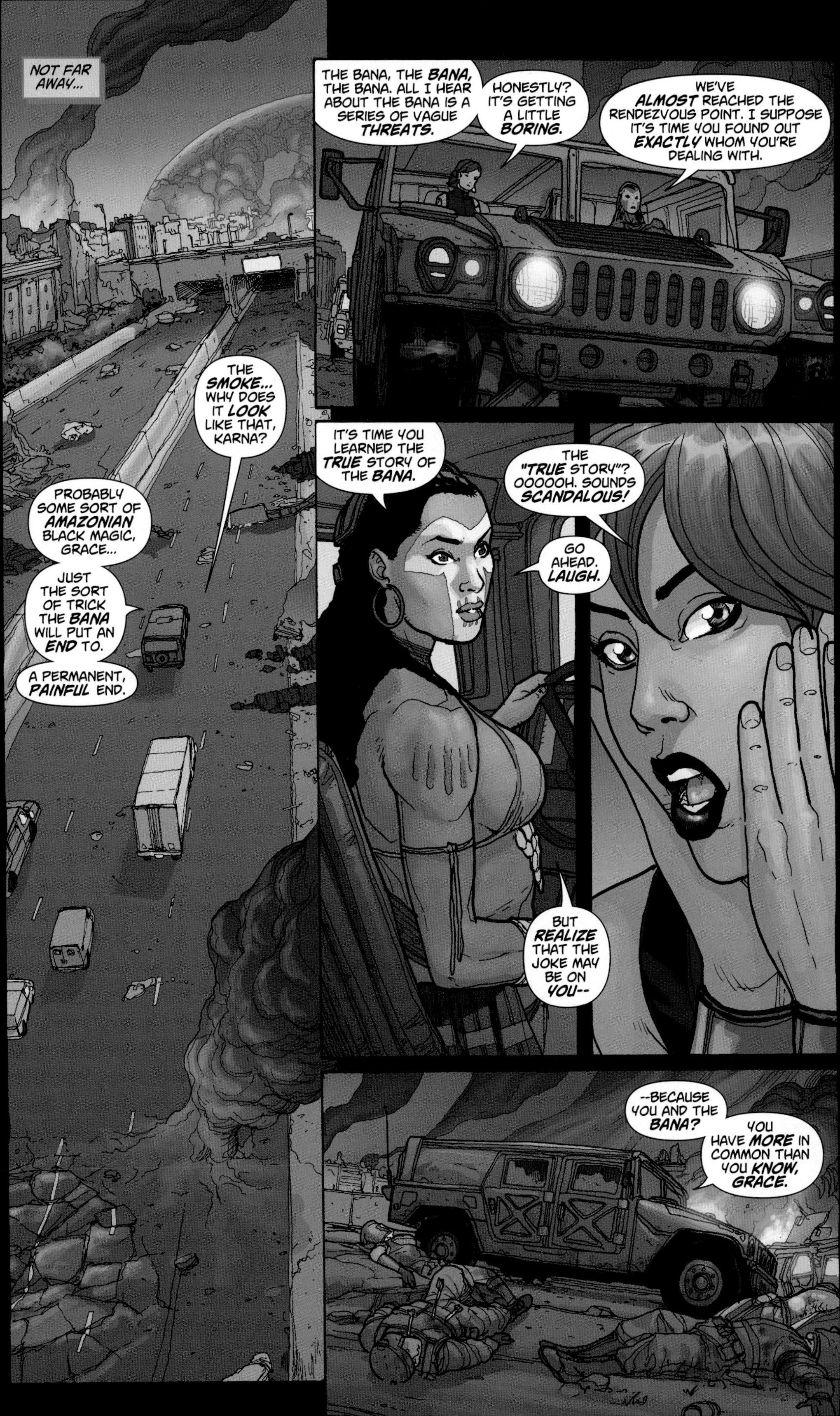
NOT FAR AWAY...
THE BANA, THE BANA, THE BANA. ALL I HEAR ABOUT THE BANA IS A SERIES OF VAGUE THREATS.
HONESTLY? IT'S GETTING A LITTLE BORING.
WE'VE ALMOST REACHED THE RENDEZVOUS POINT. I SUPPOSE IT'S TIME YOU FOUND OUT EXACTLY WHOM YOU'RE DEALING WITH.
THE SMOKE... WHY DOES IT LOOK LIKE THAT, KARNA?
PROBABLY SOME SORT OF AMAZONIAN BLACK MAGIC, GRACE...
JUST THE SORT OF TRICK THE BANA WILL PUT AN END TO.
A PERMANENT, PAINFUL END.
IT'S TIME YOU LEARNED THE TRUE STORY OF THE BANA.
THE "TRUE STORY"? OOOOOH. SOUNDS SCANDALOUS!
GO AHEAD. LAUGH.
BUT REALIZE THAT THE JOKE MAY BE ON YOU--
--BECAUSE YOU AND THE BANA?
YOU HAVE MORE IN COMMON THAN YOU KNOW, GRACE.

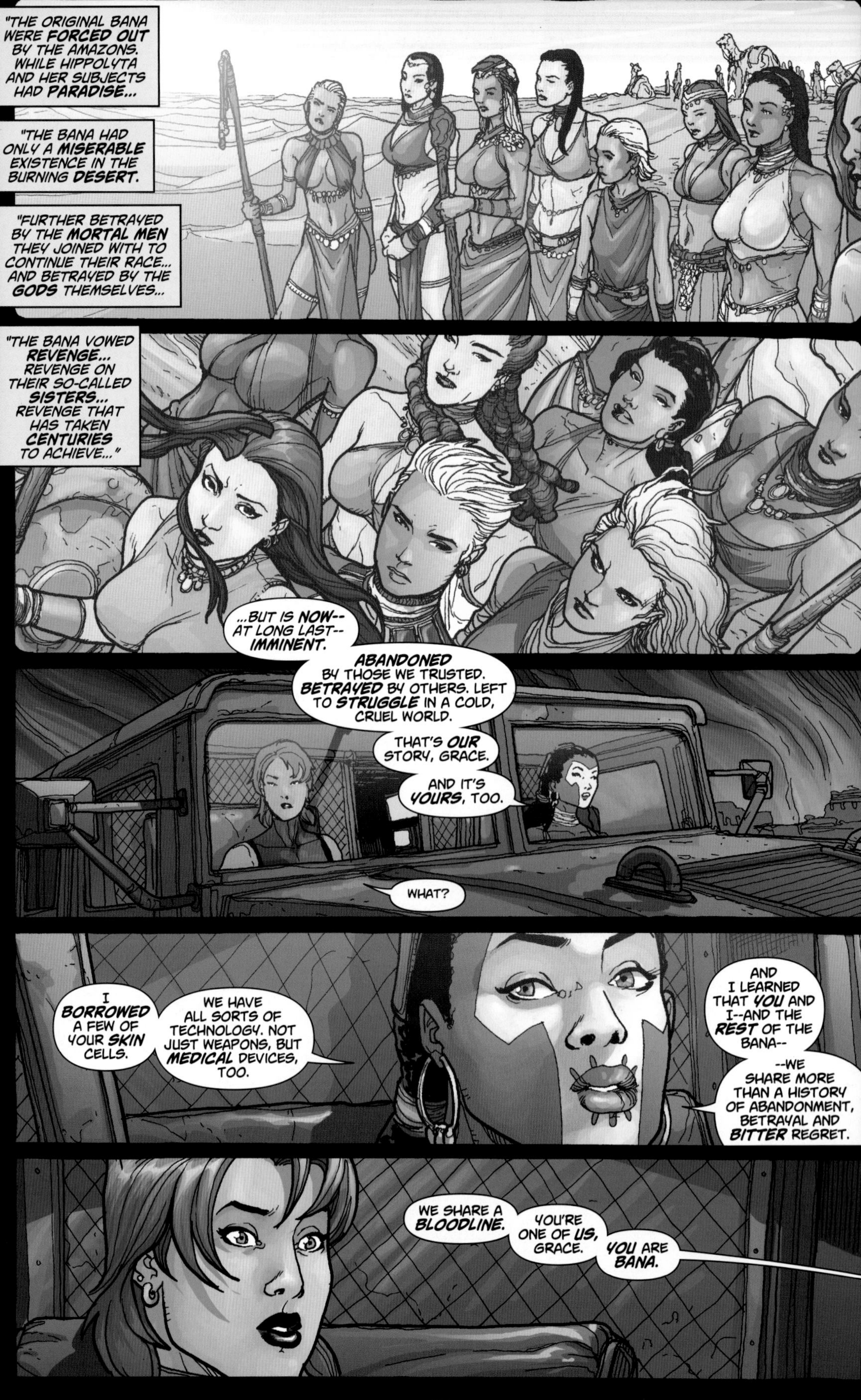

"THE ORIGINAL BANA WERE FORCED OUT BY THE AMAZONS. WHILE HIPPOLYTA AND HER SUBJECTS HAD PARADISE...
"THE BANA HAD ONLY A MISERABLE EXISTENCE IN THE BURNING DESERT.
"FURTHER BETRAYED BY THE MORTAL MEN THEY JOINED WITH TO CONTINUE THEIR RACE... AND BETRAYED BY THE GODS THEMSELVES...
"THE BANA VOWED REVENGE... REVENGE ON THEIR SO-CALLED SISTERS... REVENGE THAT HAS TAKEN CENTURIES TO ACHIEVE..."
...BUT IS NOW--AT LONG LAST--IMMINENT.
ABANDONED BY THOSE WE TRUSTED. BETRAYED BY OTHERS. LEFT TO STRUGGLE IN A COLD, CRUEL WORLD.
THAT'S OUR STORY, GRACE.
AND IT'S YOURS, TOO.
WHAT?
I BORROWED A FEW OF YOUR SKIN CELLS.
WE HAVE ALL SORTS OF TECHNOLOGY. NOT JUST WEAPONS, BUT MEDICAL DEVICES, TOO.
AND I LEARNED THAT YOU AND I--AND THE REST OF THE BANA--
--WE SHARE MORE THAN A HISTORY OF ABANDONMENT, BETRAYAL AND BITTER REGRET.
WE SHARE A BLOODLINE.
YOU'RE ONE OF US, GRACE.
YOU ARE BANA.

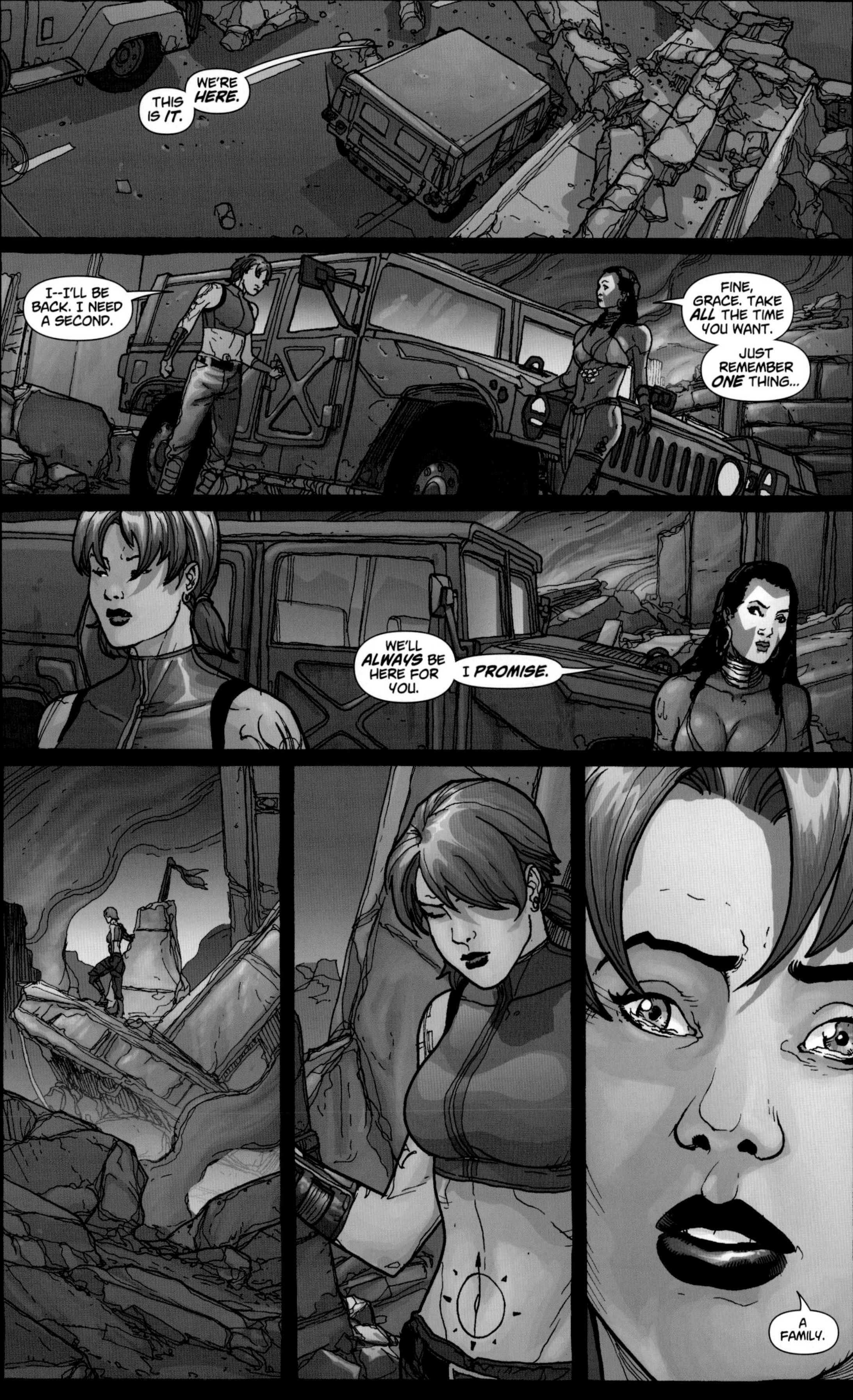
THIS IS IT.
WE'RE HERE.
I--I'LL BE BACK. I NEED A SECOND.
FINE, GRACE. TAKE ALL THE TIME YOU WANT.
JUST REMEMBER ONE THING...
WE'LL ALWAYS BE HERE FOR YOU.
I PROMISE.
A FAMILY.

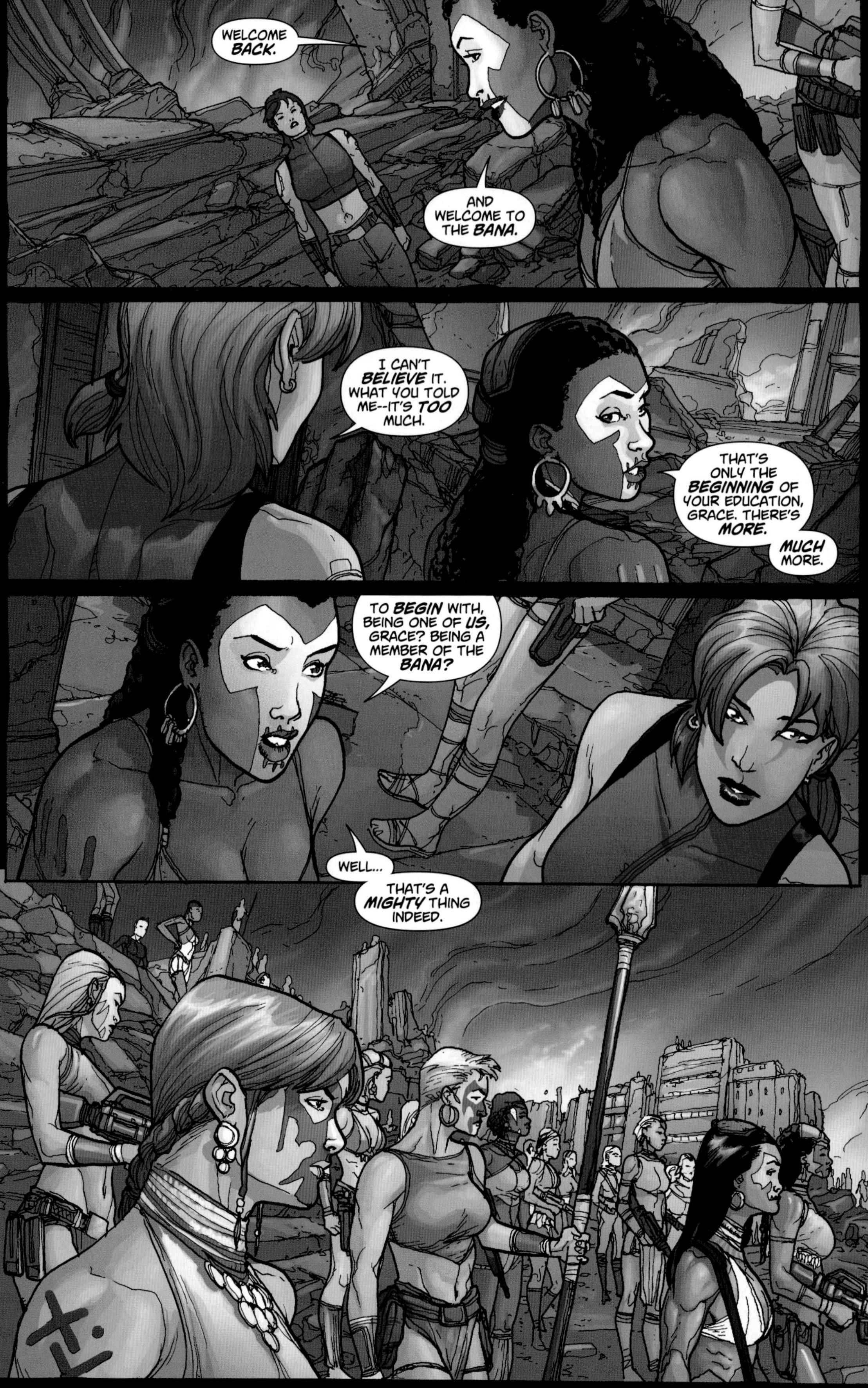

WELCOME BACK.
AND WELCOME TO THE BANA.
I CAN'T BELIEVE IT. WHAT YOU TOLD ME--IT'S TOO MUCH.
THAT'S ONLY THE BEGINNING OF YOUR EDUCATION, GRACE. THERE'S MORE.
MUCH MORE.
TO BEGIN WITH, BEING ONE OF US, GRACE? BEING A MEMBER OF THE BANA?
WELL...
THAT'S A MIGHTY THING INDEED.

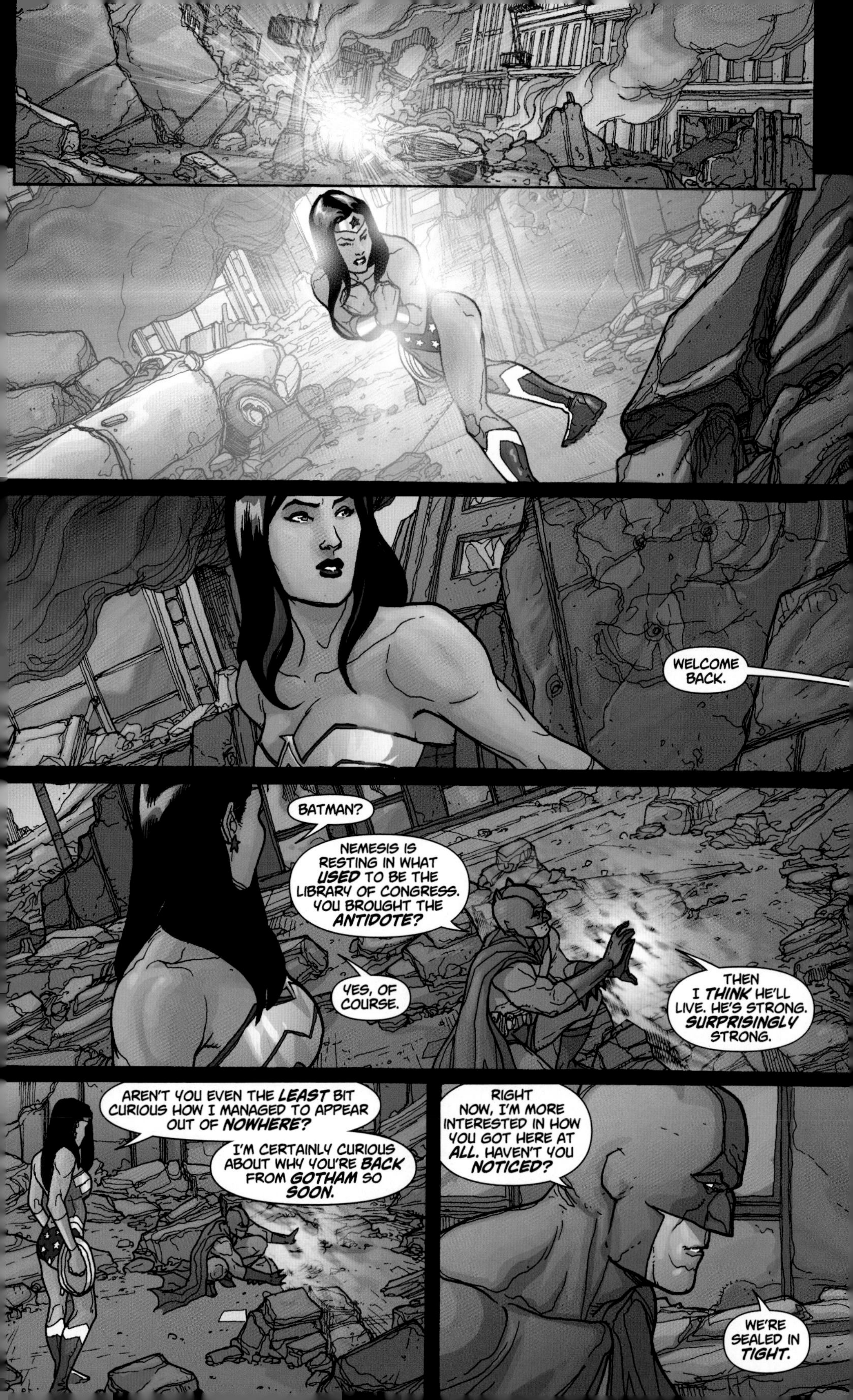
WELCOME BACK.
BATMAN?
NEMESIS IS RESTING IN WHAT USED TO BE THE LIBRARY OF CONGRESS. YOU BROUGHT THE ANTIDOTE?
YES, OF COURSE.
THEN I THINK HE'LL LIVE. HE'S STRONG. SURPRISINGLY STRONG.
AREN'T YOU EVEN THE LEAST BIT CURIOUS HOW I MANAGED TO APPEAR OUT OF NOWHERE?
I'M CERTAINLY CURIOUS ABOUT WHY YOU'RE BACK FROM GOTHAM SO SOON.
RIGHT NOW, I'M MORE INTERESTED IN HOW YOU GOT HERE AT ALL. HAVEN'T YOU NOTICED?
WE'RE SEALED IN TIGHT.

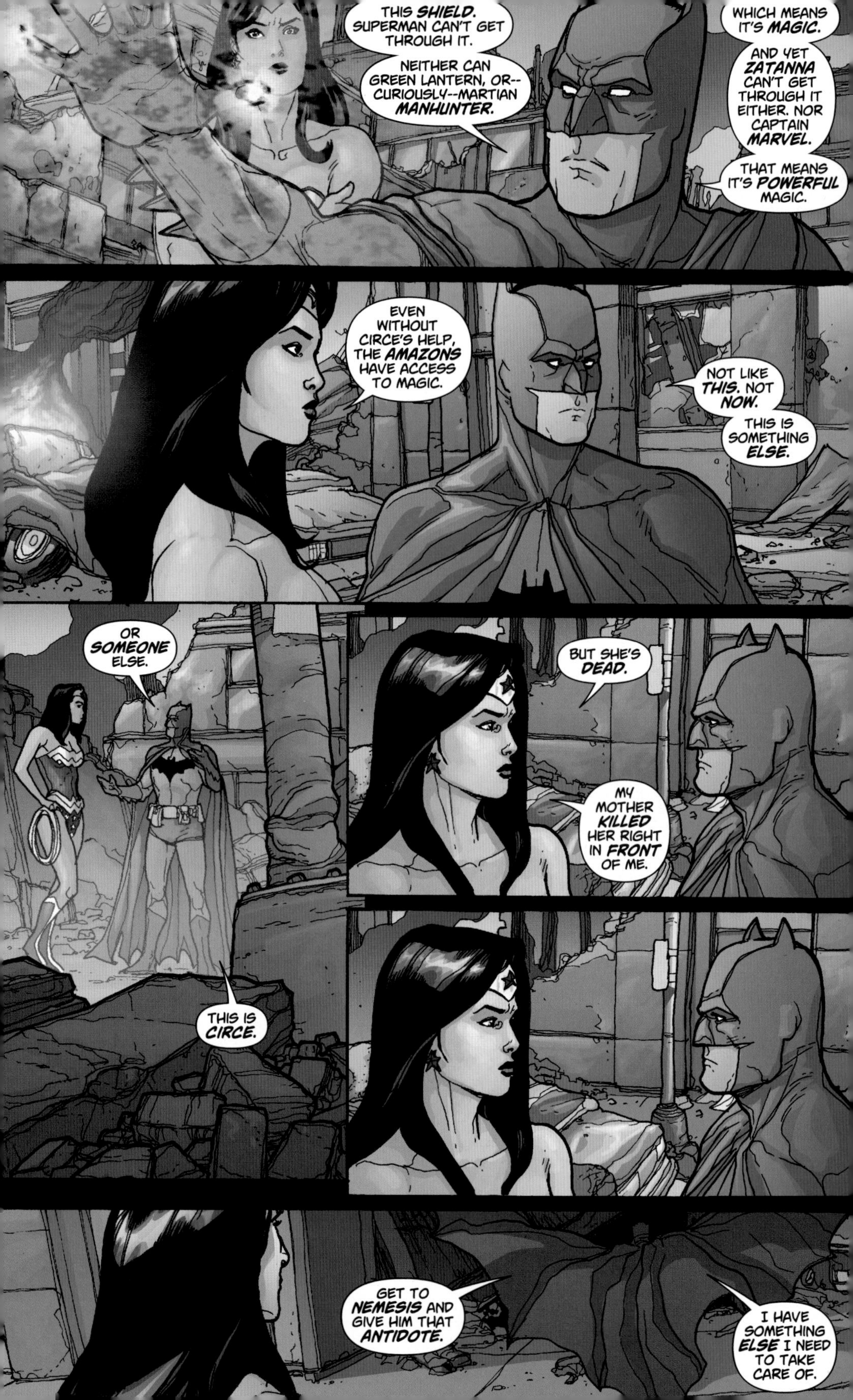
THIS SHIELD. SUPERMAN CAN'T GET THROUGH IT.
NEITHER CAN GREEN LANTERN, OR--CURIOUSLY--MARTIAN MANHUNTER.
WHICH MEANS IT'S MAGIC.
AND YET ZATANNA CAN'T GET THROUGH IT EITHER. NOR CAPTAIN MARVEL.
THAT MEANS IT'S POWERFUL MAGIC.
EVEN WITHOUT CIRCE'S HELP, THE AMAZONS HAVE ACCESS TO MAGIC.
NOT LIKE THIS. NOT NOW.
THIS IS SOMETHING ELSE.
OR SOMEONE ELSE.
THIS IS CIRCE.
BUT SHE'S DEAD.
MY MOTHER KILLED HER RIGHT IN FRONT OF ME.
GET TO NEMESIS AND GIVE HIM THAT ANTIDOTE.
I HAVE SOMETHING ELSE I NEED TO TAKE CARE OF.

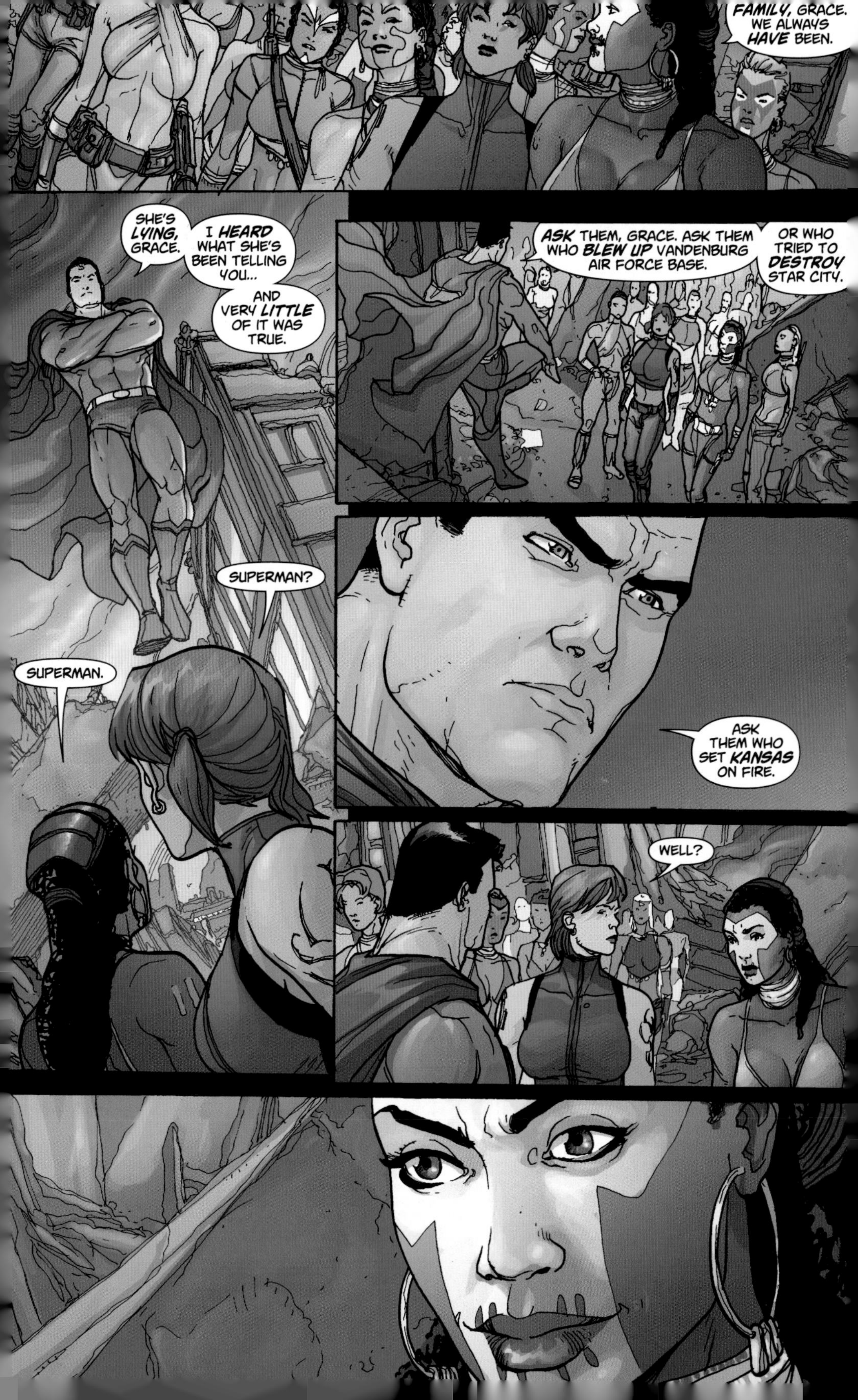
FAMILY, GRACE. WE ALWAYS HAVE BEEN.
SHE'S LYING, GRACE.
I HEARD WHAT SHE'S BEEN TELLING YOU...
AND VERY LITTLE OF IT WAS TRUE.
ASK THEM, GRACE. ASK THEM WHO BLEW UP VANDENBURG AIR FORCE BASE.
OR WHO TRIED TO DESTROY STAR CITY.
SUPERMAN?
SUPERMAN.
ASK THEM WHO SET KANSAS ON FIRE.
WELL?

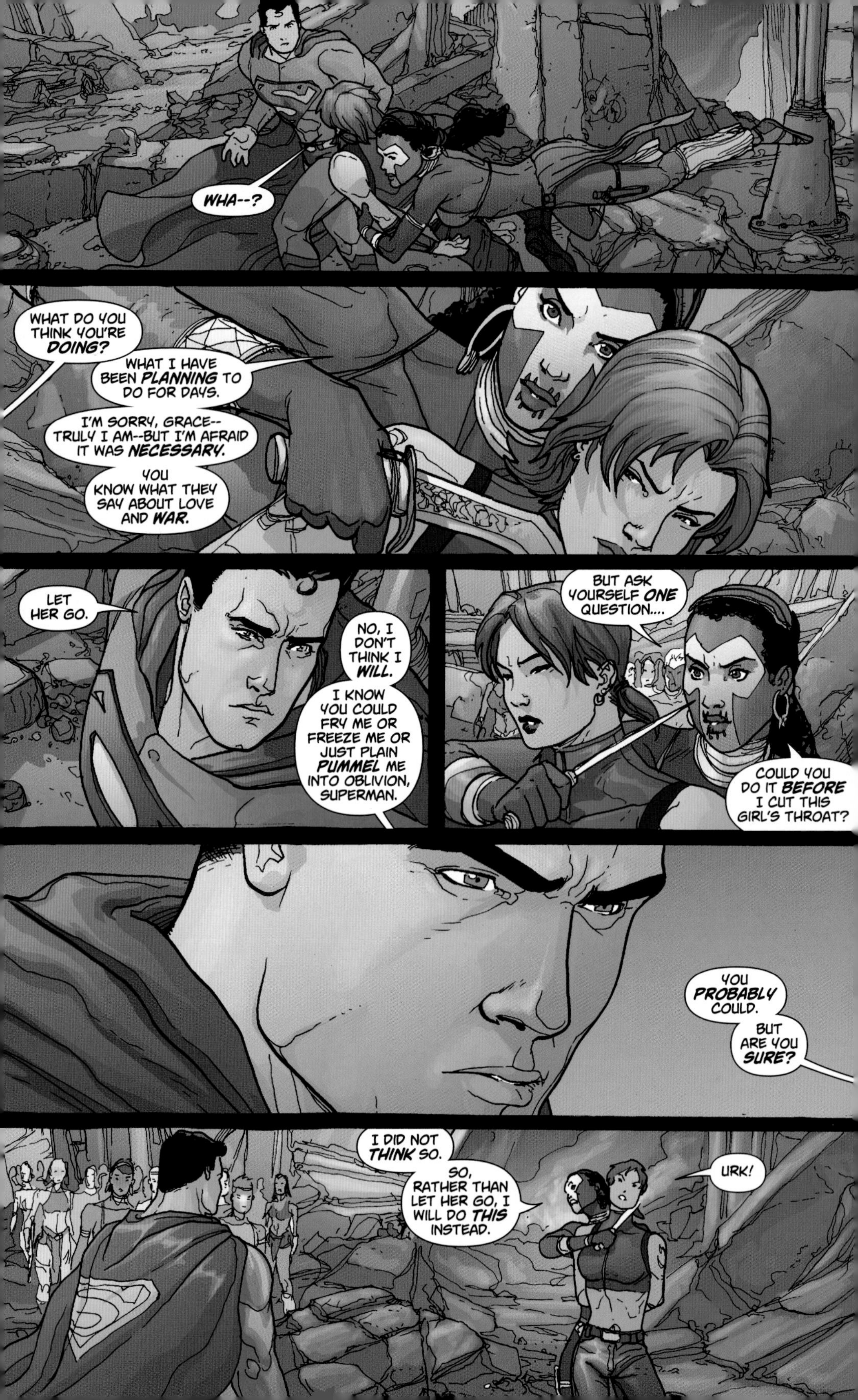
WHA--?
WHAT DO YOU THINK YOU'RE DOING?
WHAT I HAVE BEEN PLANNING TO DO FOR DAYS.
I'M SORRY, GRACE-- TRULY I AM--BUT I'M AFRAID IT WAS NECESSARY.
YOU KNOW WHAT THEY SAY ABOUT LOVE AND WAR.
LET HER GO.
NO, I DON'T THINK I WILL.
I KNOW YOU COULD FRY ME OR FREEZE ME OR JUST PLAIN PUMMEL ME INTO OBLIVION, SUPERMAN.
BUT ASK YOURSELF ONE QUESTION....
COULD YOU DO IT BEFORE I CUT THIS GIRL'S THROAT?
YOU PROBABLY COULD.
BUT ARE YOU SURE?
I DID NOT THINK SO.
SO, RATHER THAN LET HER GO, I WILL DO THIS INSTEAD.
URK!

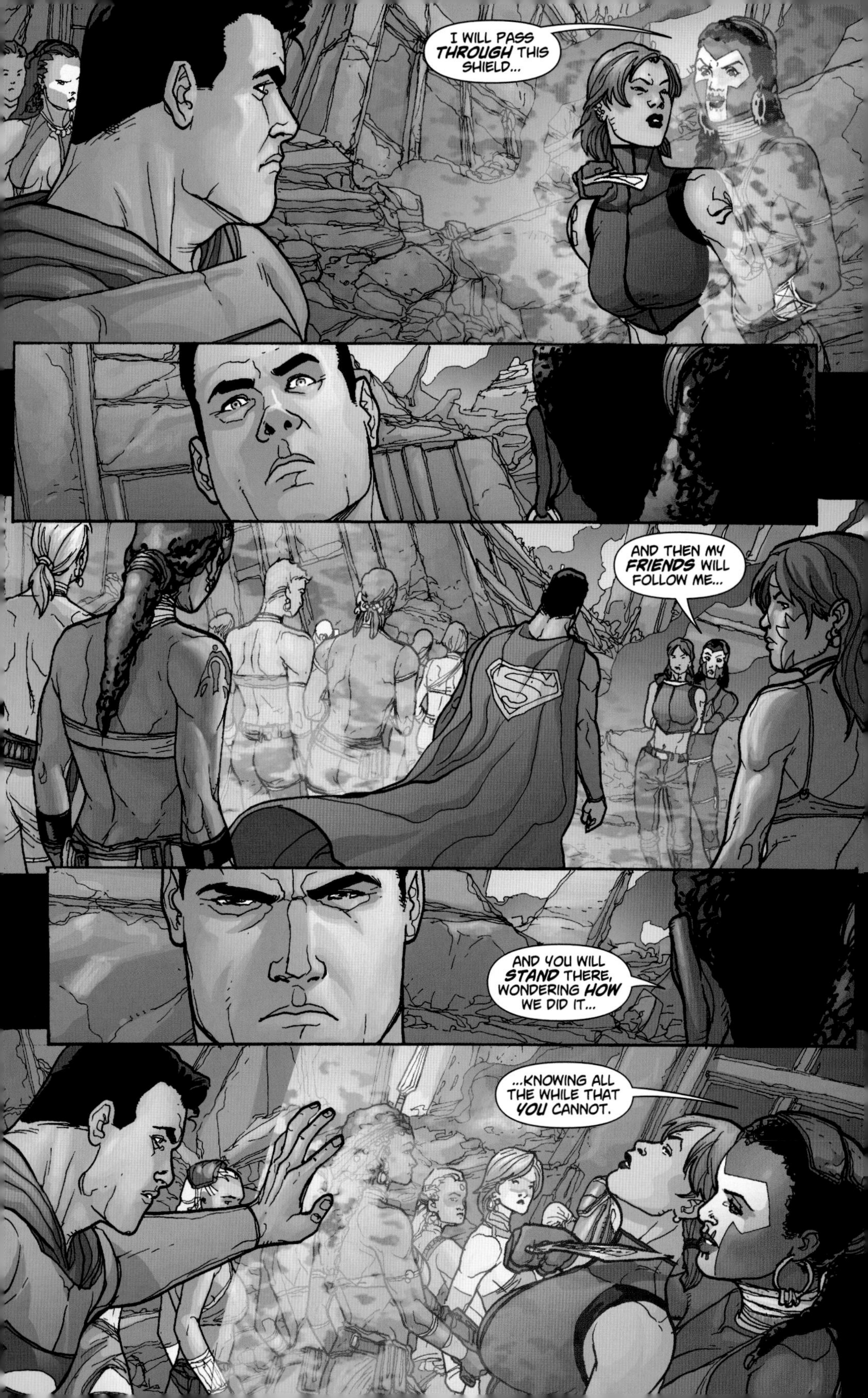
I WILL PASS *THROUGH* THIS SHIELD...
AND THEN MY *FRIENDS* WILL FOLLOW ME...
AND YOU WILL *STAND* THERE, WONDERING *HOW* WE DID IT...
...KNOWING ALL THE WHILE THAT *YOU* CANNOT.

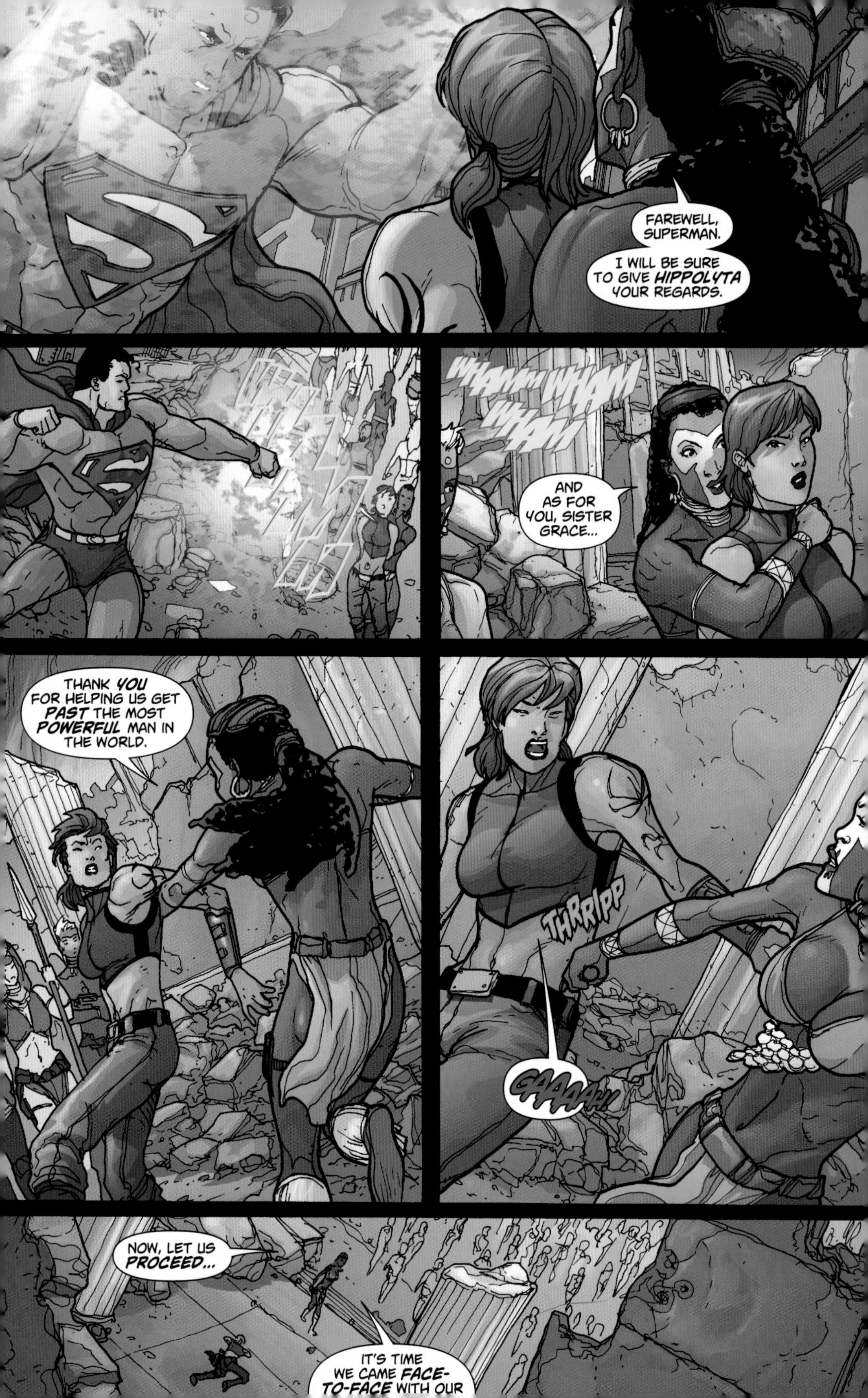
FAREWELL, SUPERMAN.
I WILL BE SURE TO GIVE HIPPOLYTA YOUR REGARDS.
WHAM WHAM WHAM
AND AS FOR YOU, SISTER GRACE...
THANK YOU FOR HELPING US GET PAST THE MOST POWERFUL MAN IN THE WORLD.
THRRIPP
GAAAAH!
NOW, LET US PROCEED...
IT'S TIME WE CAME FACE-TO-FACE WITH OUR

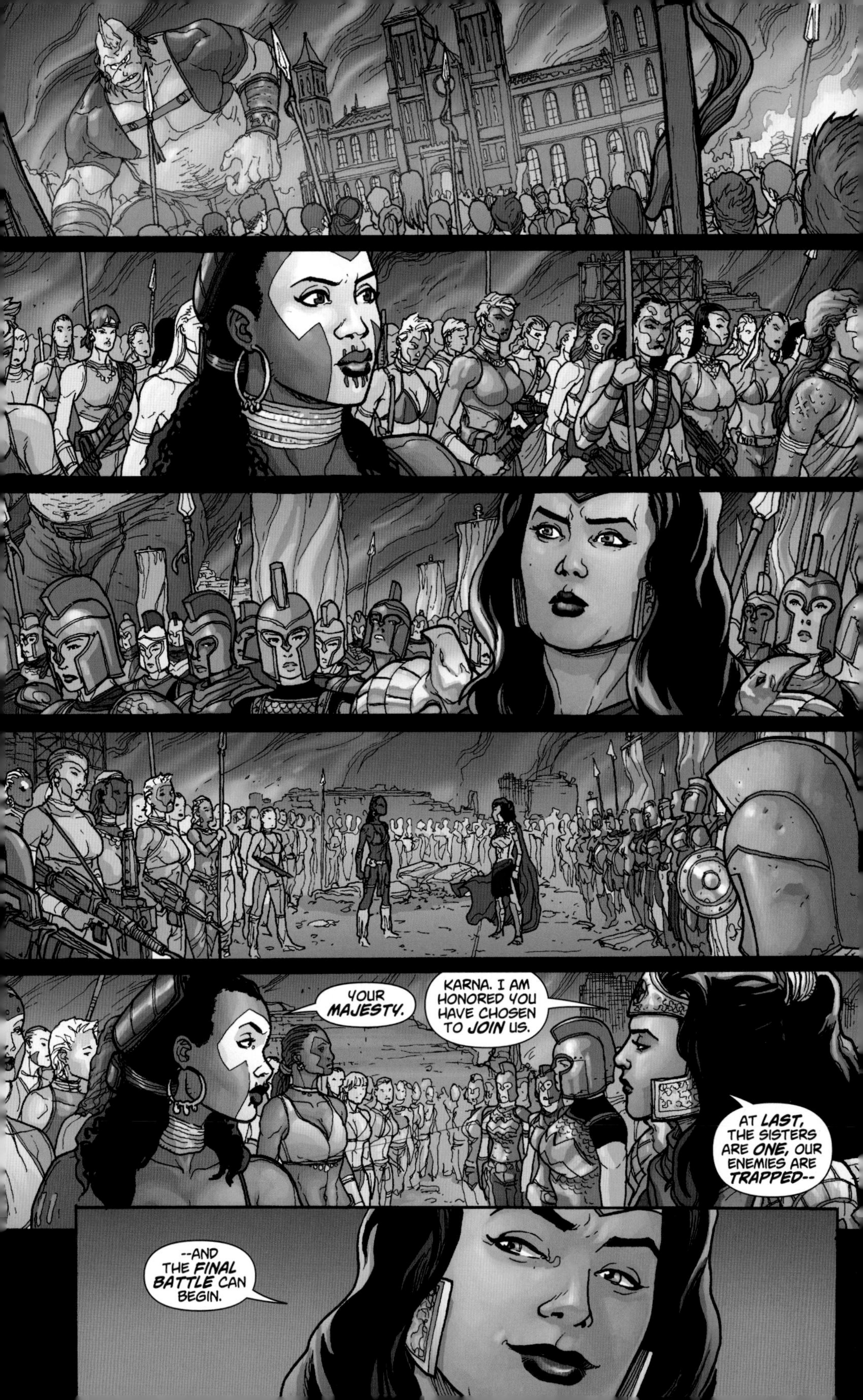
YOUR MAJESTY.
KARNA. I AM HONORED YOU HAVE CHOSEN TO JOIN US.
AT LAST, THE SISTERS ARE ONE, OUR ENEMIES ARE TRAPPED--
--AND THE FINAL BATTLE CAN BEGIN.

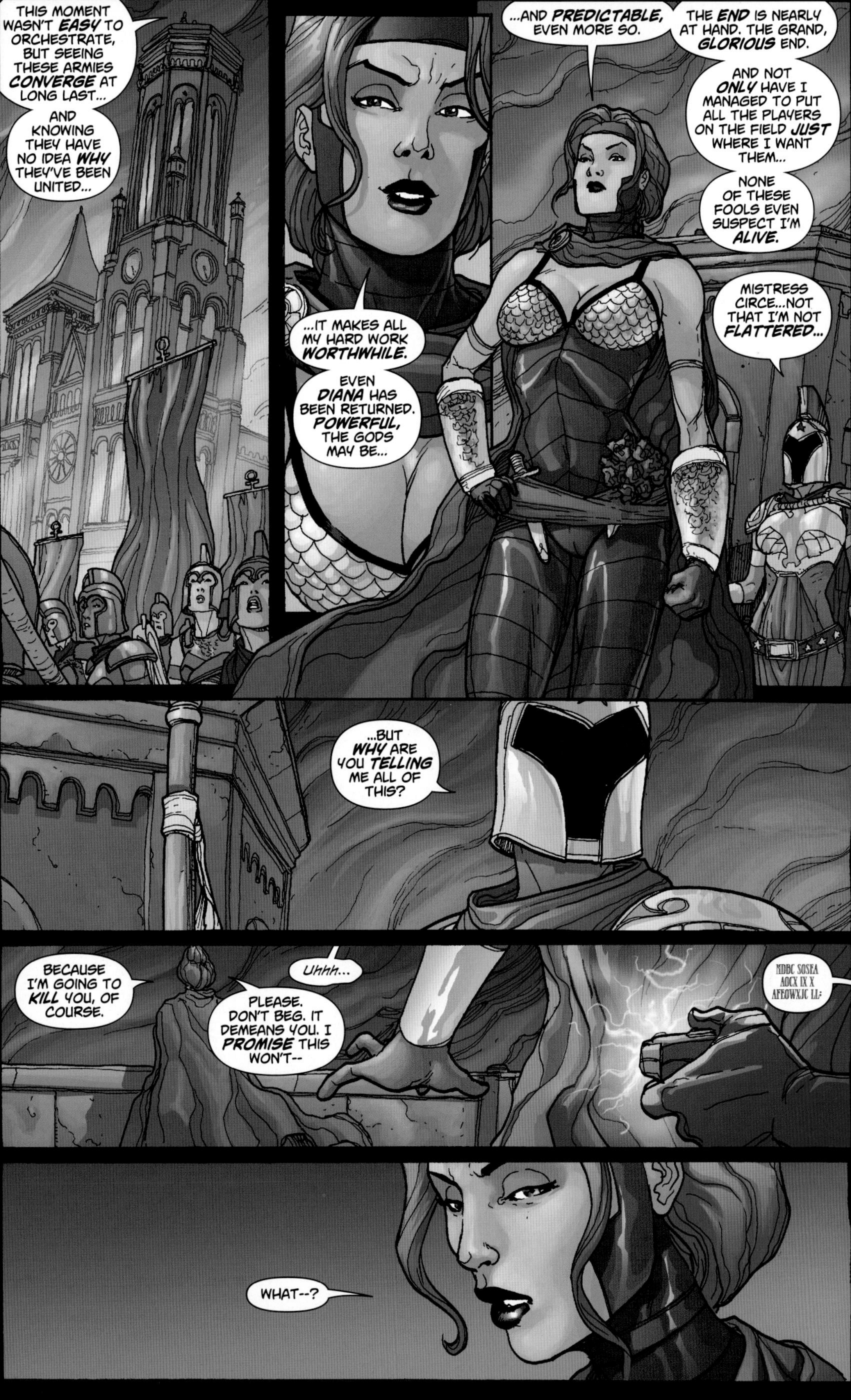
THIS MOMENT WASN'T EASY TO ORCHESTRATE, BUT SEEING THESE ARMIES CONVERGE AT LONG LAST...
AND KNOWING THEY HAVE NO IDEA WHY THEY'VE BEEN UNITED...
...IT MAKES ALL MY HARD WORK WORTHWHILE.
EVEN DIANA HAS BEEN RETURNED. POWERFUL, THE GODS MAY BE...
...AND PREDICTABLE, EVEN MORE SO.
THE END IS NEARLY AT HAND. THE GRAND, GLORIOUS END.
AND NOT ONLY HAVE I MANAGED TO PUT ALL THE PLAYERS ON THE FIELD JUST WHERE I WANT THEM...
NONE OF THESE FOOLS EVEN SUSPECT I'M ALIVE.
MISTRESS CIRCE...NOT THAT I'M NOT FLATTERED...
...BUT WHY ARE YOU TELLING ME ALL OF THIS?
BECAUSE I'M GOING TO KILL YOU, OF COURSE.
Uhhh...
PLEASE. DON'T BEG. IT DEMEANS YOU. I PROMISE THIS WON'T--
MDBC SOSEA AOCX IX X AFEOWXJC LL:
WHAT--?

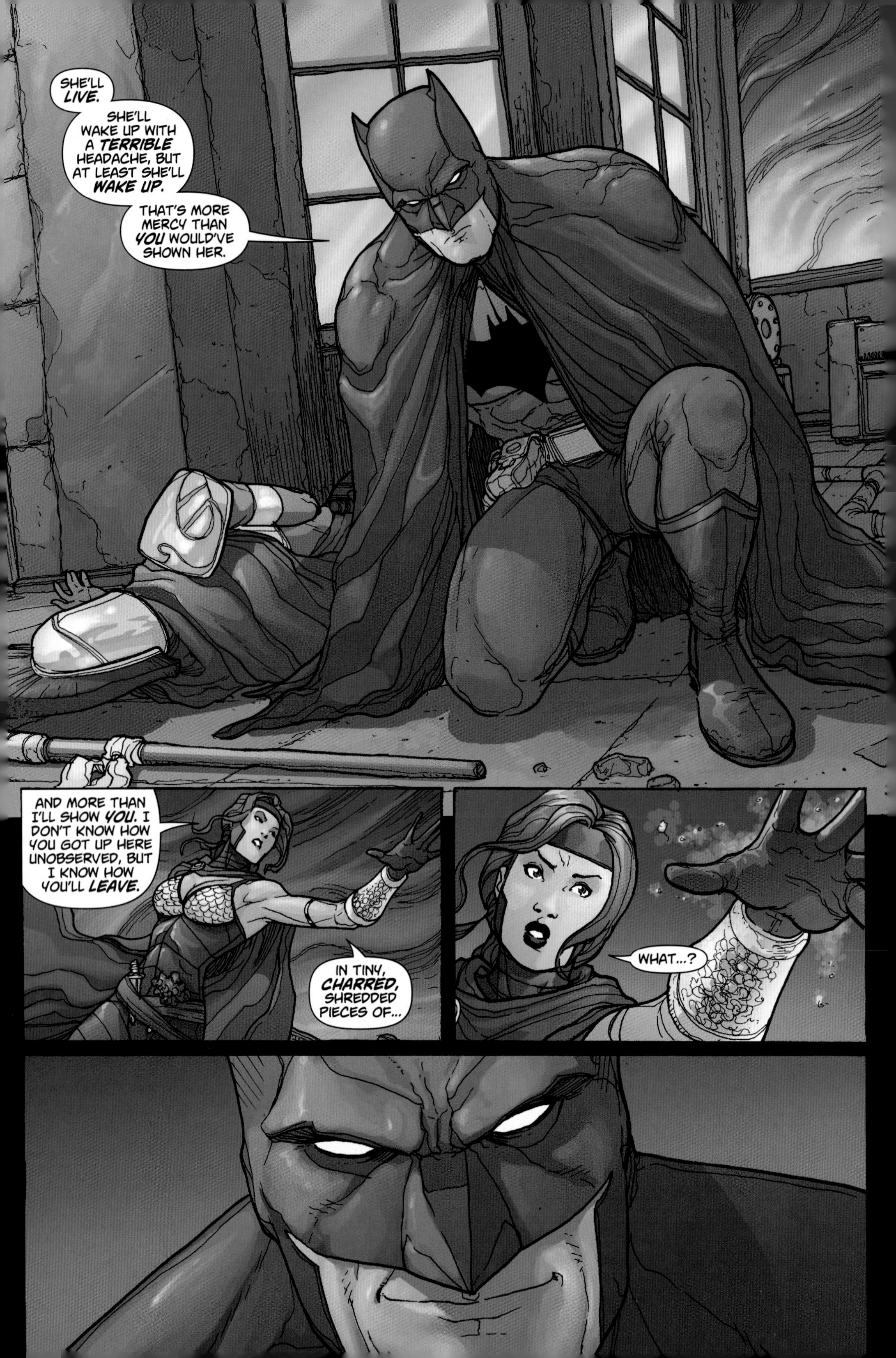
SHE'LL LIVE.
SHE'LL WAKE UP WITH A TERRIBLE HEADACHE, BUT AT LEAST SHE'LL WAKE UP.
THAT'S MORE MERCY THAN YOU WOULD'VE SHOWN HER.
AND MORE THAN I'LL SHOW YOU. I DON'T KNOW HOW YOU GOT UP HERE UNOBSERVED, BUT I KNOW HOW YOU'LL LEAVE.
IN TINY, CHARRED, SHREDDED PIECES OF...
WHAT...?

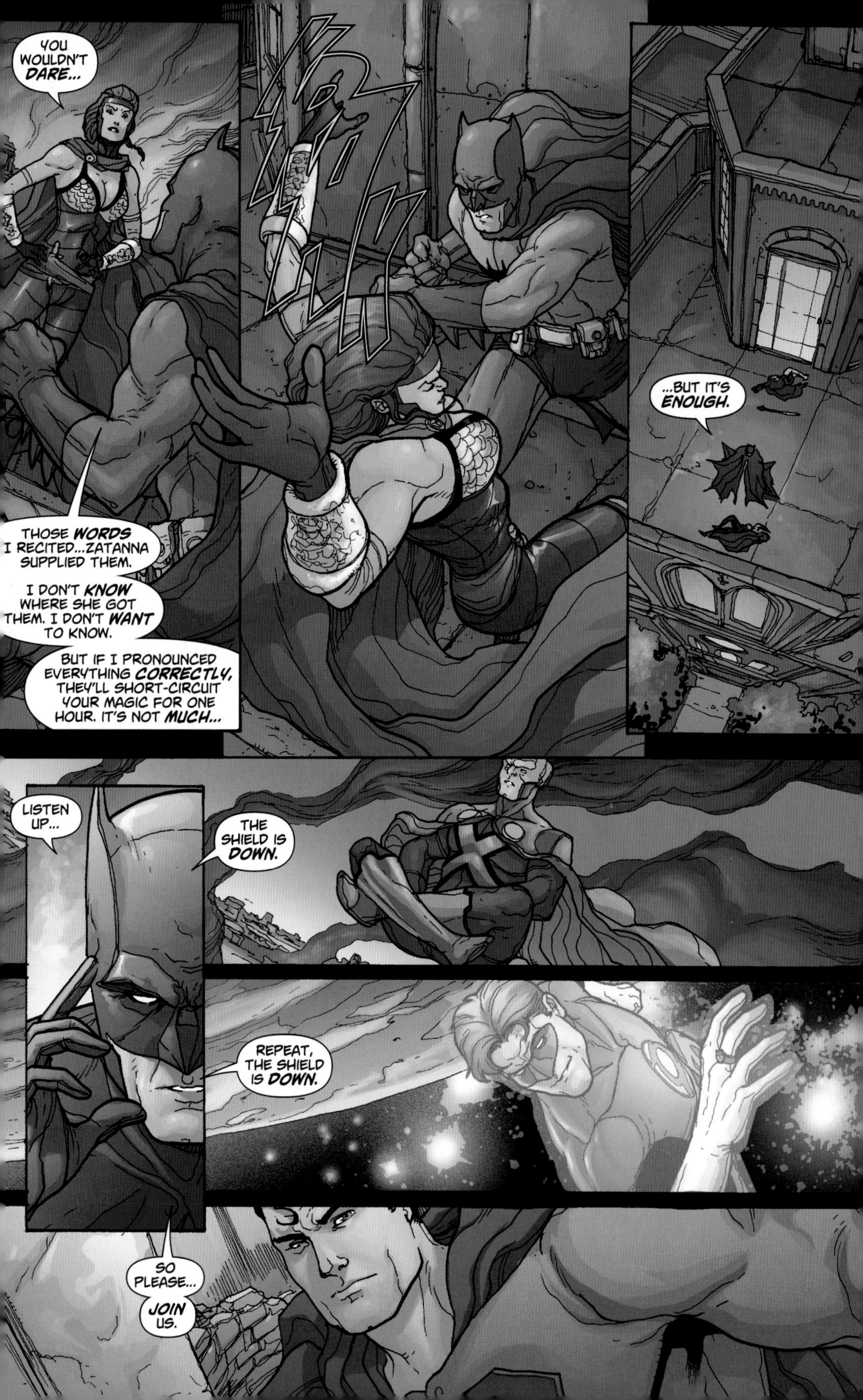

YOU WOULDN'T DARE...
THOSE WORDS I RECITED...ZATANNA SUPPLIED THEM.
I DON'T KNOW WHERE SHE GOT THEM. I DON'T WANT TO KNOW.
BUT IF I PRONOUNCED EVERYTHING CORRECTLY, THEY'LL SHORT-CIRCUIT YOUR MAGIC FOR ONE HOUR. IT'S NOT MUCH...
...BUT IT'S ENOUGH.
LISTEN UP...
THE SHIELD IS DOWN.
REPEAT, THE SHIELD IS DOWN.
SO PLEASE...
JOIN US.

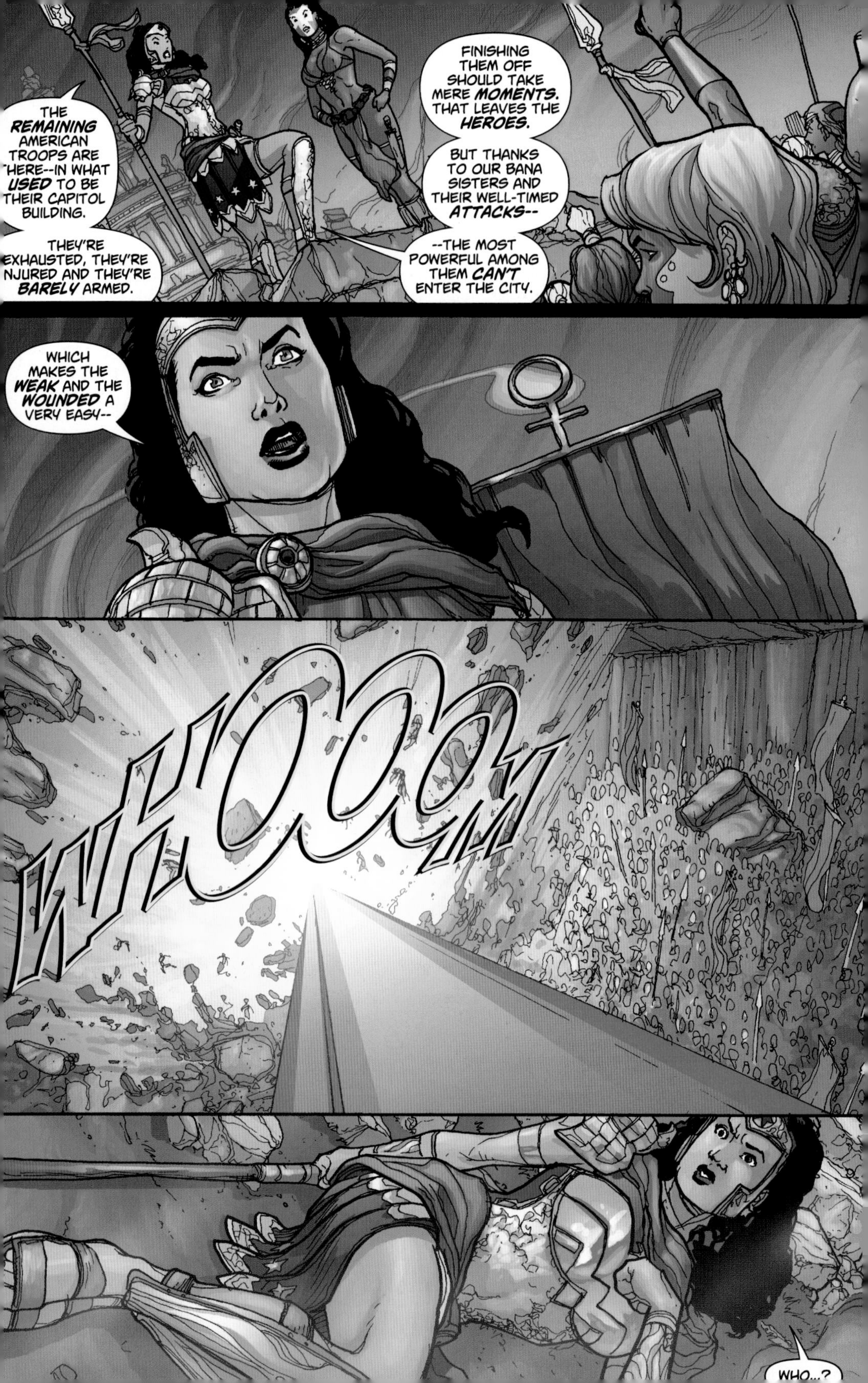
THE REMAINING AMERICAN TROOPS ARE HERE--IN WHAT USED TO BE THEIR CAPITOL BUILDING.
THEY'RE EXHAUSTED, THEY'RE INJURED AND THEY'RE BARELY ARMED.
FINISHING THEM OFF SHOULD TAKE MERE MOMENTS. THAT LEAVES THE HEROES.
BUT THANKS TO OUR BANA SISTERS AND THEIR WELL-TIMED ATTACKS--
--THE MOST POWERFUL AMONG THEM CAN'T ENTER THE CITY.
WHICH MAKES THE WEAK AND THE WOUNDED A VERY EASY--
WHOOOM
WHO...?

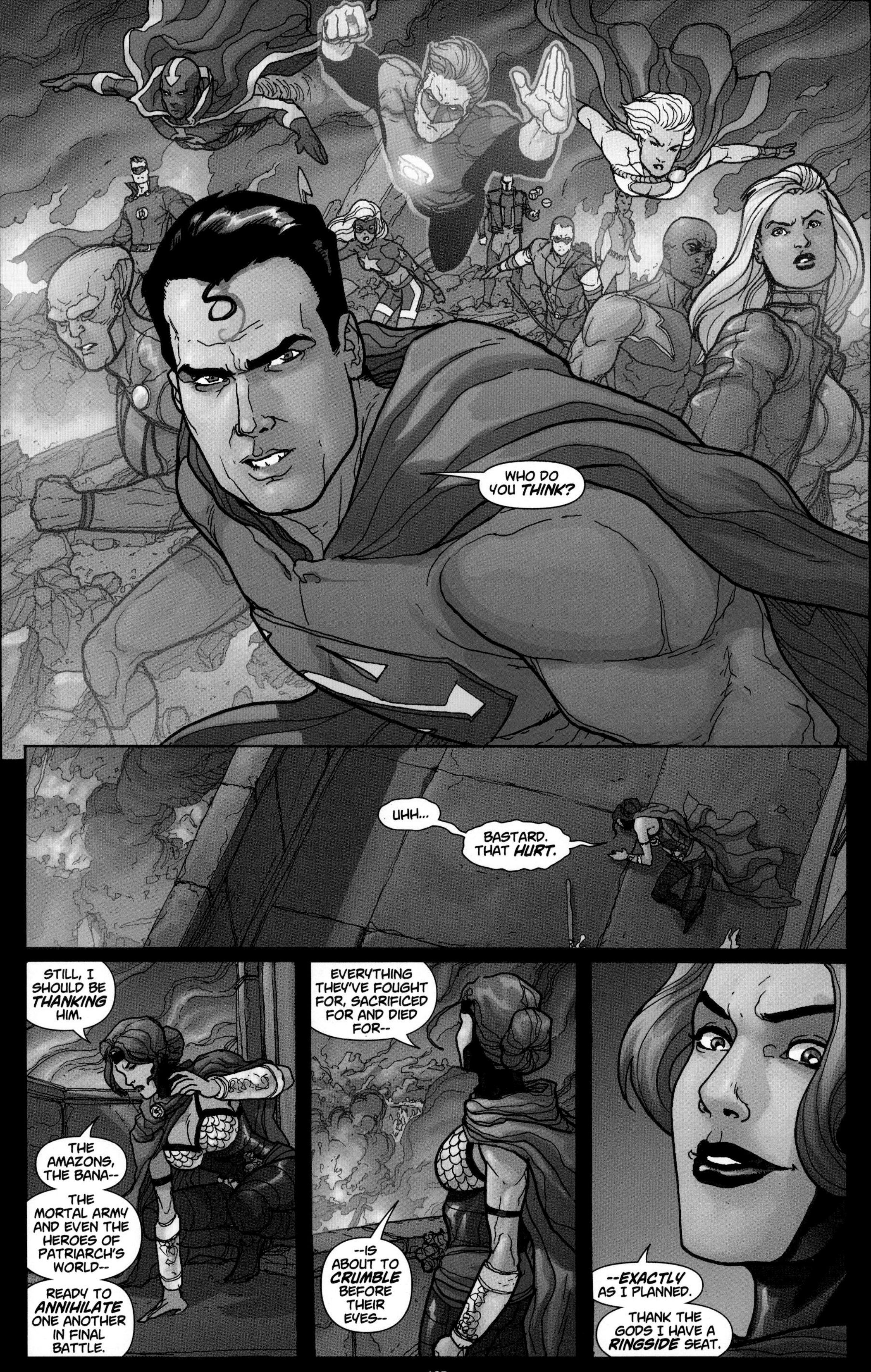
WHO DO YOU THINK?
UHH...
BASTARD. THAT HURT.
STILL, I SHOULD BE THANKING HIM.
THE AMAZONS, THE BANA--
THE MORTAL ARMY AND EVEN THE HEROES OF PATRIARCH'S WORLD--
READY TO ANNIHILATE ONE ANOTHER IN FINAL BATTLE.
EVERYTHING THEY'VE FOUGHT FOR, SACRIFICED FOR AND DIED FOR--
--IS ABOUT TO CRUMBLE BEFORE THEIR EYES--
--EXACTLY AS I PLANNED.
THANK THE GODS I HAVE A RINGSIDE SEAT.

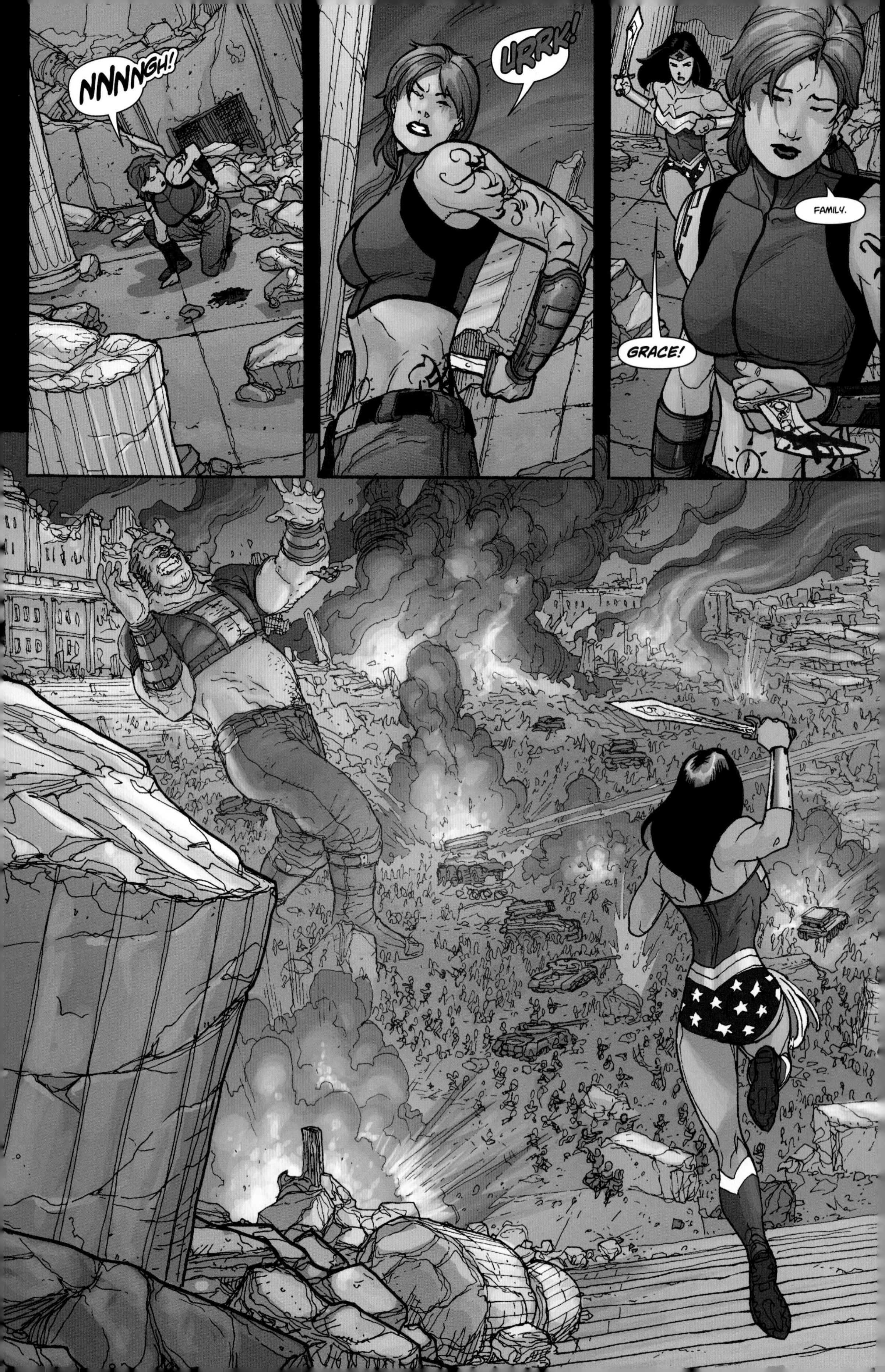
NNNNGH!
URRK!
FAMILY.
GRACE!

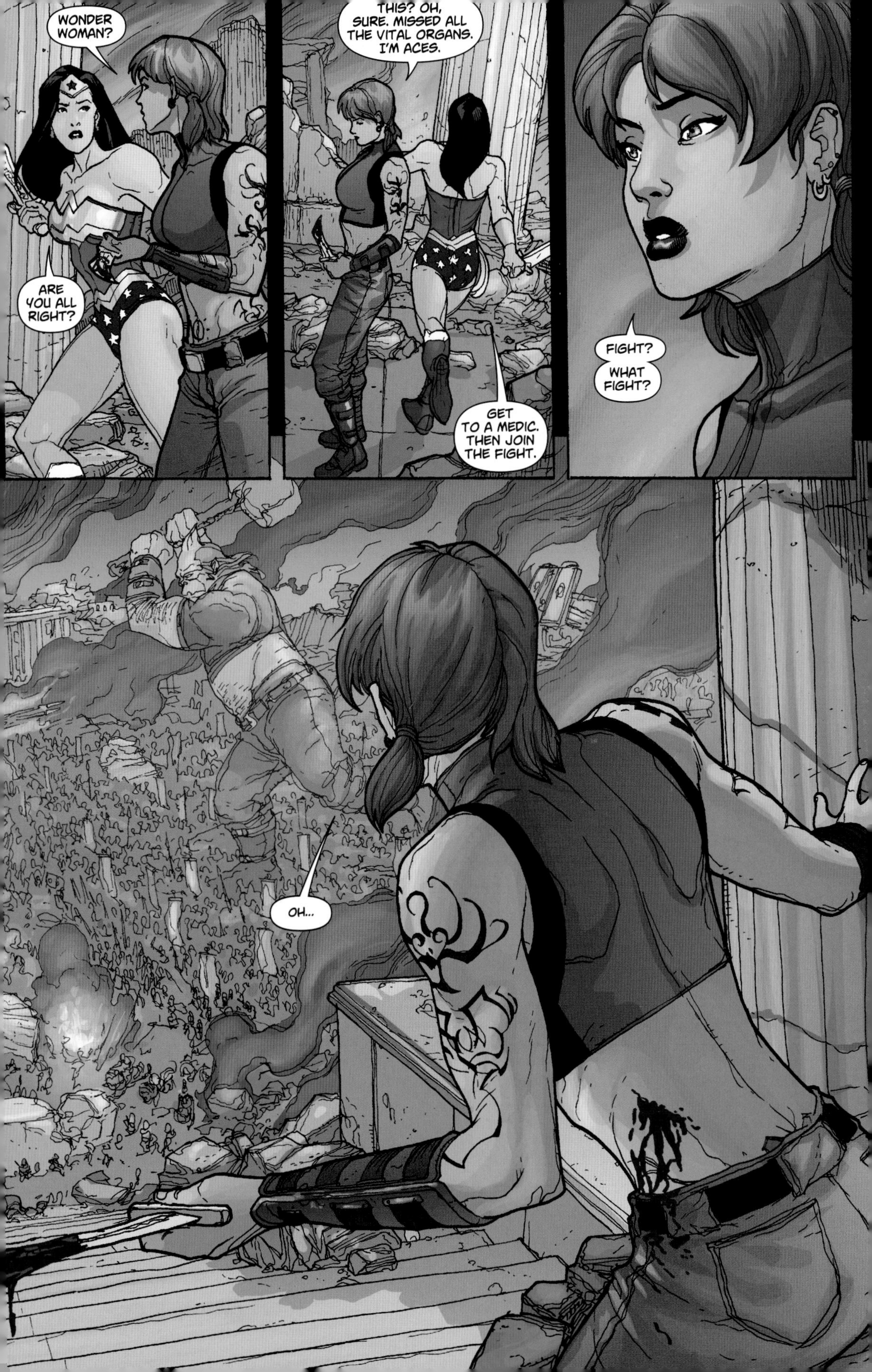
WONDER WOMAN?
ARE YOU ALL RIGHT?
THIS? OH, SURE. MISSED ALL THE VITAL ORGANS. I'M ACES.
GET TO A MEDIC. THEN JOIN THE FIGHT.
FIGHT?
WHAT FIGHT?
OH...

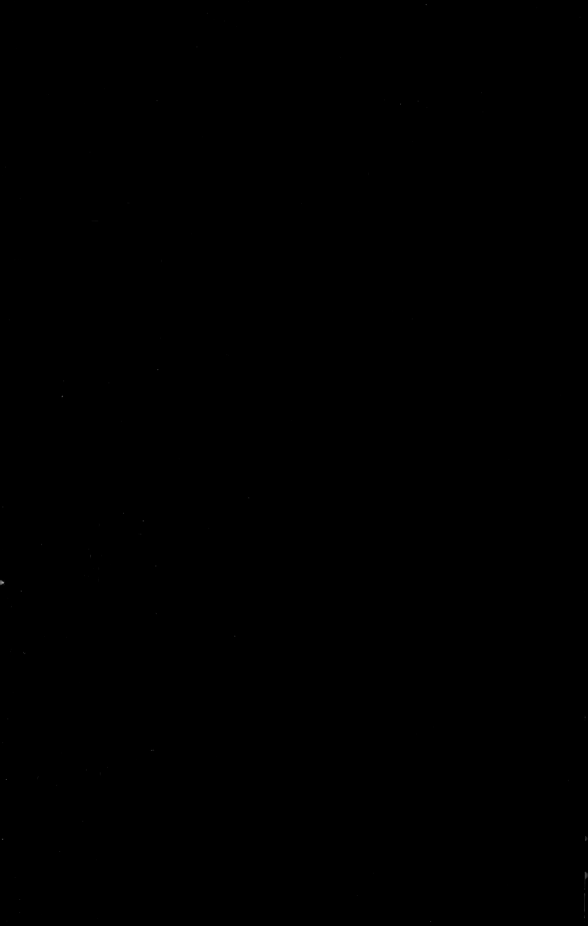

Chapter Six

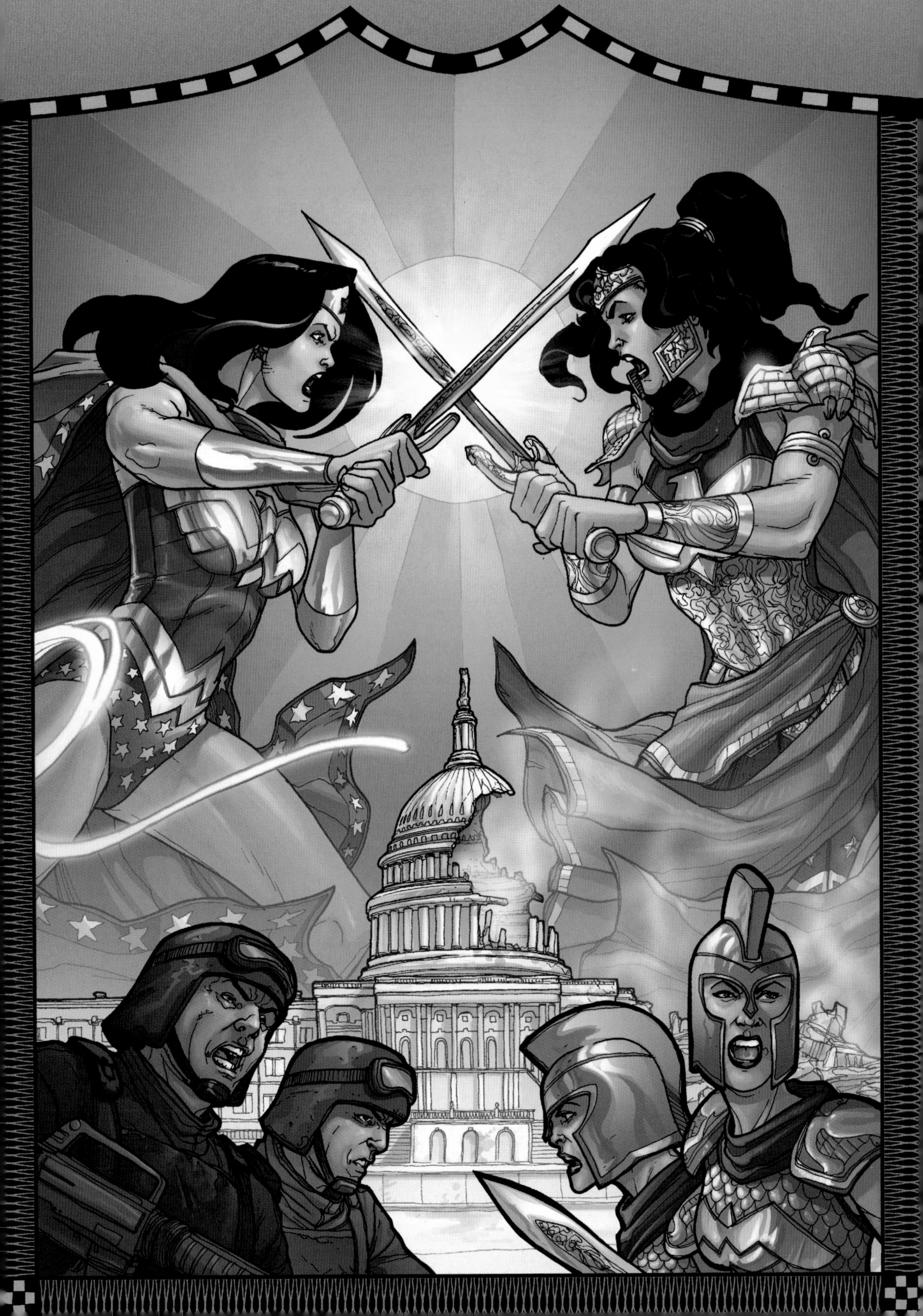

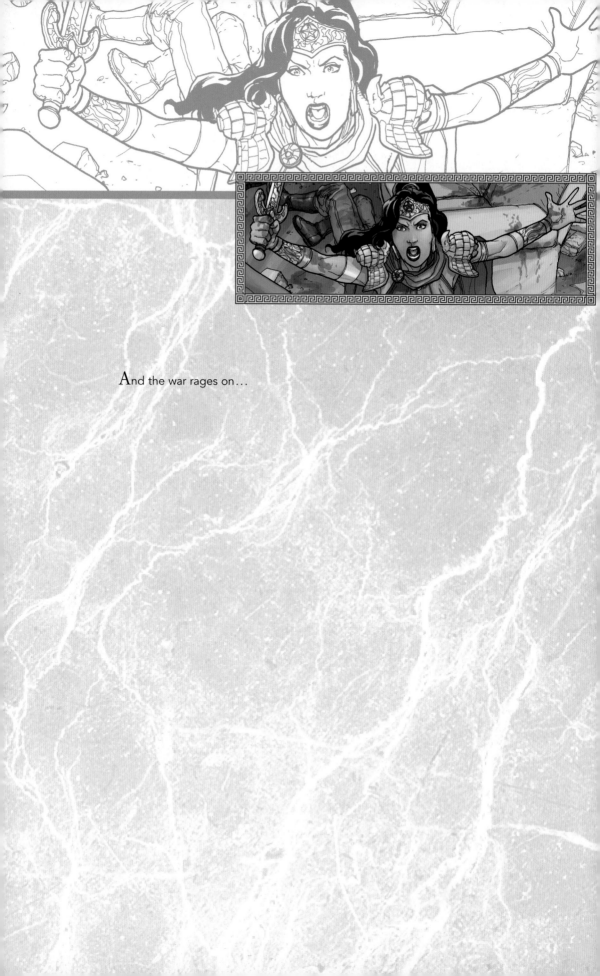

And the war rages on...

CHAPTER 6:

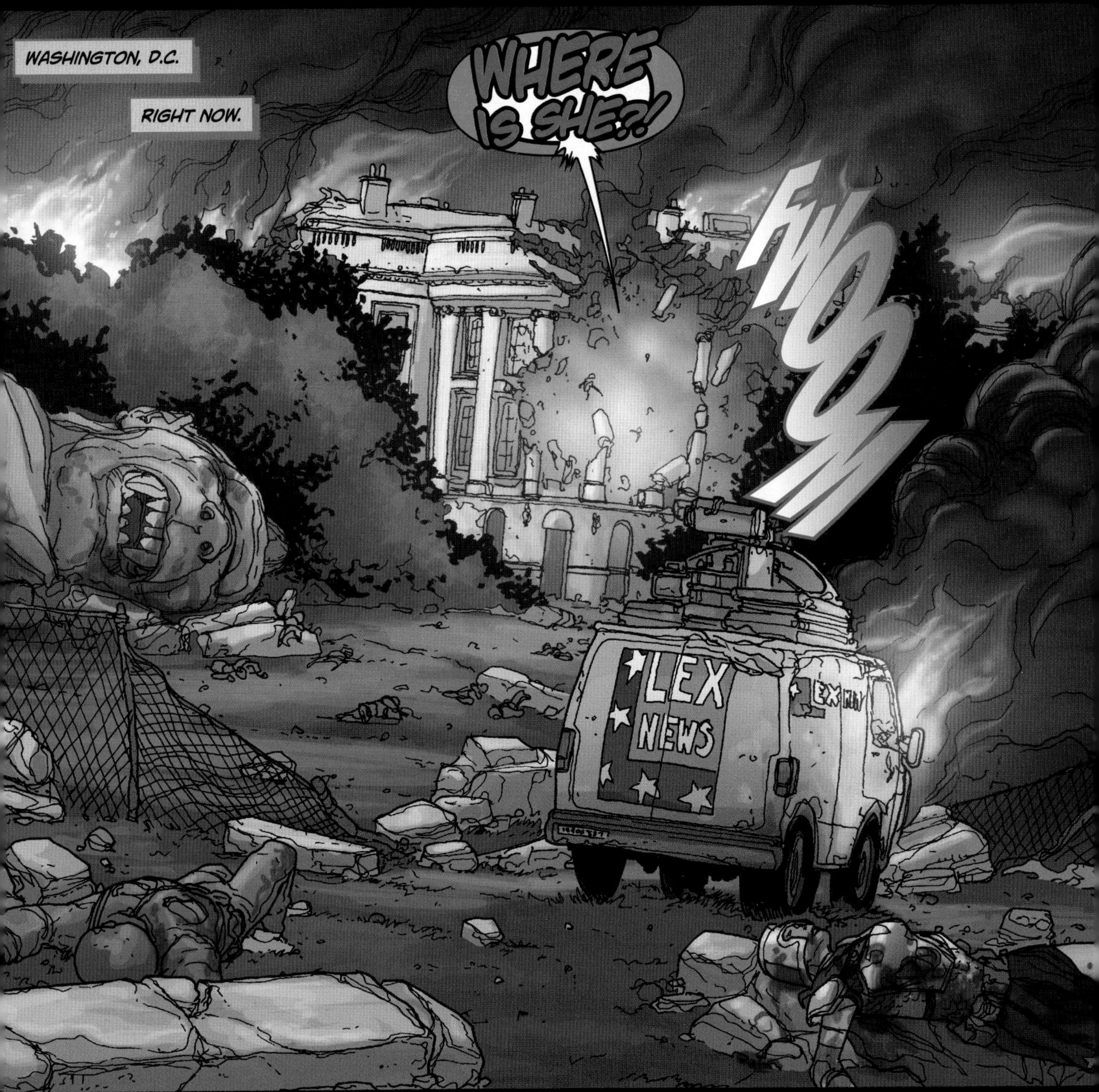

WASHINGTON, D.C.
RIGHT NOW.
WHERE IS SHE?!
FWOOM
LEX NEWS

PYRRHIC VICTORY

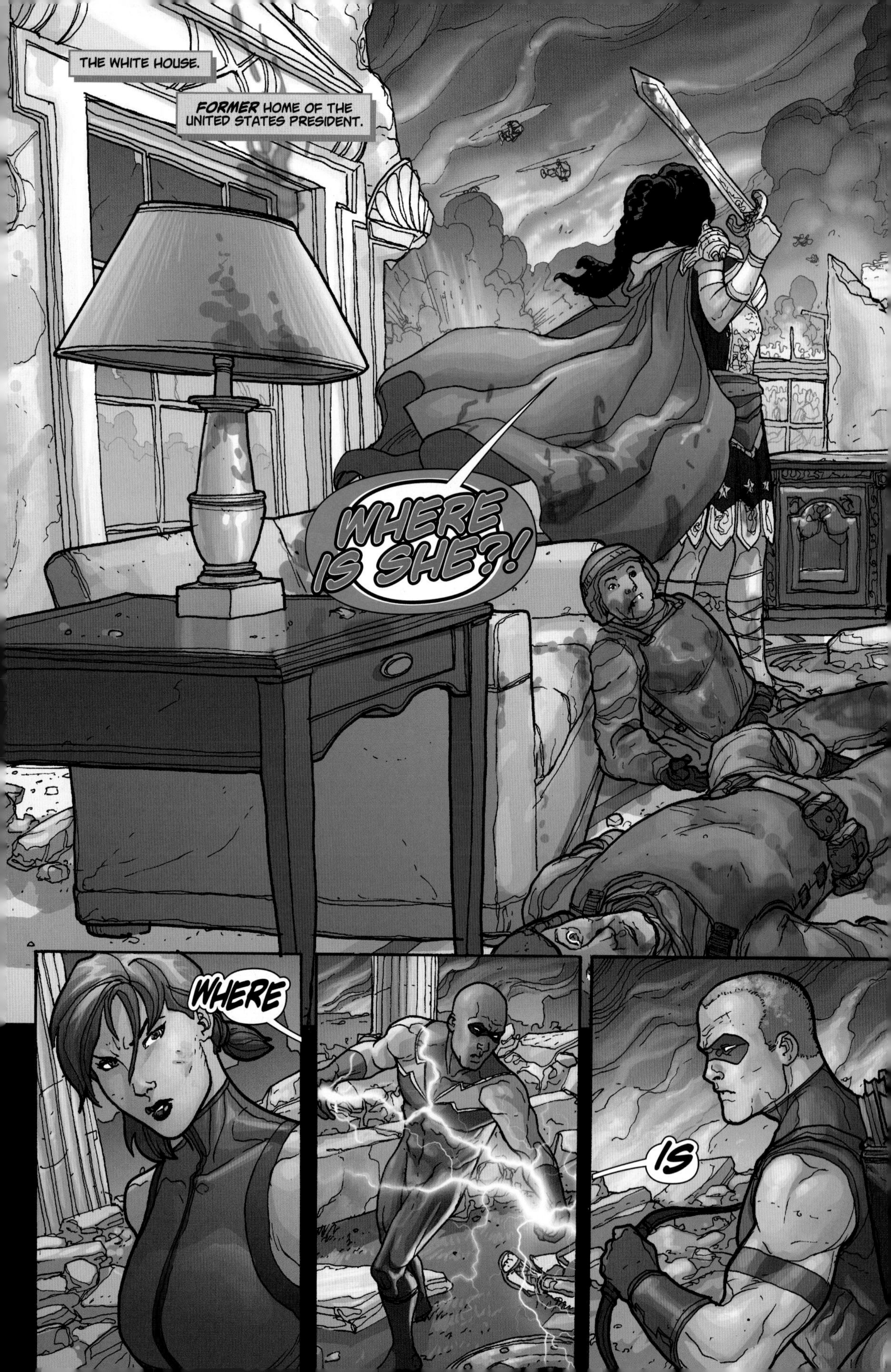
THE WHITE HOUSE.
FORMER HOME OF THE UNITED STATES PRESIDENT.
WHERE IS SHE?!
WHERE
IS

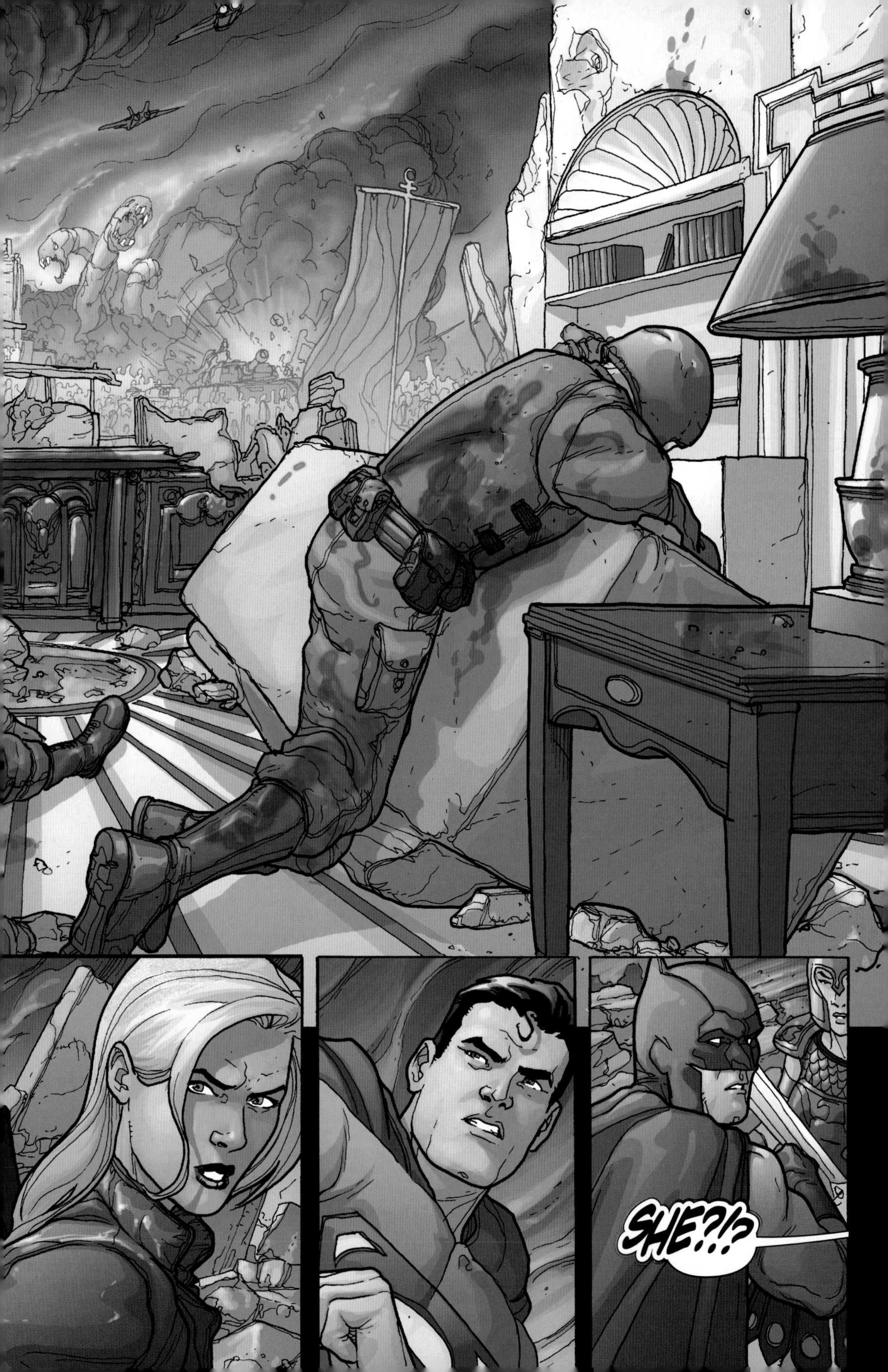
SHE?!?

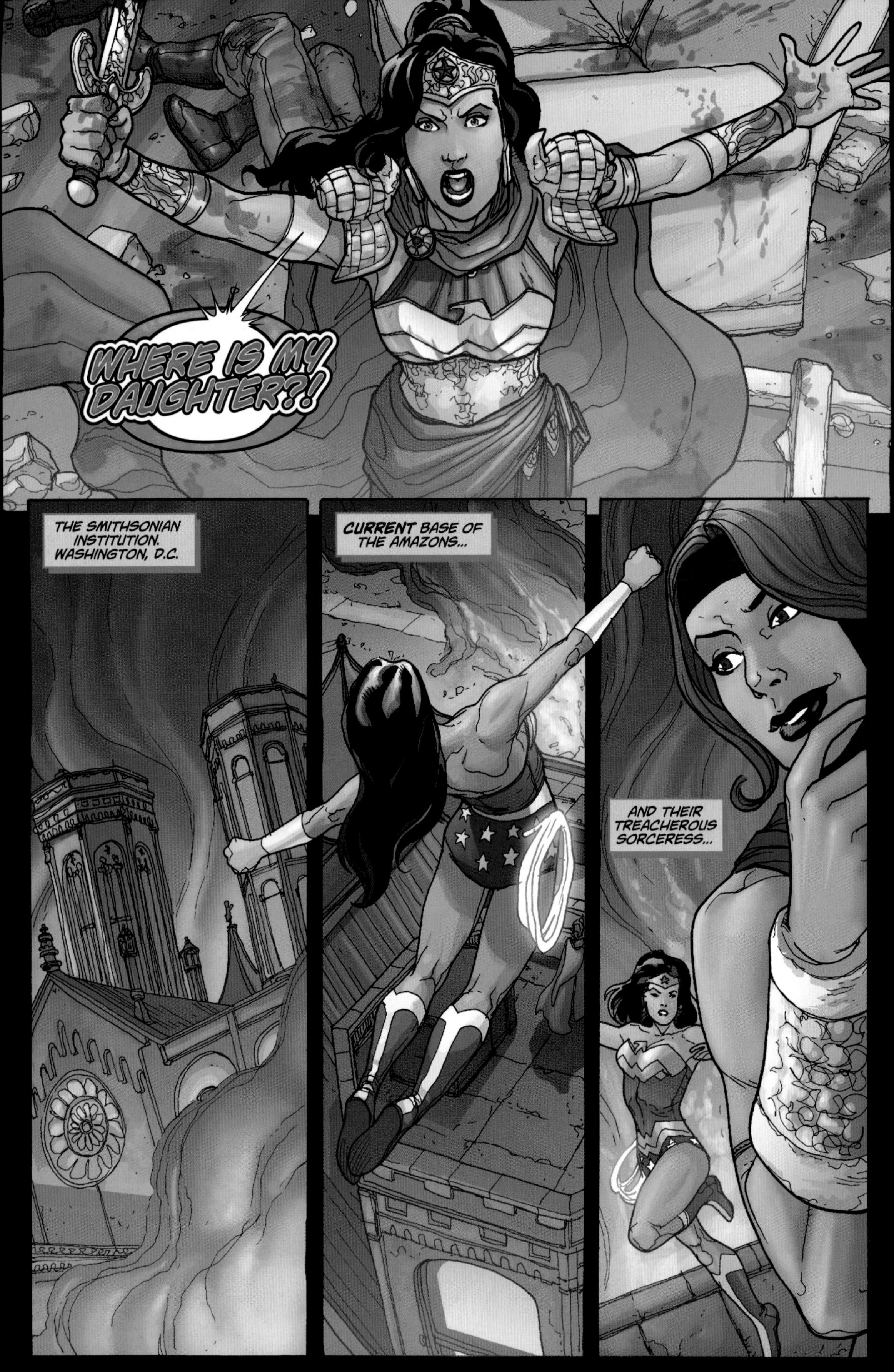
WHERE IS MY DAUGHTER?!
THE SMITHSONIAN INSTITUTION. WASHINGTON, D.C.
CURRENT BASE OF THE AMAZONS...
AND THEIR TREACHEROUS SORCERESS...

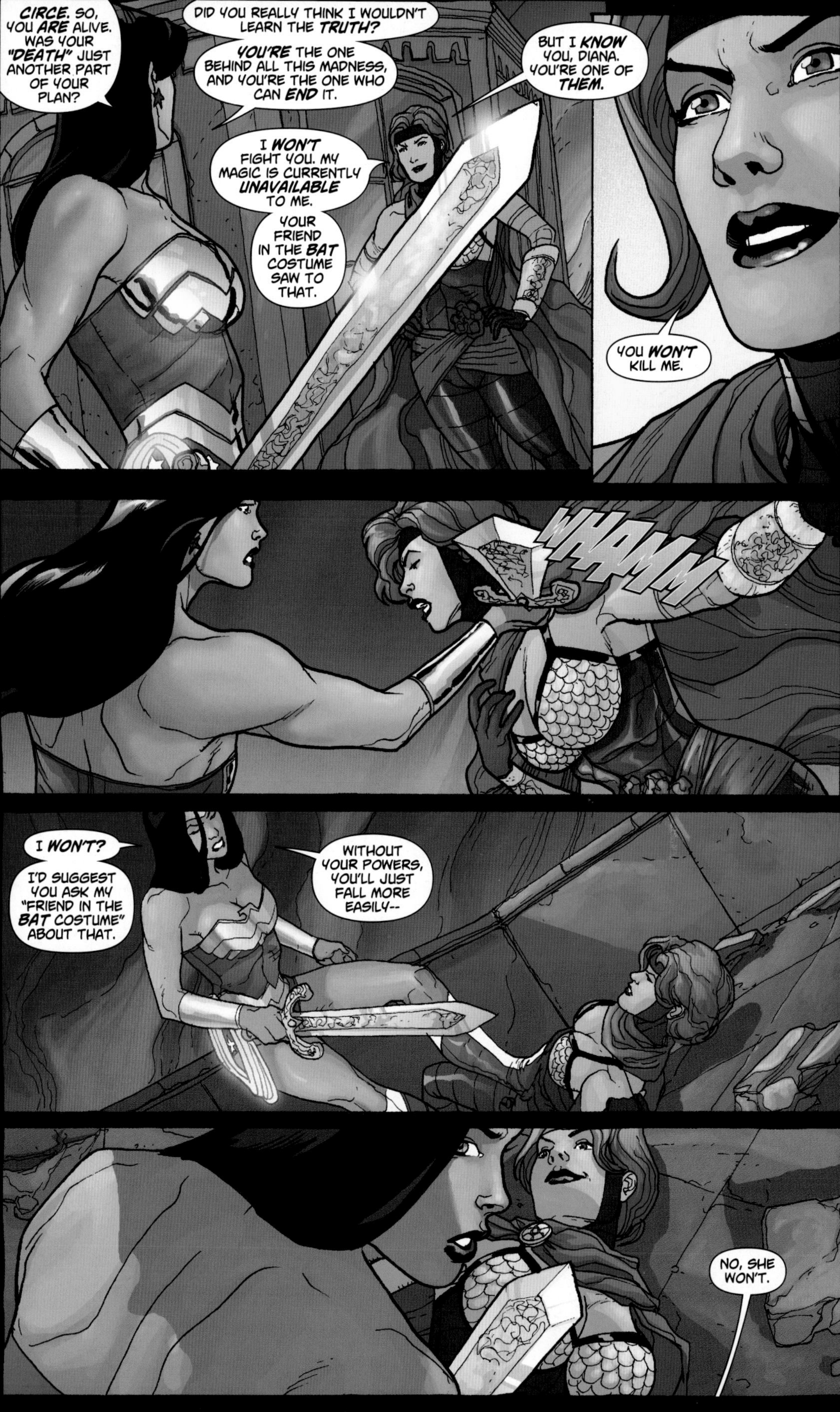
CIRCE. SO, YOU ARE ALIVE. WAS YOUR "DEATH" JUST ANOTHER PART OF YOUR PLAN?
DID YOU REALLY THINK I WOULDN'T LEARN THE TRUTH?
YOU'RE THE ONE BEHIND ALL THIS MADNESS, AND YOU'RE THE ONE WHO CAN END IT.
I WON'T FIGHT YOU. MY MAGIC IS CURRENTLY UNAVAILABLE TO ME.
YOUR FRIEND IN THE BAT COSTUME SAW TO THAT.
BUT I KNOW YOU, DIANA. YOU'RE ONE OF THEM.
YOU WON'T KILL ME.
WHAMM
I WON'T?
I'D SUGGEST YOU ASK MY "FRIEND IN THE BAT COSTUME" ABOUT THAT.
WITHOUT YOUR POWERS, YOU'LL JUST FALL MORE EASILY--
NO, SHE WON'T.

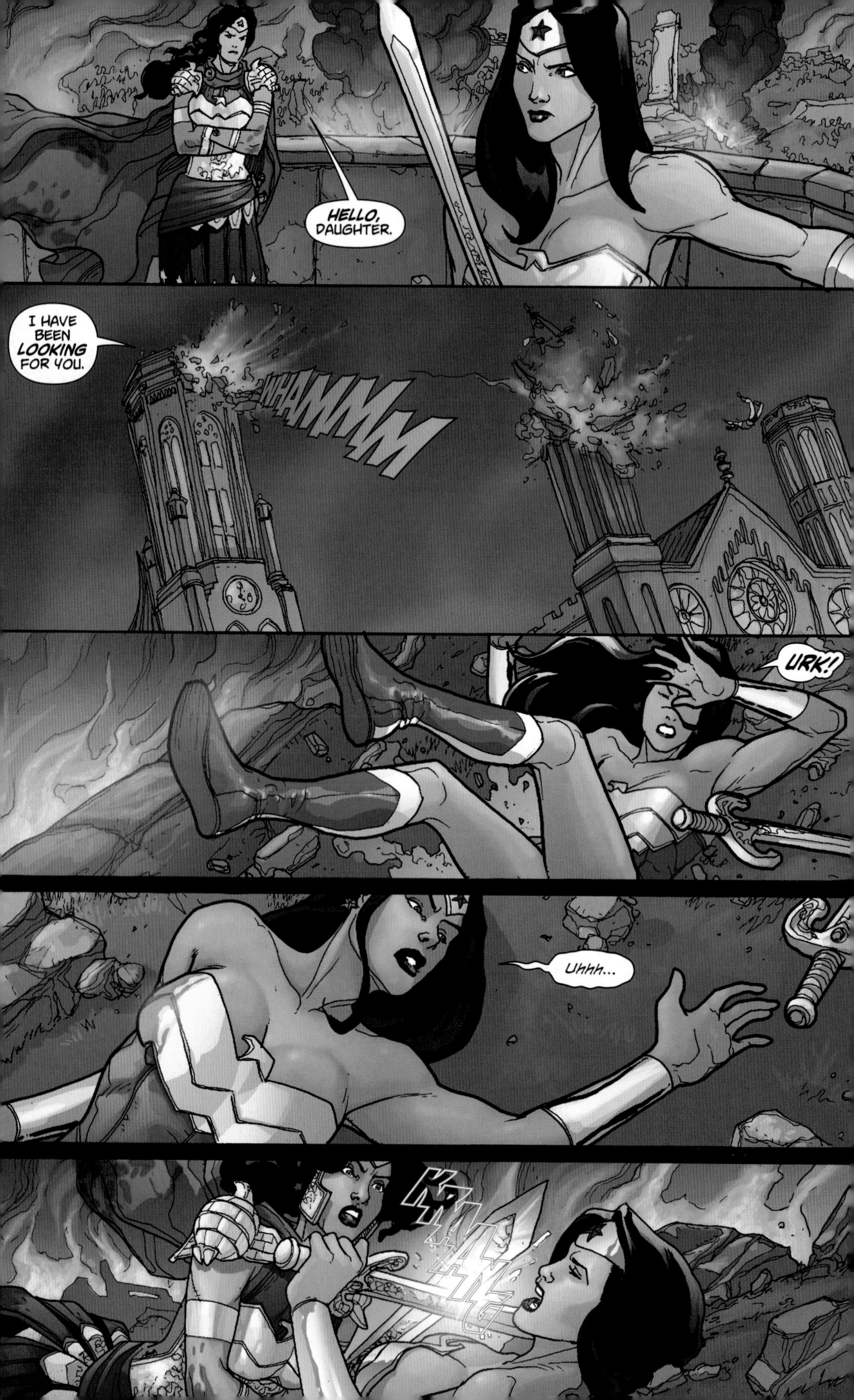
HELLO, DAUGHTER.
I HAVE BEEN LOOKING FOR YOU.
WHAMMM
URK!
Uhhh...

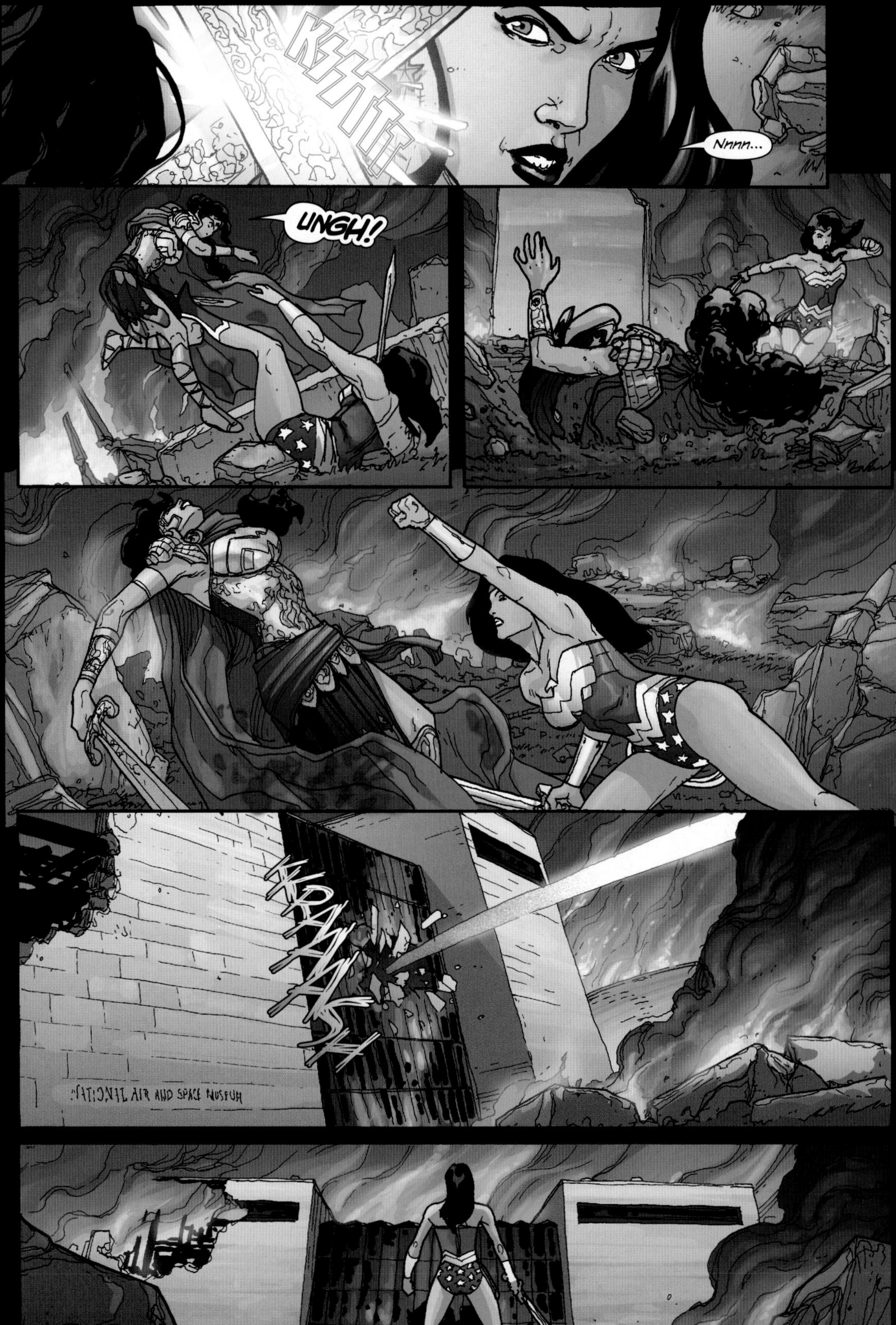
KSSSHH!
Nnnn...
UNGH!
KKRAAASSSH
NATIONAL AIR AND SPACE MUSEUM

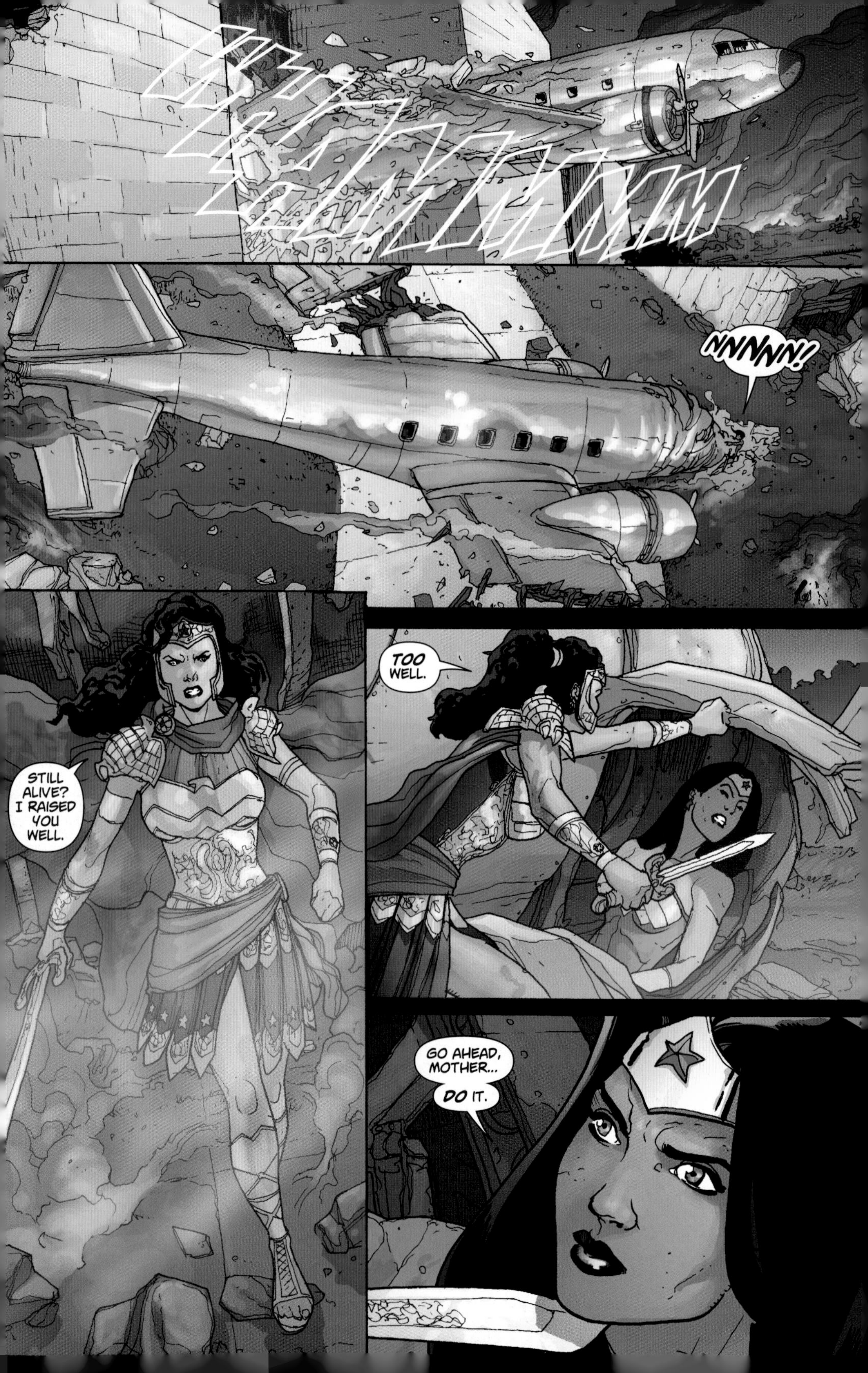

CRUNNNNNNCH
NNNNN!
STILL ALIVE? I RAISED YOU WELL.
TOO WELL.
GO AHEAD, MOTHER...
DO IT.

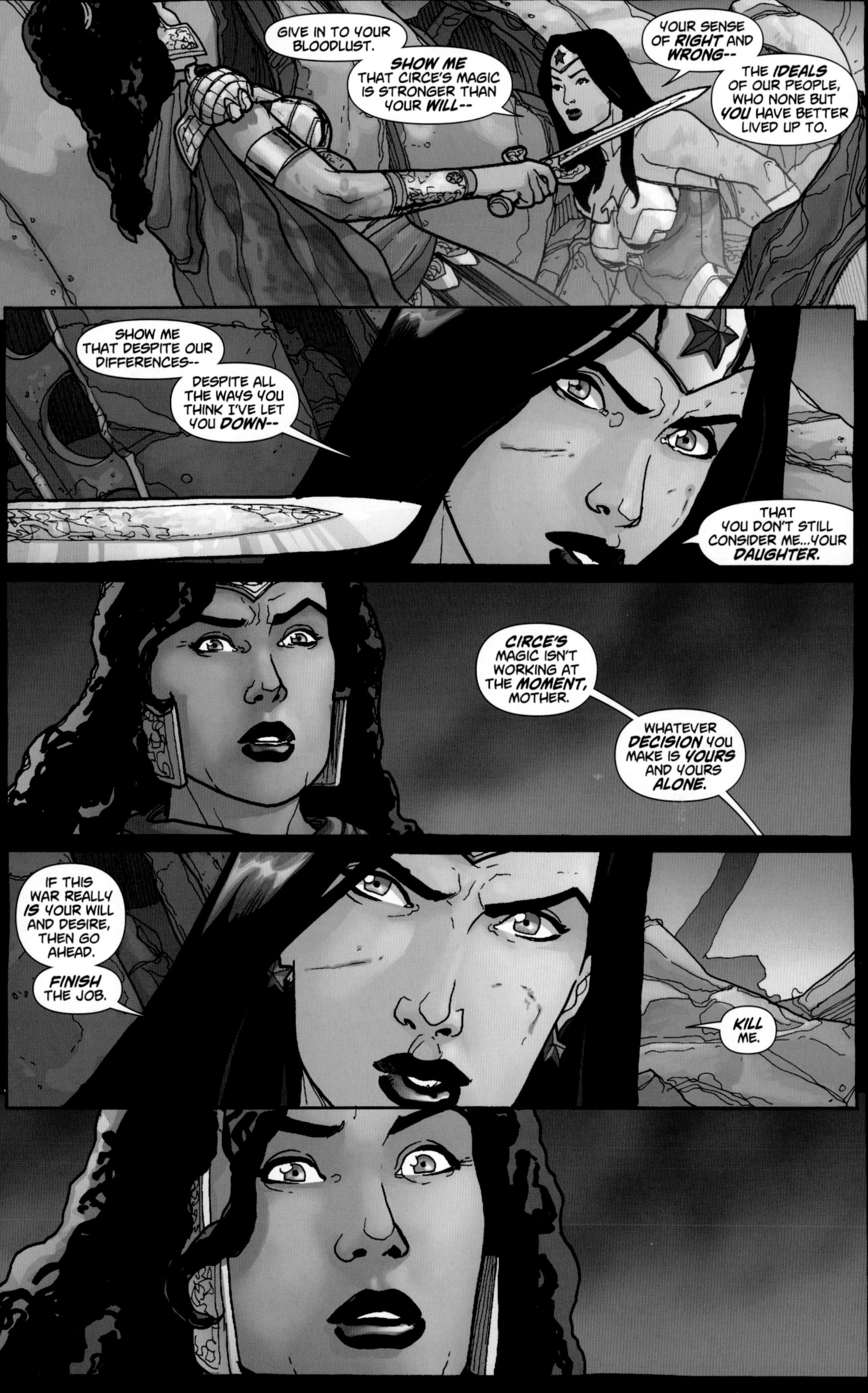
GIVE IN TO YOUR BLOODLUST.
SHOW ME THAT CIRCE'S MAGIC IS STRONGER THAN YOUR WILL--
YOUR SENSE OF RIGHT AND WRONG--
THE IDEALS OF OUR PEOPLE, WHO NONE BUT YOU HAVE BETTER LIVED UP TO.
SHOW ME THAT DESPITE OUR DIFFERENCES--
DESPITE ALL THE WAYS YOU THINK I'VE LET YOU DOWN--
THAT YOU DON'T STILL CONSIDER ME...YOUR DAUGHTER.
CIRCE'S MAGIC ISN'T WORKING AT THE MOMENT, MOTHER.
WHATEVER DECISION YOU MAKE IS YOURS AND YOURS ALONE.
IF THIS WAR REALLY IS YOUR WILL AND DESIRE, THEN GO AHEAD.
FINISH THE JOB.
KILL ME.

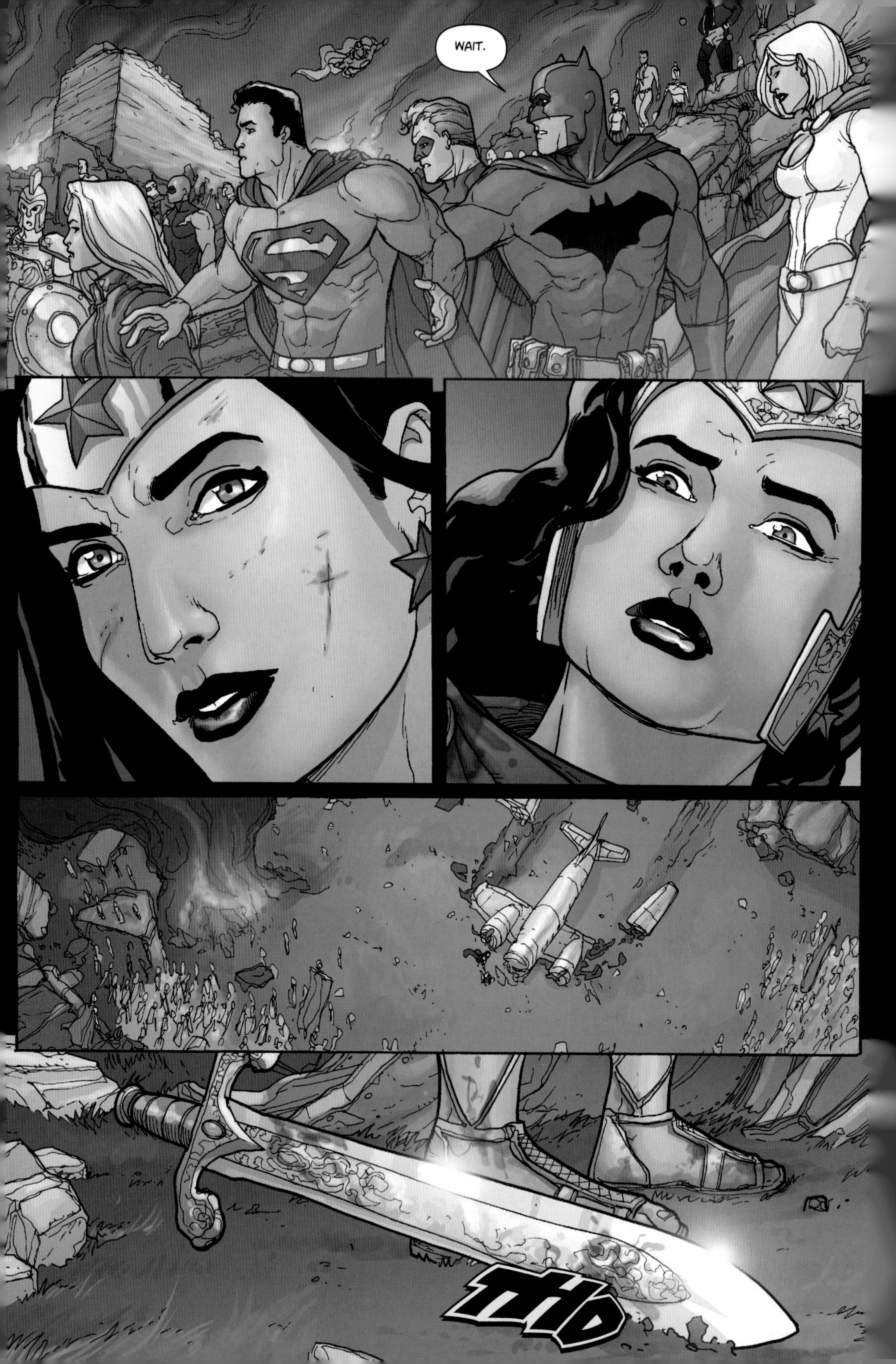
WAIT.
THD

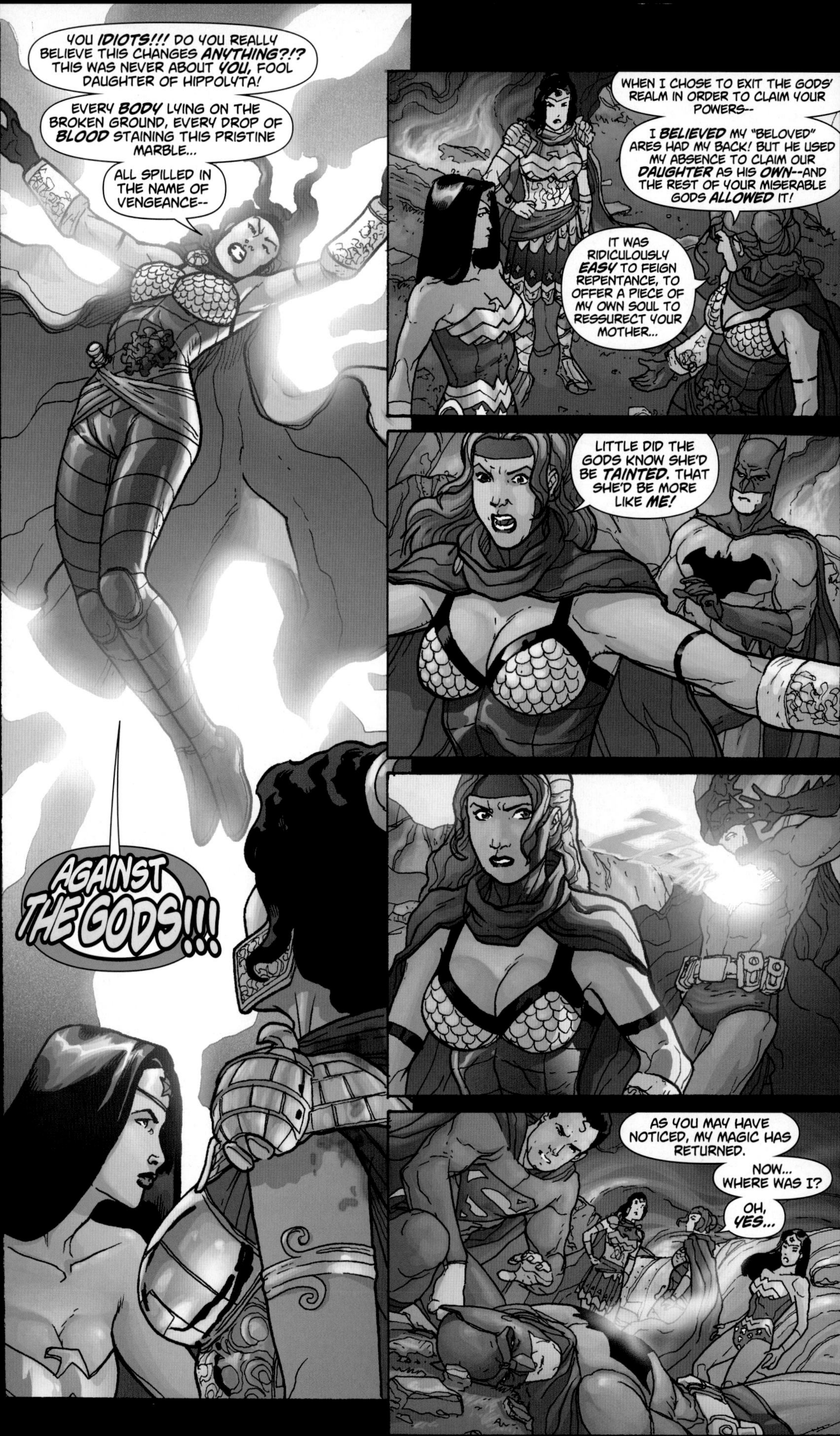
YOU IDIOTS!!! DO YOU REALLY BELIEVE THIS CHANGES ANYTHING?!? THIS WAS NEVER ABOUT YOU, FOOL DAUGHTER OF HIPPOLYTA!
EVERY BODY LYING ON THE BROKEN GROUND, EVERY DROP OF BLOOD STAINING THIS PRISTINE MARBLE...
ALL SPILLED IN THE NAME OF VENGEANCE--
AGAINST THE GODS!!!
WHEN I CHOSE TO EXIT THE GODS' REALM IN ORDER TO CLAIM YOUR POWERS--
I BELIEVED MY "BELOVED" ARES HAD MY BACK! BUT HE USED MY ABSENCE TO CLAIM OUR DAUGHTER AS HIS OWN--AND THE REST OF YOUR MISERABLE GODS ALLOWED IT!
IT WAS RIDICULOUSLY EASY TO FEIGN REPENTANCE, TO OFFER A PIECE OF MY OWN SOUL TO RESSURECT YOUR MOTHER...
LITTLE DID THE GODS KNOW SHE'D BE TAINTED. THAT SHE'D BE MORE LIKE ME!
AS YOU MAY HAVE NOTICED, MY MAGIC HAS RETURNED.
NOW... WHERE WAS I?
OH, YES...

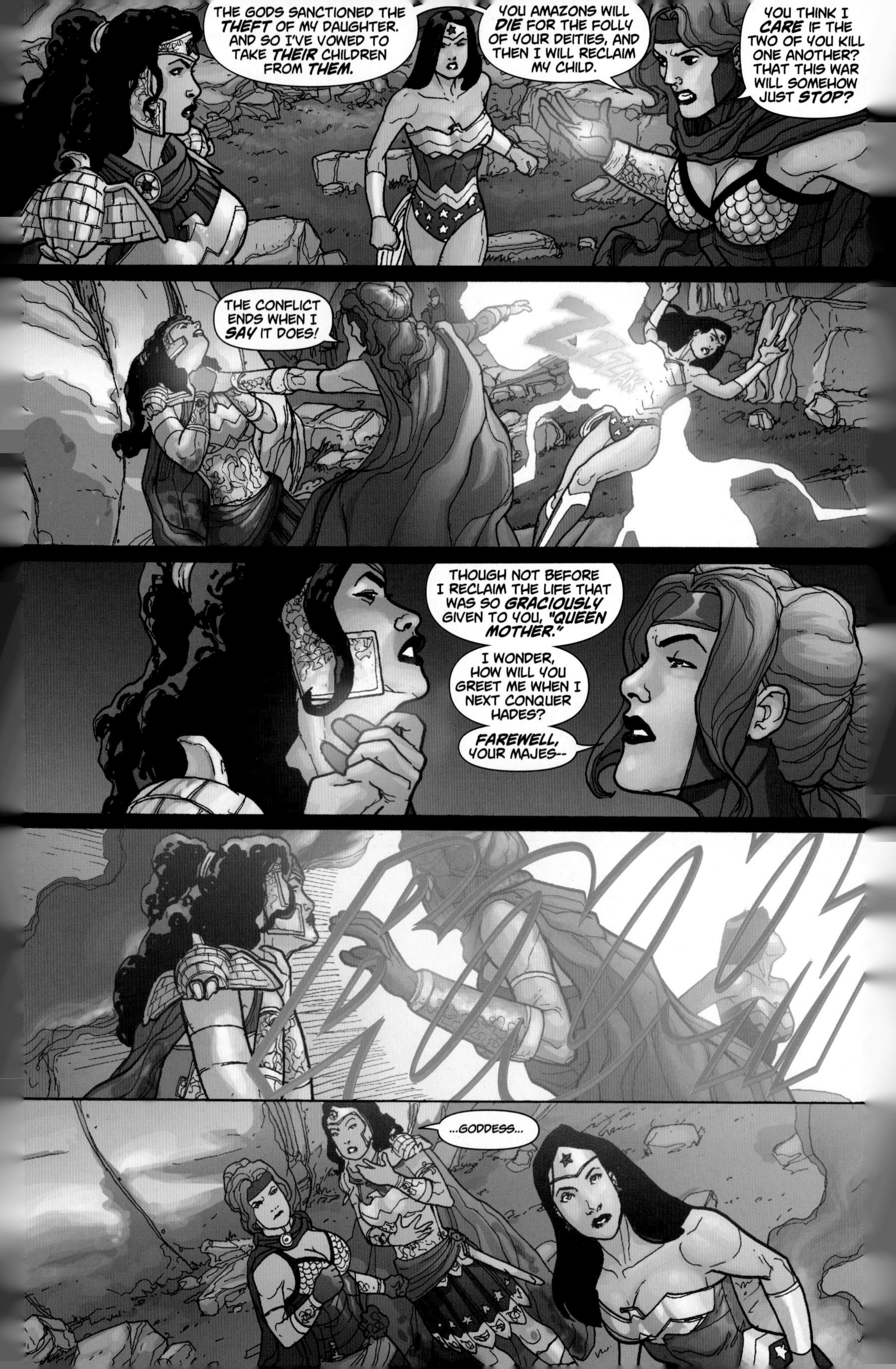
THE GODS SANCTIONED THE THEFT OF MY DAUGHTER. AND SO I'VE VOWED TO TAKE THEIR CHILDREN FROM THEM.
YOU AMAZONS WILL DIE FOR THE FOLLY OF YOUR DEITIES, AND THEN I WILL RECLAIM MY CHILD.
YOU THINK I CARE IF THE TWO OF YOU KILL ONE ANOTHER? THAT THIS WAR WILL SOMEHOW JUST STOP?
THE CONFLICT ENDS WHEN I SAY IT DOES!
THOUGH NOT BEFORE I RECLAIM THE LIFE THAT WAS SO GRACIOUSLY GIVEN TO YOU, "QUEEN MOTHER."
I WONDER, HOW WILL YOU GREET ME WHEN I NEXT CONQUER HADES?
FAREWELL, YOUR MAJES--
...GODDESS...

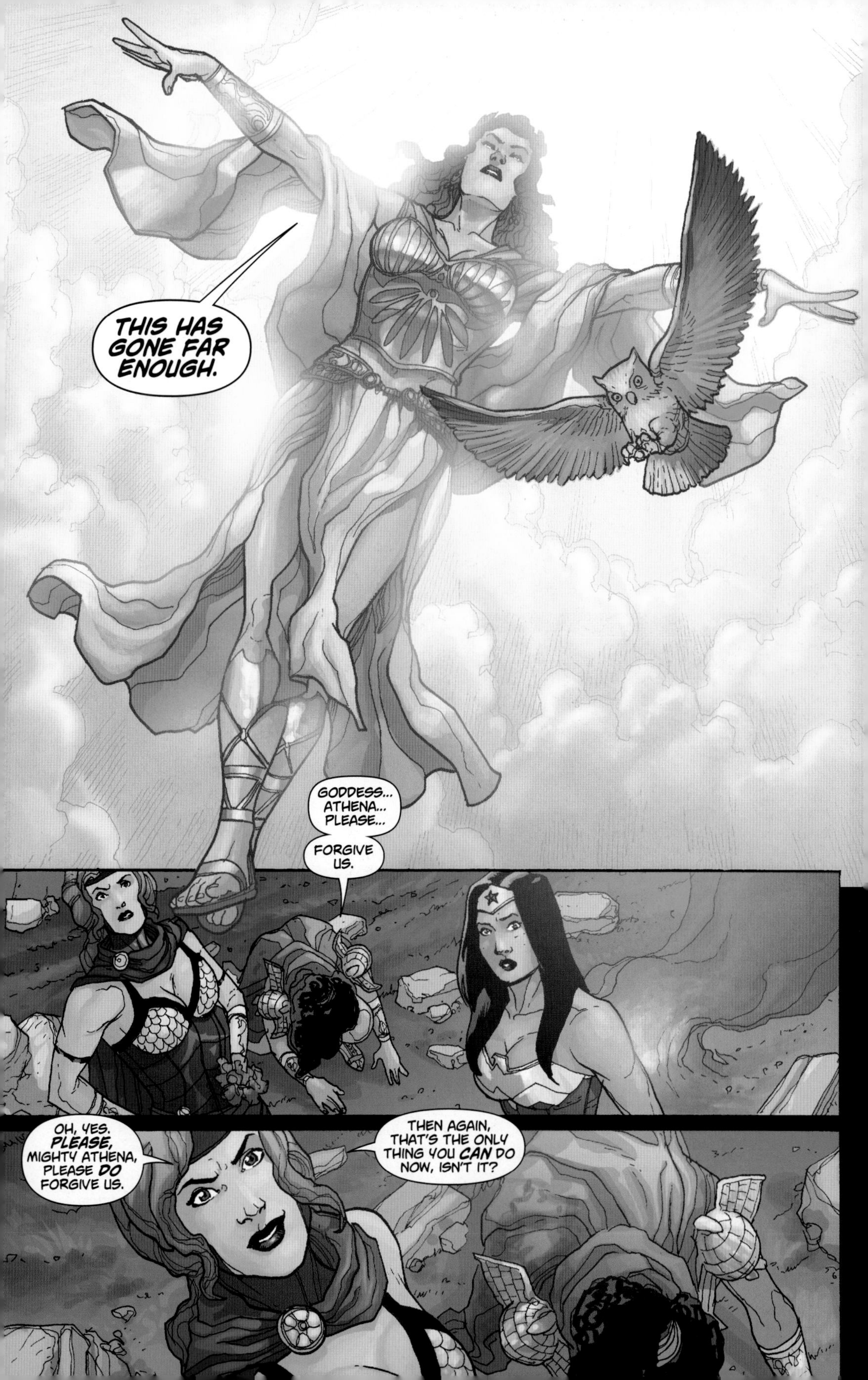
THIS HAS GONE FAR ENOUGH.
GODDESS... ATHENA... PLEASE...
FORGIVE US.
OH, YES. PLEASE, MIGHTY ATHENA, PLEASE DO FORGIVE US.
THEN AGAIN, THAT'S THE ONLY THING YOU CAN DO NOW, ISN'T IT?

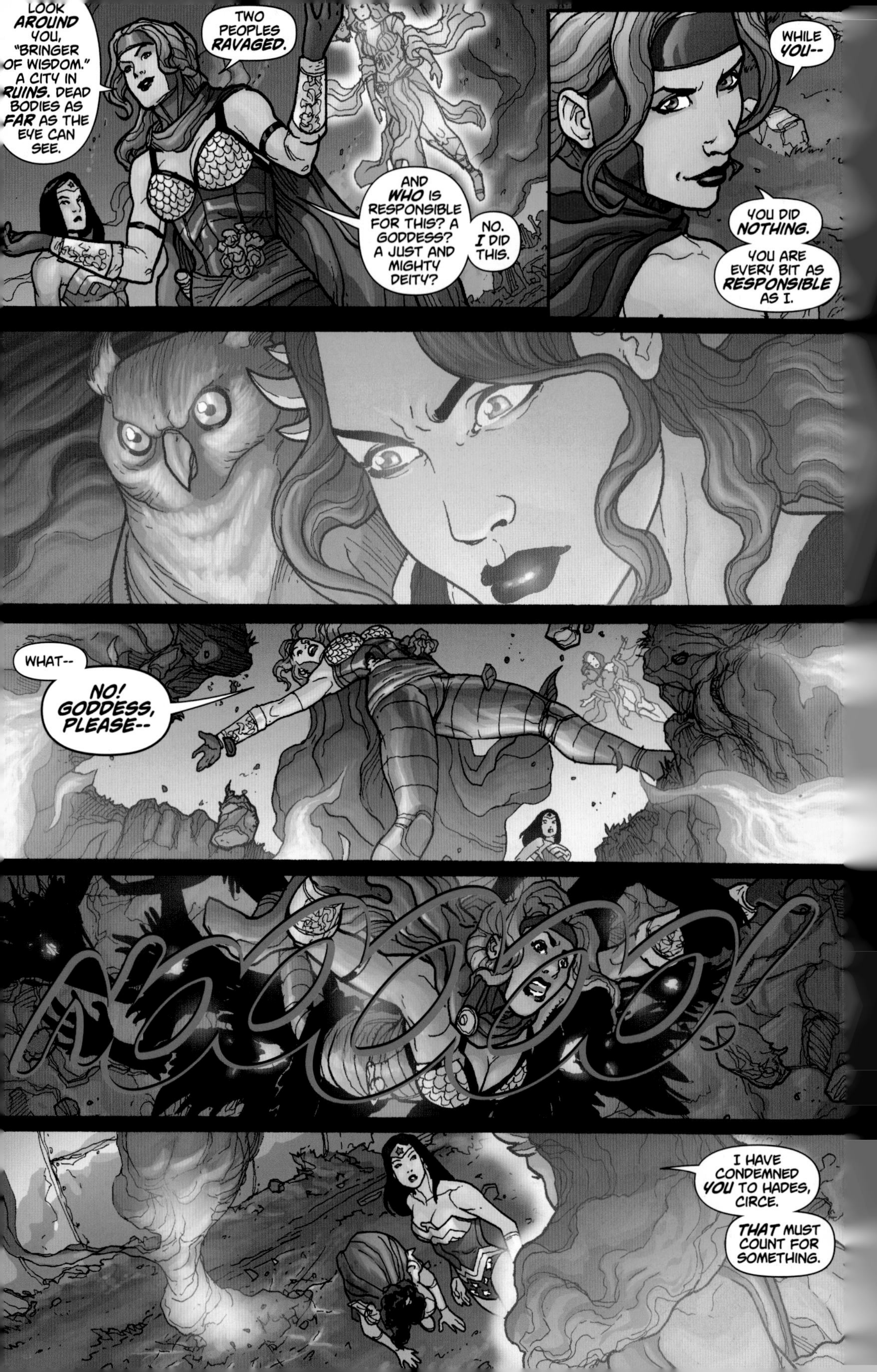
LOOK AROUND YOU, "BRINGER OF WISDOM." A CITY IN RUINS. DEAD BODIES AS FAR AS THE EYE CAN SEE.
TWO PEOPLES RAVAGED.
AND WHO IS RESPONSIBLE FOR THIS? A GODDESS? A JUST AND MIGHTY DEITY?
NO. I DID THIS.
WHILE YOU--
YOU DID NOTHING.
YOU ARE EVERY BIT AS RESPONSIBLE AS I.
WHAT--
NO! GODDESS, PLEASE--
I HAVE CONDEMNED YOU TO HADES, CIRCE.
THAT MUST COUNT FOR SOMETHING.

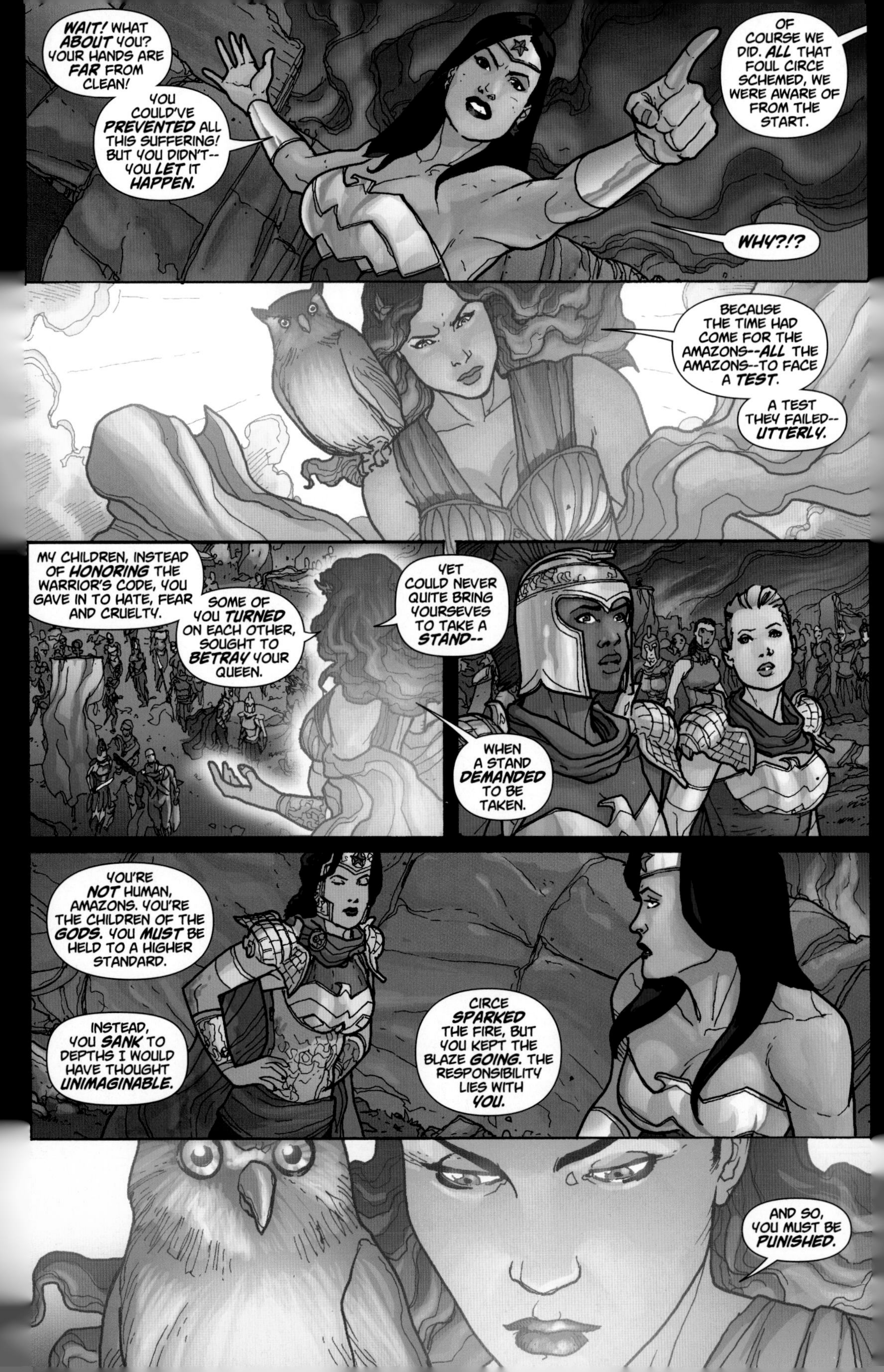
WAIT! WHAT ABOUT YOU? YOUR HANDS ARE FAR FROM CLEAN!
YOU COULD'VE PREVENTED ALL THIS SUFFERING! BUT YOU DIDN'T--YOU LET IT HAPPEN.
OF COURSE WE DID. ALL THAT FOUL CIRCE SCHEMED, WE WERE AWARE OF FROM THE START.
WHY?!?
BECAUSE THE TIME HAD COME FOR THE AMAZONS--ALL THE AMAZONS--TO FACE A TEST.
A TEST THEY FAILED--UTTERLY.
MY CHILDREN, INSTEAD OF HONORING THE WARRIOR'S CODE, YOU GAVE IN TO HATE, FEAR AND CRUELTY.
SOME OF YOU TURNED ON EACH OTHER, SOUGHT TO BETRAY YOUR QUEEN.
YET COULD NEVER QUITE BRING YOURSEVES TO TAKE A STAND--
WHEN A STAND DEMANDED TO BE TAKEN.
YOU'RE NOT HUMAN, AMAZONS. YOU'RE THE CHILDREN OF THE GODS. YOU MUST BE HELD TO A HIGHER STANDARD.
INSTEAD, YOU SANK TO DEPTHS I WOULD HAVE THOUGHT UNIMAGINABLE.
CIRCE SPARKED THE FIRE, BUT YOU KEPT THE BLAZE GOING. THE RESPONSIBILITY LIES WITH YOU.
AND SO, YOU MUST BE PUNISHED.

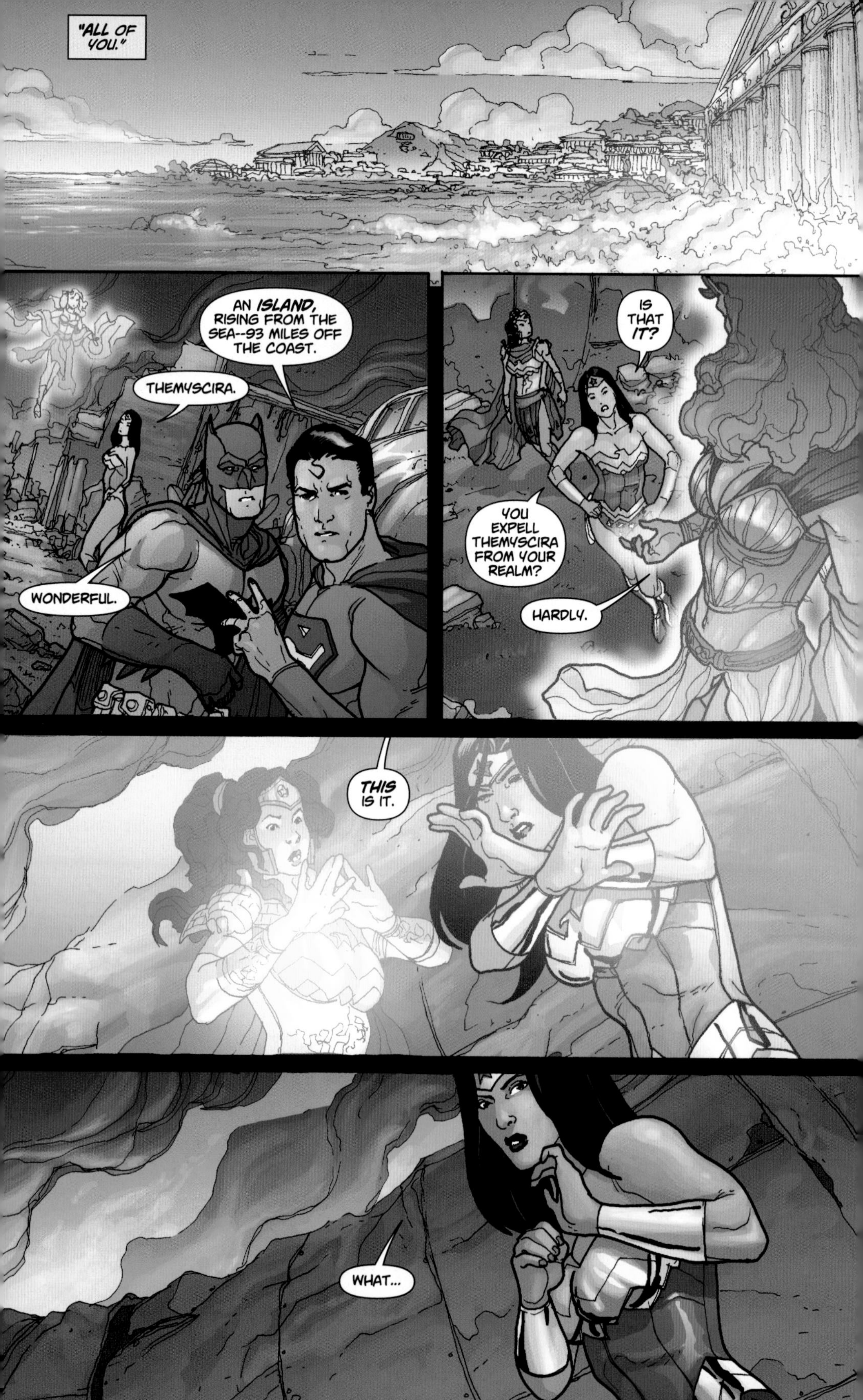
"ALL OF YOU."
AN ISLAND, RISING FROM THE SEA--93 MILES OFF THE COAST.
THEMYSCIRA.
WONDERFUL.
IS THAT IT?
YOU EXPELL THEMYSCIRA FROM YOUR REALM?
HARDLY.
THIS IS IT.
WHAT...

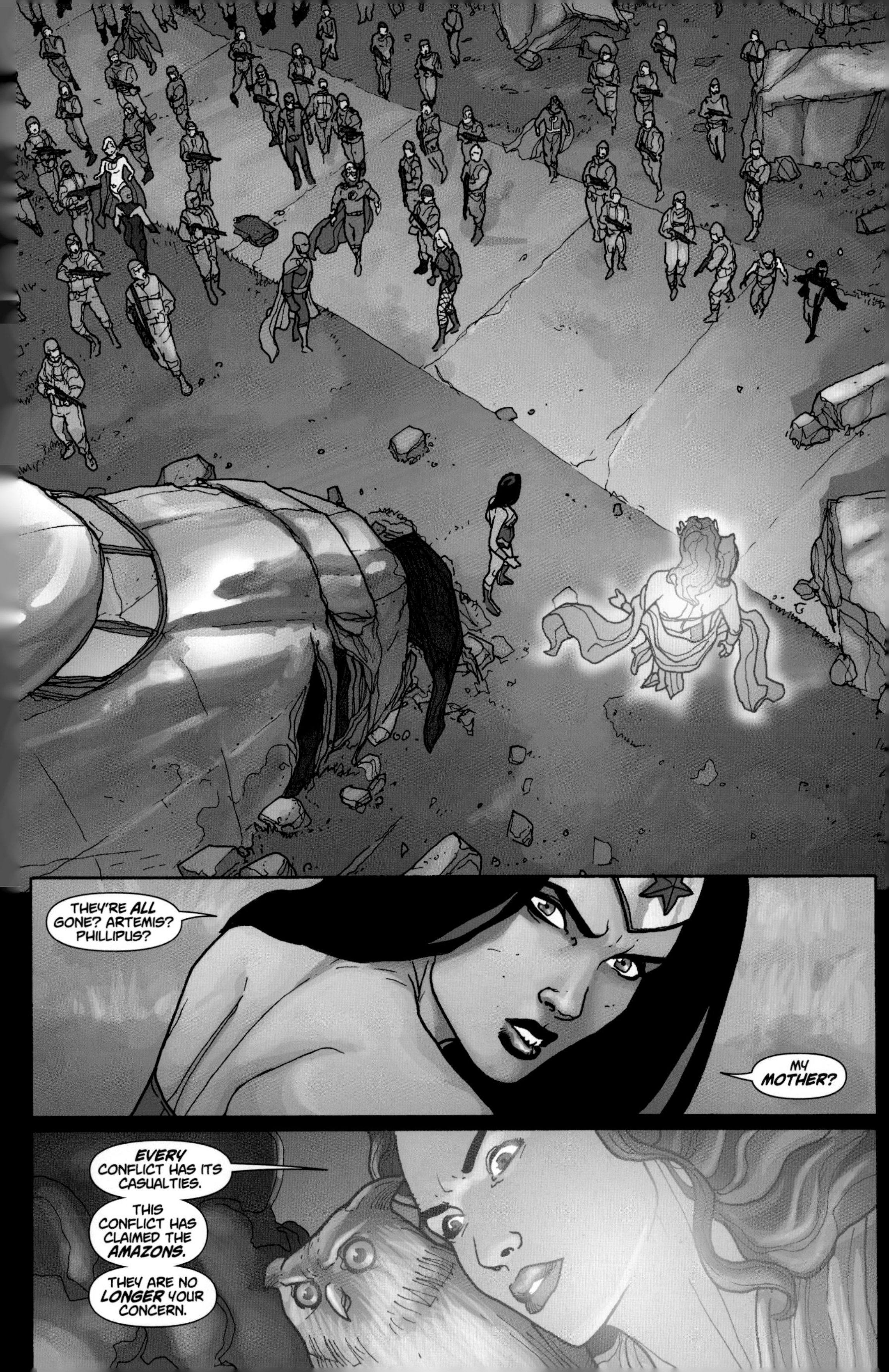
THEY'RE ALL GONE? ARTEMIS? PHILLIPUS?
MY MOTHER?
EVERY CONFLICT HAS ITS CASUALTIES.
THIS CONFLICT HAS CLAIMED THE AMAZONS.
THEY ARE NO LONGER YOUR CONCERN.

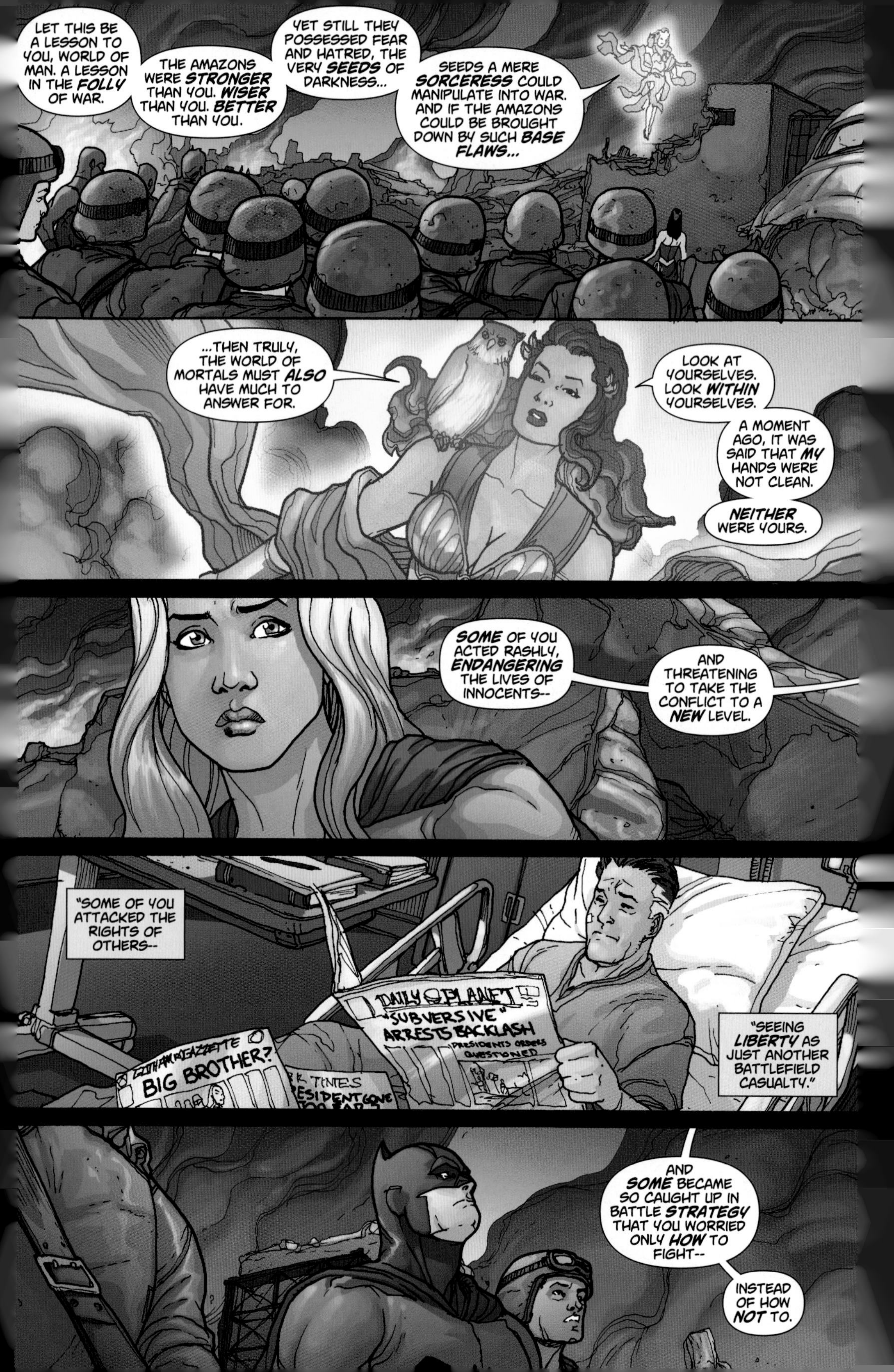
LET THIS BE A LESSON TO YOU, WORLD OF MAN. A LESSON IN THE FOLLY OF WAR.
THE AMAZONS WERE STRONGER THAN YOU. WISER THAN YOU. BETTER THAN YOU.
YET STILL THEY POSSESSED FEAR AND HATRED, THE VERY SEEDS OF DARKNESS...
SEEDS A MERE SORCERESS COULD MANIPULATE INTO WAR. AND IF THE AMAZONS COULD BE BROUGHT DOWN BY SUCH BASE FLAWS...
...THEN TRULY, THE WORLD OF MORTALS MUST ALSO HAVE MUCH TO ANSWER FOR.
LOOK AT YOURSELVES. LOOK WITHIN YOURSELVES.
A MOMENT AGO, IT WAS SAID THAT MY HANDS WERE NOT CLEAN.
NEITHER WERE YOURS.
SOME OF YOU ACTED RASHLY, ENDANGERING THE LIVES OF INNOCENTS--
AND THREATENING TO TAKE THE CONFLICT TO A NEW LEVEL.
"SOME OF YOU ATTACKED THE RIGHTS OF OTHERS--
DAILY PLANET
"SUBVERSIVE" ARRESTS BACKLASH
PRESIDENTS ORDERS QUESTIONED
BIG BROTHER?
"SEEING LIBERTY AS JUST ANOTHER BATTLEFIELD CASUALTY."
AND SOME BECAME SO CAUGHT UP IN BATTLE STRATEGY THAT YOU WORRIED ONLY HOW TO FIGHT--
INSTEAD OF HOW NOT TO.

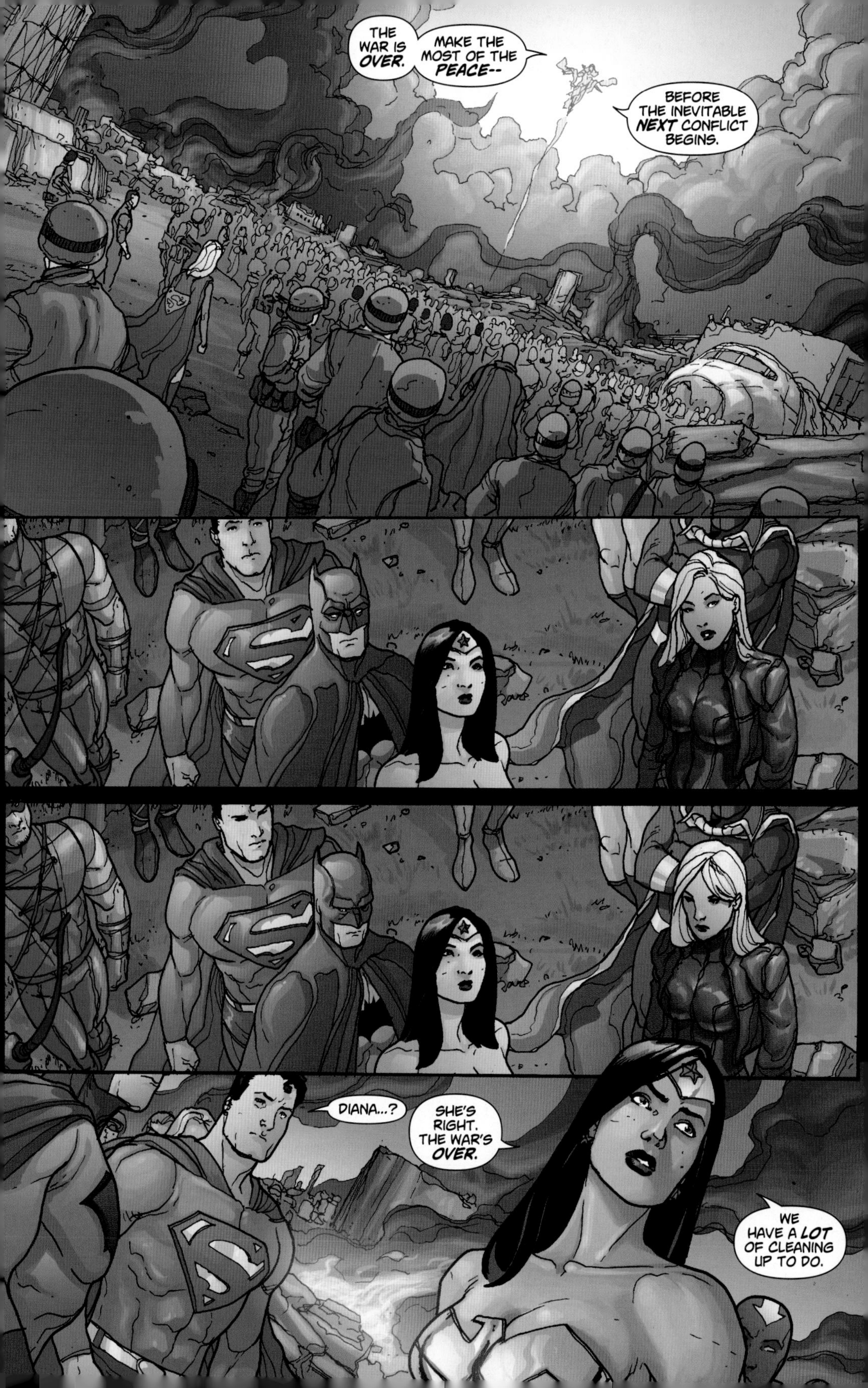
THE WAR IS OVER.
MAKE THE MOST OF THE PEACE--
BEFORE THE INEVITABLE NEXT CONFLICT BEGINS.
DIANA...?
SHE'S RIGHT. THE WAR'S OVER.
WE HAVE A LOT OF CLEANING UP TO DO.

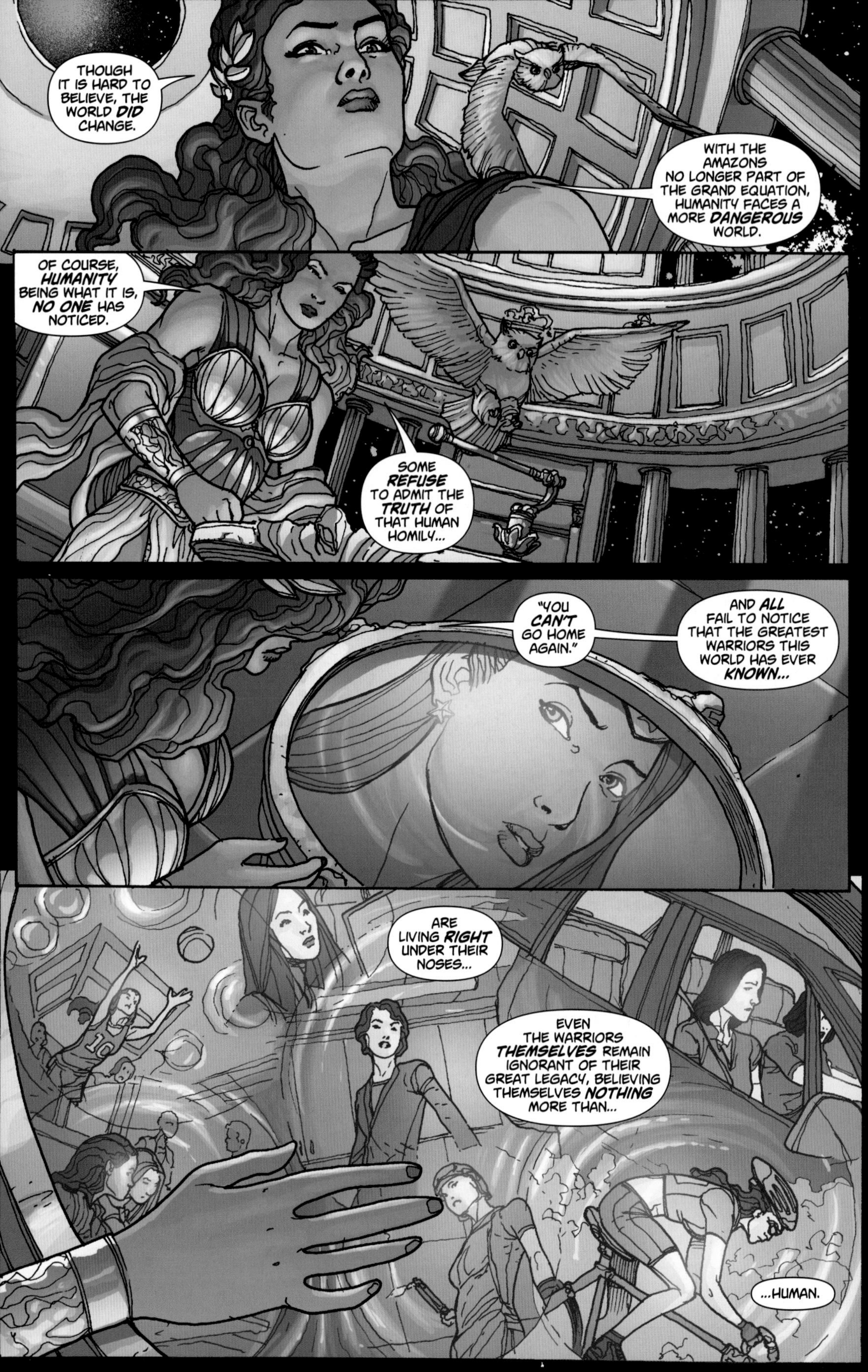
THOUGH IT IS HARD TO BELIEVE, THE WORLD *DID* CHANGE.
WITH THE AMAZONS NO LONGER PART OF THE GRAND EQUATION, HUMANITY FACES A MORE *DANGEROUS* WORLD.
OF COURSE, *HUMANITY* BEING WHAT IT IS, *NO ONE* HAS NOTICED.
SOME *REFUSE* TO ADMIT THE *TRUTH* OF THAT HUMAN HOMILY...
"YOU *CAN'T* GO HOME AGAIN."
AND *ALL* FAIL TO NOTICE THAT THE GREATEST WARRIORS THIS WORLD HAS EVER *KNOWN...*
ARE LIVING *RIGHT* UNDER THEIR NOSES...
EVEN THE WARRIORS *THEMSELVES* REMAIN IGNORANT OF THEIR GREAT LEGACY, BELIEVING THEMSELVES *NOTHING* MORE THAN...
...HUMAN.

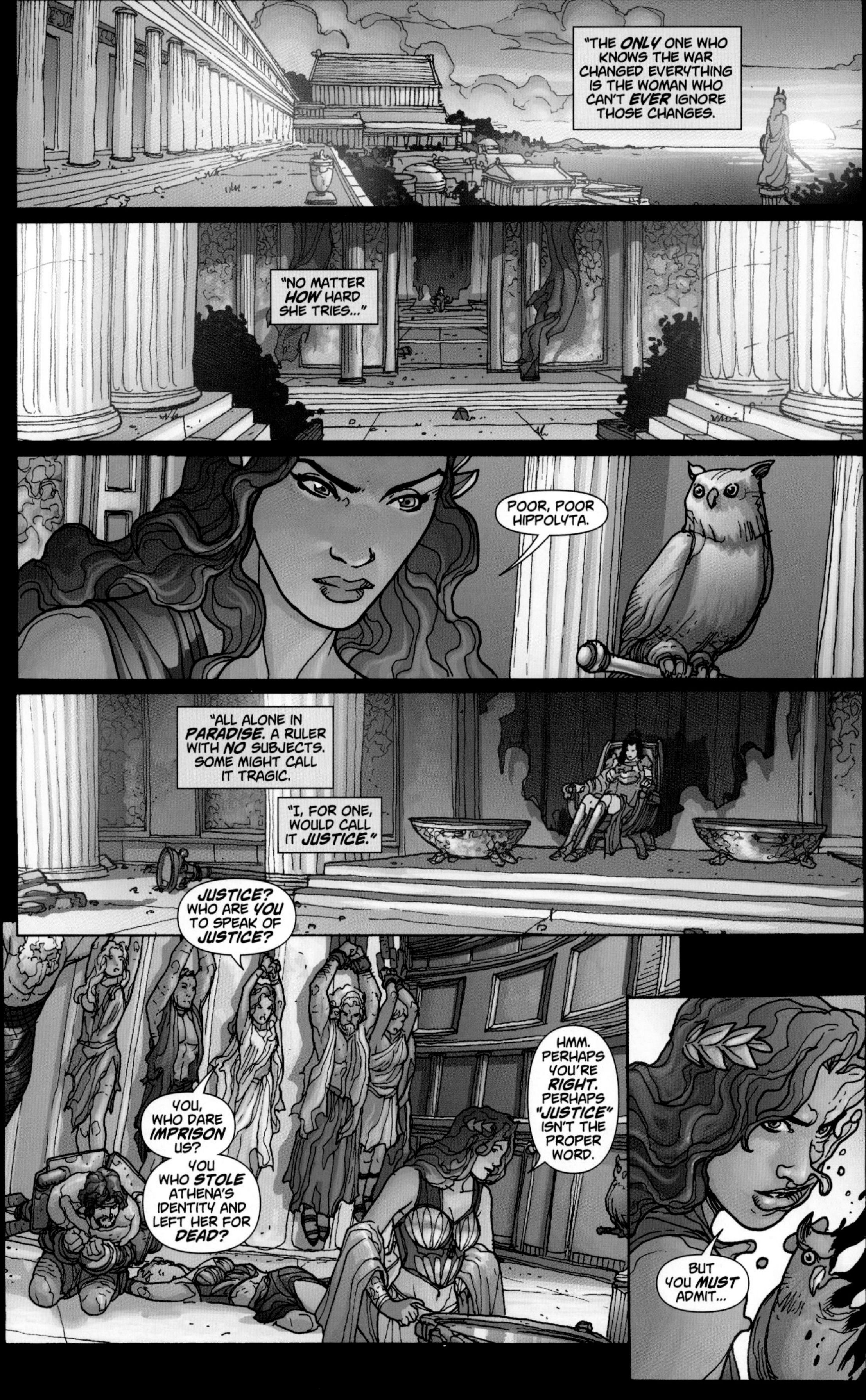
"THE ONLY ONE WHO KNOWS THE WAR CHANGED EVERYTHING IS THE WOMAN WHO CAN'T EVER IGNORE THOSE CHANGES.
"NO MATTER HOW HARD SHE TRIES..."
POOR, POOR HIPPOLYTA.
"ALL ALONE IN PARADISE. A RULER WITH NO SUBJECTS. SOME MIGHT CALL IT TRAGIC.
"I, FOR ONE, WOULD CALL IT JUSTICE."
JUSTICE? WHO ARE YOU TO SPEAK OF JUSTICE?
YOU, WHO DARE IMPRISON US?
YOU WHO STOLE ATHENA'S IDENTITY AND LEFT HER FOR DEAD?
HMM. PERHAPS YOU'RE RIGHT. PERHAPS "JUSTICE" ISN'T THE PROPER WORD.
BUT YOU MUST ADMIT...

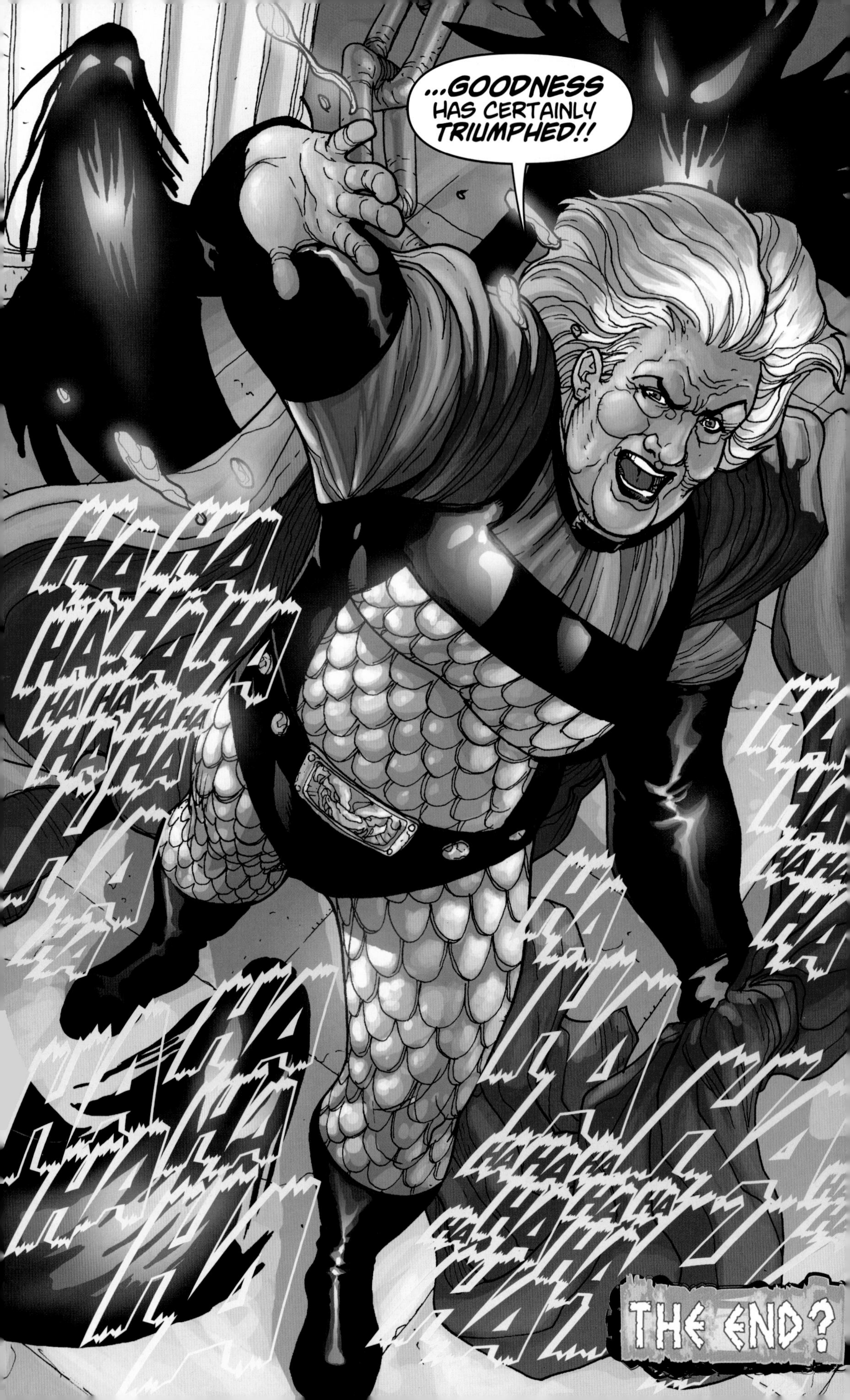
...GOODNESS HAS CERTAINLY TRIUMPHED!!
THE END?

And so we discover the true mastermind behind the war...Granny Goodness — headmistress of the military schools on Apokolips who answers to the almighty Darkseid. Darkseid...dictator and would-be ruler of the universe, who is instrumental in the upcoming "Great Disaster" to befall humanity.

But why would Granny Goodness manipulate the Amazons into a war on mankind? And why is she also using Amazon-inspired battered women's centers around the world to recruit new female fighters? These mysteries and more will reach far across the DC Universe, counting down towards a cataclysmic Final Crisis.

The war has ended...but the apocalypse has just begun.

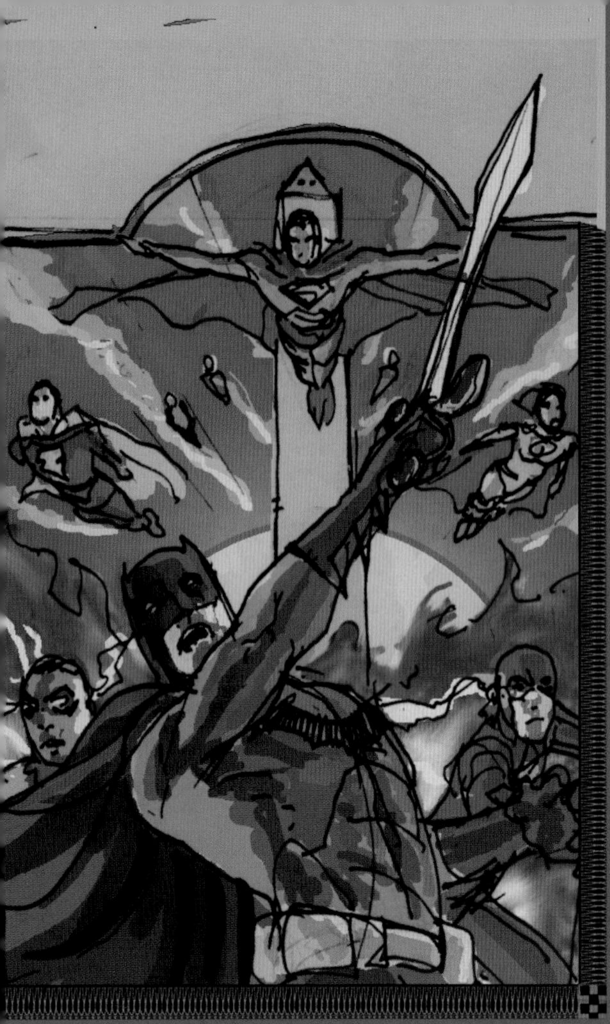

SKETCHES

BY PETE WOODS

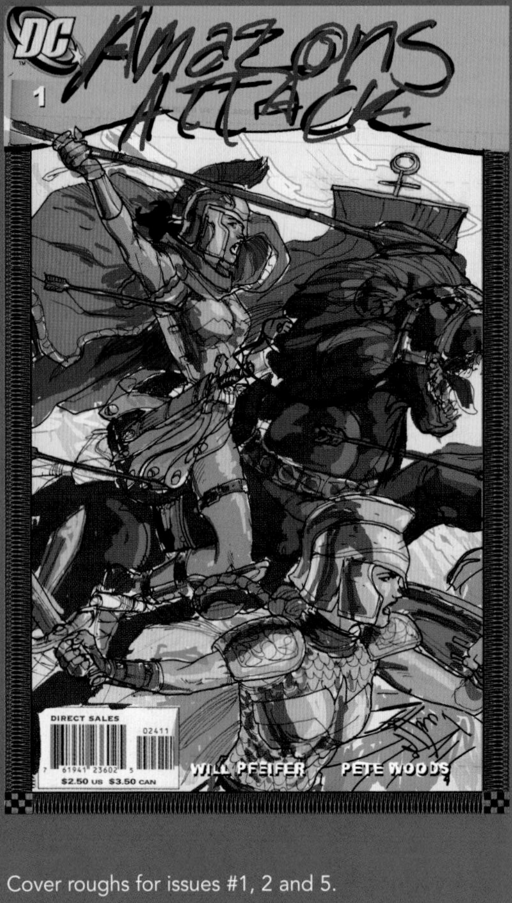

Amazons Attack
1
DIRECT SALES
$2.50 US $3.50 CAN
WILL PFEIFER
PETE WOODS

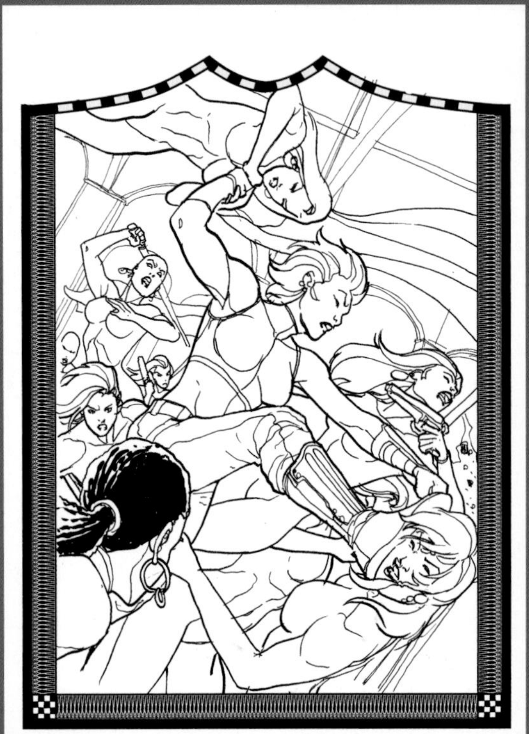

Cover roughs for issues #1, 2 and 5.

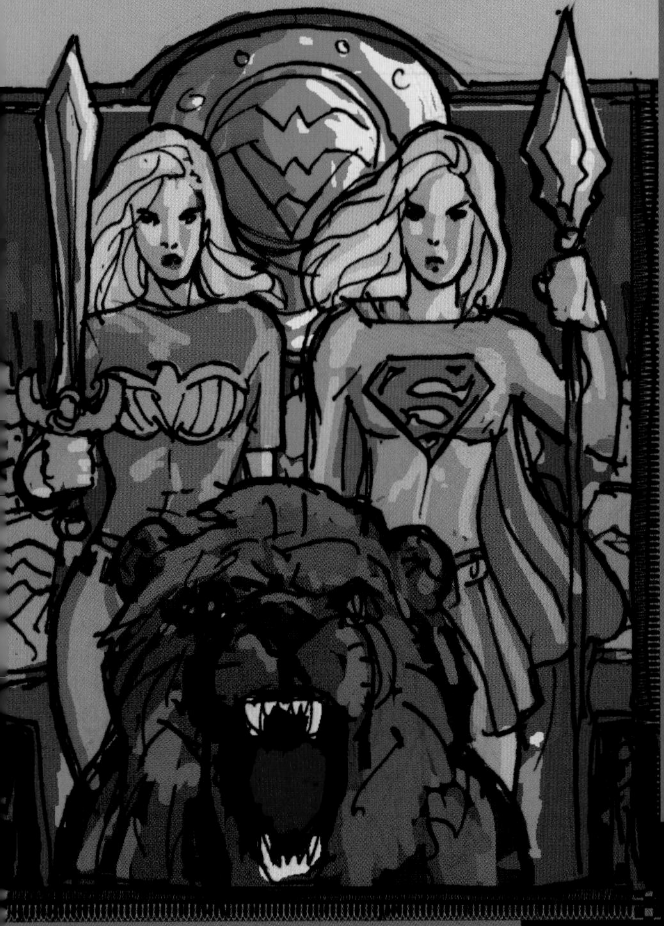

Cover roughs for issues #3 and 6, and an unused cover concept.

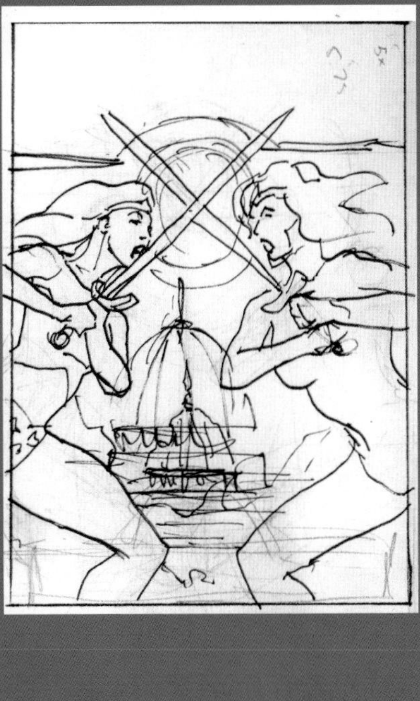

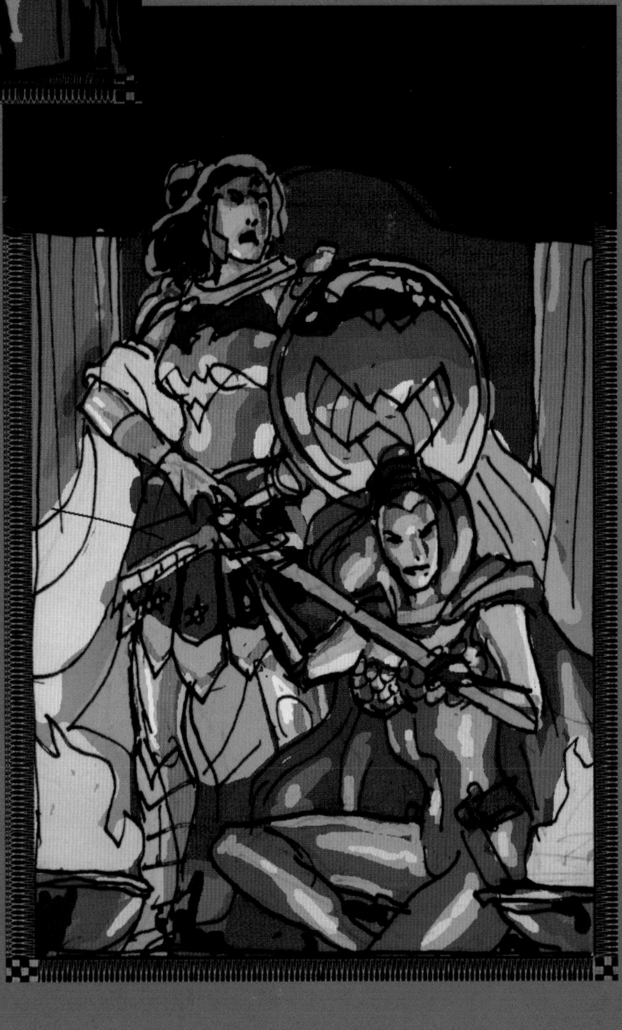

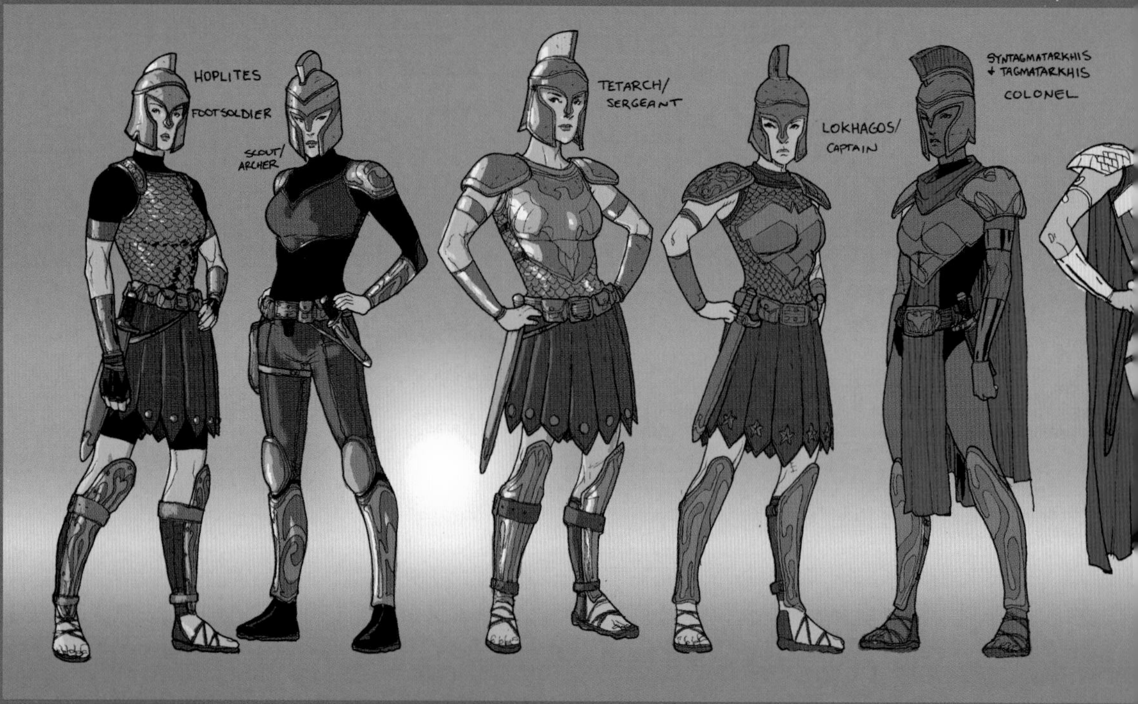
HOPLITES
FOOTSOLDIER
SCOUT/
ARCHER
TETARCH/
SERGEANT
LOKHAGOS/
CAPTAIN
SYNTAGMATARKHIS
+ TAGMATARKHIS
COLONEL

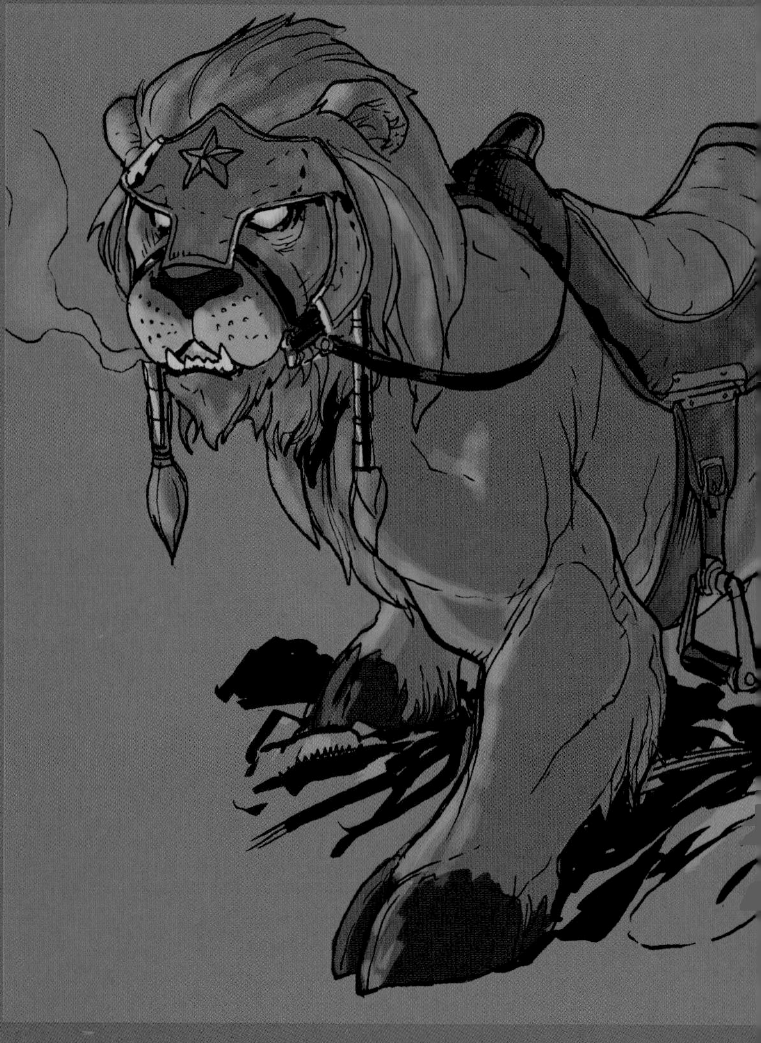

Right:

The Amazons ride the mythical Chimera.

The Amazons' queen,
Hippolyta.

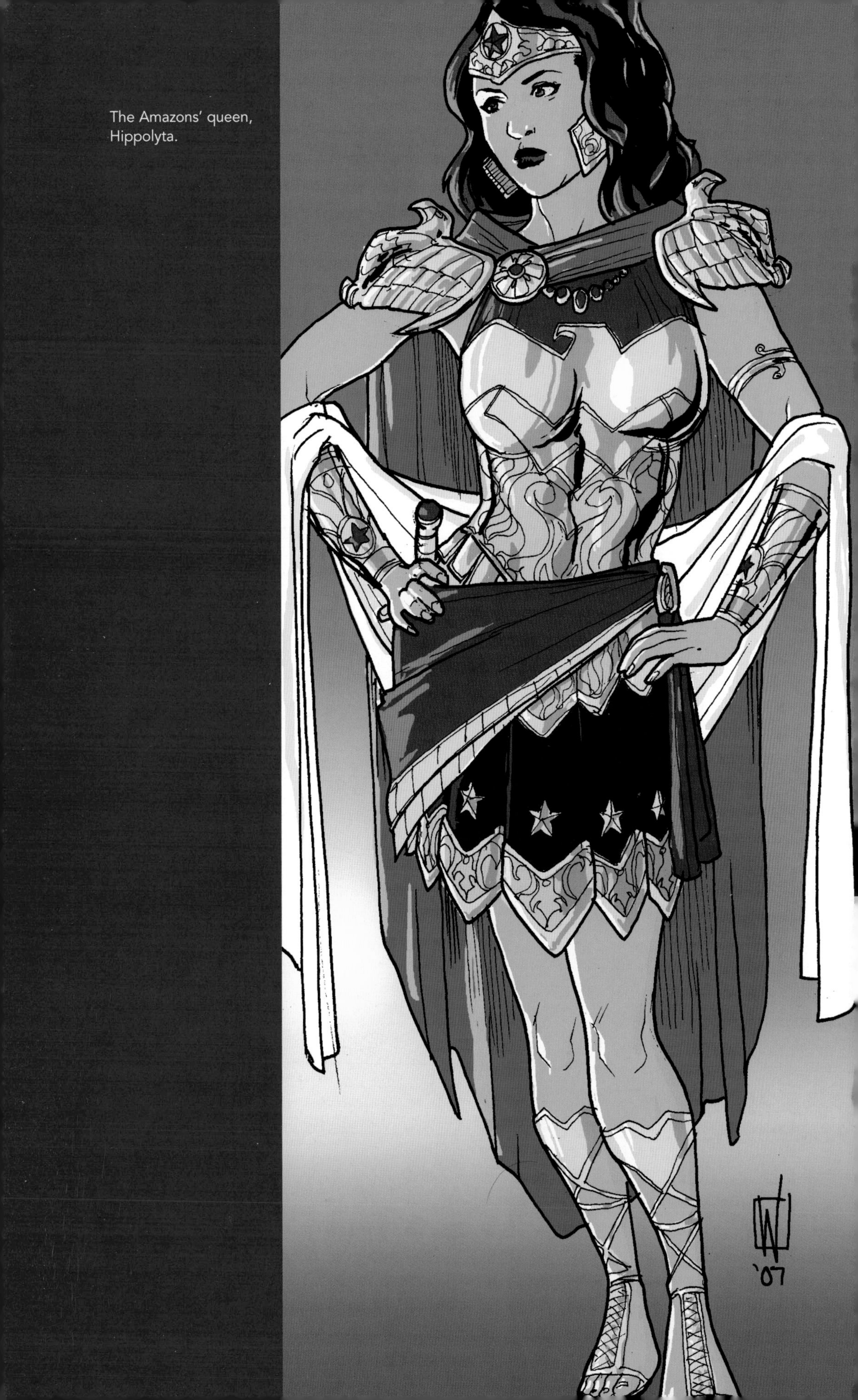
'07

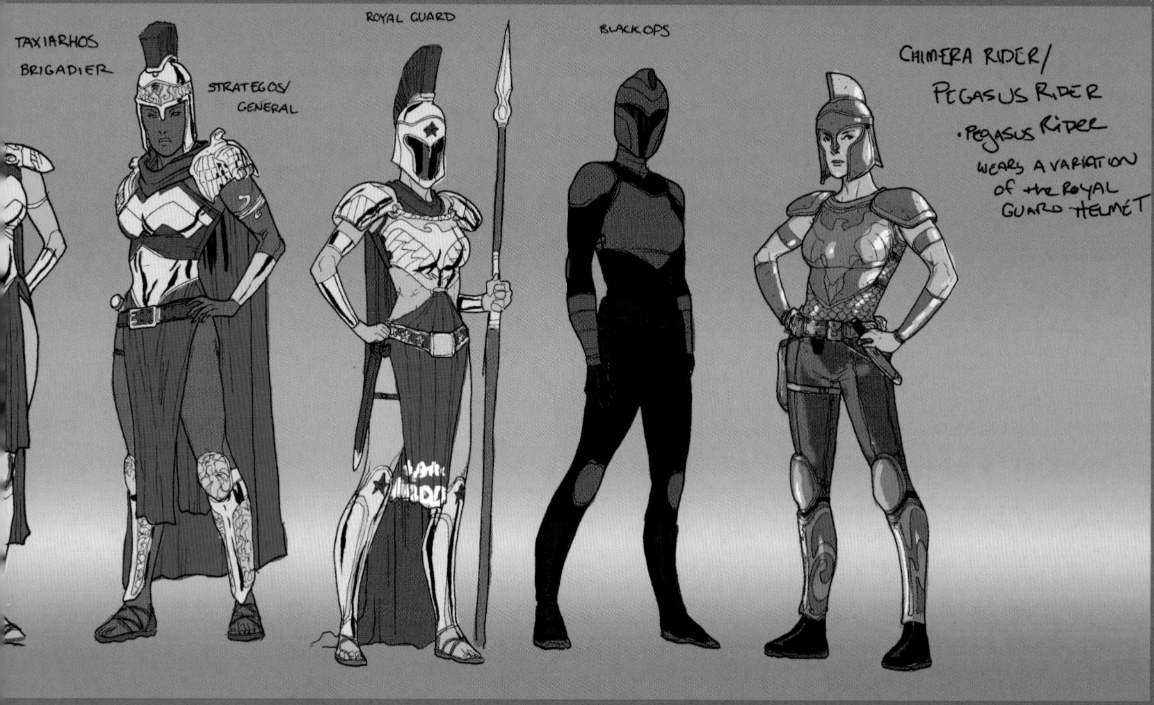
TAXIARHOS
BRIGADIER
STRATEGOS/
GENERAL
ROYAL GUARD
BLACK OPS
CHIMERA RIDER/
PEGASUS RIDER
·Pegasus Rider
WEARS A VARIATION
of the ROYAL
GUARD HELMET

Above:

Character designs for various Amazons.

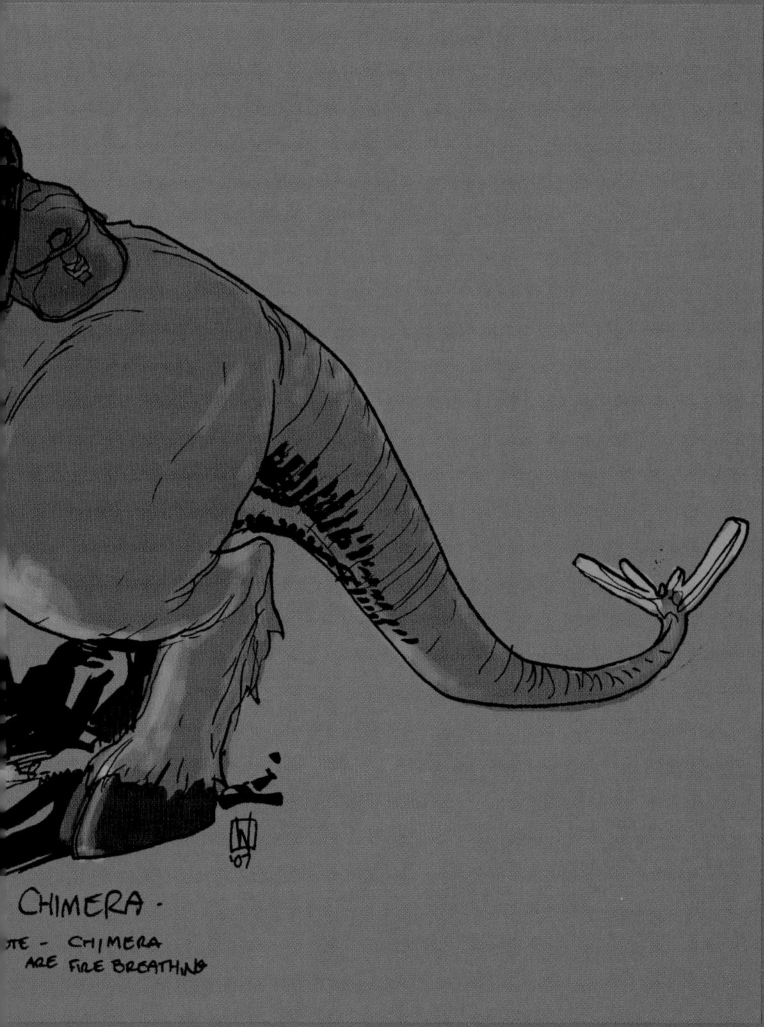
CHIMERA ·
TE - CHIMERA
ARE FIRE BREATHING

READ MORE ADVENTURES OF YOUR
FAVORITE HEROES IN THESE
COLLECTIONS FROM DC COMICS:

KINGDOM COME

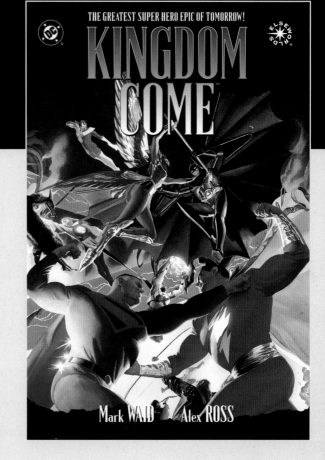

THE GREATEST SUPER-HERO EPIC OF TOMORROW!

KINGDOM COME

Mark WAID   Alex ROSS

Mark Waid and Alex Ross deliver a
grim tale of youth versus experience,
tradition versus change and what
defines a hero. KINGDOM COME is
a riveting story pitting the old guard —
Superman, Batman, Wonder Woman
and their peers — against a new,
uncompromising generation.

WINNER OF FIVE EISNER AND
HARVEY AWARDS, INCLUDING
BEST LIMITED SERIES
AND BEST ARTIST

IDENTITY CRISIS

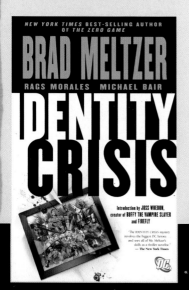

BRAD MELTZER
RAGS MORALES
MICHAEL BAIR

CRISIS ON INFINITE EARTHS

MARV WOLFMAN
GEORGE PÉREZ

DC: THE NEW FRONTIER VOLUME 1

DARWYN COOKE
DAVE STEWART

DON'T MISS THESE OTHER GREAT TITLES FROM AROUND THE DCU!

SUPERMAN: BIRTHRIGHT

MARK WAID
LEINIL FRANCIS YU
GERRY ALANGUILAN

BATMAN: DARK VICTORY

JEPH LOEB
TIM SALE

WONDER WOMAN: GODS AND MORTALS

GEORGE PÉREZ
LEN WEIN/GREG POTTER
BRUCE PATTERSON

GREEN LANTERN: NO FEAR

GEOFF JOHNS
CARLOS PACHECO
ETHAN VAN SCIVER

GREEN ARROW: QUIVER

KEVIN SMITH
PHIL HESTER
ANDE PARKS

TEEN TITANS: A KID'S GAME

GEOFF JOHNS
MIKE McKONE

SEARCH THE GRAPHIC NOVELS SECTION OF